THE

Territorial Press

O F

New Mexico

*1834-1912*

THE
# Territorial Press
OF
# New Mexico

*1834-1912*

*BY*
PORTER A. STRATTON

*ALBUQUERQUE*
UNIVERSITY OF NEW MEXICO PRESS

Manufactured in the United States of America by the
University of New Mexico Printing Plant, Albuquerque
Library of Congress Catalog Card No. 78-78556
Standard Book No. 8263-0141-x

*First edition*

# PREFACE

In this study of the press of territorial New Mexico the writer has sought to show not only the traits of the newspapermen and their journalism but also their editorial influence upon the development of New Mexico in these years. The first three chapters of this work contain the story of the most interesting and most important territorial newspapers. The information in each chapter corresponds to a particular era in the development of the economy and culture of New Mexico. In each period an effort has been made to analyze the characteristics and concepts of the journalists, the content and evolving styles of their newspapers, and the mechanical and business practices employed in the production of their newspapers. The final chapters seek to evaluate the contributions of the journalists in converting the wild and backward frontier of 1848 into the placid but progressive state of New Mexico of 1912. These chapters trace the attitudes and actions of the editors with regard to the most important of the territory's political, economic, cultural, and social problems and evaluate the efforts of the press to solve these problems.

In the preparation of this work the writer has become indebted to many persons. Professor Lawrence L. Graves of Texas Technological College made excellent suggestions concerning organization and improvements in style. Professor W. C. Holden of Texas Technological College gave valuable advice as to research procedures and organization. Professors J. William Davis, Lowell L. Blaisdell, Timothy P. Donovan, all of Texas Technological College, and Merton L. Dillon of Ohio State University also closely read the work and made many helpful recommendations.

The various university libraries in New Mexico courteously lent their facilities and files of territorial newspapers. James Dyke and Peggy Tozer, librarian and reference librarian at Eastern New Mexico University, secured a great many microfilmed newspapers on inter-library loan. David O. Kelley, librarian at the University of New Mexico, and his staff provided a great deal of information and made available the large collection of territorial papers of that institution, many of them on inter-library loan. Chester A. Linscheid, librarian at New Mexico State University, allowed the writer to examine the Amador collection of newspapers, which at that time were being arranged for microfilming. William S. Wallace, librarian at New Mexico Highlands University, made available the Mills collection of newspapers and the files of the Las Vegas *Daily Optic*. William Farrington, New Mexico State Library, Norris K. Maxwell, University of New Mexico library, and Mildred Barrett, New Mexico State University library, spent a great deal of time and effort checking the Appendix against the newspaper holdings of their libraries. I am also grateful to Irma Youngblood of New Mexico Institute of Mining and Technology library, Nobel La Fond of Wester.1 New Mexico University library, and Myra Ellen Jenkins of the New Mexico State Records Center and Archives for help with research materials.

Numerous New Mexico county clerks provided working space and access to territorial newspapers filed in their offices. Albert Stubbs, editor of the Roswell *Daily Record,* and Frank Pfeiffer, publisher of the Raton *Range,* gave the writer free use of microfilmed files of their papers. Gordon Greaves, editor of the Portales *News-Tribune,* gave many helpful suggestions. L. A. File, of the New Mexico Institute of Mining and Technology, provided information about early New Mexico towns. Jack D. Rittenhouse, of Albuquerque, who had started a similar project, graciously lent his collected information and many copies of territorial newspapers. The writer is deeply indebted to his wife, Mary Carter Stratton, who read numerous drafts and advanced many suggestions for improvement of the work.

# CONTENTS

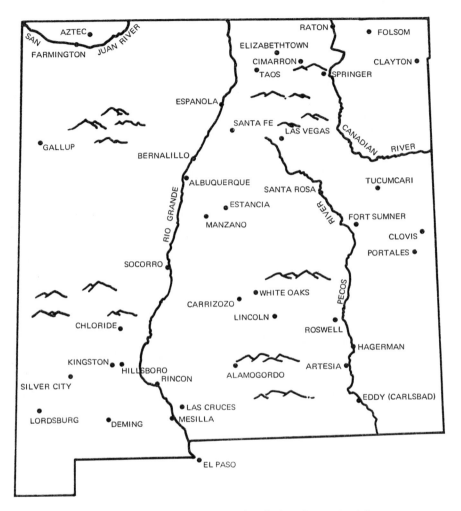

The principal towns of New Mexico during the territorial era.

# THE EARLY PRESS

## 1834-1879

JOURNALISM WAS LATE in coming to New Mexico because of the isolation, poverty, and illiterate population of that territory. All of these factors help to account for the fact that no newspapers were founded there during the long Spanish rule, from 1598 to 1821, and that only three papers were published in the relatively brief Mexican era from 1821 to 1846.

First settled in 1598 by the Spanish under Don Juan de Onate, New Mexico remained an isolated outpost under more than two centuries of Spanish rule. The Spanish failed to find the mineral wealth that had lured Onate to New Mexico; but the population grew, nourished by a subsistence type of agriculture with little exterior outlet for its products. When Mexican rule began in 1821, trade was soon opened with the United States via the Santa Fe Trail, and the economy of New Mexico was improved by this outlet for products. In 1848 the area was ceded to the United States, and territorial agriculture gained a large local market as the result of the needs of hundreds of soldiers and horses on military posts. The ensuing period of economic improvement was interrupted by the American Civil War and a large-scale renewal of Indian warfare. During the Civil War, California and New Mexico volunteers subjugated the Indians, eliminating a menace to a great portion of the New Mexican people. After the Civil War, the territory began to gain its first sizable permanent Anglo-American population. Many of the California Volunteers remained in New Mexico, mineral discoveries at Elizabethtown and near Silver City brought miners to the territory, and cattlemen came to use the vast range. Most of New Mexico, however, remained an isolated frontier region until railways reached it late in 1878.

Journalism in the early American period was somewhat amateurish, pursued by men who usually also followed another career but who were interested in the political utility of the press. Nevertheless, these jour-

nalists were well educated, vigorous, independent men of wide interests
and allegiances. As a result, the journalism of this era had great vitality
and reflected diverse opinions on public questions. Thus, despite a lack
of potential profits in an area of great poverty and illiteracy, the territorial public was well served by its few papers in the years from 1847
to 1879.

Although in these years journalism expanded rapidly elsewhere in
the United States only sixty-three newspapers were published in New
Mexico.[1] Furthermore, many of these papers survived for only one issue
and others for only a few weeks, so that in January, 1879, fifteen newspapers, seven of them relatively stable and long lived, were being published in the New Mexico territory. The publishers of these papers had
been motivated by the prospects of political spoils, mineral discoveries
which promised to sustain newspapers, and anticipation of great economic growth for New Mexico when railways reached the territory.
With so few newspapers, their editors became exceptionally important
and influential. Their small numbers also gave them a sense of comradeship despite vigorous battles for political spoils and the insulting
exchanges so common between journalists in the papers of that day.
Thus, these first editors reflected the spirit of the American frontier;
they were self-sufficient, rugged individualists who were inherently
democratic and optimistically believed a great reward would be theirs
once railways entered New Mexico and ended its isolation.

In frontier New Mexico during the Spanish and Mexican eras, there
were no public and very few parochial schools, and the resulting illiteracy made it an inhospitable area for journalists. Nevertheless, three
Spanish-language papers appeared in Santa Fe during the Mexican era.
*El Crepusculo de la Libertad* was published for four weeks in 1834, and
*La Verdad* was issued for about sixteen months in 1844 and 1845. Later
in 1845, *El Payo de Nuevo Mejico* appeared for several months.[2] Then,
even before annexation, came the founding of the first English-language
journal, the Santa Fe *Republican*. An issue of January 1, 1847, was evidently a prospectus,[3] and regular publication began September 10, 1847,
with this notice to the public:

> The want of some medium through which the public can be informed of the
> earliest and most authentic news from the States, the movements of the ARMY,
> and of stirring events of the WAR have been severely felt throughout New
> Mexico, both by the American and Mexican population, and we have deter-
> mined to try and supply this desideratum.[4]

The printing plant of the *Republican* was owned by the United States
Army, and soldiers were assigned to the paper as printers. Since the
army did not wish to subsidize the paper indefinitely, however, it sold

the plant to the founders of the Santa Fe *New Mexican,* who published their paper intermittently in 1849 and 1850.[5] In June, 1851, the Santa Fe *Weekly Gazette* was established, becoming the first long-lived New Mexico paper.[6] Although this paper had various editors and publishers, James L. Collins, its founder, was closely associated with it until his death in 1869.[7] Two other short-lived papers appeared in the 1850s. *Amigo del Pais,* established at Albuquerque in 1853, moved in a few weeks to Santa Fe where it soon lapsed. In 1857 this shop was used to publish the Santa Fe *Democrata* for the duration of a political campaign.[8]

In the 1850s Anglo-Americans had also entered southern New Mexico, and this element became jealous of the political power of northern territorial towns such as Santa Fe and Albuquerque. New Mexico then included the present state of Arizona, whose rich mineral discoveries near Tucson brought an influx of miners and increased population for all southern New Mexico. Mesilla, with a population of 2,420, was the largest town of the area. First settled in 1849, Mesilla soon attracted hundreds of Spanish American farmers, who used the Rio Grande waters for irrigation. In the late 1850s residents of Mesilla and Tucson jointly attempted to escape the control of northern territorial counties, proposing that southern New Mexico be made a separate territory with the name of Arizona. The Mesilla *Times* was launched in October, 1860, as a spearhead for this movement. After Congress had rejected several pleas from this area for statehood or a separate territorial status, the Arizonians petitioned the Southern Confederacy to annex them. Shortly after, Texas troops invaded the area and a *Times* headline read: "ARIZONA IS FREE AT LAST!" When California federal troops marched toward New Mexico late in 1862, however, the Texans retreated. With them went *Times* publisher B. C. Murray, who abandoned his paper.[9]

Even while the Civil War raged in New Mexico, new journalistic ventures were launched. In 1862 a second Santa Fe *Republican* was founded, but the general commanding the federal forces soon closed it for disclosing troop movements.[10] A second Santa Fe *New Mexican* was launched in January, 1863, and was sold in November, 1863, to W. H. Manderfield. In May, 1864, Manderfield took in Thomas Tucker as a co-publisher.[11] These two published the *New Mexican* until 1880, making it the leading territorial paper of the 1860s and 70s. The advent of a second Santa Fe journal started a competitive struggle; out of that battle arose the *Daily New Mexican,* launched in 1868 with this optimistic greeting:

Following up the progressive spirit of the age, we this day present to our readers, and the public generally, the first issue of a daily newspaper in New

Mexico. . . . Last November we greatly enlarged the size of the NEW MEXICAN weekly; we determined then to follow up our improvements and enlarge our enterprise as soon as opportunity offered. Hence when the question of a telegraph line between Santa Fe and Denver was first proposed we gave it our hearty commendation and support. We saw the DAILY NEW MEXICAN then in our mind's eye.[12]

A heated journalistic competition continued at Santa Fe for the remainder of the pre-railroad era. This struggle and the ill health of the publisher of the *Weekly Gazette* led to its sale in October, 1869, when it became the *Weekly Post* under a new owner.[13] As the battle became more intense, a *Daily Post* emerged in June, 1870. The *Daily Post* was suspended in March, 1872, and in July the *Weekly Post* also lapsed. The editors of the *New Mexican,* hoping for the permanent death of their competitor, wrote: "Requiescat in pace."[14] Nevertheless, the plant, which was sold at a sheriff's auction, was used in August, 1872, to found the *New Mexico Union.* This paper finally was bought by the owners of the *New Mexican* early in 1874, probably to insure that its shop would not be used again at Santa Fe.[15]

During the 1870s several short-lived rivals competed with the *New Mexican* for the business of the largest territorial town and the public printing of the capital. Published from 1873 to 1875, the fortnightly *Regimental Flag* featured military news.[16] The semi-weekly *News,* launched in September, 1874, was published for about sixteen months.[17] The weekly *News,* a Democratic campaign paper, lasted about one month in 1878.[18] The *Illustrated Monthly,* a magazine initiated in January, 1878, was converted in July, 1878, to a weekly newspaper, the *Rocky Mountain Sentinel.*[19] For several months in the autumn of 1879 this paper was published as a daily, but on Christmas Day, 1879, it was closed by its mortgagors—the publishers of the *New Mexican.*[20] The *New Mexico Co-operator* began as a weekly in July, 1876, but in March, 1878, it became the daily *New Mexico Advertiser.* This paper apparently soon returned to a weekly status and continued thus until 1880.[21] The *New Mexican* subdued all of its competitors of the 1870s. But the decade had not dealt kindly with the ambitions of W. H. Manderfield and Thomas Tucker, for on December 31, 1877, they announced the suspension of the *Daily New Mexican:*

With the issue of the DAILY NEW MEXICAN today it has been published nine years and six months. With slight exceptions during this whole period, it has been a losing investment to its proprietors. With the close times of the past year, and the indisposition of advertisers to continue their support of its columns, the conviction is forced upon them that the loss incident to its publication is greater than in justice they can submit to. It is with reluctance that

they come to this conclusion. . . . Whenever it shall seem practical its publication will be resumed.[22]

Albuquerque journalism lagged far behind that of Santa Fe in the
1860s. Although founded in 1706, Albuquerque, a small farming and
trading center, had by 1860 a population of only 1,203 and thus gave
little encouragement to journalists. Despite these discouraging facts,
H. S. Johnson[23] in January, 1863, launched the *Rio Abajo Weekly Press*
in Albuquerque. Compared to the usual bombast of initial editorials,
Johnson's editorial was quite modest:

. . . we [do not] think the brilliance of our style of writing will throw any considerable number of readers into ecstatic raptures, or set the Rio del Norte on
fire. . . . However, . . . we can master enough simple English words to manifest our meaning to the generality of the readers of the language.[24]

Although during the next decade the Albuquerque paper had several
names and publishers, Johnson apparently retained control. William
McGuiness, publisher of the paper from 1870 to 1880, edited the paper
under very trying conditions. Until 1876 it was the *Republican Review,*
but at that time McGuiness dropped *Republican* from its flag.[25]

Because of equally discouraging conditions, only two short-lived
weeklies were published in the Mesilla Valley from 1863 to 1871. A
Mesilla *Weekly Times* was launched in 1867, but soon was abandoned
after it failed to receive promised support from a political candidate.[26]
Its plant, that of the earlier Mesilla *Times,* was moved to Las Cruces in
1869 and used by an almost equally short-lived *Rio Grande Gazette.*[27]
Two years later, N. V. Bennett gave Las Cruces, which had a population
of 1,304 in 1870, its first stable newspaper, the *Borderer.* Bennett, as his
first editorial showed, was one of the most imaginative of the early
editors:

THE BORDERER rises from his easy chair—a box that was once used for the
transportation of candles—places his hand gently on the empty barrel that forms
his desk, scrapes his moccasin on the adobe floor of his sanctum and with a
majestic inclination of his head says to Mr. Public, Mrs. Public and Miss Public, "Your most obedient! We wish for a long and happy acquaintance—a
pleasant association with your family for a hundred years to come. . . ."[28]

Bennett, a zealous Democrat, used his paper to revive the post-Civil
War Democratic party in New Mexico before ill health forced him to
suspend the *Borderer* in 1875.[29]

Meanwhile, new journalists had arrived in the Mesilla Valley. Lawrence Lapoint launched the Mesilla *News* in September, 1873, and made
Ira M. Bond a co-publisher early in 1874. These partners in August,
1874, established at Las Cruces the *Eco del Rio Grande,* which they pub-

lished until 1878.[30] Further journalistic rivalry in this populous irrigated area was provided by the Mesilla *Valley Independent,* published
from June, 1877, until July, 1879.[31] Another newspaper was added in
1878 by schoolmaster S. H. Newman with his Mesilla *El Democrata,* a
campaign weekly. This paper successfully rallied the Mesilla Valley
Democracy for electoral victory. Disgruntled Republicans then seized
the press of *El Democrata* and threw it into the Rio Grande. Undaunted
by violence, Newman obtained another press and began the Las Cruces
*Thirty-Four,* named for the Democratic margin of election victory in
Dona Ana County.[32]

Both Las Cruces and Las Vegas were relatively young towns; the
latter, founded in 1833, had grown slowly as a supply center for sheep
ranchers and had a population of 1,090 in 1870. Here again, journalism
was late in starting. The first paper in Las Vegas, the *Acorn,* published
by A. V. Aoy, was not founded until 1869. Soon renamed the *New Mexico Advertiser,* it was issued, sometimes briefly as a daily, until 1880,
although in 1878 it was moved to Santa Fe.[33] The next paper in Las
Vegas, the *Mail,* was published in 1871 and 1872. A month after the
*Mail* suspended, Louis Hommel used its plant to launch the *Gazette.*[34]
The course of the *Gazette,* like that of the *Mail,* was troubled, for under
Hommel it was suspended in 1873, and then revived in 1874. However,
after 1875 it gained stability under J. H. Koogler, its publisher until
1883.[35] Another Las Vegas journal, *Revista Catolica,* founded in 1875
by the Jesuits, was still in publication in 1912.[36]

Several mining discoveries after 1869 led to the founding of new
towns totally unlike a placid agricultural town such as Las Vegas. In
the territorial northeast were Cimarron and Elizabethtown, while in
the southwest were the camps near Silver City. At these places several
papers arose to serve the miner population. The first paper at Elizabethtown was the short-lived *Moreno Lantern,* which about one month
after its founding in 1869 was succeeded by the *National Press and Telegraph.*[37] The Elizabethtown *Argus,* a competitor founded in 1871, soon
merged with its rival to form the *Railway Press and Telegraph.*[38] Meanwhile, at nearby Cimarron the *News* was founded in 1870. By 1874
Elizabethtown mining had slowed, and the *Railway Press and Telegraph* was moved to Cimarron to combine with the *News* as the *News
and Press,* a combination surviving until 1882.[39] Journalism was slower
in coming to Silver City, and the *Mining Life,* first paper of that camp,
was not launched until 1873. Its editor immediately assumed the duty of
promoting the growth of the town and camp as his salutatory editorial
illustrates:

We offer the Mining Life to the people of Grant County and the territory
of New Mexico, as a medium through which the world may learn of our where-

abouts . . . and the treasures of our mines, our soil and the congeniality of our climate and the rapid growth of our population.[40]

The *Mining Life* was suspended early in 1875 because its publisher concluded that a paper could not be profitable at Silver City. Within a month, however, the *Grant County Herald* was launched using the plant of the *Mining Life* and soon became the most lucrative territorial paper.[41] Serious competition never existed at Silver City, and the *Grant County Herald* rivaled the Santa Fe *New Mexican* as this era's most profitable territorial paper—despite the *New Mexican's* monopoly of territorial public printing. Other publishers, on the contrary, having neither rich mines nor political printing spoils, strove to maintain their papers until the railways had reached New Mexico, bringing the expected great economic development and flood of people.

The adventurous journalists of the pre-railway era were by nature opportunists, men who, because of the extreme poverty of New Mexico, sought through journalism the rewards of politics. As a necessary corollary the political affiliations of the journalists of a dependency such as New Mexico changed with the changing fortunes of the national political parties, for national power controlled territorial political rewards. As a result, northern Republicans dominated the territorial press when the North gained national political and economic dominance after 1860. Despite their opportunism, however, the journalists, on the whole, were well educated and competent. In addition, they held in high esteem their positions as editors or publishers. Because of such self-esteem, it was easy for the editors to follow the current custom of personal journalism. Nevertheless, heated exchanges between journalists did not prevent a feeling of fraternity among them, nor did political differences breed unfriendliness unless the editors were located in the same town.

Many who became editors and publishers had come to the territory for other than journalistic reasons but found it politically expedient or profitable to enter journalism. This certainly was true of H. S. Johnson, publisher of the Albuquerque *Rio Abajo Weekly Press.* Johnson followed an older brother to New Mexico and became an apprentice printer at Santa Fe. Later he became publisher, legislator, and district judge. Most of the various editors and stockholders of the Santa Fe *Weekly Gazette* were both territorial officials and part-time journalists.[42] On the other hand, W. H. Manderfield and Thomas Tucker, publishers of the Santa Fe *New Mexican,* were practical printers when they arrived in the territory. Yet they too soon allied themselves with the dominant political group for a share of the political spoils.[43] The journalistic careers of A. J. Fountain and N. V. Bennett also had strong political motivation. Fountain arrived in New Mexico with the California Volunteers and remained to enter journalism and politics.[44] Bennett apparently came to New Mexico for his health and founded a paper which became an exponent of a southern New Mexico Democratic faction led by his brothers. Both Bennett and Fountain, however, had previous newspaper experience before they arrived in the territory. On the contrary, some of the mining town editors had little evident interest in political rewards; they were attracted to the territory by its mineral wealth. Nevertheless, politics was the principal reason for the entry of a majority of the territorial editors into journalism.

Politics also appeared to have an influence on the geographic origins of the early journalists. Before the Civil War many political appointees who also became editors were southern Democrats; after 1860 most editors were northern Republicans. An example of this trend is provided by S. M. Baird, publisher of the Santa Fe *Amigo del Pais* and *El Democrata;* he came to New Mexico from Kentucky via Texas.[45] Further examples are provided by the prevalence of southerners on the Santa Fe *Weekly Gazette:* J. L. Collins was from Kentucky and Missouri, John T. Russell was from Virginia,[46] and S. M. Yost and Dav. J. Miller were former Texans.[47] After 1860 the trend was from the North: N. V. Bennett from New York; J. H. Koogler from Iowa; and W. H. Manderfield, H. S. Johnson, and S. M. Ashenfelter from Pennsylvania.[48] A few journalists were from neither section. There were several native journalists and some Europeans who had drifted to the frontier, as was the case with Louis Hommel of Germany.[49] William McGuiness was from Ireland,[50] and A. V. Aoy came from Spain via Cuba and Mexico. Despite these exceptions, the origins of a majority of the early journalists followed the patterns noted above. The basic reason for this trend appears to have been politics. From 1853 until 1861, the Democratic party was in power nationally; southerners, dominant in that party, obtained appointments for southerners in New Mexico. In the later period, the Republican party was dominant, and northerners received New Mexico appointments. In addition, the economically expanding North pushed westward, building railways, investing in mines, and bringing with it northerners as supervisors and workers.

Another characteristic of the early editors, their high regard for their positions and the power of the press, was shown by the attitudes and ideas of several of them who believed that the occupant of the editorial chair was expected to be very wise and might be called upon to answer almost any question.[51] The concepts these editors held of their positions are shown by S. M. Ashenfelter's attitude; he believed an editor's duties included:

. . . the careful moulding and directing of public thought leading into the same exalted frame of mind and capacity for making sound judgments which are characteristic of the average editor himself. . . . [He should] . . . pay great heed to the malice in the conversations of the street corner oracles . . . and make his journal the mouthpiece of their peculiar wisdom. This gratifies the malicious few and serves to create among the craven many a proper respect for the editor himself, and in fact is one of the methods of "independent journalism."[52]

Closely coupled with the high regard of the editors for their position was their concept that all newspapers were valuable community assets which the public had a duty to support with subscriptions, advertising, and, if necessary, direct contributions. The publishers believed that their papers were valuable promotional tools for any town. For example, one editor wrote: "We will make all effort to forward Grant County. We see a bright future for our area and modestly believe that a well conducted journal can contribute much to help."[53] As another illustration, J. H. Koogler of the *Gazette* at Las Vegas claimed:

In our sister territory of Colorado, the first thing the early settlers did was to see that the papers of the Territory were well supported and encouraged, and the wisdom of that course is now seen in the thrift of the population and the growth of the Territory. Without newspapers Colorado would have yet been an unknown land, traversed only by a few hunters. . . . The people supported the papers, and the papers made the Territory.[54]

This high regard of the editors for their positions and the prestige of the press apparently brought most of them to announce that they would not indulge in personal journalism, the practice of sharp criticism of fellow editors commonly followed by most rural American journalists of that period. To illustrate, the Santa Fe *New Mexican* adopted a policy of "live and let live."[55] S. M. Ashenfelter, upon assuming the editorship of the Silver City *Grant County Herald,* strongly stated his policy:

We propose to avoid controversy with other journals, deeming that it would be a species of presumption, not to say dishonesty, on our part to burthen the columns of the HERALD with such matter, to the exclusion of local or general news.[56]

H. S. Johnson of the Albuquerque *Rio Abajo Weekly Press* warned fellow editors against critical personal journalism but stated he would reply in kind if attacked.

And now a few words to our editorial brethren. Dearly beloved, we do not consider you generally knaves bullies and blackguards, ready to sell yourselves to the highest responsible bidder, frighten greenhorns and abuse your contemporaries. Nevertheless it behooves us to say to you, that we are like unto yourselves as God made us. We may jostle and controvert opinions, but beware of personalities. "People who live in glass houses should not throw stones!" Editorially we belong to the church militant, and will return "good for evil;" that is, if you give us a knock, we will give you as good as we get. Draw it mild.[57]

Despite the good intentions of these early editors, controversy, criticism, and abuse were common—particularly in competitive situations. For example, the Santa Fe *New Mexican* greeted the loss of the postmastership by the editor of the Santa Fe *Post* with this editorial headed "At Last":

We published last night one of the most welcome dispatches that has ever been brought into this Territory by the electric telegraph, . . . the telegram announcing the removal of Mr. A. P. Sullivan, Postmaster, from the office . . . that has been used so basely and traitorously . . . against the Republican party. . . . Democratic leaders . . . immediately perceived in his arrogant self sufficiency, inordinate vanity, destitution of judgement and discretion and his rule or ruin ambition the means of producing dissension in the party.[58]

A great deal of the abuse directed toward other editors appeared in the form of unsigned letters which, if not written by the editor, certainly had editorial approval. A series of unsigned critical letters appearing in the Silver City *Mining Life* and Mesilla *News* displays this practice. O. L. Scott of the *Mining Life* published numerous letters signed "Gila Pete," "P. Encil," or other fictitious names. Some of the letters were critical of N. V. Bennett of the Las Cruces *Borderer*. The Mesilla *News* used letters signed "Jee Whilikins," "Truth," and "Impecunious" abusing Scott and Bennett and with an occasionally inserted editorial comment that any responsible person could learn the identity of the letter writers upon application at the *News* office. Scott made several efforts to learn the name of his literary assailant and at length received a reply which he published along with his answer.

O. L. Scott, Esq.
Dear Sir—we are not in the habit of giving the name of our correspondents upon a simple request by letter.
We have interviewed the correspondent signed "Impecunious" and he authorized us to say, if you desire to hold him personally responsible, and make personal application in our office, we shall give you his name in full.
We hope you are satisfied we have done all we could in this matter.
Very respectfully
Your Obt. Srvt's
Lapoint & Bond

Ira M. Bond, Esq.
La Mesilla, N. M.
Dear Sir—Impecunious is an ungentlemanly and cowardly scrub, and you're *ditto*.
Yours very truly
O. L. Scott[59]

Despite a tendency to be sharply critical of one another, the early territorial editors displayed an over-riding spirit of fraternalism and comradeship. A thorough reading of the editorial columns of these newspapers reveals that among the subjects most discussed were the actions, accomplishments, and failings of the territorial editors. The tenor of these comments appears to place the journalists in an elevated position in territorial society. Although many of these editors actually had very little status in that society, the frequency of press accounts about journalists made them public figures about whom the newspaper audience knew more than it did of all but a few of the most prominent New Mexico political figures. Thus, the interest of the editors in each other, their comparative rarity because of the small number of papers, and their tendency to place themselves in a special, superior category bound them in a unique comradeship despite their frequent quarrels.

Perhaps the fraternalism of the editors was increased by their better-than-average education. Their superior education can be deduced from the nature of their prior professions which they often continued to practice while editors. Some of the varied professions in which territorial editors had gained experience were as territorial officials, fourteen; practicing lawyers, ten; ministers of the gospel, five; doctors of medicine, two; schoolteachers, seven. On the other hand, among all American journalists of this period, a majority had moved into the editorial chair from the printshop, where they had usually started as young apprentices and educated themselves.[60] In New Mexico only from eleven to fifteen out of eighty editors had either printing or journalistic experience before they moved into their editorial chairs. Thus, on the whole, territorial editors of this era were above average in education and had a wide background which broadened their perceptions.

Possibly it was the better educational backgrounds of editors which produced a better-than-average journalism. Of course, like the writers of that period, they were inclined toward wordiness, and flowery, stilted language. But their writing was generally clear, and there was a minimum of glaring errors in grammar, spelling, and typography. One incident, showing that high standards were expected and maintained, concerned A. V. Aoy, a self-trained printer who was relatively unfamiliar with the English language and more error-prone than most editors. William McGuiness criticized his sloppiness, and emphasized his point by publishing Aoy's answer to his criticism:

The Edtr of that uodle sheet the Albur-Review has our thans for his critisdnim. We are sorry to see such an elegant fiery stump orator occupy such a humdle pos.ition and controlled by a ring and clique in which he dares not call his soul his own. He should return to the land of potatoes and weild his pen and passions in behalf of his country and so put to shame the eloquence of the

O'Donnels, O'Donogougghes and all the rest of the celedrated O's. We beg him to continue to advertise us and send us his bill io the editors of the Co-Operator, a copy of which will be found safely ledged at the next Centenial, in spite of all the growls of our esteemed contemporary of the immediate collapse.[61]

The capabilities of the early territorial journalists, however, were not best represented by Aoy, for generally they were competent in their craft and well educated. These qualities made them unique in New Mexico a uniqueness increased by the rarity of journalism on the frontier. All of this, in turn, generated a spirit of fraternalism and, at the same time, a high self-esteem. From such self-esteem it was easy for the editors to fall occasionally into the sharp criticism characteristic of the currently common personal journalism. Such bitterness was increased by the battles of these opportunistic editors for political positions or rewards. Thus, a survey of the predominant traits of the early editors shows them to be well educated, capable, politically alert, and both friendly and critical in their relations with one another.

But these capable editors faced severe limitations. Among the handicaps of the early territorial papers was the language problem presented by the mixed population of New Mexico, as well as the customs of contemporary journalism which resulted in papers unattractive in content, style, and makeup compared to present-day newspapers. The small space available for the information and entertainment of readers was cut in half by the necessity of reporting the news in Spanish and English. Dominating the meager space remaining were the editorials. Following the editorials in a declining order of importance and space were territorial news, local events, national news, and special features. Inadequate news sources also hampered the editors, for they obtained information, usually very late, from other papers, volunteer correspondents, and from a very frequently interrupted Associated Press service. Considering the handicaps, the quality of territorial journalism was good.

Journalism in New Mexico in this era presented the unique problem of a predominantly Anglo-American press serving a population overwhelmingly Spanish-American. The first paper edited by an Anglo-American, the Santa Fe *Republican,* set the pattern for most of the early papers by dividing its pages between the two languages. Although there were some efforts to break away from this by printing a paper in each language in areas of heavy Spanish-American population,[62] most territorial editors followed the bilingual practice. Despite the heavy usage of the Spanish language in newspapers, only about 12 per cent (ten out of eighty) of the journalists were Spanish-Americans. Apparently other Spanish-Americans were employed only to translate the English-language copy into Spanish. Bilingualism reduced by one-half the space available for editorials, news, and features, for the Spanish-language portion was largely a translation of the English-language copy. Moreover, it was usually a translation of the previous week's English copy.[63]

On the other hand, many southern New Mexico mining area papers did not follow the bilingual practice. The Tubac and Tucson *Arizonian,* Mesilla *Times,* Silver City *Mining Life,* and *Grant County Herald* were published in English alone. Most of these papers apparently believed they had little to gain from bilingualism, since the majority of the population they served was Anglo-American. Nevertheless, the great majority of papers of this era was bilingual.

The present-day newspaper reader, accustomed to a varied fare of news in a wide range of topics and with numerous special features, would find the early territorial journals very dull reading, for they were heavy in editorials and limited in news. The editorial columns were of greatest interest and importance with their colorful language and personalized topics which served to increase reader interest. Perhaps this motivated personal journalism, for disputations of the well-known editors lent color and increased reader interest in the editorials. Next after the editorials in importance and proportion of space was the general news of the territory. News was usually obtained by clipping stories from other papers; often, however, stories were reported by voluntary correspondents. In some instances such correspondents proved unreliable, but the editors, who often also served as reporters, business managers, and mechanical staff, had neither time nor facilities to verify facts. In addition, the lack of reliable news sources and poor communications led editors to publish mere rumors and to depend heavily on unconfirmed facts.[64]

Local news was usually limited to the most important events; social items and sports events were rarely reported. Least prominent was national and international news. Most territorial editors borrowed this news from other papers, although the Santa Fe *New Mexican* and Silver City *Grant County Herald* subscribed to the Associated Press service for short periods. This service, a 500-word daily telegram, was a brief account of the chief news stories of the day and was usually presented to the readers as a news summary.

The type and consistency of special features used by the territorial editors followed no regular pattern. One wasteful feature, considering the limited space of the papers, was the publication of a directory of territorial and county officers, which required eight to ten inches of space and usually ran unchanged week after week. This feature, more common later, was used only by the Silver City *Mining Life* and the Mesilla *News* in these decades.[65] A more useful feature, used by the Albuquerque *Republican Review,* Silver City *Mining Life,* and Silver

City *Grant County Herald,* was the publication of a current list of food prices.

Various types of literary features were prominent in some of the papers. Fiction, used by many American weeklies at this time, was uncommon in New Mexico. The Albuquerque *Rio Abajo Weekly Press,* the only notable user of fiction, published one short novel and then abandoned the practice.[66] Several years later the Albuquerque *Review* ran a serialized history of New Mexico.[67] Literary efforts were confined mainly to humor and poetry. Most humor was in the form of satires upon the other editors or brief puns. An example of the latter is the following: "DEFINITION—A spare rib: a thin wife."[68] One of the best humorous articles, headed "WHISTLE TIME," appeared in the Silver City *Grant County Herald*:

> Silver City, besides apparent time, mean time, meal time, treble time, has whistle time, which is kept by the mill men and regulated by the organ of digestion of the several engineers "on watch" and is far meaner time than mean time or any other time.
> . . . . . . . . . . . . . . . . . . . . . . . . . . . . . . . . . . . . . . . . . . . . . . . . . . . . . . . . . . . .
> An engineer afflicted with tape worm makes any other day in the year as long as the 21st of June, not because solar time is chopped off by the irregular motion of the sun, but because the snake is restless and requires its victim to call the "relief" before the usual time for breakfast.
>
> There seems to be a laudable rivalry among the mills. No sooner does one whistle toot, than the engineers of all the other mills, rush for the several clocks, set them to correspond with the sound of the first whistle and then awaken the echoes by announcing that they too, are on time; thus giving Silver City absolute time, which does away with the necessity of considering time in relation to the heavenly bodies and their motion.[69]

Poetry, another literary feature popular in the American press in these years, was prominent in only three territorial papers: the Albuquerque *Republican Review,* the Silver City *Mining Life,* and the Silver City *Grant County Herald.* All three used a great deal of poetry. Most of this poetry was contributed, but some of it was unsigned and possibly the work of the editors. The following selection, entitled "NO KISS," is one of the better humorous poems:

> "Kiss me Will," sang Marguerite
> To a pretty little tune,
> holding up her dainty mouth,
> Sweet as roses born in June.
> Will be ten years old that day
> And he pulled her golden curls
> Teasingly, and answer made:
> "I'm too old—I don't kiss girls."

> Ten years pass and Marguerite
> Smiles as Will kneels at her feet,
> Gazing fondly into her eyes,
> Praying, "Wont you kiss me, sweet?"
> 'Rite is seventeen today;
> With her birthday ring she toys
> For a moment, then replies:
> "I'm too old—I don't kiss boys!"[70]

Poetry of a more serious mien was also frequent, and the following, "WHAT IS LIFE," is an example of this type:

> A little crib beside the bed,
> A little face below the spread,
> A little frock behind the door,
> A little shoe upon the floor.
>
> A little lad with dark brown hair,
> A little face blue eyed and fair,
> A little lane that leads to school,
> A little pencil, slate and rule.
>
> A little blithesome winsome maid,
> A little hand within is laid,
> A little cottage, acres four,
> A little old-time household store.
>
> A little family gathered round,
> A little turf-heaped, tear dew'd mound:
> A little added to His soil,
> A little rest from hardest toil.
>
> A little silver in his hair,
> A little room and easy chair;
> A little night of earth-lit gloom,
> A little cortege to the tomb.[71]

Just as the extensive space devoted to poetry by some territorial journals is in striking contrast with current practices, so are the journalistic styles of the territorial editors. Today in journalism, the first paragraph of a news story summarizes the important facts and contains the chief point of the article. Territorial papers, and the general American press of this era, might place the important facts anywhere in a long story. Where modern journalism strives for clarity by the use of simple sentence construction and simple and concise language, territorial journalism is noted for its verbosity, flowery and stilted language, as well as long and complicated sentence structures. Modern headlines are set in large type, to attract readers and to emphasize the chief point of a news story. The headlines of territorial newspapers were usually in small type, only one line deep and one column wide, and often unrelated to the chief point of the story. In the mid-seventies, however, multi-tiered headlines, already being used by the eastern press, began to appear in New Mexico.[72]

The page makeup of the territorial papers likewise would be considered very poor by present standards. The left-hand columns of the first page were given to advertising; and if the paper was well supported by the town merchants, advertising might occupy over three-quarters of the first page and all of the last page. Page two contained the editorials along with some advertising and news stories. In bilingual papers news space on pages three and four was reserved for the Spanish-language copy. Since the papers were generally only four pages and bilingual, large headlines and artwork to provide a balanced makeup were impractical. Thus, both by custom and necessity these papers were poor in style and format and used small headlines.

Hampered as they were by poor makeup, limited space, the necessity of dividing that space between two languages, and the shortcomings of the journalistic practices of that age, it is remarkable that the territorial journals enjoyed circulations as large as they did. Perhaps the emphasis on editorials was the wisest course, for the editors, who made themselves well-known public figures, shared their thoughts on an interesting personalized basis with their readers. Since general news was often stale and skimpy, the editorial interpretations of territorial life became the most important and enjoyable feature of the early territorial journals.

The success of a newspaper lies neither in the brilliance of its editorials nor the excellence of its news stories and features alone; a newspaper is also a business whose production costs must be met by advertising and circulation sales. The conditions for the economic success of early territorial newspapers were made difficult by tedious and time-consuming printing methods. Business success was further curtailed because the high rate of illiteracy in the territorial population held subscriptions down and reduced advertising effectiveness. In addition, high advertising rates further reduced revenues and ultimate profits.

The American press derived supplementary income from commercial printing during this era, but in New Mexico the only important business of this type was the territorial public printing. Battles for this extra income led to a fierce competitive struggle at Santa Fe, accounting for the failure of several newspapers there. Most newspaper failures in the territory, however, were the result of the difficult conditions of journalism in New Mexico in this period.

Throughout the early territorial period very crude and tedious printing methods prevailed. From the little information available about the one printing press in the territory during the Mexican era, it can be deduced that this press was changed little from that used by Gutenberg almost four centuries earlier.[73] The earliest press of the Anglo-American New Mexicans was small.[74] By the 1860s, most New Mexico newspapers were using a Washington model hand press, capable of making 250 impressions of a two-page form per hour.[75] Thus, printing a four-page paper with 1,000 subscribers required the labor of two men for at least eight hours. Probably a longer time was actually needed, for fatigue would eventually slow the workers. The first cylinder model mechanical press was brought to New Mexico in 1875 for *Revista Catolica* at Las Vegas. Although this Fairhaven press could be operated by steam power, its Jesuit owners operated it manually at a speed of about 250 impressions an hour.[76] It was probably easier, however to maintain such a rate on this press than it was on the Washington hand press. These slow press speeds made large circulations impractical and improbable, retarding territorial journalism.

Composition of type was another handicap, thousands of tiny pieces of type were assembled by hand and locked in a form before the printing of the paper could begin. After the printing of the paper, the type was returned to its proper niche in the type cases—an operation almost as time consuming as composition. Skilled printers set about ten column inches of news type per hour.[77] Type setting, printing the four small-size pages used by most territorial weeklies, and redistributing the type probably required the full time of one printer five days a week. For example, when H. S. Johnson was the entire staff of his Albuquerque *Rio Abajo Weekly Press,* he printed the paper in the daylight hours but worked late each night preparing copy.[78] Since many territorial editor-publishers were their entire staffs, publication of these newspapers required exceedingly long and tedious hours. Hence the shortcomings of many territorial editors are more understandable.

Editors who wished to devote more time to editing found it very difficult to recruit printers, for such skilled workmen were rare in frontier New Mexico. To illustrate, Santa Fe *New Mexican* publisher W. H. Manderfield probably made Thomas Tucker, a printer on the competing Santa Fe *Weekly Gazette,* a partner because he needed a compositor.[79] William McGuiness taught his wife, a native of New Mexico, the trade; and one week, during his illness, she published the paper alone.[80] Some publishers sought to train native New Mexicans as printers.[81] This was very difficult since few of them were literate in Spanish, and fewer yet were literate in English. Thus, the isolated publishers often had little recourse but to become their own compositors.

Another obstacle was the expensive and time-consuming haul by wagon to bring supplies to isolated New Mexico. Since practically all territorial papers were undercapitalized, they were able neither to maintain an ample stock of newsprint, nor to get dependable delivery on small lots. As a result, every paper of this era surviving over a year missed issues or printed on brown wrapping paper because newsprint failed to arrive when expected. When an issue was missed, subscriptions and advertising contracts were extended, reducing revenues and increasing expenses of the publishers.

Apparently to offset the high expenses of publishing and the limited sources of revenue, the publishers adopted very high advertising rates. Most early New Mexico journals printed their rates in their papers. The published rates of the Santa Fe *Republican,* for example, were $1.50 per square, about one column inch, and $1 per square for each subsequent insertion of the same type.[82] The Santa Fe *Weekly Gazette* in 1853 charged $1 and 75 cents for this arrangement.[83] The rate of the Albuquerque *Rio Abajo Weekly Press* was $1 and 50 cents. This tabloid weekly, however, sold an entire column for $100 per year, which amounted to about 12 cents per column inch.[84] Evidently copy changes in the advertisement were severely limited in the course of that year. The rates of the Santa Fe *Daily New Mexican* were $1.50 and $1, which was less than the rates of the *Weekly New Mexican* at $2.50 and $2.[85] Probably the rates of the weekly were higher because of higher circulation. The highest advertising rate of the pre-railway era was the $4 and $2 rate of the Silver City *Grant County Herald,* higher than the present rate of any New Mexico newspaper.[86]

Eastern American rural weeklies at this time sold space for as high as $1.40 per column inch for a first insertion, and an entire column for one year for as little as $25.[87] Possibly the high rates of the territorial papers prevented their receiving national advertising, for very little such advertising was to be seen in these journals, despite the fact that most of them were represented by a national advertising agent.[88]

The published advertising rates of the New Mexico papers were quite high, considering their small circulations, the current purchasing power of the dollar, and the rates of comparable eastern papers. Yet, there were reasons for these high rates. The excellent rag-content newsprint used was expensive, and high freight rates over the Santa Fe Trail increased costs of all supplies. In fact, high freight costs inflated all prices in New Mexico, forcing publishers in turn to charge high advertising and subscription rates.

In addition to maintaining exceptionally high rates the publishers were quite slow to adopt the improvements in advertising techniques developed by papers in the eastern United States, and thus their advertisements were often unappealing. For example, in the 1847 Santa Fe *Republican* most advertisements were similar to present day classified advertising, being composed of small blocks of the body type of the paper. By the 1860s and the 1870s, large-type display advertisements were more popular; and newspapers sought especially to sell full-column or half-column standing advertisements for one year. Standing advertisements sometimes produced strange results. For example, a Bean Brothers' Saloon advertisement in the Mesilla *Times* announced for over a year the arrival of a new shipment of whiskey.

By the 1870s some eastern American papers were publishing multi-column advertisements, and advertisers were beginning to demand frequent copy changes. Since this increased interest in the advertisements, it was beneficial to both publishers and advertisers.[89] The scarcity of printers evidently led publishers to encourage standing advertisements, which appealed to merchants because of their much lower prices. Thus, this was an almost universal practice. Publication of acts of Congress and army notices asking for bids on supplies provided income for some papers.[90] Most advertising revenue, however, came from display advertisements, and encouragement of standing advertisements both curtailed revenue and limited advertising effectiveness, discouraging increased advertising budgets. Thus, standard practices limited the growth of advertising revenues.

Exceptionally high subscription rates also limited newspaper income, for this restricted the circulation of territorial papers. The annual subscription rate of the first Santa Fe *New Mexican* was $7 and the rate for the *Daily New Mexican* was $16.[91] Both papers were small four-page tabloids. The rates of weekly papers were gradually reduced over the years until by 1879 most were $3 annually. Considering that most of these papers had a consistent four-page format, these prices were very high. Thus, high prices along with high illiteracy rates kept circulation of these papers quite small. The Santa Fe *Republican* claimed a circulation of 750, but this probably was exaggerated.[92] In view of the low circulation figures reported to *N. W. Ayer and Son's Newspaper Annual* in the mid-eighties, it is doubtful if any territorial paper of the seventies had more than 500 subscribers.[93]

An achievement of larger circulations of these papers would not automatically have increased their profits, for few subscribers paid in advance. Publishers had great difficulty with collections; William Mc-Guiness of the Albuquerque *Review,* for example, constantly lamented unpaid accounts.[94] Even the prosperous *Grant County Herald* in booming Silver City was troubled with delinquent subscribers, for S. M. Ashenfelter informed his readers after nine months as publisher that unpaid subscriptions amounted to $2,000.[95] Apparently 80 to 90 per cent of his subscribers were delinquent. Thus, not only were circulations small, but poor collections further reduced revenue.

Non-journalistic printing, or "job work" in the jargon of publishers, offered a supplementary income which all territorial publishers sought. The greatest profits were from printing for territorial and federal agencies, the United States Army, and the legislature. While the first two provided more consistent income, legislative printing was extensive and very profitable during a short period. All bills introduced in the legislature and the laws finally approved were printed in Spanish and English. The Santa Fe *New Mexican,* because of its political influence and location, monopolized governmental printing after 1870.[96] Therefore, job work provided little income for other territorial papers.

Monopoly of the territorial public printing, while profitable for the *New Mexican,* brought with it the disadvantage of almost continual competition. Competive struggles between territorial newspapers were rare in this era except at Santa Fe, where between 1863 and 1879 seventeen papers were published. Although only about one-half of them survived long enough to provide effective competition for the dominant *New Mexican,* even the short-lived rivals absorbed part of the community subscriptions and advertising. Santa Fe papers did not fight competition by reducing circulation and advertising rates as present-day papers sometimes do; they apparently fought by offering additional services. The most prominent of the additional services was daily publication. While this proved effective for the *New Mexican* against the *Weekly Gazette,* the daily *Post,* and the weekly *Post,* the efforts of three papers to use daily publication against the *New Mexican* proved ineffective and they soon were driven into bankruptcy.

Competition was not without its benefits to society, for without it, possibly no daily newspaper would have been published at the territorial capital. In addition, the territory enjoyed the advantage of the Associated Press telegrams for several years, providing early news of the outside world. On the other hand, it is quite possible that without rivalry Santa Fe would have been served better by only one journal— a newspaper freed from the necessity of political subservience.

Competition and the harsh conditions imposed upon journalism in New Mexico led to many newspaper failures. Of sixty-six papers founded before January, 1879, only fifteen survived, and another five of them lapsed before the end of that year. In view of these conditions, why were so many papers established? Several reasons can be assigned. First, papers were established by opportunists who hoped to transform the prestige of a publishership into political preference, either as spoils or as offices. Second, the editors, like their frontier neighbors, were inherently optimistic, believing that mineral development or the magic of railway transportation would in the future make New Mexico into a prosperous empire from which they would benefit more than the latecomers because of their early arrival. Third, the simple machinery and limited supplies needed to launch a newspaper made it easy for these optimistic opportunists to found papers.

Few of the editors, however, profited from their efforts to advance themselves through politics. The competitive struggle for printing spoils at Santa Fe illustrates one facet of this, and few of them were rewarded with offices. Thus, on the whole the rewards promised by politics failed to materialize. Similarly, most of those who anticipated gains from the economic growth of New Mexico found few rewards. Of all who had published papers before 1879, only three remained publishers in New Mexico for another five years, and only two of the newspapers published in January, 1879, survived that long.[97] Nevertheless, these men were incurable optimists who believed in a great and prosperous future for themselves. An editorial by William McGuiness, written shortly before the railways reached Albuquerque, provides an example of their optimism:

We have fought long, hard and faithfully, have experienced many severe struggles, and many painful sacrifices. . . . [and soon] . . . . We will be in on the reward.[98]

Optimism comes easy when the price is low, and the cost of founding newspapers in this area was very low indeed. At least that seems to be the case with A. V. Aoy of the *Acorn* at Las Vegas, for as the Santa Fe *New Mexican* noted:

Mr. Aoy commenced publication . . . with no more skill as a printer than might have been expected from an office devil who had spent three months sweeping the office, as carrier and ink dauber and with no more type and material than might have been packed on a man's back.[99]

The low initial cost of entry into the newspaper business was one of the few advantages of the territorial journalists and was offset by many handicaps. Obsolete hand-powered presses and hand composition of type require long hours of tedious labor, which, because of a shortage of printers, usually was performed by the editor-publisher himself. The largely illiterate and impoverished population held down circulation and advertising revenues. Irregular, slow, and expensive freight interrupted publication and further reduced profits.

In addition to the mechanical and business difficulties territorial papers were limited by bilingual publication, poor page makeup, headlining, and writing styles. Little space was devoted to local news, and other news was often late or unreliable. Consequently, the core of these papers became the editorials, which were made interesting by the prestige and insight of the editors and their strongly partisan support of political allies—support usually given to obtain political preferment. The ensuing rivalry was valuable, for the educated, individualistic, frontier editors espoused varied causes, delving fearlessly into most public questions. As a result, the public was well served. Such was the position of the territorial press at the end of the pre-railway era and in the first years of the next decade.

# THE TERRITORIAL PRESS
# IN TRANSITION
## 1879-1900

FOR THE TERRITORIAL PRESS the years from 1879 to 1900 were a period of change. The opportunistic amateur journalists of the pre-railway era rapidly gave way to a group of equally opportunistic professional newsmen. This new group, seeking commercial rather than political profits, quickly launched dozens of new papers. But by 1900 economic depression in the territory again forced journalists to turn to politics for sustenance. In this period the development of territorial journalism was retarded, and newsmen lagged behind in accepting new journalistic styles, mechanical methods, and business techniques. Thus, despite an early optimism induced by development of the railway, by 1900 the receding frontier and poor economic conditions had transformed territorial papers into routine country weeklies and dull and backward dailies.

The era of change began in December, 1878, when a Santa Fe Railway subsidiary reached the New Mexico border. Within three years this line had been extended southwestward to Las Vegas, Albuquerque, and present-day Rincon where it divided, one branch going to Deming and the other via Las Cruces to El Paso.

Simultaneously, from the west the Southern Pacific Railroad advanced across southwestern New Mexico; and from the north a Denver and Rio Grande line, projected to Albuquerque, El Paso, and Mexico City, halted at Espanola, twenty-four miles north of Santa Fe.[1] In 1880 the Atlantic and Pacific Railroad launched the western end of its proposed transcontinental line from Albuquerque toward California.

Opened to the world by four major railways, New Mexico now had an outlet for its products; and a wave of immigrants came to the territory to exploit its wealth. Following the railway construction crews came miners to begin exploiting the low-grade ores that could be marketed by using the cheap railway transportation. Cattlemen were attracted by vast free ranges, easy access to markets, and exceptional profits resulting from high cattle prices. Lured by potential profits to be derived from the new exploiters of New Mexican wealth, merchants came by almost every train. Close behind all these groups trailed a swarm of saloon keepers, card sharps, petty gunmen, and prostitutes to pander to the baser desires of frontier New Mexicans. Thus, New Mexico, a rugged frontier for almost three centuries, quickly assumed a new vitality, roughness, and rawness, and became even more of a frontier area. Mining towns quickly sprang up at White Oaks, Chloride, Hillsboro, Kingston, Raton, and Gallup, and the sleepy village of Socorro became the fourth largest territorial town. Albuquerque and Las Vegas prospered as railway centers and distribution points. Most of the new arrivals were Anglo-Americans, who soon grew from a small fraction to one-third or more of the population—completely altering territorial life.

Then the prosperous '80s gave way to the bleak '90s. Inflated cattle prices fell; reduced silver prices closed many of the territorial mines; and reductions in the tariff on wool curtailed the profits of sheep raisers. The great depression, which gripped the entire nation from 1893 to 1897, was extremely harsh in New Mexico since the territory had already lost one major industry, and two others were crippled before the national depression began. Nevertheless, even in the midst of depression there were signs of future prosperity for New Mexico. Irrigation projects brought hundreds of farmers to the Pecos and San Juan River valleys, and the frontier of homesteading farmers advanced into the northeastern corner of the territory—developments that later would bring New Mexico even greater wealth and population.

Under the impetus of the new population and industry there was a tremendous growth of territorial journalism between 1879 and 1900. In this period 283 new journals were launched, making a total of 294 different papers published in these years compared to 66 in the pre-railway era. In January, 1879, New Mexico had no daily paper, but in 1900 there were five stable dailies among sixty-three papers then being published. Since the proportion of failures was lessening and the proportion of long-lived papers increasing, a greater stability of the press in this era is indicated. A great many of those papers that failed did so as a result of economic conditions, particularly in the mining centers. On the other hand, many of the failures can be attributed directly to harsh competition; confined largely to Santa Fe in the early period, it raged generally throughout the territory in this era. Politics played a part in this severe competition, for almost every town had a newspaper representing the interests of one of the major political parties. If one party lacked newspaper representation, it would often publish its own paper for the duration of a political campaign. Thus, despite greater overall stability for journalism in this era, competition and depression brought many trials to the newsmen.

Las Vegas journalism mirrored all the troubles of the new era. Competition was rife, political quarrels were frequent, and in the nineties depression left its mark. The booming prosperity of East Las Vegas and West Las Vegas boosted the combined population to 5,697 by 1890 and attracted many journalists. As a result forty-four different papers were published in Las Vegas between 1879 and 1900. Fierce competition began with the launching of two new weeklies, the *New Mexico Herald* and the *Optic,* in June and July respectively, in 1879. The *Gazette,* a weekly, quickly retaliated by adding a daily issue.[2] Then in October, 1879, Russell Kistler, editor of the *Optic,* converted his struggling weekly into a daily—apparently foolhardily. But surprisingly enough the paper was soon operating profitably.[3] In January, 1880, the *New Mexico Herald* moved from Las Vegas to less competitive Santa Fe,[4] and J. H. Koogler, evidently believing that the *Optic* would win the battle, sold his Las Vegas *Gazette* in 1883 to a group headed by Jefferson Raynolds, local banker.[5] The *Gazette* then had many short-term editors and several suspensions before it died permanently in May, 1886.[6] Meanwhile, the *Daily Optic* had survived with great difficulty. During the political campaigns of 1880 and 1886, originally Republican Kistler, in need of funds, had sold his support to the Democrats,[7] causing the Republicans in the next several years to retaliate with campaign weeklies.[8]

The founding of papers in Las Vegas was not dependent on political motivation only, for in this era all types of weeklies were founded, sopping up some of the funds available for newspaper advertising and subscriptions. The mining industry had as its trade publication the *Mining World,* published intermittently in the '80s.[9] Cattle and sheep men could turn to the pages of the *New Mexico Livestock Journal,* founded in 1882 and succeeded in 1884 by the *New Mexico Stock Grower.*[10] Real estate dealers began several advertising sheets to be sent to prospective immigrants. In addition, the lack of a Sunday issue by Las Vegas dailies led to the founding of several briefly flourishing Sunday weeklies. The *Sunday Herald,* the *Sunday Morning Mountain Breeze,* the *Sunday Courier,* and the *Sunday Morning Review* all competed for Las Vegas revenues.[11] Nevertheless, politics motivated the most serious threats to the *Daily Optic.* The political campaign of 1884 was featured by the foundation of the *Daily Chronicle,* which later became a weekly.[12] The desire of Republicans for a newspaper voice led J. A. Carruth in March, 1891, to found the *Free Press,* which was published first as a weekly and then as a daily until November, 1892.[13] Politics apparently fostered in January,

1895, a weekly *Examiner,* founded by the owners of the prosperous *New Mexico Stock Grower.* The *Examiner* became a daily in June, 1895, but weakened by the ensuing battle it was turned over in January, 1897, to a company headed by J. A. Carruth. Finally in February, 1898, the exhausted combatants merged, apparently forced to do so by their creditors, and the *Daily Examiner* was absorbed by the *Daily Optic.* Kistler lost control of the paper to George T. Gould, who represented a company of prominent Las Vegas Democrats.[14] Republicans, still determined to control a Las Vegas paper, then retaliated in October, 1900, with the *Daily Record.*[15]

Politics also led to the founding of two good Spanish-language papers in Las Vegas, still further increasing journalistic strife there. *La Voz del Pueblo,* founded at Santa Fe in 1888 by Nestor Montoya and E. H. Salazar, was purchased in June, 1890, and moved to Las Vegas by the Union People's party. Then in March, 1894, Salazar left *La Voz* to found *El Independiente.*[16] These two prosperous weeklies absorbed still another part of available circulation and advertising funds of the town, making journalism in Las Vegas even more competitive.

Initially, optimistic pioneer publishers at Las Vegas launched papers of all types, seeking to garner a portion of the commercial revenue of the town. This dispersion of revenue among many papers weakened all combatants and led them to seek political subsidy. Politicians without newspaper representation fostered new journals, adding to the intensity of the rivalry. The ultimate result was that the *Daily Optic,* the best territorial paper of these years, failed to develop into a strong daily paper which could have provided necessary civic and business leadership for the town.

As compared with Las Vegas and the Santa Fe newspaper battles before 1879, competition did not play as important a part in capital city journalism. Rail connections failed to bring the prosperity anticipated by the city, and it thus had less appeal to journalists. The lessened commercial importance of the town, which had been the largest in the territory in 1880, is shown by a decline in the population from 6,185 in 1880 to 5,603 in 1900 and 5,072 in 1910.[17] Under these circumstances journalstic rivalry soon reverted to the struggle for public printing contracts. During this era the Santa Fe *New Mexican* battled twenty-two other short-lived papers for political power and the public printing. At the end of the era the *New Mexican* remained the most important territorial paper because it was still the most politically influential.

Expectations of commercial rather than political profits motivated the first competitors of the Santa Fe *New Mexican.* The Las Vegas *New Mexico Herald* was the first to arrive, becoming at Santa Fe the *Era Southwestern.*[18] J. G. Albright[19] bought this paper in September, 1880, publishing it as the weekly and daily *Democrat* until September, 1882. His blast at the town when the *Daily Democrat* was suspended in August, 1882, indicates the lack of commercial profits:

> With this issue the DAILY DEMOCRAT wearily closes its leaves, and takes a Rip Van Winkle sleep—not for twenty years we predict, but until the people of this drowsy town come to a sense of understanding and realize the necessity of supporting an enterprise that is entirely devoted to their interests.[20]

Initially, the owners of the *New Mexican* apparently expected it to gain commercial profits and also to provide them with political influence. Early in 1880 a group of Santa Fe railway officials bought this paper, revived the *Daily New Mexican,* and placed Charles W. Greene in charge. Despite the efforts of Greene and later managers, the *New Mexican* proved unprofitable; and in May, 1883, its owners abandoned it, moving the plant to Kansas.[21] At this time the Santa Fe Ring, a political clique which had allied itself with the *New Mexican,* entered directly into Santa Fe journalism. W. H. Bailhache and Max Frost, members of the clique and co-owners of the Albuquerque *Evening Review,* sold shares in their paper to ring members and moved it to Santa Fe as the *New Mexican Review.*[22] In 1885 a Democratic territorial administration dismissed many of the politico-owners of the *New Mexican;*[23] they then left the territory, selling much of their stock to Max Frost. The Democratic administration also awarded territorial public printing to short-lived Democratic papers which sprang up. As a result the *New Mexican* survived with great difficulty until the Republicans returned to power in 1889.[24]

The *New Mexican* survived and remained politically powerful through the bleak '90s as a result of the efforts of Max Frost, who became editor and publisher in 1889. Frost, an able editor and an astute politician, kept the *New Mexican* on a profitable basis while it competed with its greatest rival of these decades, the Democratic Santa Fe *Sun.*[25] When in 1893 Democrats regained control of the territorial administration, the clever Frost leased the *New Mexican* to Democratic office-holders. This group, which desired to use the paper as a propaganda medium, merged the *New Mexican* and the *Sun,*[26] thereby eliminating for the *New Mexican* a rival that could have been tremendously strengthened by printing contracts it might have been awarded by Democrats. With the return of the Republicans to power in 1897, Max Frost again resumed control of the *New Mexican.*[27] Thus, despite Santa Fe's declining population, the depression, Democratic administrations, and almost incessant competition, the *New Mexican* survived and remained the most politically influential of all territorial papers.

Albuquerque, unlike Santa Fe, grew rapidly in the new era; it became a center for railway construction crews, railway shops, and whole-sale merchants. As a result, by 1900 Albuquerque had become the largest territorial town,[28] and many ambitious journalists were attracted to it. Although Albuquerque had fewer newspapers than Las Vegas, news-paper competition in the two towns was equally fierce. Between 1882 and 1900, two or more excellent dailies constantly battled for newspaper revenue in Albuquerque. During this heated contest many ambitious newsmen were left behind in the race to own or control the dominant daily in the town.

William McGuiness, who since 1870 had endured poverty to maintain the Albuquerque *Review* in anticipation of a reward from a railway-induced prosperity, evidently foresaw the intense rivalry when with bitter irony he invited others to share his bounty:

Now is the time for impecunious scribes, overwhelmed with a devouring ambition to acquire fame and fortune, to establish a score or more of papers in Albuquerque. We are getting rich . . . won't press the invitation further.[29]

Soon his invitation was accepted and McGuiness abandoned jour-nalism. In June, 1880, the *Daily Golden Gate* was launched and came under the control of J. A. Spradling. Financed by Albuquerque mer-chants,[30] Spradling bought a new plant and renamed the paper the *Daily Journal*.[31] Thomas Hughes, who gained control of the paper the following year, made it the *Morning Journal*.[32] Meanwhile, W. H. Bailhache purchased the *Review,* and in February, 1882, added a daily issue as the *Evening Review*.[33] This was the beginning of a keen rivalry which became sharper in September, 1882, when J. G. Albright moved his *Daily Democrat* from Santa Fe to Albuquerque.[34] The ensuing strug-gle soon forced the *Review* to move to Santa Fe and brought a rapid shifting of editor-managers[35] at the *Morning Journal* until it was sus-pended in December, 1886.[36]

The demise of the *Morning Journal* did not bring the struggle in Albuquerque to an end, for Albuquerque Republicans had already found a new champion, the *Daily Citizen*. Launched by C. L. Hubbs, the *Citizen* came under the control of Thomas Hughes and W. T. Mc-Creight in May, 1887.[37] Competition from the *Citizen* and loss of sup-port of the Democrats made Albright the next victim of the battle. His failure to support a Democratic delegate to Congress alienated his fel-low partisans. They, in turn, encouraged the founding of a weekly, and later a daily, the *Times,* depriving Albright of sorely needed revenues. The *Times* was suspended in 1894,[38] but in less than one year Albright lost the *Morning Democrat* when T. B. Catron foreclosed a mortgage he held on its plant. Subsequently, at a sheriff's auction, the *Democrat* was purchased by A. A. Grant, an Albuquerque capitalist.[39] During the rest of the decade, the *Citizen* and *Democrat* appeared to be almost equal in strength and quality. Thus, in 1900 these two dailies shared the Albuquerque journalistic field with several small weeklies, for the rivalry had resulted in a draw.

For some reason not immediately apparent, the merchants of Las Cruces, a relatively large town drawing on a nearby irrigated area that was populous, gave meager support to their newspapers. The short lives of numerous journals and the troubled course of the *Rio Grande Republican* appear to confirm this. Seven months after J. A. Spradling and prominent local political figures began the *Rio Grande Republican* in May, 1881, Spradling sold his interest in the paper, stating that since the paper was unprofitable "our pencil refuses to keep up to scratch."[40] Meanwhile, in July, 1881, *Newman's Semi-Weekly,* which had been operating at a loss, moved from Las Cruces to El Paso, Texas. The *Rio Grande Republican* continued, though with great difficulty, undergoing nine changes of management between 1882 and 1900.[41] The fate of two small tabloid dailies founded in 1889 was even worse. One, the *Daily Times,* lasted one month; and the other, the *Daily News,* survived ten months.[42]

Lacking adequate merchant support, Las Cruces publishers relied heavily on political rewards and were often politically motivated. The Las Cruces *Mesilla Valley Democrat,* for example, was launched in August, 1886, shortly before its owner announced himself as a candidate for the legislature. Eventually suspended in 1890, this paper was revived in 1892 as the *Independent Democrat* by A. B. Fall to advance his political career. It survived until 1899, perishing shortly before Fall became affiliated with the Republican party.[43] The numerous Spanish-language papers serving this area were, with two exceptions, short-lived political campaign papers. The exceptions, *El Tiempo,* founded in 1882, and *El Labrador,* launched in 1896, survived with great hardship.[44] The papers at both Las Cruces and Santa Fe thus illustrate that the prosperity of the railway era was not evenly distributed among the territorial journalists.

Mineral development near Silver City was encouraged by the cheap new transportation the railroads afforded, and the town quickly gained population,[45] including a flood of journalists who founded eight new papers between 1879 and 1883. The *Grant County Herald,* a weekly, menaced by a daily rival in March, 1880, began the *Daily Southwest,* only to suspend it in August of that same year. The weekly was enlarged in April, 1881, and renamed the *New Southwest and Grant County Herald.* Apparently this was an effort to combat two rivals, the *Telegram* and the *Mining Chronicle,* both of which lapsed that year.[46] In 1882, however, a new daily and four new weeklies challenged the supremacy of the *New Southwest*. In March, 1883, four of the five Silver City papers were consolidated as the *Southwest Sentinel,* purportedly independent but in fact Democratic. This left in opposition a Republican weekly, the *Enterprise,* founded October 24, 1882.[47]

The *Enterprise* and the *Southwest Sentinel* dominated Silver City journalism throughout the remainder of this era, for one new daily and several weeklies which were founded soon failed.[48] The *Enterprise* survived with few difficulties under two able publishers.[49] The career of the *Southwest Sentinel* was more troubled. There were frequent changes of publishers from 1883 until 1898, when W. B. Walton, son-in-law of S. M. Ashenfelter, became editor-publisher. During this period the *Southwest Sentinel* had been issued both as a daily and semi-weekly for short intervals and in 1896 had been renamed the *Independent.*[50] Since both major parties were represented by these two strong weeklies in the economically depressed 1890s, there were few efforts to establish new papers at Silver City.

Deming, unlike Silver City, grew not from the development of mines but of railways. A division point (local operating unit) of the Southern Pacific Railroad, the town also expected to become a division point or terminus of the Texas Pacific, the Santa Fe line to Guaymas in Mexico, and the line to Arizona via Silver City. Anticipating great growth for Deming, J. E. Curren founded the weekly *Headlight* there in June, 1881,[51] and soon other journalists sought a share of the revenues. In response to the weekly *Tribune* launched by Charles W. Greene in October, 1883, Curren made the *Headlight* a daily.[52] Curren soon left, but the *Daily Headlight* defeated the *Tribune* and again became a weekly before S. M. Ashenfelter bought it in September 1889.[53] This paper then became a leading territorial Democratic journal under the editorship of first, former Governor E. G. Ross, and second, W. B. Walton.[54]

The failure of the Deming *Headlight* to become the great and profitable paper of which J. E. Curren had dreamed did not kill his high optimism. In 1884 an exchange of his Deming paper for the Kingston *Clipper* thrust him into the midst of the booming Sierra County mining camps. Curren now sought to make his fortune by establishing a chain of small papers in Kingston, Hillsboro, and Lake Valley. Once a paper was well established Curren left it in the charge of others and moved on to found another. By 1887 his Hillsboro *Sierra County Advocate* and Kingston *Shaft* had subdued all rivals, but Curren apparently foresaw a bleak future for the area and sold out.[55]

The fluctuating fortunes of mining affected the careers of Sierra County newspapers for a number of years. The *Shaft,* for example, passed from hand to hand until J. P. Hyland bought it in March, 1889. By late 1893 low silver prices had closed Kingston's mines and it was a dying town. Hyland then moved the *Shaft* to Rincon, where in January, 1895, he abandoned it.[56] The *Sierra County Advocate* was also briefly owned by a series of publishers before P. J. Bennett acquired it in 1891. He remained its publisher until 1900 and then sold it to W. O. Thompson, a former publisher of the Chloride *Black Range*.[57] This paper, which Thompson had edited from 1885 to 1897, was abandoned when he lost all hope for higher silver prices.[58] Thus, to the publishers of Sierra County papers, declining silver prices and dying mining towns were much more of a problem than was newspaper competition.

White Oaks became a thriving mining camp after the discovery of gold nearby in 1880 and soon attracted a number of journalists. The first paper of the town was the *Golden Era*, founded in December, 1880. After a period of rapidly changing editor-publishers,[59] it was moved in 1884 to nearby Lincoln.[60] The next stable paper at White Oaks was the *Lincoln County Leader*. Founded by Lee H. Ruidisille in October, 1882, it was sold to William Caffery in 1883. Published by Caffery until his death in 1893, the *Lincoln County Leader* was soon suspended.[61]

J. E. Sligh,[62] earlier an editor of the *Golden Era*, launched the *New Mexico Interpreter* in 1885, publishing it for two years before selling it to William Watson.[63] Watson retained an equity in the paper or its mortgage until it was sold in 1897 to S. M. Wharton and J. A. Haley. Meanwhile, it had been renamed successively *Old Abe Eagle* and White Oaks *Eagle*.[64] With the depletion of its gold deposits, White Oaks also began to die, leading to the suspension of the *Eagle* in 1902.

A much more attractive site for journalists was the town of Raton, which rapidly gained population as a railway division point, the site of extensive coal mining, and the center for a thriving cattle industry. The *Comet*, Raton's first paper, was founded in January, 1881, by O. P. McMains. It was succeeded in September, 1881, by the *Guard*, evidently issued from the same shop by different owners.[65] In October, 1881, George F. Canis and Thomas Henderson moved the Cimarron *News and Press* to Raton and renamed it the *New Mexico News and Press*. The two Raton papers, sharply divided in politics and other matters, competed vigorously. Then in July, 1882, McMains bought the *Guard* and renamed it the *Comet*. Later that year when McMains became a candidate for territorial delegate to Congress, the *New Mexico News and Press*, then owned by Canis alone, strongly opposed him. Because McMains was very popular at Raton, the biting editorials of Canis infuriated many of his followers. They forced Canis to flee to Las Vegas, where he issued his paper until its suspension in November, 1882.[66] McMains soon sold the *Comet*, and Raton journalism became more placid. The *Comet*, renamed the *Range* in 1887, remained the leading paper of the town—especially during the editorship of T. W. Collier from 1891 to 1900.[67] Meanwhile, other journalists competed for income at Raton. The daily and weekly *Independent* was published from 1883 until 1889.[68] In 1890 the weekly *Reporter* was launched by G. B. Beringer. Before 1900 this paper became, successively, a tri-weekly, a semi-weekly, and a weekly again.[69] In addition, five less important weeklies were published at Raton in the 1890s.[70] In summary, high income from industry and agriculture as well as sharp political conflicts made Raton journalism more competitive than that of the dying mining towns.

Springer had few of the advantages of Raton, but its being named the county seat soon brought it a newspaper, the *Colfax County Stockman*. Three years later, in 1885, this paper came into the possession of Henry W. Sturges and his son, P. F. Sturges. Upon the death of the elder Sturges in 1891, J. F. Hutchinson became and remained the principal owner of the paper into the new century.[71]

In western New Mexico exploitation of low-grade coal deposits at Gallup led to its rapid growth in the late 1880s. After 1887, four weeklies competed there. The *Gazette, Register,* and *News-Register* were short lived, but the *Gleaner,* founded in 1888, endured a competitive flurry and then remained unopposed for over a decade.[72]

Gallup, like many of the older towns, was badly hurt economically by the depressed '90s. On the other hand, despite the depression a new wave of immigrants came in the '90s to exploit northeastern New Mexico's dry farming areas and the irrigation potential of the San Juan and Pecos River valleys. As a result such new towns as Roswell, Eddy, and Clayton were founded and new papers were launched, offsetting the decline in journalistic activity in the older towns. Without these new enterprises, the number of territorial newspapers being published in the '90s would have been greatly reduced.

San Juan River irrigation, developed very slowly by a series of small projects, did not provide a great economic stimulus to the area which explains the fact that although six papers were launched in the San Juan River Valley, only two of them survived through the troubled '90s. The Aztec *San Juan County Index* was founded in 1889 and continued under five publishers until 1900. The Junction City *Times,* founded in 1891, became the Farmington *San Juan Times* in 1893 and also frequently changed publishers before 1900.[73]

The lower Pecos Valley irrigation district, unlike that of the San Juan Valley, was developed rapidly by large companies and soon an extensive acreage was under cultivation. As a result both Roswell and Eddy enjoyed rapid growth which lured newsmen. The first paper of this region was a weekly, the Roswell *Pecos Valley Register,* founded in November, 1888, by J. A. Erwin and L. O. Fullen. This Republican weekly was sold two years later and became simply the Roswell *Register.*

Before 1900 it had had six owners. The Democratic weekly, the Roswell *Record,* was launched in 1891 and had a more stable career. It was published until 1899 by J. D. Lea, who made Lucius Dills the editor. Three short-lived weeklies also were established at Roswell in this decade.[74]

Further south along the Pecos at Eddy, the first paper was the Republican weekly *Argus,* founded in 1889 by the Pecos Irrigation and Development Company. From 1895 to 1900, L. O. Fullen represented this company as its editor and publisher.[75] Five other papers were launched at Eddy in this period, of which the most important was the Democratic *Current.* Established by W. H. Mullane in 1892 as the *Daily Eddy Current,* it retreated from its overambitious beginning by becoming a semi-weekly in 1894 and a weekly in 1895.[76] Here as at Roswell the chief competitive elements became two long-lived and stable papers representing the major political parties.

Farmers of a type different from those of the Pecos Valley were drawn into northeastern New Mexico. The Denver and Fort Worth Railroad in this area, provided access to markets and sped the immigration of dry farmers. Again small towns arose as trading centers and newspapers were established. The Clayton *Enterprise,* founded in May, 1888, led the parade of small weeklies launched in this region. J. E. Curren, who had published two small Colorado papers since leaving Sierra County, returned to New Mexico to establish the Folsom *Idea* in July, 1888. In 1890 Curren acquired the Clayton *Enterprise* and then followed practices similar to those he had used in Sierra County, publishing as many as three papers with editor-managers. Of ten papers founded in this area, the *Enterprise* was the most stable. Seven out of the ten were published at Clayton, providing almost continuous competition for the *Enterprise* from 1893 until 1900.[77]

From this survey of the founding of about 300 papers in the short period between 1879 and 1900, and in such a sparsely settled area as New Mexico, it may be seen that instability accompanied by intense competition was the most striking feature of territorial journalism. More newspapers were founded in the years from 1879 to 1885 than in the period between 1886 and 1900. The earlier years were a time of marked instability because many over-optimistic but under-capitalized publishers failed in this period of harsh and incessant competition. In the later years the competition became more intense, for depression reduced available revenues and made the contest more heated. The fierceness of the battle can be seen by the fact that such able and entrenched publishers as Russell Kistler of the Las Vegas *Daily Optic* and J .G. Albright of the Albuquerque *Morning Democrat* failed. As depression raged and the field narrowed, the publishers, who found it difficult to maintain themselves solely on advertising and subscription revenues, became more dependent upon the support of the politicians, who endeavored to maintain in most towns at least one paper favorable to their party.

This, then, was a period of transition in territorial journalism, an era of change from the independent, opportunistic, frontier editors of the 1870s toward the subdued and controlled press of 1900 dominated by territorial political figures. In this transitional period the personal journalism, warm fraternalism, and high self-esteem of the journalists of the 1870s were considerably moderated. Thus, the fading of the frontier, intense competition, and harsh depression had robbed the press of the independence of the frontier editor but had not yet given it the financial independence of the modern New Mexico press.

Independent and optimistic pioneer journalists of the early 1880s founded dozens of papers in small New Mexico towns anticipating prosperous futures when the towns and territory were fully developed. They were sustained initially by an equally optimistic merchant group and Anglo-American population. The merchants at first advertised heavily to introduce their firm names and to encourage newspapers, believing that newspapers were community assets that would attract new capital and immigrants to their town. And the Anglo-American immigrants, having a friendly interest in their new neighbors and homeland, generally became cash subscribers to their newspapers.[78] The large revenue resulting from advertising and circulation sustained a belief among newsmen of the '80s that most profits would come from commerce rather than from political subsidy.

Declining cattle, silver, and wool prices, as well as the general economic recession of the 1890s, dampened the enthusiasm of territorial journalists. The best evidence of this is the decline in the number of papers founded in the depression decade. In the '80s, 168 new papers were established, whereas in the '90s only 115 were launched. However, pioneering continued in some areas, and 28 of the new papers of the '90s were founded in the Pecos or San Juan River valleys, in new gold mining camps near Taos, or in the new dry farming areas. Despite the fact that there were some pioneer journalists in the 1890s, however, these bleak years robbed the territorial press corps of the frontiersman's optimism which had been so characteristic of them in the early 1880s.

Reduced commercial income led territorial journalists to seek, through politics, greater income from government posts or public printing. Illustrating this trend is the large number of journalist-postmasters in the '90s. Only two active journalists were postmasters in the 1880s: C. B. Hayward of the Santa Fe *New Mexican Review* and Thomas Hughes of the Albuquerque *Morning Journal*. On the other hand, six active journalists were postmasters in the 1890s: T. W. Collier of the

Raton *Range,* L. O. Fullen of the Eddy *Argus,* A. M. Swan of the Gallup *News-Register,* George T. Gould of the *Daily Optic* at Las Vegas, J. A. Carruth of the *Daily Examiner* at Las Vegas, and Don H. Kedzie of the Lordsburg *Western Liberal.*[79] The duties of postmasters were so light that the editors could easily hold both positions. A postmastership was considered by politicians as both a reward for past political support and as bait for future cooperation.

The general territorial public printing subsidy was monopolized by the Santa Fe *New Mexican* journalists, but at the county levels lesser journalists competed for the public printing, which by the '90s had increased considerably in volume.

In this decade counties published delinquent tax lists. Sometimes as many as twenty pages were filled with legal notices, along with the minutes of the meetings of the county commissioners. Printing of these legal notices, minutes, and other county matters, as well as the need for office supplies, were rewards given by county commissioners to politically faithful newspapers.[80] In addition, by the '90s journalists were rewarded with printing contracts from the new territorial colleges. Newspapers in the depressed '90s, therefore, sought legislation to increase public printing, cooperated with the politicians to receive printing contracts, and in the process became ever more subservient to their political benefactors.

Territorial political leaders increased their control of the press in several other ways. The number of campaign papers was increased from ten in the 1880s to twenty-five in the 1890s. Politicians also went beyond the campaign papers, becoming publishers themselves in order to get long-term newspaper support. Prominent examples of this latter trend were the purchase of the Las Cruces *Independent Democrat* by A. B. Fall, the purchase of the Las Vegas *Voz del Pueblo* by Union People's party leader Felix Martinez, the leasing of the Santa Fe *New Mexican* by Governor W. T. Thornton and Democratic officeholders, and the attempt of Republican leader T. B. Catron to acquire the Albuquerque *Morning Democrat* through a mortgage foreclosure. Increased political control also was indicated by changes in party affiliations of newspapers. The number of Republican papers decreased from fifty-six in the 1880s to thirty-six in the 1890s. On the other hand, Democratic papers increased from thirty-eight to forty-five, and nine new People's party papers appeared.[81] No doubt, popular dissatisfaction with Republican policies led to an increase in Democratic and Populist papers; however, control of public printing by those parties in some counties also allowed them to subsidize papers. In either case, their survival was dependent upon adherence to the party line and shows the increase in political control of the press.

The political control of rural papers so characteristic of American journalism in this period[82] was a new trend in New Mexico. The pre-railway era journalists had been political opportunists who used the press to advance personal political careers. Newsmen of the '80s had turned away from politics to commercial rewards for advancement. Then came the political subservience of editors during the '90s, which indicated, at least in part, a decline of frontier influence.

While the newsmen of this era were not the independent opportunists in politics that the journalists of the pre-railway era had been, their places of origin were but slightly different. The editors of the early era came mainly from the northern seabord states and, so far as could be determined, editors of this new era came from the northern Midwest. Although no effort was made to investigate thoroughly the geographic origins of all journalists of this era, thirty-four American journalists were checked. Seven were from Ohio; five, from Illinois; six, from Kansas; two, from Iowa; one each was from Nebraska and Colorado; and four were from Missouri, three of these were Republicans and represent a northern Midwest attitude. From the eastern seaboard states, two journalists came from Pennsylvania and one from New York. The South was represented by three Kentuckians and two Texans. Foreign lands continued to be represented among the territorial journalists with one each from Mexico, Austria, England, and Canada. Although these journalists were diverse in origin, it appears that they were predominantly from the northern Midwest.[83] The origins of Spanish-language journalists were more easily checked since there were few Spanish-language papers. However, the Spanish journalists, constituting only a small part of the press corps, were rather limited in their influence.

In the years after 1880 the prevalent bilingualism of the pre-railway era papers gave way to a predominantly English-language press. Only sixteen bilingual and thirteen Spanish-language papers were published in the '80s. However, by the '90s a larger number of native New Mexicans were literate in the Spanish language, having been educated in that tongue in an increaing number of Catholic schools. As a result, thirty-five Spanish-language and eleven bilingual papers were published in the '90s—a decade of reduced journalistic efforts in the territory.

Most of the Spanish-language and bilingual papers were short lived; many were only campaign papers. Nevertheless, there were several stable and well-edited papers being published in 1900. For example, *El Tiempo* of Las Cruces was launched in 1882; at Santa Fe the *Boletin Popular* and *El Nuevo Mexicano* were founded in 1885 and 1890, respectively; and at Albuquerque the *Nuevo Mundo* and the *La Bandera Americana* were established in 1897 and 1894 respectively.[84] The two best Spanish-language journals were the Las Vegas *La Voz del Pueblo* and *El Inde-*

*pendiente,* which were founded in 1888 and 1894, respectively. The quality of Spanish journalism in Las Vegas was a reflection of its able newsmen. Personnel of *La Voz del Pueblo* included Felix Martinez and Ezequiel Cabeza de Baca, both of whom were prominent territorial political figures. E. H. Salazar, founder and publisher of *El Independiente,* learned printing and journalism from W. H. Manderfield of the Santa Fe *New Mexican.*[85] These able men gave new prestige to the Spanish-language press.

Most territorial editors of this period retained a high estimate of the position of capable journalists in society. For example, one editor wrote: "The profession of journalism is co-ordinate and co-equal with that of law, medicine or divinity. . . ." Later he wrote: "Quarrels between newspapers are neither dignified nor profitable, and they impair the influence of the press as the great public mentor."[86] Other newsmen believed that mere participation in journalism did not automatically entitle all journalists to the respect due editors of integrity and ability. Evidence of this was a resolution offered by T. W. Collier at the territorial press convention in 1890. He asked that a committee be established to judge the fitness of any journalist to be a member of the New Mexico Press Association.[87] Thus, territorial journalists moved toward a more moderate concept of their position in society, a belief that journalists should be judged individually rather than as a class but that the better journalists were due the esteem accorded other professions.

This new practice of judging editors individually rather than as a class was an element in the decline of journalistic fraternalism. Editors of the early '80s shared the common experience of establishing and publishing papers in a frontier area, and their editorial columns often contained notes about the activities of other editors. But by 1900, editors infrequently noted the actions of other journalists and then usually limited themselves to remarks about personnel of nearby papers, or to comments by dailies about dailies and weeklies about weeklies. Fraternalism between all journalists was giving way to fraternalism between those possessing comparable power, wealth, or ability.

A survey of New Mexico Press Association activities shows the trends noted above. In 1881 pride of profession and fraternalism born of common experience led to the organization at Albuquerque of a press association. This spirit sustained the association through 1882, but only a small group attended the 1883 meeting. Until 1889 this group, principally Albuquerque newsmen, continued to hold annual meetings during the Territorial Fair days at Albuquerque. Then the territorial legislature passed a severe libel law; in the same period New Mexico entered an economic depression. Interest in repeal of the libel law and obtaining increases in public printing apparently led to a revival of the press association, and meetings from 1890 through 1893 were well attended. In 1893 the libel law was repealed, and public printing at county levels had been greatly increased. Since the prime motives for maintaining the association were removed and journalistic fraternalism had declined, the press association lapsed until 1900. Accounts of press association meetings tell of gay dinners with freely flowing liquor furnished by merchants of the host town and of the election of association officers. Editors mention little of actions with regard to the libel law or public printing, but such discussions may be deduced from pre-convention editorial comment. In short, fraternalism led to the founding of the New Mexico Press Association; common needs led to its revival; but division of interests and declining fraternalism again brought its lapse.[88]

Coincidentally, fraternalism and personal journalism reached a peak in the '80s. Heated exchanges between the editors in those years were often vulgar, obscene, and sometimes sacrilegious. One illustration of this is the attack of the Las Vegas *Daily Optic* on the editor of the Santa Fe *New Mexican* headed "AN EDITORIAL ASS":

> The writer of the second page of the Santa Fe New Mexican has about as much idea of the courtesy due a gentleman as an ass has of manners. . . . When the fellow charges THE OPTIC with being an "organ of the New Mexico boodlers," and having been bribed in its utterances, . . . he lies in his throat! . . . Booby Spradling, whose imbecility of mind is shown by the silly paragraphs he pens, at the bidding of his keepers, is painful evidence that he is a bound slave to onanism, and therefore the time server should not be held accountable for what he says or does. Outside of his office he is a man whom God hates (a sneaking coward) and in his office he is a blubbering fool, who is to be pitied and not blamed for his unjournalistic utterances. . . . .

The *New Mexican's* reply brought another *Daily Optic* blast at the "syphilitic nimbeferous Spradling management . . . of the Santa Fe excuse for a newspaper . . . and its penetentiary deserving gang. . . ."[89]

In competitive situations editors were particularly sensitive, as the heated battle between the Gallup *Gleaner* and the *News-Register* indicated. W. T. Henderson of the *Gleaner* wrote of *News-Register* editor A. M. Swan:

> An evidence of the underhanded sneak, liar, ruffian, the two faced scarecrow, whose whiskers are leaking for need of a bath, is given in the last issue of the hypenated bladder . . . it says we made anarchist [sic] speeches to the strikers and several other damphool statements.

The *News-Register* reply was in the form of a curse:

> May fortune flee from him, and evil cling to him all of his days; may death rob him of family; friends forsake him; disease waste his flesh; ghosts of women

haunt his sleep, and in the end poor, miserable, loathed of men and despised by God may the wretch sink into the grave and hell receive his soul.[90]

Violent editorial language sometimes brought physical violence in return, as the following item illustrates:

Newman carries a leaded cane, a speck of newspaper war is brewing at Las Vegas. There are traces of blood on the journalistic moon at Socorro. Editor Sturges of the Springer Stockman wears a steel breast plate. Editor Leonard of the Silver City Enterprise licked a citizen last week. An Albuquerque woman has been after the city editor of the Democrat with a rawhide. Editor Hughes threatens to shoot editor Albright "with a pistol like a dog be gad!" . . . At Albuquerque editor Dunbar is slowly recovering from bruises received at the hands of editor Albright.[91]

In the '90s editorial comments became more moderate. An editorial of the Albuquerque *Daily Citizen* in 1893 shows the new trend: "Space in this newspaper is entirely too valuable to waste in wrangling with other newspapers. When we have anything to say about our genial contemporaries we say it in as few words as possible." Late in the decade comments became more on the order of this Santa Fe *New Mexican* note of 1898: "A more or less esteemed contemporary over in Union County is barking at the NEW MEXICAN. A dog baying at the moon so as to speak."[92] Thus, New Mexico editors belatedly followed national trends of reducing personal journalism.[93] In this, as in other matters, the territorial press was losing its frontier character and approaching the norms of rural American journalism.

If one were to construct a composite of the most prominent characteristics of all territorial newsmen in this transitional period, it would have been a profile of a man of the northern Midwest who had abandoned the bilingual publication of his predecessors to issue an English-language paper. In the 1880s he would have been an optimistic pioneer confident that he would receive most of his rewards from private business. By the 1890s, however, he would have lost his optimism and sought political rewards to supplement his meager income, becoming increasingly subservient to the territorial politicians. In addition, with the fading of the frontier he would have lost his fraternal feeling for fellow editors, but at the same time he would have been more moderate in personal journalism. He also would have come to recognize that merely publishing or editing a newspaper did not entitle one to the respect due a journalist of integrity and ability. Territorial journalism still retained traces of frontier and Spanish tones in 1900, but it was fast approaching the norms of rural American journalism.

Although not far behind other American country newsmen of that day, the style, writing, and news coverage of the territorial journalists

appear crude when compared to current practices. Editorials in the territorial papers were usually long, occupied a disproportionate space in
the newspaper, and were less concerned with territorial problems than
those of the earlier editors. Entertaining features, humor, and poetry
appeared less frequently than in the 1870s and had been almost eliminated by 1890. On the other hand, news coverage, improved slightly.
Several of the dailies subscribed to the brief Associated Press telegram;
and territorial news coverage improved with the increase in newspapers,
since the territorial news was obtained mainly by clipping copy from
other papers. Also in this era more space was devoted to local news, and
it was perhaps here that the territorial papers made their greatest
progress.

With rare exceptions, the editorials of the territorial journalists would
be assessed unfavorably by modern editors. First, editorials were unduly
long, usually taking up all available space on one page. Furthermore,
with hundreds of problems in the towns and in the territory deserving
editorial comment, editorials were usually concerned with topics of
little interest to territorial readers. A comment in the *Daily Optic* at Las
Vegas best describes the general practice: "The Albuquerque Democrat
again bores its readers with a column and a half editorial read by no one
except the fellow who wrote it and the unfortunate proof reader who
probably went to sleep in the process of this narcotic exercise."[94] While
the Santa Fe *New Mexican* used excessive space for its editorials, its
editors at least concentrated on territorial political matters which readers probably found more interesting than many of the topics used by
other editors. Only two papers, the Albuqurque *Evening Review* and
the *Daily Optic,* devoted a reasonable amount of space to editorials—
which generally consisted of editorial comments on local or territorial
matters.

The most effective and sound editorial approach of the era seemed to
be that of W. F. Saunders, editor of the Albuquerque *Evening Review.*
His handling of a local sanitation problem provides an illustration of his
effectiveness. In 1882 Albuquerque's drainage system consisted of an
open irrigation canal extending along its main street. Townsmen threw
slops, garbage, and refuse of all types into the canal rather than carry
them to the garbage dump. The canal, as a result, soon became a
nauseous ditch. In his first weeks as editor, Saunders called attention to
the condition of the ditch and asked the county commissioners to correct it. Then almost daily he made a brief comment: "Clean out that
ditch gentlemen. It must be done." Eventually the ditch was cleaned,
and Saunders credited this result to his brief but persistent reminders.[95]

Editorials also provided one of the few instances of the use of humor in the papers of this era. Personal journalism, for example, was often intended to be amusing. A few editors in the early '80s saw humor in the suffering of others, particularly fellow editors, and filled their editorial columns with this type of "humor." one of the most able of these "humorous" editors was C. J. Hildreth of the Las Cruces *Rio Grande Republican*. When the Silver City *Watch Dog* was launched, he quipped: "Its bark commences with 'Our Bow.' It should have been 'Our Bow Wow.' " Later he noted: "The *Watch Dog* is enlarged, its growls are more ferocious than ever. May he never want for a bone and be long in reaching the sausage makers." When J. E. Curren boasted of improvements in his Deming *Headlight* and claimed to have started with the poorest town, press, and types in the United States, Hildreth commented: "This reminds us of the fruit vendor who came to Chicago twenty years ago with all of his stock and trade in one basket and now he owns a handcart."[96]

The most humorous paper in the territory in this era was the Manzano *Gringo and Greaser,* a tiny semi-monthly. It was edited by Charles L. Kusz, who was also postmaster, miner, stockman, and assayer at Manzano. Since it had almost no advertising, it evidently was intended for the personal amusement of Kusz. The *Gringo and Greaser,* whose title insulted all its readers, emphasized humorous anecdotes such as the following:

> Dolores Sedillo is out of luck; he fell in love with a piece of Las Vegas calico, that is visiting here, but his love was spurned, he then skedaddled, taking with him a mule, the mule died on the plains and left him on foot. The last seen of him, he was making a jackass of himself, being saddled up and trying to ride himself out of the country. A busted heart will raise hell with any man.[97]

The use of humorous quips such as these declined with the fading of the frontier; instead, most territorial editors sought to entertain readers with better news coverage.

The space devoted to national and international news was increased during this period. For such copy, daily papers continued to rely on a brief daily telegram from the Associated Press and on stories clipped from Colorado and midwestern papers. The use of the Associated Press service was limited by its high cost, however, for press service and telegraphy charges were more than $3,000 annually. This cost made the service too expensive for many short-lived dailies; even the Las Vegas *Daily Optic* used it only when threatened with competition.[98] The Albuquerque dailies and the Santa Fe *New Mexican* (daily) were consistent Associated Press subscribers after 1890, with the result that national and international news coverage generally increased in the daily press. The weekly press and a few dailies relied on news clipped from exchanges, but by 1900 the weekly press was leaving national news to the dailies and devoting more space to local news.

Most territorial papers improved local news coverage and made significant advances. The best examples were the *Daily Optic* and the Albuquerque *Evening Review*. In the early years of the *Daily Optic,* Russell Kistler was unable to afford the Associated Press service; since the competing Las Vegas *Daily Gazette* did, however, use the service, Kistler sought to counter it by providing superior local news coverage. In addition, *Daily Optic* reporters met every train and interviewed travelers, particularly prominent ones, for territorial news.[99] These practices enabled the *Daily Optic* to steal subscribers from the *Daily Gazette* and eventually led to the suspension of that paper. The Albuquerque *Evening Review* also gave heavy emphasis to local news and was not an Associated Press subscriber. While most other papers confined themselves only to the most important local news, such coverage was gradually extended.

Space devoted to general territorial news was increased even more than that given to local news, for such matter was obtained easily from other territorial papers and was more extensive because of the increased number of papers. Occasionally the Las Vegas *Daily Optic* sent a reporter to the legislative session at Santa Fe, and the Albuquerque *Morning Democrat* assigned one to report the constitutional convention in 1889.[100] But most editors continued to rely on exchanges for their territorial news.

Many New Mexico weeklies had non-territorial stories on pre-printed pages, often called "patent pages" or "ready print," which were sold to them by such companies as A. N. Kellogg or Western Newspaper Union. National advertising sold by these companies was surrounded by feature stories and printed on half of the pages of newsprint sold to rural weeklies. This advertising paid part of the printing and newsprint costs and allowed the country publisher to offer his subscribers a larger paper. The first use of this service in New Mexico was noted by the Albuquerque *Review* with the following comment: "The *New Mexico Co-operator* is . . . one of those emasculated humbugs, one half is printed in the states, the other half here."[101] Other papers, short of printers, used boiler plate (that is, stereotyped news matter) which could be inserted directly into the printing forms. Both devices were used by undercapitalized publishers who frowned on them as makeshift or as avoidance of an editor's responsibilities and discontinued them as soon as possible.

The style and headlines used by even the most conscientious editors would not have been pleasing to modern newspaper readers; they were improved only slightly over practices of the pre-railway era. Most headlines consisted of one line of print and were one column in width but were set in small type. However, for important news stories a few papers used multi-deck or multi-tiered headlines arranged in inverted pyramids. The need to conserve space evidently made the small headlines mandatory, and under such conditions balanced makeup was impractical.

Generally, news stories were written in a rambling, verbose style without lead paragraphs. The Albuquerque *Evening Review* and the Las Vegas *Daily Optic,* however, used brief stories and were able to publish a variety of accounts. For the general press, however, the journalistic styles developing in the major eastern American cities had little influence on New Mexico newspapers in this era.

Nevertheless, in the opinion of many New Mexico newsmen the quality of territorial dailies was equal to that of dailies in towns of the same size elsewhere in America. One editor believed there were no better dailies published in any United States territory than the Albuquerque *Daily Citizen,* the Albuquerque *Morning Democrat,* and the Las Vegas *Daily Optic.* Another editor compared favorably the Albuquerque dailies with those of Kansas City and Denver.[102] No doubt, this last was an exaggeration. However, comparison of the territorial dailies with the general small-town dailies of this era described by a leading authority on American journalism leaves the impression that the New Mexico dailies were only slightly inferior in quality.[103]

Even though territorial journalism was not far behind rural American journalism in general, the practices of New Mexico newsmen were only slightly improved over those of the pre-railway era. National and foreign news was still limited to the brief daily Associated Press telegrams and borrowed stories. Editorial comment still occupied a disproportionate amount of available space. The coverage of local and territorial news was but slightly improved, and few advances in journalistic style and headlining were made. Many of the poorer weeklies relied on pre-printed pages and had little space for local news. Finally, the friendly humor in the editorial columns of the early 1880s declined, apparently as a consequence of the decline in frontier influence and the gloom of the 1890s. By the end of the century many of the territorial papers had lost their frontier vitality and had become routine country weeklies.

Numerous problems faced by the journalists heavily influenced the transition from a vital frontier press to a routine country press. First of all, crude methods of printing retarded the development of sound journalistic practices. Next, financial problems beset publishers. First, newspaper incomes decreased with a general reduction in subscription rates. Nor was this reduced income offset by any considerable increase in circulation. In addition, subscribers were still slow in paying their subscriptions. Second, a general reduction in advertising rates in this era also helped keep down the income of the publishers. A third general problem was the excessive competition, which placed a severe burden on most publishers. Fourth, a high-illiteracy rate among Spanish-Americans apparently made publishing unprofitable in towns that were heavily Spanish-American. Finally, the uninhibited language of the editors apparently motivited the legislature to enact the severe but short-lived libel law of 1889. These manifold problems of the publishers contributed to the relatively slow progress of territorial journalism in the '80s and '90s.

Poor printing methods retarded all American journalism before the 1890s, but conditions were much worse in New Mexico. Since most territorial papers were undercapitalized, they were launched with the crudest of equipment that was improved very slowly. For instance, the Las Vegas *Daily Optic* was launched in 1879 with a small army press. The Albuquerque *Daily Journal* and the *Evening Review* were founded with Washington hand presses.[104] The Deming *Headlight* was launched with a small treadle-powered job press, although it soon acquired a Washington hand press.[105] The dailies soon purchased cylinder presses, but continued to operate them at slow speed by hand power. By 1887 the Santa Fe *New Mexican* had replaced a water-power drive with steam-power and by the end of the century was using an internal-combustion engine. Other dailies soon followed the lead of the *New Mexican;* however, in 1900 many territorial weeklies were still relying on the Washington hand press. Hand composition of type continued to be the rule for New Mexico weeklies, although in the late 1890s the dailies acquired linotypes. The Albuquerque *Morning Democrat* in 1896 became the first territorial paper to own one of these mechanical typesetting machines.[106]

Labor relations never became a great problem for New Mexico publishers, although early in this era unions were formed and strikes occured at the Albuquerque *Morning Journal*, Santa Fe *New Mexican* and *Daily Gazette* as a result of disputes over wages and working conditions. Other than these instances, labor and management relations appeared cordial. While unions were the rule for territorial dailies, this was not true of weeklies, probably because their printer-publishers could easily have broken strikes by doing their own work. Despite some crude practices, the printing methods and labor relations of the territorial press appeared to be almost abreast of the contemporary rural American press as described by one authority on the development of American journalism.[107]

In the 1880s territorial newspapers developed several new sources of revenue unavailable to American newspapers in general. In the territorial southwest, legal notices concerning mining claims and cattle-brand advertisements provided additional revenue.[108] By contrast papers in the northeastern part of the territory had a great deal more cattle-brand advertising, and their legal notices concerned homesteaders instead of miners.[109] Shortly before the drastic drop in cattle prices, three of the eight pages of the Raton *Comet* were devoted each week to cattle-brand advertisements. By 1894 most newspaper revenue from cattle and mining advertisements had vanished. Merchant advertising was still largely of the single-column type, and for months such advertisements were published unchanged; full-column length advertisements used in the 1870s were rare. Apparently it was the preference of the merchants rather than the rules of the publishers that the one-column advertisement continued, for multi-column advertisements were published occasionally.[110] Although publishers were slow to adopt the large-size advertisements used in papers in the eastern part of the country, this was probably because New Mexico merchants did not want them.

Advertising rates were high in the early eighties but much lower in the '90s. In the early '80s the advertising rates of weeklies ranged from $1.25 to $2 per column inch per issue, but in 1890 the New Mexico Press Association asked a standard rate of $1 and $2.50 per column inch per month for weeklies and dailies, respectively.[111] According to this, column inch rates were less than 25 cents for weeklies and 10 cents for dailies. Few papers published their advertising rates in the '90s; evidently prices were often settled by bargaining. The rates asked by the press association were higher than current advertising rates, which accounts for the poverty of some territorial dailies—despite the high percentage of space devoted to advertising.

The circulation figures reported to *N. W. Ayer and Son's American Newspaper Annual* for territorial newspapers were quite low, indicating a small income from this source. Some papers made no report of circulation to *Ayer and Son's Annual,* probably neither wishing to reveal their deficiency nor to lie about it. Other publishers claimed much higher circulations than they truly had. For instance, the Albuquerque *Morning Democrat* in 1895 reported 2,500; and the next year, under new management, 700. After strenuous efforts by the new management, circulation increased to 1,500 in 1899. The reported circulation of the Albuquerque *Daily Citizen* ranged from 1,100 to 1,900 from 1895 to 1899. The Las Vegas *Daily Optic* fell from a high of 1,930 in 1892 to a low of 900 in 1899.[112] Many of the circulation figures reported by territorial papers to *Ayer and Son's Annual* should be discounted by 30 to 50 per cent.

An additional trouble to publishers was the fact that subscribers were still reluctant to pay for their papers, and in a few instances publishers even resorted to law suits to collect subscriptions. Prices of weekly subscriptions declined in the early '80s from the usual $3 per year to about $2 in 1900. Annual mail subscription rates of dailies declined from $10 to $8, but city carrier rates remained at 25 cents per week in this period. While circulation rates were lower than those of territorial papers of the 1870s, they were generally higher than rural papers elsewhere in America in this era.[113] Thus, low circulation and poor collection, more than subscription rates, restricted the income of territorial papers from subscriptions.

One of the greatest troubles of the publishers of this era was the harsh and incessant competition. In the booming territorial towns of the 1880s, Socorro newspapers best illustrate this evil. Journalism began at Socorro in 1880 with the launching of the *Sun*. At the same time railway construction neared the town and development of nearby mines was intensified. An ancient, sleepy Spanish-American village before 1880, Socorro by 1885 was the fourth largest town in New Mexico with a population of 4,049,[114] rivaling Albuquerque and Las Vegas. However, during these years it did not develop a strong newspaper. From 1880 until 1889, fifteen different papers were launched at Socorro; or if variations in title and changes in frequency of publication are counted, twenty papers. Ten attempts to sustain dailies were made during those years. The *Sun*, after battling a series of rivals, lapsed in 1884. That year the Socorro *Daily Chieftain* was launched. With great effort this paper subdued its rivals until in 1889 only one competitor was left. Depression made daily publication impractical, but the *Chieftain* continued to overshadow its weekly rival, the *Industrial Advertiser*, which in 1899 left the then dwindling town for Albuquerque.[115]

The early establishment of a daily paper at Socorro strong enough to become a community leader might have provided the guiding force to promote the projected railway branches. If these branches had been completed, Socorro could have become a distribution center rivaling Albuquerque and Las Vegas. But strong rivalry prevented any paper in Socorro from gaining such a foothold, and the lack of strong editorial leadership crippled efforts of the town to expand its trade. Although this was not the chief reason for Socorro's decline, it constituted an important contributory factor. Albuquerque at one time had fewer assets than Socorro, Bernalillo, or Los Lunas, but it quickly gained two strong daily papers financed by local business groups. These papers provided leadership and coordinated community efforts and were important assets in making Albuquerque the largest town in New Mexico by 1900. Although competing newspapers provided contrasting views, they crippled efforts to provide strong leadership at crucial times during the development of some towns.

In sharp rivalries the most apparent competitive method of weeklies was to launch a daily paper, while among the long-established dailies the chief method was an attempt to monopolize the Associated Press franchise. A weekly confronted with a new competitor or perhaps the new weekly itself often launched a daily to drive out the rival. This has been already pointed out in several instances and accounts for ten daily papers in less than ten years at Socorro. At Albuquerque the *Morning Democrat* fought the *Daily Citizen* by holding both morning and evening Associated Press franchises. Once while the Las Vegas *Daily Gazette* was suspended, its chief owner, banker Jefferson Raynolds, continued to hold and pay for the press franchise, hoping to force the *Daily Optic* into a merger. The *Daily Optic,* however, did not subscribe to the press service until a few years later; the service was used only when the paper was faced with the prospect of a daily competitor, and was abandoned as soon as the threat had passed.[116] There were no indications of competition by reductions in subscription or advertising rates, although the latter probably occurred, since in many cases rates seemed to be set by bargaining with advertisers. Daily publication by a weekly and monopoly of Associated Press services by a daily apparently were the chief competitive tactics used by newspaper publishers.

Towns mainly Hispano in population did not support newspapers nearly so well as Anglo-American towns of the same size. Probably the high illiteracy rate of the Spanish-Americans was responsible; illiteracy limited circulation revenues and advertising effectiveness. Merchants were reluctant to buy advertising because unread advertisements did not produce results. C. J. Hildreth, publisher of the *Rio Grande Republican* at Las Cruces, noted a lack of support for his paper and blamed the Hispanos:

. . . in this town there are nearly fifty firms and individuals doing business who ought to advertise, and who, if they were in a live American town would advertise. Of this number our columns barely show ten or a dozen, three-fourths of which are small cards placed at our lowest rates.[117]

When J. G. Albright complained of a lack of support for his Santa Fe *Daily Democrat,* Hildreth advised him "to move to some young American city where his energy and perseverance would be appreciated."[118] Within a year after Albright had followed this advice, the Santa Fe *Daily New Mexican* was suspended. The success of the later *New Mexican* was the result of the ability of Max Frost to obtain territorial printing contracts. The lease of the *New Mexican* to Democrats in 1894 by the ardently Republican Frost, who could foresee bankruptcy without public printing, confirms the conclusion that political subsidy was necessary to sustain a daily paper at the populous territorial capital. Nor did Taos, another large town predominantly Spanish-American, support journalism. Eight short-lived papers operated there from 1879 to 1900.[119] Here again, lack of support for journalism seems to be explained by the high rate of illiteracy among the Hispanos. The conditions discouraging to journalism in areas of predominantly Spanish-American population in this era apparently account for the relative lack of newspapers in Bernalillo, Belen, Espanola, and Rio Arriba County. Furthermore, many Hispanos were literate only in the Spanish language, adding another handicap to the many already faced by newspaper publishers.

In the 1880s, libel suits posed no particular problem for the territorial editors, for despite their use of abusive language, such suits were rare. Frontier juries probably did not look harshly upon editorial abuse or poorly substantiated charges and were reluctant to award damages against newspapers. Possibly the public attitude was that of a Colorado editor who apparently believed that the worst that could be written about New Mexico politicians would be milder than the truth, for he wrote: "New Mexico editors seem to court libel suits but know what they are about, for New Mexico's prominent men can't be libeled."[120] Such an attitude evidently motivated legislators to enact the libel law of 1889. This law made it a penal offense to publish news stories stating that a candidate for office had committed a crime or a disgraceful act; or that he had any moral vice, physical or mental defect, or disease—if such publication would bring him public contempt. In such cases, and some were listed in the law, the truth of the story was not a defense against the charge of libel.[121]

Friends of publishers in the legislature sought unsuccessfully to amend or defeat this bill before it became a law. It was vetoed by Governor E. G. Ross, a former editor, but his veto was overridden. Except for the most loyal Republican editors, all of the territorial press vigorously attacked the Republican-dominated legislature. Most editors believed with Kistler of the Las Vegas *Daily Optic* that the libel law was an attempt to gag the press, for he wrote:

No doubt they have felt the lash of the press for their wrongdoings of the past, and have determined to bind, for the future, the arm that wielded it. They have become wearied of paying certain venal members of the press for suppressing accounts of their nightly debauches, so they are determined that the sleepless watch dog of the people should be muzzled; that the great conservator of morals should be silenced.[122]

Republican editors defended the law on the following grounds: Texas had a similar law, publishers would be protected by the jury trials guaranteed under the law, grand juries would not indict a reputable newsman for reasonable statements, and the law was better than the previous common-law rule that the greater the truth the greater was the libel.[123]

When an attempt was made to repeal the libel law in 1891, territorial councilman T. B. Mills of Las Vegas proposed an amendment "permitting Senator Catron, or any other aggrieved citizen, to go after the acrimonious editor, manager or writer with a cactus club."[124] The efforts of publishers to have the law repealed were successful in 1893.

One of the most notable libel cases of this period was an 1898 charge of criminal libel against George T. Gould of the Las Vegas *Daily Optic* for his attack on Max Frost. Under the common-law concept that truth was no defense, admission of publication of the editorial by Gould was sufficient to convict him of breach of the peace, and he was fined $300.[125]

Newspaper income reflected two sharply divergent trends in this period. The '80s were years of boom and prosperity. The '90s, on the other hand, were a decade of depression, with falling advertising and subscription rates. Circulation figures remained low despite lower rates and a reduced number of papers. Because of the low incomes resulting from all these factors, most territorial papers in these years were unable to take advantage of the mechanical advances in printing. Thus the financial stability of the territorial press, as well as the mechanics of printing, lagged slightly behind the rural press of America.

For the territorial press the years 1879 to 1900 were an era of transition from a raw frontier press to a rather placid, country journalism. Publishers of the revitalized New Mexican frontier of the 1880s reflected its spirit with increased personal journalism, intense competition, and optimistic confidence in the future prosperity of New Mexico. At the same time frontier friendliness continued to influence relationships between newsmen. In this spirit and with the increase of journalists, the first territorial press association was organized. Frontier friendliness was also mirrored in the humorous exchanges between editors. The humor, vitality, and freshness of New Mexico journalism faded with the economic collapse of the 1890s, and newsmen came to depend on politicians to secure governmental subsidies.

By 1900 the territorial press, as was true of the rural American press in general, was subservient to the politician. The newsman, who had lost the independence, daring, and vitality of pioneers, moved through the 1890s without improving methods and techniques of journalism or adopting the new styles being developed in the eastern American cities. Thus, a large part of the New Mexico press had degenerated; what had once been a vigorous pioneer press had turned into a stolid, country press. Some large papers, however, adopted the new mechanical techniques and made possible much better newspapers, and in the final territorial decade they led the New Mexico press toward an improved journalism.

# III

# THE BEGINNING OF MODERN
# NEW MEXICO JOURNALISM
## 1901-1912

AFTER 1900 GREAT economic, social, and technical changes swept the territorial press toward a modern journalism which was vastly different from the weak, depression-ridden, and politically subservient press of the 1890s. The twentieth-century press became strong in a time of great economic prosperity, its vigor restored by many new pioneer newsmen. Improvements in printing, journalism, and business techniques allowed the press to exploit its new strength and a prosperous economy permitted it to become free and modern.

This was an era of growth, development, and prosperity in New Mexico. The end of the national depression in the late 1890s brought a general improvement in the territorial economy. But more significant was the westward flow of eastern American capital to finance the building of railways. In less than a decade territorial railway mileage was more than doubled, and much of eastern New Mexico was made accessible by rail. Then, within a few years, thousands of homesteading dry farmers, promised a rail outlet for their products, pre-empted millions of acres of the public domain in eastern New Mexico. Dozens of towns sprang up to serve as trading points for the railway workers and farmers; and older towns, particularly Albuquerque, grew as distribution centers to serve the new population. Mainly as a result of the new immigration, the territorial population by 1912 had increased almost 70 per cent.

The new immigrants wrought several significant social changes. First, the Anglo-American portion of the population became almost one-half of the total. Next, this last wave of the American frontier was composed of vigorous, daring, and enterprising people who reinvigorated New Mexican society. Finally, most of the newcomers were from the Midwest, both north and south, the area of the greatest Populist discontent in the 1890s. Accustomed to dissent and recognizing the necessity for reform, they heartily supported the contemporary nationwide progressive movement. Journalists of the same nature, supported by this public attitude, became reformers and were critical of the politicos who had ruled the press of the 1890s.

Adventurous journalists of this type readily adapted themselves to dramatic changes occurring in journalism in these years. The perfection of the linotype and better presses left publishers free to increase easily the number of pages in their papers. This enabled them to make their journals more attractive and to offer more news and features, which in turn made possible larger circulations. In these years also, enterprising retailers in eastern New Mexico and Albuquerque discovered the effective use of advertising to increase sales and began to use newspaper space on a scale undreamed of by earlier publishers. For the newspapermen the key to capturing this new revenue was to provide the largest circulation, thereby contacting the most customers for the merchant. To gain subscribers, the alert New Mexico journalists began to copy the innovations of other American journalists of this era. Notable among the changes were more attractive front pages freed from advertising and with large display headlines and balanced makeup; improved content brought about by better reporting, greater use of the Associated Press service, and special news features; and, most important, a relatively independent stand in politics. In this era a large part of the territorial press was revitalized and freed from its former political subservience.

Independent journalism, however, would have been impossible without the prosperity that had been sparked by railway construction. The Pecos Valley Northeastern, built in 1898 from Roswell to Amarillo, Texas, was the first of the new roads. Along this line arose the towns of Elida, Portales, and Texico to serve as trading centers for homesteaders. Another railway launched in 1898, the El Paso Northeastern, sponsored the towns of Alamogordo, Carrizozo, Capitan, Vaughn, Santa Rosa, and Tucumcari. Failure of the Capitan mines to supply enough coking coal led to an extension of the line from Tucumcari to Dawson, near Raton. Then two lines of the Rock Island from Dalhart and Amarillo, Texas, were built to Tucumcari to make that town a thriving railway center. Later the railway originally named the El Paso Northeastern was extended westward to Douglas, Arizona, to carry Dawson coal to the copper smelters. In the territorial northwest a Denver and Rio Grande branch was built down the San Juan Valley to give a rail outlet to irrigation farmers there. From Santa Fe the New Mexico Central pushed south to Estancia and Torrance; and to complete the era of railway construction, the Santa Fe's New Mexico Eastern was built across the center of the territory from Belen to Texico. Along these new lines arose railway shops and division points; the development of irrigation was hastened by improved connections to markets; and in large sections of eastern and central New Mexico dry farming was made feasible by access to markets for farm production. Following the railway workers and farmers came enterprising merchants and journalists to serve the new population.

In the areas developed or helped as a result of railway construction approximately 110 new papers were founded, many of them stable and long-lived. Since in this decade a total of only 259 papers were published, and many of them very briefly, those published in the areas of recent immigrants represented a large portion of the territorial press corps. These publishers, like those of the early 1880s, anticipated greater profits from private enterprise than from government subsidy. They also had a characteristic of the earlier pioneers, intense optimism, which led them to found papers in small villages. They hoped that these towns would soon grow into metropolises with the full development of the area.[1] Such was the character of the journalists who founded the first papers at Portales.

Along with Elida and Texico, Portales was founded in 1898 as a railway construction town and survived as a cattle shipping and farmers' trading center. Here in 1901, John Pipes, a tuberculous printer, launched the first of the plains area papers, the Portales *Progress*.[2] This paper lasted less than six months, but it was succeeded by the Democratic *Herald* in 1902. The next year the *Herald* had a Republican competitor, the *Times*.[3] Evidently because partisan advantage had been pre-empted, no other papers were founded at Portales before 1912. Of the various editor-publishers of these papers, the most interesting were Munsey Bull,[4] W. C. Hawkins, and E. P. Alldredge. Bull, who founded the *Times,* was a representative of that fading breed of tramp printers who were capable of performing either as skilled printers or country editors. Hawkins,[5] successor to Bull at the *Times,* was the owner of several pioneer country weeklies and apparently hoped that one of the towns he had chosen was a future metropolis. Alldredge, the most outstanding editor of the *Herald,* was a highly educated man of great vigor and enthusiasm unusual in a country editor.[6] At the two other Roosevelt County towns, Elida and Texico, four weeklies were launched. Notable among them were the Elida *News* and Texico *Trumpet,* both of which were published from 1904 until 1912.[7]

Close behind the founding of the Roosevelt County towns came that of Tucumcari. The town mushroomed as a farmer's trading center, a junction and division point for four railways, and the site of railway shops. J. E. Curren,[8] perennial pioneer editor, was attracted by the prospects of Tucumcari and founded there in February, 1902, the first paper in Quay County, the *Pathfinder*. Renamed the *Quay County Democrat* in 1903, it later became the *Actual Settler*. Curren's son, Arthur E. Curren, purchased the Republican Tucumcari *Times* in December, 1903,[9] in a family effort to control all Tucumcari journalism. However, there evidently was insufficient revenue to sustain both papers, and J. E. Curren in July, 1905, suspended the *Actual Settler*, moving its plant to Sunnyside, New Mexico.[10] Then the prospect of Tucumcari's growth lured S. M. Wharton to found the Republican *News* there in October, 1905.[11] A fifteen-month battle ended with the purchase of the *Times* by the *News* in January, 1907. Within a year local Democrats sponsored the weekly *Sun*, which then competed with the *News* for the rest of the territorial era.[12] Fifteen other papers were launched in the nine small villages which arose in Quay County. Vigorous rivalry led to three mergers, but in January, 1912, there were still ten papers in the small towns.

To the southwest of Tucumcari, the older Pecos Valley towns of Puerta de Luna and Fort Sumner were both off the railway routes. As a result, a new town, Santa Rosa, arose on the lines of the El Paso Northeastern opposite Puerta de Luna. At Santa Rosa five papers were published before 1912. Because of its predominantly Spanish-American population, three were Spanish-language journals. The most important newspaper of the town, the Santa Rosa *Sun*, was a bilingual publication.[13] Fort Sumner, on the other hand, kept its old name when moved to the New Mexico Eastern lines, although for several years some inhabitants called it Sunnyside. Here late in 1905 J. E. Curren launched his Sunnyside *Sun* but soon moved to more promising Melrose. Three other papers were published at Fort Sumner before 1912. The most important, the *Review*, was founded in 1908 by A. Clausen.[14]

East of Fort Sumner on the new Santa Fe line the small villages of Lalande, Taiban, and Tolar grew up. In these towns four papers were founded, with three of them still in publication in 1912. Melrose, farther to the east, became very attractive to journalists, for the Santa Fe planned to make Melrose its main center in eastern New Mexico with extensive railway repair shops. A Santa Fe Gulf Coast line was to cross the New Mexico Eastern at Melrose, making it a division point on both lines. Enticed by such promise of prosperity, J. E. Curren launched the first paper at Melrose and gave it the name of his first New Mexico venture, the *Headlight*.[15] Before 1912 three additional papers had been founded at Melrose.

Since Melrose lacked a suitable water supply, Clovis was the town which received all the railway prizes. Arthur E. Curren, who had just sold his Tucumcari *Times,* learned that Clovis was to be both a railway shop site and a division point; and in May 1907, he launched the Clovis *News.* Within six months five other papers had joined the *News* at Clovis. Of all these papers the *News, Post,* and *Journal* were the most stable. During a period of intense competition all three papers issued short-lived dailies. Then in July, 1909, the *Post* was bought by the owners of the *Journal,* and soon this Democratic weekly alone faced the Republican *News,* which in 1912 still belonged to A. E. Curren.[16] From 1909 until 1912 Thomas J. Mabry published the *Journal.*[17]

Meanwhile, the New Mexico Central railway was built south from Santa Fe across the center of the territory to join the lines of the El Paso Northeastern. Estancia, which arose as a trading center for farmers settling in the region, became in 1905 the site of the area's first paper, the *News.* From April, 1911, to January, 1912, it was the daily *Morning News.* Its chief rival was the *Daily Herald,* published from March, 1909, until June, 1911, when it became a weekly.[18] There were two other weeklies at Estancia in these years and nine weeklies at seven nearby small towns.

Most of the towns discussed above were founded along the sites of the new railways and grew as trading centers for dry farmers. Along the lines of the El Paso Northeastern in south central New Mexico, however, two towns had risen outside the areas suitable for dry farming. Alamogordo began as a railroad division point and shop site, and Carrizozo grew simply as a trading center for ranchers and miners in Lincoln County. This town gained its papers from less fortunate Lincoln County towns. One of these towns, Capitan, boomed as the result of the discovery of a seam of coking coal but soon declined, for the nature of the deposit prevented large-scale operations. Four weeklies were published at Capitan, but after two mergers the *News* was the sole survivor. This Democratic journal moved to Carrizozo in 1908 to become the Carrizozo *News.*[19] The first paper at Carrizozo, however, was the Republican *Outlook,* moved there in 1906 from the dying town of White Oaks. Both these papers were still being published in 1912.[20]

Alamogordo grew more rapidly than Carrizozo because of the extensive revenue it derived from railway employees. As a result, Alamogordo lured many journalists, and between 1900 and 1912 four weeklies and a tabloid daily battled each other there. Of them the Democratic weekly *Otero County Advertiser* and the Republican weekly *News* were the most important survivors. Five weeklies were established at other Otero County towns, but the sole survivor in 1912 was the Tularosa *Valley Tribune.*[21] An initial wave of railway prosperity led to the founding of many weeklies in Otero County, but since the area had little future from irrigation or dry farming they rapidly faded.

Railroads brought great development, prosperity, and the founding of many towns in large areas of the territory. The most thriving towns of this region were those which had a railroad payroll. This income, provided by the train crews who lived at the division points and the workers in the railway shops, became the basis of a thriving retail business. In addition, these towns became regional trading centers. When the homestead areas of eastern and central New Mexico became heavily populated, rail centers such as Tucumcari or Clovis were provided with a large additional retail trade.[22] Many smaller towns also arose and prospered in this region because with rail connections they became trading centers for homesteaders.

In northeastern New Mexico near Clayton there was an influx of homesteading dry farmers less influenced by railways. This area, which had obtained railways in 1888, had lost farm population in the 1890s because of drought and low agricultural prices. Better prices and a wet cycle in the first years of the twentieth century induced a new flow of immigrants to the area. As a result new journalistic ventures were launched. Six papers were founded at Clayton in this era, but only the *Citizen* and *Enterprise* were long-lived.[23] Folsom, which had lost all its papers in the late 1890s, had five short-lived weeklies in this decade. Along the new railway from Tucumcari to Dawson several small towns grew up. In these towns and others that served the homesteaders fifteen small weeklies were founded. Most of these papers had very brief lives—including a revived Cimarron *News and Press*.[24] At nearby Springer, J. F. Hutchinson, publisher of the *Colfax County Stockman* since 1891, suppressed three short-lived competitors and continued to dominate Springer journalism until 1912.[25]

Immigration was encouraged in the irrigation farming areas by improved rail access to markets, just as it had been in the dry farming areas. The lower Pecos Valley profited from a direct rail connection to the markets of the northern Midwest. The San Juan Valley, which had no rail outlet earlier, could now easily transport its products to Pueblo, Denver, and midwestern points. Improved marketing conditions in turn encouraged the extension of irrigation in both areas. In the San Juan Valley several small projects diverted San Juan River waters to orchards and fields. In the lower Pecos Valley farmers began an extensive use of ground waters by pumping from a shallow stratum in some areas and by utilizing a deep stratum of artesian waters in others. These developments brought a new flood of pioneer farmers, closely followed by merchants, journalists, and others to share the wealth from this new irrigated farm production.

Roswell, the trading center of the Pecos Valley and its largest town, became the scene of several journalistic battles between 1900 and 1912.

In August, 1902, C. E. Mason and H. F. M. Bear bought the weekly *Record.* The following December the weekly *Journal* was launched; thus, with the well-established *Register,* three weeklies competed in Roswell. In March, 1903, each began to issue a tabloid daily. Mason and Bear[26] soon bought both rivals; then, encouraged by long-term advertising contracts from Roswell merchants, they subscribed to the Associated Press service and continued the Democratic *Daily Record.* The partners maintained as weeklies a *Record* and the *Register*—the latter as a Republican paper with Mason in charge.[27]

In January, 1906, Roswell Republicans, believing the *Register* was not truly Republican, inspired the launching of the weekly *Tribune.* Having failed to prevent the founding of a Republican paper, the *Register* had lost its usefulness and was sold to the *Tribune.* The result was the *Register-Tribune,* which endured as a Republican weekly until 1912. Most of these years B. F. Harlow was its business manager and the capable Will Robinson its editor.[28] Apparently Mason's brand of Democracy did not please some Roswell Democrats, for prominent party members[29] bought the *Register-Tribune* in August, 1911, and began issuing the *Morning News.* The group continued the Republican *Register-Tribune,* however.[30] Despite these competitors, the *Daily Record* remained the best paper in eastern New Mexico and a leader for its Democrats. There were two other short-lived weeklies at Roswell and four at other Chaves County towns in these years.[31]

Discovery of a stratum of artesian water in southern Chaves and northern Eddy counties led to the founding and rapid growth of Artesia, which soon acquired newspapers. The Democratic *Advocate,* launched in August, 1903, preceded the Republican *Pecos Valley News* by three years. Both weeklies represented very well the territory's vigorous new Anglo-Saxon element until 1912.[32]

Further south along the Pecos lay Eddy, a town of 963 people, which in 1900 adopted the name of the famous German spa, Carlsbad, hoping to exploit nearby mineral springs. Two stable and three short-lived weeklies competed in the increasingly prosperous town which by 1910 had a population of 1,736. W. H. Mullane, who had sold the *Current* in 1900, re-entered journalism in May, 1905, with the *New Mexico Sun.* This paper merged with the *Current* in August, 1907, with Mullane functioning as editor and publisher until 1912. Opposed to these Democratic weeklies was the Republican *Argus.* L. O. Fullen, its editor since 1895, was succeeded by W. T. Reed in January, 1907. Reed, who had purchased the paper in 1902, continued as editor and publisher until 1912.[33] Six other weeklies, most of them Democratic, were published in smaller Eddy County towns and added to the growing Democratic-press representation in the territory.

The San Juan Valley, like the lower Pecos country, benefitted from improved marketing conditions resulting from railway construction. The prospects of greater profits hastened the development of irrigation and the flow of immigrant farmers. At Farmington and Aztec, the largest towns of San Juan County, there was an increase in newspapers as a result of this new prosperity. At Farmington the *Times* gained a competitor in January, 1901, with the launching of the *Hustler*.[34] Two years later these weeklies were merged as the Democratic *Times-Hustler*. Democratic monopoly invited a Republican rival, and in 1905 Frank Staplin founded the *Enterprise*.[35] As late as 1912 the ensuing journalistic battle was still being waged in the small town of about 800 population. At Aztec the *San Juan Democrat* was launched in 1906 to compete with the long-established *San Juan County Index;* both papers were still publishing in 1912.[36]

The newspapers discussed to this point either arose to meet the needs of the new immigrant population or were influenced by it. This portion of the territorial press then had the characteristics of a pioneer press. On the whole, the editors of these areas were enterprising, daring, modern, and optimistic. Because of the nature of the journalists and the people they served, the newspapers of these areas were more inclined to dissent, to support progressive reforms, and to assert political independence. Since more than one third of the papers in this era were published in the regions of these twentieth-century pioneers, territorial journalism as a whole necessarily was reinvigorated and hastened toward modernization.

Most territorial journalists were aided by the revived prosperity of New Mexico; some beneltted from the prospects of irrigation projects; and the publishers of one mining district experienced an unprecedented prosperity. Nevertheless, the central and western portions of New Mexico were much less influenced by the extensive Anglo-American immigration into the territory. For example, Belen in this era benefitted from railway construction, railway shops, and an irrigation project. Yet, its population remained predominantly Spanish-American; and despite its prosperity, Belen's journalism exhibited little of the vigor of the eastern New Mexico papers. Of three papers founded in Belen, the *Tribune* was the most stable and important.[37]

As at Belen, the prospects of more water for irrigation increased journalistic activity in the Mesilla Valley, but support for newspapers remained scanty. At Las Cruces the *Dona Ana County Republican* was renamed the *Progress* in 1902, and two years later it was merged with the *Rio Grande Republican*. In February, 1911, O. A. and Josephine Foster purchased this paper and by September had made it a semi-weekly. Lawrence Lapoint, apparently the same man who founded the Mesilla

*News* and the *Eco del Rio Grande* at Las Cruces in the 1870s, launched the *Citizen* in 1902. From 1910 to 1912 his son, Will Lapoint, published this paper.[38] In this decade six other weeklies were also issued at Las Cruces, which by 1910 had become a town with a population of 3,836.[39]

The general prosperity and prospects of a ground-water irrigation project boosted the population of Deming to 1,864 by 1910 and quickened the pace of journalism, providing stable opponents for the *Headlight*. The most important editor of this Democratic weekly in this era was G. L. Shakespeare, who was also the publisher from 1898 to 1911. A competing weekly *Herald* launched in 1900 was replaced in 1903 by the weekly *Graphic*, which was continued into the new era.[40] At Deming, as with Belen and Las Cruces, new immigrants came late in this era and had only a very minor influence on journalism.

The economy of Raton improved more than that of Deming or Las Cruces because of an increased demand for the high-grade coking coal mined nearby. As a result of the town's greater prosperity and an increase in population from 3,540 in 1900 to 4,539 in 1910, journalism was highly competitive. The *Range,* foremost paper of Raton, had several publishers before it was purchased by O. A. and Josephine Foster in 1905. In 1906 the Fosters briefly issued the daily *Republican* and in 1908 began the *Daily Range* to compete with three short-lived dailies launched in 1908 and 1909. They sold the *Range* and *Daily Range* in 1910; and in January, 1911, the *Daily Range* was discontinued. The weekly *Reporter,* which survived until the 1930s, was published by G. B. Beringer from 1890 until 1910.[41] There were four other weeklies at Raton in this era, all of which endured for relatively short periods.

Gallup mining activity declined in this decade, and as a result its population dropped from 2,296 in 1900 to 2,204 in 1910. Since the town did not experience the high prosperity of Raton, the pace of its journalism continued to be slow. In 1902 W. T. Henderson sold the *Gleaner* to a Republican group, who renamed it the *McKinley County Republican.* In 1911 this paper gained a competitor, the *Independent,*[42] ancestor of Gallup's excellent present-day daily.

The mining of silver as of low-grade coal at Gallup was not appreciably increased in the decade after 1900; and the economy of the silver mining towns was aided little by higher beef and wool prices. The conditions for journalism thus remained poor in these towns. At Socorro, which by 1910 had a population of only 1,560, the *Chieftain* was purchased in 1900 by local Republican businessmen who placed E. A. Drake, a New Mexico School of Mines professor, in charge as editor until 1912. A Democratic Spanish-language weekly, the *Defensor del Pueblo,* competed with the *Chieftain* after 1905.[43] At Silver City the Democratic *Independent* and the Republican *Enterprise* continued routine existences. W. B. Walton[44] remained editor-publisher of the *Independent,* and Fred A. Bush edited the *Enterprise* from 1901 to 1912.[45] At Hillsboro W. O. Thompson bought the *Sierra County Advocate* in 1900 and was still publishing it in 1912. Apparently Hillsboro Democratic leaders wanted a more enthusiastic advocate for their party and launched the *Sierra Free Press* in 1911.[46] In these towns that were little affected by the new prosperity, politics continued to have a strong influence on journalism and newspaper competition.

Spanish-language journalism, unlike that of the quiet silver mining towns, was more affected by the trends of the new era, although it was also influenced by trends notable in the 1890s. First of all, there was a large increase in the number of Spanish-language journals. The increased literacy in Spanish, noted in the 1890s, probably was partially responsible, as well as the generally improved territorial economic conditions. But possibly the large and hostile Anglo-American immigration of this decade brought new urgency to the desire of the Hispanos to preserve their culture.[47] As in the past, however, Spanish-language journals faced very severe difficulties in some areas, apparently by reason of the high rate of illiteracy and poverty among Hispanos.

The northern counties of Taos, Rio Arriba, and Mora, which were predominantly Spanish-American in culture, gave meager encouragement to Spanish-language journalism but more than in the past. At Taos the only stable paper of the period was the *Revista de Taos.* Founded in 1902, this paper soon absorbed the older *Cresset,* and was still in publication in 1912. In Rio Arriba County at Tierra Amarilla the bilingual *Republicano* was published intermittently from 1901 until 1907, and *El Nuevo Estado* was issued from 1908 until 1912. In Mora County the Wagon Mound *Combate,* published from 1903 until 1911, became in the latter year the bilingual weekly *Mora County Sentinel* and *El Combate.*[48]

In other areas there was in this decade a more notable increase of Spanish-language journals. At Las Vegas *La Voz del Pueblo* was continued by Felix Martinez and E. C. de Baca, while *El Independiente* was issued by E. H. Salazar and others.[49] At Las Cruces *El Labrador* was continued through this period, and in 1905 the *Eco del Valle* was launched. After 1910 this paper was ably edited by Isadoro Armijo, Jr.,[50] and in 1911 it absorbed *El Tiempo*—the oldest Spanish-language paper in New Mexico.[51] At Albuquerque in 1901 *La Bandera Americana* and *El Nuevo Mundo* were merged. Nestor Montoya[52] then edited this paper as *La Bandera Americana* until 1912. Among several other Spanish-language papers at Albuquerque, *La Opinion Publica* was the most important. Elfego Baca[53] became a co-publisher and, for a brief time, editor of this paper. In addition, the New Mexican Publishing Com-

pany continued *El Nuevo Mexicano* at Santa Fe. By 1912 territorial
Spanish-language weeklies had reached a peak, attaining a greater number and a higher quality than in all prior decades.

Santa Fe journalism, as had the Spanish-language press, benefitted
from the general territorial prosperity despite the city's decrease in
population from 5,603 to 5,072 between 1900 and 1910. In addition,
prospects of statehood increased political activity and Santa Fe journalistic enterprises as well; in these years four new and relatively stable
weeklies were established. The most important of these was the *Eagle*,
founded in 1906 by A. J. Loomis.[54] This paper absorbed *El Boletin
Popular* in 1908[55] and continued into the new era. Despite a loss of
political subsidies in this decade, the *New Mexican* was enlarged and
improved. Max Frost and his successor in 1909, Paul A. F. Walter, continued to support the Republican party although patronage was withdrawn.[56]

Just as Santa Fe had lost its wholesale and distribution business to
Albuquerque and Las Vegas with the advent of railways, the second
period of railroad building initiated an era of economic decline for Las
Vegas and an evermounting ascendancy for Albuquerque. In the early
1880s the trade area of Las Vegas extended over large parts of central
and eastern New Mexico, including White Oaks and Seven Rivers. As the
most convenient rail connection for such a large region, the town was a
major shipping point for cattle, wool, and hides. Each railroad constructed after this time, however, removed part of this trade area, and by
1908 it had been vastly reduced.

The economic decline of Las Vegas was very slight at first. The general prosperity of the era and a population increase (of the combined
towns) from 5,319 to 6,934 between 1900 and 1910 kept Las Vegas attractive to journalists. As in prior decades newspaper rivalry was intense.
The battle between the *Daily Optic* and the *Daily Record*, begun in
1900, terminated with a merger in 1903.[57] But before this was consum-
mated, the *Advertiser* was launched. Beginning as a weekly, the *Advertiser* became a daily on May 1, 1903. Earl Lyons, its editor-publisher,
obtained financial support from Jefferson Raynolds, a Las Vegas banker
and former principal owner of the early *Daily Gazette*. But Raynolds
soon withdrew his support, and then in quick succession the *Advertiser*
became a weekly and lapsed.[58]

Despite the *Advertiser's* experience, the launching of new papers
continued. In 1905 and 1906, Russell Kistler, former *Daily Optic* owner,
published the weekly *News*. In 1909 Kistler began the *Homesteader*,
which was very short-lived.[59] Meanwhile, during all these years the two
Spanish-language Las Vegas weeklies, *La Voz del Pueblo* and *El Independiente*, were well supported, absorbing a large part of available

advertising and circulation funds. Thus, excessive competition continued to be an important facet of Las Vegas journalism until 1912.

Whereas the new railroads diverted trade away from Las Vegas to Texas points or the new territorial towns, one road, the New Mexico Eastern, had by 1909 extended the Albuquerque trading zone across central New Mexico to the Texas line. By 1900 enterprising businessmen had already made Albuquerque the largest territorial town, its population was 6,238. In this era of general prosperity and territorial growth, Albuquerque gained new trade and wealth; by 1910 its population had grown to 11,020. As a result the prosperous town was the scene of the greatest newspaper competition of the era. Here between 1900 and 1912 six dailies and fifteen weeklies were published—with nine of the weeklies in Spanish. In addition to these general newspapers, there were seven specialized journals, which drew all or part of their sustenance from the town. Towering above all these papers were the *Journal-Democrat* and the *Daily Citizen* and its successors.[60]

Initially the two Albuquerque dailies were evenly matched, but a vigorous new management for the *Journal-Democrat* and the death of Thomas Hughes changed the balance. Hughes, since 1881 a leading Albuquerque journalist, sold the *Daily Citizen* in 1905 because of ill health. Purchased by a group headed by banker W. S. Strickler, this Republican paper was continued until 1909. At this time a Democratic group, which had launched the *Tribune* a month earlier, bought the *Daily Citizen* and combined both papers as the *Tribune-Citizen*.[61] This group also suffered severe financial losses and in 1911 sold the paper to Republican leaders who renamed it the *Evening Herald*.[62]

The *Journal-Democrat* under an active new management was the chief source of trouble for the *Daily Citizen*. After the death of A. A. Grant, D. A. Macpherson gained control of the *Journal-Democrat*. Macpherson was the nephew of Grant and the administrator of his estate. In 1903 under the new management, W. S. Burke, an associate editor, was made editor-in-chief. Within a few months the name of the paper was changed to the *Morning Journal,* and it began to move toward the improved twentieth-century journalism. The latest reporting styles and headlines gradually were adopted, and the full leased wire service of the Associated Press soon was obtained. In politics the *Journal* became independent Republican, which left it free to criticize everyone—which it frequently did. By 1912 the *Journal,* except for occasional lapses, was following modern journalistic styles. In its business policies this paper also adopted the latest techniques. The purchase of a modern press made it possible to increase circulation, and between 1903 and 1912 the number of subscribers tripled.[63] Apparently because of its superior circulation, advertising sales climbed to new heights. Thus, the *Journal* editorially, journalistically, and in business practices was a stable, modern newspaper. It became a near-at-hand example of the success of the new journalism for other papers to admire and copy.

The stability shown by the Albuquerque *Morning Journal* in this era was characteristic of the entire territorial press. The short-lived political campaign papers had passed out of vogue, and most newly founded papers now survived for at least a year or longer. One example of the stability of the press was the large number of papers in existence in 1912. At the beginning of the decade 58 weeklies and five dailies were being published in the territory, while on the eve of statehood there were 115 weeklies and seven dailies. Nevertheless, newspaper failures and intense competition were as common as in the earlier period. To illustrate, from 1901 to 1912, 197 new papers were launched, compared to 252 founded in all the years before 1901. The decade thus displays the old trait of excessive competition as well as greater stability.

Just as the general territorial press exhibited traits of both the old and the new journalism, so too did the careers of individual editors and publishers. In this decade the trait of pioneer optimism recurred, but it was coupled with a more practical attitude about newspaper business practices. And in politics also both the old and the new were apparent, for the editors not only showed some of the old subservience but also some of the new spirit of independence in politics. The origins and backgrounds of the newsmen also reflected great diversity. Furthermore, there was diversity of opinion, editorial capability, pride of profession, journalistic fraternalism, and personal journalism. A trend away from the old ideas and practices toward twentieth-century journalism was clearly discernible.

That pioneers were still to be found in the twentieth century may seem improbable to many, but such seemed to be the case in eastern New Mexico. There the homesteaders lived under very trying conditions while they turned the sod into cultivated fields and were forced by the aridity of the area to learn new farming methods. The journalists who followed the farmers to eastern New Mexico were pioneers too, for many filed homestead claims which they worked while they published weekly newspapers. At any rate, the journalists adopted some of the characteristics of their pioneer neighbors, such as exceptional optimism and independence. At the same time in being enterprising and practical they displayed another pioneer trait. They took advantage of the friendliness and curiosity of their pioneer neighbors to sell many newspaper subscriptions. A newspaper with good circulation became a tool suited for the use of enterprising, optimistic, pioneer merchants, who followed the latest retail practices of increasing sales through large advertisements.[64] Thus, as in the early 1880s, many of the new publishers foresaw greater prospects of profits from private enterprise than from politics.

Although the influence of politics on territorial journalism was declining, its role was still important. Politicians still entered journalism in order to use newspapers as political tools. One illustration of this was the founding of the Albuquerque *Tribune* by such political figures as A. A. Jones, H. B. Fergusson, Felix Martinez, and O. N. Marron.[65] In another instance, the Roswell *Morning News* was founded by Roswell Democrats who were dissatisfied with the political policy of the Roswell *Daily Record*.[66] Some publishers, as has been pointed out, sought to prevent competition by providing a journal for avid partisans of both major political parties. This was true of H. F. M. Bear and C. E. Mason at Roswell with their Democratic *Record* and Republican *Register*. J. E. Curren and his son, A. E. Curren, duplicated this feat with politically opposed papers at Tucumcari and Clovis.[67] In other cases publishers changed their politics to suit their opportunities. One example occurred when life-long Democrat P. J. Bennett launched the Republican Deming *Herald* to compete with the Democratic Deming *Headlight* simply to gain local Republican support. Perhaps such cynicism as these instances show eventually helped to curtail the support avid partisans had given papers simply because they had displayed a party label. At any rate, in this era a great many newspapers were founded to give a political voice to one party of another as shown earlier in this chapter.

Prospects of political spoils continued to lead to the launching of newspapers. Most of the Republican papers founded in eastern New Mexico anticipated as their reward a monopoly of the legal notices required of homesteaders in the area.[68] And, as in the past, Republican publishers received political appointments as rewards for their party loyalty. For example, Leroy Loomis of the Texico *Trumpet,* James Corry of the Springer *Sentinel,* and Paul A. F. Walter of the Santa Fe *New Mexican* became postmasters. Wesley McCallister of the Lovington *Leader,* A. E. Curren of the Clovis *News,* and W. C. Hawkins of the Montoya *Republican* were appointed officials in the United States Land Office; and for his loyalty to the party, Frank Staplin was rewarded with a post as United States court commissioner.[69]

Republican journals outnumbered Democratic papers 112 to 64 in this era, and several factors account for the resurgence in Republican strength. First, the dissent of Populists and silverites had faded with the prosperity of the twentieth century, and many former Republicans had returned to the party. But perhaps more important was the fact that territorial Republicans controlled political spoils because there was a national Republican administration in these years. As a result the party could reward journalists with political appointments, territorial public printing contracts, and a monopoly of homesteaders' legal notices. This last was so profitable that there were almost as many Republican as Democratic papers in heavily Democratic eastern New Mexico. Nevertheless, Democratic press strength also grew during the period, principally because of the heavily Democratic immigration into southeastern New Mexico.

Of great political import was the fact that newspapers in general were more independent in this era. Some papers chose to list themselves as affiliated with neither party; many of them perhaps awaiting the highest bid from the politicians, and others probably hoping to placate partisans of both parties. Among these, twenty-seven listed themselves as independent; thirty-eight as non-political; and Prohibitionists, labor, and Socialists each had one journalistic champion.[70] However, many papers which were listed as affiliated with a major party rejected political control and were relatively independent. Increased income from circulation and advertising, as shown, made publishers less dependent on political income.[71]

The political affiliations of newspapers perhaps reflect the diverse origins of the journalists of this era, although no attempt was made to check the origins of all journalists. The group which appears to have been most prominent was that of Anglo-American journalists with a decade or more of residence in New Mexico. Newspapersmen with this background were to be found in all parts of the territory, but they were more numerous in the areas that had long been settled. Next most prominent were southerners, who published and edited many of the papers of southeastern New Mexico. Next were the Spanish-American journalists of the enlarged Spanish-language press of this decade. Finally, the northern Midwest continued to be well represented among the newsmen who immigrated to the territory in this era. Thus, three regional and two cultural elements were represented in the New Mexico press corps: western, southern, and northern midwestern Anglo-Americans, and the Spanish-American. As a result the territorial press was more cosmopolitan than at any earlier date.[72]

The cosmopolitan background of the newsmen may have helped them gain a more realistic attitude concerning the position of the journalist in society. While some believed the position of the editor was very important, few of them any longer considered themselves great arbiters of public morals and affairs. Wrote one country editor: "A newspaper is not such an important affair that it should turn a man's head. . . ."[73] On the other hand, when Will Robinson of the Roswell *Register-Tribune* was offered the New Mexico governorship by a high official of the Interior Department, he rejected it with this comment: "I am a newspaperman and would rather work on a newspaper than be president of the United States."[74] On the whole, editors assumed a more reasonable view of the power and prestige of their position than in the earlier periods. However, this must be deduced more from a lack of boastful statements about editorial importance and the power of the press, so prevalent earlier, than from editorial comments denying the power of the press.

The quality of editorial personnel in this decade varied from the superior to the decidedly inferior, and, as a result of the large number of new weeklies, printer-trained editors were the most prominent. The superior qualifications of some newsmen are reflected by their distinguished later careers. For example, T. J. Mabry left the Clovis *Journal* to study law and eventually served as both chief justice of the Supreme Court and governor of the state of New Mexico. E. C. de Baca of Las Vegas *La Voz del Pueblo* also served as a New Mexican governor. William A. Keleher, the noted Albuquerque lawyer and New Mexico historian, was a city editor of the Albuquerque *Morning Journal*.[75] Roy Bedicheck, Texas author and naturalist, served briefly as editor of the Deming *Headlight*.[76] E. Dana Johnson of the Albuquerque *Morning Journal* and Will Robinson of the Roswell *Register-Tribune* continued distinguished careers in New Mexico journalism.[77] In addition, the territorial press corps was improved in this era by the large number of college-trained members. Among the college-trained editors were such men as Isadoro Armijo of the Las Cruces *Eco del Valle*, H. F. M. Bear of the Roswell *Record*, O. N. McBride and E. P. Alldredge of the Portales *Roosevelt County Herald;* and E. A. Drake of the Socorro *Chieftain* was a former college professor.[78] As a general rule the quality of editorial personnel of dailies and larger weeklies was improved; however, among the smaller weeklies some editors were as inferior as the worst of the past, probably because they had learned journalism as apprentice printers and had little formal education.

The widening gap between the good and the poor journalists quickened the decline in journalistic fraternalism in New Mexico, but the opposite trend could be noted in eastern New Mexico where frontier friendliness prevailed and a spirit of fraternalism was encouraged by the common experiences and hardships shared by the pioneer newsmen. The contrast between the levels of journalistic fraternalism in the two areas was pointed up by press association activities.

The New Mexico Press Association was reorganized for the third time in September, 1900, when it met at Albuquerque and elected as its president William Berger of the Santa Fe *Capitol*. The next February Thomas Hughes of the Albuquerque *Daily Citizen* was elected president, and he evidently served through 1902. The association then seems to have disintegrated again. Although an effort was made to revive it in 1908, New Mexico had no general press association until 1912.[79] The activities of eastern New Mexico newsmen offer a contrasting picture. The Pecos Valley Press Association was organized in Roswell in August, 1907, with Will Robinson of the Roswell *Register-Tribune* becoming the first president. Subsequent meetings at southeastern New Mexico towns were well attended, and news accounts reflect the spirit of camaraderie of the conventions.[80]

Spanish-language journalists, united by a common cultural background, seemed to be exceptions to the decrease of fraternalism in the older New Mexican areas. Early efforts to maintain a Spanish-language press association evidently failed because of the small number of stable Spanish-language papers. Such efforts were renewed in 1911, and an association was formed at Albuquerque. Nestor Montoya of the Albuquerque *La Bandera Americana* was elected president, and Elfego Baca of the Albuquerque *Opinion Publica* became treasurer.[81] In 1912 this association in cooperation with eastern New Mexico weekly editors organized a newsmen's group which later became the present New Mexico Press Association.[82]

The various press associations had no startling achievements to their credit. Probably their chief accomplishments were the discussion of common problems and their efforts to revive the fading journalistic fraternalism.

The decrease in personal journalism in this decade was partially a result of the decreasing fraternalism among territorial editors. They were less likely to abuse someone whom they believed too insignificant to be worthy of attention. Another characteristic of personal journalism at this time was that the exchanges between editors were more often factual than abusive. An example of factually based labels was the Santa Fe *New Mexican* naming the Albuquerque *Morning Journal* "a rotten corporation sheet" because it belonged to the corporation-owning Albuquerque public utilities. The *Morning Journal* countercharge that the *New Mexican* was the organ of the Plunderbund[83] and was the territorial administration almanac was based on its constant defense of Republican leaders and its refusal to adopt readily the new journalistic styles. In other instances editors used clever editorials to ridicule their adversaries rather than countering with vile abuse. One example of this technique was a reply of Thomas Hughes of the Albuquerque *Daily Citizen* to a charge of dishonesty by J. H. McCutcheon of the Albuquerque *Industrial Advertiser:*

> The public is warned against Johnny McCutcheon. He is not honest. We bought him last year for $37.50 and he will not stay bought. Why we paid the extra $37.00 for a maverick of Johnny's sort is almost unexplainable. He came

and insisted upon selling himself and the bargain counter instinct caused us to buy a chunk of living rummage that is really not worth thirty cents in Mexican money.

We had no earthly use for Johnny in any way whatever, but the opportunity to buy a Democratic editor at bargain sale rates led us to invest. The idea that we could tell the fellow to crawl in our vest pocket was probably worth fifty cents, but looking back on the transaction we are convinced that when we paid $37.50 for such a sniveling, snarling, whining deadbeat, we recklessly threw away good money.[84]

Thus, it appears that while the era of personal journalism was not finally ended, personal editorial exchanges were rarer and milder.

In addition to a milder personal journalism, the territorial press corps of this decade had several notable traits. New elements made it more cosmopolitan. Perhaps this helped to lessen the former dominance exerted by the politicians over the territorial press. The improved educational background and capability of many editorial personnel were other notable traits. Despite their better qualifications, however, territorial editors achieved a more realistic and reasonable attitude toward the power and importance of their profession. In this more sophisticated press corps the spirit of friendliness and fraternity among editors declined, except among the pioneer newsmen of eastern New Mexico and the members of the Spanish-language press. Fraternalism among the latter journalists, born of shared atitudes and experiences, led to the founding of press associations more enduring than the New Mexico Press Association. In general, as statehood approached, the press was increasingly sophisticated, cosmopolitan, independent, and impersonal.

With a more capable press corps in this era, substantial improvements were made in territorial journalism, moving it along the road toward a more modern press for New Mexico.

Following national developments toward an improved press, territorial newsmen in this decade began to use the style and techniques developed by the yellow journalists. Some sought to exploit the sensationalism of this new journalism. Others began to use large headlines, photography, balanced front-page makeup, and other features to make their papers more interesting. At the same time, there was a general improvement in content brought about by more extensive use of Associated Press services. Territorial and local news coverage was also improved. While these innovations were being used to improve the dailies and the better weeklies, however, many weeklies retreated into a routine country journalism. In both cases the New Mexico press was following national trends.

The techniques of the yellow journalists, already adopted by the general American press, were used in this decade to modernize the territorial press. There is a generally held concept that yellow journalism was altogether bad, but it was not without some redeeming features. The original yellow journalists, W. R. Hearst and Joseph Pulitzer, are remembered for stretching the truth and placing a heavy emphasis on the sensational, particularly in dealing with sex and crime. But this is not the whole story. These men, realizing that a large circulation is the key to newspaper profits, took advantage of the innovations in composition, printing presses, and paper to increase the circulation of their journals.

Along with sensationalism, other techniques were developed to attract readers. New composition methods provided almost unlimited newspaper space, making it possible to use many large headlines and photoengravings.[85] Order was brought to front pages by excluding advertising and providing balanced makeup. Interesting additions were made, such as sports news, comics, and feature stories. Newspapers gained a lively and interesting appearance. In many ways newspapers were not a great deal more sensational than in the past, but the blaring headline, the skillfully written lead paragraph, and photography so increased the impact of the sensational that the readers were impressed as never before.

Nor was sensationalism an unmixed evil, for many of the stories were informative. A new interest in crime made the public aware of its extent, opening the possibility of a demand for reform. Sensationalism was also used to expose incompetent or corrupt officials. Generally the yellow journalists backed the progressive movement's demand for reform, partially because it was sensational. Good or bad, sensationalism and the wide variety of news stories presented in the new manner made newspapers more interesting, timely, and lively than ever before. As a result millions of new readers were attracted. Seeing the success of men such as Hearst, American journalists began to adopt their methods.[86] Territorial newsmen were no exception and followed the trend toward modern journalism.

Only two territorial papers used yellow journalism extensively. The most notable user of sensationalism to increase circulation was the Las Vegas *Advertiser*. From the inception of this paper, editor Earl Lyons sought to use the ethnic clashes between East and West Las Vegas for his benefit. Since West Las Vegas was an unincorporated town, its post office was merged in 1903 with that of East Las Vegas, the newer town; and a $10,000 Carnegie Library grant for Las Vegas was accepted by the East Las Vegas City Council, which located the library in its town. Efforts were being made to combine the two towns, but some East Las Vegas residents objected to the incorporation of the slum areas of West Las Vegas. Lyons charged or implied that discrimination against the predominantly Spanish-American population of West Las Vegas was a partial motivation for the actions of the leaders of East Las Vegas. Successful exploitation of these issues helped the weekly *Advertiser* to grow. Then it gained financial support and launched a *Daily Advertiser*.

Having fully exploited the cultural conflict, Lyons turned his attention to a grisly incident at the territorial insane asylum at Las Vegas. A doctor at the asylum had taken the skeleton from the body of a deceased patient without family permission. The bones were placed in a barrel of lime water on the grounds and were found by an inmate who threw them over the asylum wall. Lyons learned of this, and, in a series of sensational stories and editorial comments, charged asylum officials with cruelty to patients. Again, his primary motive appeared to be to exploit the affair for circulation growth. Lyons lost his financial support because his backer, banker J. S. Raynolds, was a member of the asylum board. The *Advertiser* then reverted to weekly publication and was soon suspended. Although all these events were newsworthy and editorial comment was justified, Lyons' sensationalism and inclusion of the cultural issue appeared to be designed primarily to advance his own fortunes.[87]

Yellow journalism of a more justifiable nature was used by the Albuquerque *Morning Journal*. In an editorial campaign extending over several years, the *Morning Journal* sought to break the power of Albuquerque's political boss, F. A. Hubbell. Later the paper vigorously attacked the administration of territorial Governor M. A. Otero and Republican leader H. O. Bursum. Partially as a result of the campaign of the *Morning Journal*, Hubbell's control of the Republican party at Albuquerque was curtailed; and the hold of the Otero-Bursum faction on the territorial Republican party was loosened.[88] Certainly it is the business of a newspaper to point to the faults of public officials and party leaders, but never had a territorial newspaper carried forward such an extensive campaign in such a sensational manner. The use of the other techniques of yellow journalism became more widespread. The changing style and size of headlines can be illustrated by noting the treatment of two major stories in 1901 and 1910.

In 1901 the Santa Fe *New Mexican* related the assassination of President William McKinley under a small two-column headline. By contrast President W. H. Taft's signing of a New Mexico statehood bill in 1910 produced banner headlines in almost every territorial paper, including the *New Mexican*.[89]

The Albuquerque *Morning Journal* led the territorial press in the adoption of the new headlining styles. Even this paper, did not consistently follow the new practices and occasionally placed 8 one-column headlines of the same size and type face together at the top of its front page. For brief periods the Las Vegas *Daily Optic* adopted the new styles but soon reverted to its old ways. Late in this era the Albuquerque *Tribune-Citizen* and its successor, the *Evening Herald,* adopted the new practices.[90] By 1912 most dailies had recognized the new styles by using them occasionally.

Improvements in front-page makeup were dependent on the usage of the new headline styles, and hence the improved practices in makeup of eastern American papers was not being consistently used in New Mexico in 1912. The elimination of front-page advertising aided the movement toward balanced front pages. Such leading papers as the Albuquerque *Morning Journal* and the Las Vegas *Daily Optic* began this practice early in the decade. Many weeklies also began to eliminate front-page advertising, but few of them were consistently doing so in 1912.[91] Thus, the trend toward a modern, balanced front page was well underway but not consistently followed by 1912.

Photographs, which ease the problem of achieving a balanced-page makeup, were not consistently used by territorial journals at this time. The Albuquerque *Morning Journal* and *Tribune-Citizen* and the Las Vegas *Daily Optic* at various times used news pictures furnished by national newspaper syndicates. As for local pictures, the *Morning Journal* made more use of them than did most papers, but the most consistent user of local photographs was the Santa Fe *New Mexican.* However, these were photos of leading legislators and pictures of buildings in various territorial towns rather than true news photographs.[92] Many territorial weeklies also occasionally used photos of this variety. Here again, the territorial press had adopted one of the new techniques but was inconsistent in its use.

The territorial press improved newspaper content at the same time that it began the occasional use of the new techniques to make papers more attractive. Again the most notable improvement was in the Albuquerque *Morning Journal.* In 1903 this paper doubled its Associated Press coverage and in 1906 obtained the full leased-wire service. From this time on, the *Morning Journal* had excellent coverage of national news, considering the fact that it was only a small town daily. Until 1906 the Roswell *Daily Record,* Santa Fe *New Mexican,* Las Vegas *Daily Optic,* and Albuquerque *Daily Citizen* had subscribed for a 500-word daily telegram from the Associated Press; then the last three of the above papers received a 1,000-word telegram.[93] Before 1906 the *New Mexican* published the entire telegram as a single story—a daily news summary. But the *New Mexican* began to divide the longer telegram into brief stories, a practice the other papers had adopted earlier. Local news also gained a new prominence, with the most important stories being accorded treatment equal that of the interesting national news of the day.

Local news briefs and social news were given more space and prominence than in the past.

Most territorial weeklies, on the other hand, began to concentrate on reporting the news of their locality, following practices similar to those of small-town weeklies of today. Possibly the efforts of the dailies to extend their circulation to rural areas forced weekly editors to improve local news coverage. Since they could compete with the dailies neither in freshness nor quantity of territorial and national news, they began a more detailed reporting of local events to entice the minority who wanted national news to subscribe to the weeklies as well as to the dailies.

Eastern New Mexico weeklies were the first to adopt this practice, publishing a large number of short local stories—many written by rural community correspondents. These news briefs dealt with routine matters: the coming and going of people, minor social affairs, births, marriages, and deaths of ordinary citizens.[94] Coverage of territorial political news was often limited to editorial comments or interpretation of events. Thus, by 1912 a trend which had begun in the 1890s was completed, and the weekly press of the territory became almost entirely a local press.

Both weeklies and dailies continued to rely on the news sources used in the past to obtain territorial news. Dailies made some use of the Associated Press for territorial news, but the exchange system provided fuller details almost as rapidly as that service. The dailies followed various practices in exchanging papers with weeklies, but the latter often limited their exchange of papers to nearby weeklies.[95] Personal reporting of territorial news, on the other hand, was increased only slightly, being limited for the most part to the Albuquerque *Morning Journal* which assigned reporters to cover the legislative session and other events at the territorial capital.[96] A one-page summary of New Mexico news was included among the pre-printed pages sold by the Denver branch of the Western Newspaper Union, giving some poor weeklies delayed but excellent territorial news coverage.[97] These stories apparently were also obtained by the exchange system, which worked better than in the past because local news reporting had been improved. Nevertheless, by their continued use of the exchange system the territorial press lagged behind national progress in journalism.

The territorial press also lagged behind the general development of journalism in a great many other practices. For example, most editors continued to use personalized editorial columns. The Santa Fe *New Mexican* provides the best example of the dailies which followed this practice, and almost every territorial weekly continued to use personalized editorial columns.[98] Sports coverage was almost entirely limited to the Albuquerque *Morning Journal,* which with its full leased-wire service could easily follow this news. Feature stories, another development of the new journalism, were rarely used by territorial papers.[99] Although the transition to the modern press was not complete, few of the distinctive facets of a frontier press remained. The poetry and boisterous humor of an earlier day were no longer to be seen. One exception to this, however, was a humorous column by Will Robinson, "Impressions of a Tenderfoot," which appeared in several eastern New Mexico weeklies. But on the whole, the territorial press, still hampered by limited space, devoted little effort to formalized editorial pages, sports, feature stories, humor, or poetry. It had become a workaday, no-nonsense press striving to give as much of the local and territorial news as possible. Even so it was nearer to modern journalism than the frontier press. Thus, by and large the territorial editors had moved far down the road toward modern journalism by 1912.

The quickening pace of twentieth-century American life made itself felt in territorial journalism between 1900 and 1912. While the weeklies began to limit themselves to local news, New Mexico dailies met the challenges of the new century. Under the leadership of the Albuquerque *Morning Journal,* they increased their foreign and national news coverage and experimented with the latest innovations in makeup, headlining, and style. Thus, despite their adherence to some of the old ways, the territorial press by 1912 was nearing the modern practices of journalism with regard to newspaper content and style.

The changes in American newspaper content and style during this period were closely related to the business policies adopted by newspapers, for the new journalism might not have developed without the improved printing machinery and the new merchandising and advertising concepts accepted by American retailers. Until 1890 most retail advertising simply stated the firm name and the type of goods sold; then retailers began to advertise specific items, particularly in sales promotion. This new advertising listed, described, and gave the price of the goods for sale, requiring more space than the old-style advertisement. The generally held concept—the bigger the advertisement, the bigger the bargain—helped even more to increase the size of advertisements.

Since the new advertising practice was expensive, most retailers were inclined to place their advertising in the paper with the most subscribers, because the more readers, the better the results. As a consequence a battle for circulation began between the leading newspapers of each town. And at the same time publishers began to buy the new printing machinery, enabling them to compete more effectively for the new advertising and circulation. It was under these conditions that Hearst and Pulitzer began their all-out struggle for circulation and advertising, using every department of their papers. The news and editorial phase of this struggle has been discussed as yellow journalism. The struggle for circulation led to reduced prices on subscriptions, special circulation promotion, and violent war for newsstand and street sales. With regard to advertising, the war was carried forward by keeping rates low, or at least not raising them in proportion to the increased circulation. Newspaper competition became even sharper than in the past, and many papers were forced out of business. At the same time, the large capital needed for the expensive new machinery reduced the number of new journalistic ventures. After 1910, under these conditions, the number of American newspapers has been reduced annually. This trend has been one of the significant features of modern journalism.[100]

The course of journalism at the national level was belatedly and partially repeated in New Mexico. First, many papers adopted the new printing machinery. Next, publishers sought to encourage the new large advertisements, conducting extensive circulation campaigns as a part of that effort. Finally, despite attempts of political parties to increase their control of newspapers, a large portion of the territorial press followed the national trend toward political independence. Thus, by 1912 a large part of the New Mexico press had adopted modern business practices.

While most territorial dailies had adopted modern printing techniques by 1900, many territorial weeklies lagged far behind. From 1900 to 1912 these weeklies still were printed with Washington hand presses and handset type. The acquisition of a power press was a momentous event for most territorial weeklies and one which fellow editors noted with praise or envy. The purchase of a linotype was even rarer among the weeklies. The comments of Quay County weekly publishers about the marvelously unique and expensive linotype installed at the Tucumcari *News* shows the machine's rarity, and even the ancient *Rio Grande Republican* did not install a linotype until 1911.[101]

There appear to be several reasons for the delay in adoption of the new machinery by territorial weeklies. First, the income of many of the older papers was still very limited, and they were forced to continue with the old methods. Next, numerous pioneer weeklies were founded in small eastern New Mexico villages which could not support the expensive new journalism. Since most of these publishers were undercapitalized, they purchased used equipment and continued the hand-powered methods of printing. The number of such struggling weeklies was increased by the policies of pre-print companies such as the Western Newspaper Union. Such companies would sell entire plants on an installment-payment plan. Then they supplied the publisher with pre-printed pages, reducing his expenses and allowing him to hang on. This helps to account for an increased use of pre-printed pages in New Mexico, contrary to the national trend.[102] By 1912, however, most large territorial weeklies had power presses and many had linotypes. Nevertheless, weeklies lagged well behind dailies and the national trends in the use of power machinery.[103]

The lag in the acceptance of new machinery delayed the transition to the new advertising practices, but it was also delayed by some merchants. In Albuquerque and eastern New Mexico aggressive retailers used large merchandising advertisements, especially of sales. Thus, in papers of those areas such advertisements were common. For example, after 1906 the Tucumcari *News* routinely published one-page and occasionally two- and four-page advertisements.[104] On the other hand, the transition to the new advertising was not delayed by lack of aggressive merchants alone, but also by the advertising rates of some of the old weeklies. To illustrate, the rate per column inch of the weekly Silver City *Enterprise* was $1 for one week, $2 for one month, and $12 for one year; the copy apparently was to remain unchanged throughout the period the advertisement was to run. This policy encouraged the continued use of small advertisements, the old system, but discouraged the intermittent large advertisements in which the copy was always changed because such advertising would be too costly at $1 an inch. The eastern New Mexico weeklies, on the other hand, encouraged the new advertising system. The rate of the Tucumcari *News,* for example, was 15 cents per column inch for any advertisement. Most eastern New Mexico papers had similar rates. This practice helps to account for the large retail advertisements of that area, while the lack of them in the older weeklies is partially explained by their policies.[105]

Some eastern New Mexico weeklies were additionally blessed with a large income from homesteaders' legal notices. The Portales *Times,* for example, at one time used 25 per cent of its space for the publication of such legal notices. The advertising in the pre-printed pages of the eastern New Mexico weeklies was also of interest. This advertising came usually from national firms and was principally for patent medicines such as Dr. Williams' Pink Pills for Pale People, Lydia Pinkham, Peruna, Buckingham's Mustache Dye, and others. The advertisers favored testimonials and often sought to exploit famous names. For example, Peruna advertised, "Admiral Schley endorses PE-RU-NA," with this statement, "Gentlemen: I can cheerfully say that Mrs. Schley has taken Pe-ru-na and I believe with good effect." Publishers were beginning to realize the falsity of some patent medicine advertising, but it was probably a lack of public response to such advertising—induced by "muckraker" exposure of its falsity—rather than the efforts of country publishers that led to its decline.[106]

Classified advertising, a large source of revenue for present-day papers, was not common in the territorial press. It was not until 1903 that the dailies at Las Vegas, Albuquerque, and Santa Fe began classified sections,[107] and by 1912 they still had little of such business. Nevertheless, with the new advertising practices, homesteaders' legals, and other revenues, many territorial publishers were very prosperous.

Possibly the increased prosperity of newspapers lessened the former common criticism of towns and their merchants for insufficient support of newspapers, for it was rare during this period. However, the Santa Fe *New Mexican* was an exception. Santa Fe merchants continued to provide poor support for the paper; and when it began to lose its profitable territorial public printing, the *New Mexican* began to appeal for support from the town and merchants. Most territorial editors, on the other hand, apparently adopted an attitude similar to that of Frank Staplin of the Farmington *Enterprise*. He maintained that the worst sort of advertising for a paper was that which was put in to "help the paper. The only advertising that pays the paper is that which is done for the purpose of bringing business to the advertiser, and no paper which believes in and is willing to give a square deal wants any other kind."[108] Adoption of this realistic attitude was shown by publishers' efforts to improve newspaper content and increase circulation, which increased advertising response and advertising sales.

Most publishers were aware of the necessity of offering a large circulation to their advertisers and many of them made efforts to obtain more subscribers. The easiest and first method used was to lower prices. Soon after D. A. Macpherson became publisher of the Albuquerque *Morning Journal,* for example, he lowered subscription rates to 60 cents per month by city carrier and $5 per year by mail. The other territorial dailies soon followed his lead. Approximately a year later the Las Vegas *Daily Optic* reduced its rates to 60 cents monthly by carrier and $6 annually by mail.[109] However, during these years the circulation of the *Daily Optic* advanced from 2,000 to only 2,100. The Santa Fe *New Mexican,* which in 1907 reduced mail circulation rates from $7.50 to $7, by 1912 had increased its subscribers from 1,350 to 1,600. The *Morning Journal* did not depend on lower prices alone and by 1912 had increased its circulation from 2,003 to 6,000.[110]

The subscription prices of territorial weeklies varied widely in this era. Western and central New Mexico weeklies had rates ranging from $3 to $1.50, but eastern New Mexico weeklies favored a rate of $1 per year. This was the rate of the Tucumcari *News,* Clovis *News,* Portales *Roosevelt County Herald,* and Clovis *Journal,* as well as many smaller weeklies. The rate of the Roswell *Register-Tribune* was $1.50, but it had an annual promotional period when it sold for $1 per year. The

Clovis *News,* for a short time, was sold for 50 cents a year to attract new subscribers, and the San Jon[111] *Sentinel* was sold for 25 cents a year during its first six months of publication. The lower rates and vigorous efforts of these papers produced large circulations. For example, the Tucumcari *News* reached 1,900, the Portales *Roosevelt County Herald* 3,000, and the Roswell *Register-Tribune* 2,150.[112]

Realizing the importance of circulation, many New Mexico papers began to use promotional schemes in addition to price inducements to obtain it. The Albuquerque *Morning Journal* employed a circulation solicitor to travel over the territory and sell subscriptions while he wrote news stories about the various territorial towns. The Tucumcari *Sun* promoted circulation sales by offering a $400 piano to the Quay County woman who sold the most subscriptions to the *Sun.* The Fort Sumner *Index* offered half of its original subscription sales to any church named by its subscribers.[113] Although reduced newsprint prices in this period allowed lower circulation prices, the lower subscription rates and the special efforts to increase circulation show that publishers had a new awareness of the value of a large circulation in increasing advertising sales and rates.[114] The Albuquerque *Morning Journal* was the best example of this. By 1910 it was able to boast of advertising rates twice that of any other territorial paper and the largest annual advertising linage ever published by any New Mexico paper to that time.[115] Therefore, it appears that in this period the New Mexico press was introduced to the modern concept of newspaper management that a larger circulation, even if in itself less profitable, increased advertising sales and total profits.

Although circulation, the key to increased advertising sales, became an important competitive weapon in this era, the resort to daily publication was still a widely used tactic in battles between weeklies. This was true at Estancia, where two dailies competed in a town of about 500 population. At Clovis four short-lived dailies, and at Roswell three, were published in competitive flurries. The short-lived Texico *Daily Trumpet* and Alamogordo *Daily Journal* are other examples of the use of this competitive technique. All these towns but Roswell were too small to support dailies, and they were soon forced to return to weekly publication.[116] Evidently the publishers hoped either to frighten or to force out competitors and at the same time gain the support of subscribers and advertisers with an increased service.

Another striking fact about journalistic competition in this era was that despite the increased number of papers the intensity of journalistic battles decreased, except in the towns of great prospective growth. For example, at Clovis between 1907 and 1909 nine papers were launched, but by 1911 only two had survived. This represents the general trend. In towns large enough to support more than one paper, usually competition soon was limited to two papers representing the major political parties.[117] On the other hand, some small-town publishers avoided political affiliation—evidently hoping to avoid politically motivated competition. Most journalists became increasingly reluctant to start or maintain papers for political reasons, especially since advancing wages and the greater capital requirements of newspaper plants left potential printer-publishers unwilling to struggle to sustain unprofitable papers. Furthermore, newsmen were learning that some who urged them to start papers were insincere in their offers of support and only wished to harass opposition publishers. The following colorful editorial headed "OBITUARY" illustrates these points:

> With this issue the PECOS VALLEY STOCKMAN ceases to be. It dies, peters out, alkalies, passes over the range,—anyway you prefer to put it.
>
> .  .  .  .  .  .  .  .  .  .  .  .  .  .  .  .  .
>
> The causes of this move are few and plain. Some months ago the STOCKMAN was about suspended and for sale under foreclosure, and by the advice of "friends" I bought it, hoping that by industry and economy in the mechanical department—doing my own work—I could make it pay. Becoming convinced that I nor any man can do it, I take advantage of the best offer to sell the material, preferring to enjoy the position of an humble mechanic with three square meals a day and something coming on Saturday night to the proud position of a country editor without enough revenue to pay expenses. . . . To those who promised to support me and failed to deliver the goods, I have nothing to say. They know their business and I know mine well enough not to continue a paper that does not and cannot be made to pay.[118]

This reluctance to launch competing papers was a facet of modern journalism. The founding of new papers was not only deterred by increased capital requirements but as well by the desire of merchants to patronize the paper with the largest circulation—whatever its politics. Thus, in the last territorial era there was a preview of the present day, when the preference of the advertisers for the most efficient advertising medium would limit most New Mexico towns to only one newspaper.

Since the merits of the newspaper as an advertising medium were not involved in job work, the purchasers of such printing could feel free to patronize any paper. With business prosperity in twentieth-century New Mexico, job work became an important source of newspaper revenue. Even in the smaller towns enough income was derived from this source to provide a modest living for the country publisher.[119] Throughout the period the larger papers continued to seek revenue from this source, and a few maintained a vigorous fight for territorial public printing. In 1903 the Santa Fe *New Mexican* lost its dominance of this lucrative source;

in that year the Republican governor and legislature assigned part of its public printing to the Republican Las Vegas *Daily Record.* In 1907 under the administration of Governor H. J. Hagerman, Max Frost was removed as secretary of the Bureau of Immigration, and the *New Mexican* lost its last hold on the territorial public printing. H. B. Hening, city editor of the Albuquerque *Morning Journal,* replaced Frost, and the *Morning Journal* received the printing contract of the Bureau.[120] Although until statehood the territorial public printing apparently continued to be awarded on a political basis, it was no longer used to maintain the chief party organ at Santa Fe.

Exposure of the political subsidization of newspapers at the county level apparently helped to bring an end to the practice soon after New Mexico became a state. One such exposure occurred in San Juan County. Frank Staplin, publisher of the Farmington *Enterprise,* bid $300 lower on a county printing contract than the Farmington *Times-Hustler.* Failing to receive the contract from the Democratic county commissioners, Republican Staplin sought an injunction against payment to the *Times-Hustler* for the printing. Staplin lost his suit because the *Times-Hustler* had arranged for the public notices to be published in all the San Juan County Democratic papers. The court ruled that the greater circulation justified the higher price. Nevertheless, soon after statehood was granted, such useless and wasteful practices as the publication of county commission minutes and delinquent tax notices were discountinued, probably because of exposures such as the above during an era when progressive reformers closely watched government activities.[121]

The complete loss of political subsidy was still in the future, for in this decade newspaper revenue from politically controlled sources was increased—mainly because of the legal notices of homesteaders. Nevertheless, there was a strong trend toward political independence because the readers demanded it. Since revenue from the new retail advertising depended on having the most subscribers, readers became more important than politicians. In this era of progressive reformism the public was suspicious of politicians, wished to see them questioned and exposed if they were corrupt, and subscribed to the paper which did question and expose them.

Evidently the owners of the Albuquerque *Morning Journal* correctly assessed this new attitude and made their paper politically independent. One measure of the vigor of their attack on the politicos was the numerous libel suits filed against them by the territorial politicians. Prospects of libel suits in this decade were increased when the legislature of 1905 re-enacted the harsh libel law of 1889. Under its provisions the *Morning Journal* was not only indicted for criminal libel but was sued for

$50,000 in damages by members of the ruling Republican group which had secured passage of the law. The *Morning Journal* fought a delaying action against the criminal charges and damage suits and apparently escaped with a very light fine and little or no penalty for damages.[122]

The career of the Albuquerque *Morning Journal* tells the story of the advances of territorial journalism in this decade. In 1900 the territorial press was a captive of the politicians. In content and style its journalism was that of the 1890s, lagging behind the development of the general American press. Its mechanical and business practices likewise lagged. But in this decade a vigorous new population arrived in the territory and demanded more of its newspapers. A new group of journalists also arrived, suffered through a brief competitive flurry reminiscent of early pioneer periods, and then began to follow the lead of the *Morning Journal* toward modern journalism. And the Albuquerque paper did provide leadership. It was first to adopt the new machinery, first to improve news content and style. In so doing it made large gains in circulation, enabling it to monopolize the profitable new retail advertising at Albuquerque. Then, dependent not on politicians but readers, the *Morning Journal* became politically independent. The newsmen in the areas of the vigorous new population were not long in following the lead of the *Morning Journal*, and by 1912 a great part of the territorial press had become a modern press.

By 1912 the territorial press had traveled a long road, going through three stages of development since 1834. From 1834 to 1879 New Mexico was an isolated and impoverished area. Its papers were printed with obsolete machinery and its journalism lagged behind that of eastern America. Because of the poverty of the area, opportunists who hoped to use newspapers to gain political power or spoils were the chief ones attracted to journalism in the territory. They were, nevertheless, far above the average in education, fiercely individualistic, and politically independent; and their papers were well edited and interesting.

The second stage of journalistic development in the territory, from 1880 to 1900, was a period of transition. Economic prosperity in the early 1880s led to the founding of many new papers whose editors looked for income from business rather than from politics. Then the collapse of the boom in the mining and livestock industries and the advent of a general depression forced the journalists into political subservience and caused them to lag in acceptance of new printing and journalistic techniques. The editors of this era had neither the aggressiveness nor the education characteristic of their predecessors. Their papers were therefore not as well edited, were more routine, and were obsessed with politics.

In the final phase of territorial press development, from 1900 to 1912, the pioneer period of the 1880s was re-enacted in some portions of the territory, but in the territory as a whole a strong element of political control remained. Then, inspired by national developments in journalism, the editors adopted new styles, improved the contents of their newspapers, and purchased the new machinery that allowed them to serve an expanding population, increase circulation, and capture the profitable new retail advertisements. By these activities the press was freed from the control of the politicians and accepted as its policy the fact that only by serving the desires and demands of its readers could it have the large circulation that made a newspaper a desirable and profitable advertising medium. Thus, by 1912 the territorial press had become a modern press and was ready to serve the new state of New Mexico.

# THE TERRITORIAL PRESS

# AND THE POLITICIANS

THE TERRITORIAL PRESS, as has been shown earlier, went through several phases in its relationship with the politicians. Until 1879 the press and the politicians were closely aligned, with most of the journalists being opportunists who hoped to use their profession to attain political ends. From 1880 until 1888 some newsmen rejected political domination, so that the press was partially both controlled and free. Then until about 1908 the press was generally under the influence of the politicians. But by 1912 it was rapidly becoming freed from manipulation by politicians. Thus, most of the territorial press throughout the whole period was controlled by political leaders. This subservience of the press was not unusual, for, as has been shown, much of the rural American press was dominated by politicians. On the other hand, the final freeing of the press from political control occurred under the stimuli of the progressive movement and the new concepts of American journalism. Thus, generally the territorial press merely followed the same trends as the rural American press. How the territorial press was controlled by politicians, by which politicians and for what purposes, and how their influence was eliminated will be shown in detail.

Politics, national or territorial, from 1870 to 1900 was rather meaningless, with little real difference in the policies of the two national parties. Both avoided the chief issues of American life and in their political campaigns appealed for the support of the voters with such shibboleths as the "bloody shirt," party loyalty, and loyalty to the South. Possibly the most fundamental issue of that era was who should get the rapidly increasing wealth brought by industrialization and national expansion. But the politicos of the two major parties, following the widely held concept that the only duty of the state was to be a referee in such a contest, generally avoided this issue even though it was thrust at them time and again by Greenbackers, Grangers, Populists, silverites, and labor unions. The progressives made a deeper impression on the major parties, but their chief accomplishment was to insure that the state became a fairer referee in the contest for wealth. If national politics was a meaningless jumble without real issues, territorial politics was even more so. There was little prospect that New Mexicans could solve their problems through politics, for they neither had full self-government nor could their one delegate to Congress vote and effectively influence national policy for New Mexico. Thus, there was little likelihood that territorial campaigns for congressional delegate, territorial legislative seats, and county offices would be fought over real issues.

It is the contention of Harold D. Lasswell that all politics is a battle between competing "political elites" for power and wealth, in which "symbols" rather than real issues are used to win popular support.[1] One of the first steps in the political contest is to gain effective control of communications media to be better able to present the symbols which would muster popular support for the elites. Since Lasswell's ideas appear particularly suited to a study of territorial politics, it is proposed to show how the political elite gained control of the press, to identify the elites, to illustrate the scope and appeal of the symbols they used, and to demonstrate how these symbols were used to win elections.

Although it would seem impossible to keep several hundred frontier editors under control, the territorial political leaders were able to do so, with rare exceptions, through patronage in offices and public printing, outright purchase of the loyalty of opposition papers, introduction of campaign papers, encouraging competition for opposition party papers, direct entry into the newspaper business, and by using the loyalty of party member subscribers and advertisers to reward or punish publishers. During most of the territorial era, party ties were so strong that merchants, attorneys, and newspapers were patronized or shunned because of their party allegiance.[2] As a result of this practice, newspapers were tightly bound to the party and were expected to support party candidates without regard for their qualifications. A statement of H. W. Sturges, publisher of the Springer *Colfax County Stockman,* at the 1890 territorial press convention indicates the extent and limitations of this concept.

When a candidate comes up for office with the party endorsement, the paper of that party is very properly expected to give him an unpurchased support, but if no party lines are drawn we hold that no candidate has a right to expect the paper to boost him into office without an adequate consideration.[3]

Territorial papers were expected to publish at their mastheads the names of party candidates for President, delegate in Congress, legislative seats, and county offices from the time they were nominated until the election was over. The complete territorial party platform was also published. Shortly before the election the paper was expected to endorse editorially all party candidates and to list their qualifications for office—whether or not the editor believed they had any such qualifications. Parties did not pay for such services but did reward the leading party paper in each county with a contract to print the election ballots.[4]

Additional bait to keep editors and publishers loyal to the party was the prospect of appointment to governmental positions under party control, such as postmasterships or land office positions. Another form of patronage was the awarding of public printing contracts. Although the Santa Fe *New Mexican* usually acquired the territorial public printing, lesser papers were held to the party line with prospects of county printing contracts. In the homestead areas, the printing of legal notices, part of the process of acquiring public lands, was reserved for papers loyal to the party in control of the national government.[5]

Failing to obtain support from an established paper, politicians often resorted to publishing their own papers for the duration of the campaign. Papers of this type diverted the subscriptions and advertising of loyal party followers from well-established papers and held out the threat that the campaign paper might endure as a post-election competitor. Politicians who lacked a party paper in their own town sometimes became publishers but more often encouraged the founding of a paper to reflect their partisan attitudes. Thus, the threat of diversion of revenue to campaign papers and the risk of acquiring new competition made publishers hesitate to adopt an independent attitude or support opposition-party candidates, even if they were of superior ability and qualifications.[6]

The course of Las Vegas journalism in this era provides an example of the way politics robbed editors of political independence by increasing the harshness and prevalence of competition. From the founding of the *Daily Optic* in 1879 until 1912, forty different papers, eight of them dailies, were published at Las Vegas, which in this period grew from a village of less than 1,500 people to a town with a population of 7,000. Nine of these papers, three of them dailies, were directly sponsored or encouraged by politicos. In addition, politics indirectly brought and sustained other competitors. Some Las Vegas newspapers were specifically charged with selling their editorial opinions.[7] Three of the town's journalists were postmasters, and other posts were used to reward or motivate publishers. Eventually one Las Vegas paper was even awarded part of the territorial public printing, traditionally reserved for the Santa Fe *New Mexican,* to insure that a Republican daily survived in the town. Although from 1879 to 1904 the *Daily Optic* was the best territorial paper, editorially, in circulation, and in advertising, it had a very difficult time. It twice narrowly averted mortgage foreclosures, and twice was forced into mergers. The first merger, in 1898, forced Russell Kistler, one of the best of the territorial editors, to relinquish control of the paper.[8] Thus, politicians, by encouraging excessive and unreasonable competition, prevented the development of a potentially great newspaper, damaging both Las Vegas and the territory. Under competitive conditions of this type, political independence was very difficult.

Thus, the politicos through custom, patronage used as bait, campaign papers, encouragement of competition, and often outright purchase of favorable editorial opinions induced journalists to present unrealistic symbols to the reading and voting public. The net effect was to rob territorial editors of the independence necessary to present the true issues of New Mexico politics or to compare the qualifications of candidates for office.

What sort of men were the political leaders who so tightly controlled the political policies of the press? They were men of varied occupations, most prominent of which were the federally appointed officials of the territory who were in a sense resident agents of the national party in power at the time. But in addition, they were lawyers, landowners, ranchers, merchants, and journalists. In most instances they were men in position to control newspaper publishers or gain alliances with them; and that control helped them to become leaders of the territorial political groups.

In the first years of American rule there arose two groups who sought to control the politics of the territory. The nucleus of one of these was a group of federal officials who allied themselves with prominent members of the Spanish-American community. Some of the federal officers founded and alternated as publishers of the Santa Fe *Weekly Gazette*. Opposed to this group was another led by Jose M. Gallegos, a former priest who was somewhat hostile to American rule. Allied with him was Spruce M. Baird, a former Texan and lawyer. Baird briefly published the Santa Fe *Amigo del Pais* and *El Democrata* to provide propaganda organs for his clique during political campaigns. With the coming of the Civil War, Baird returned to Texas, and Gallegos joined the opposition elite. However, a new group quickly developed, led by J. F. Chaves. He allied himself with one portion of the federal officeholders and the publishers of the recently founded Santa Fe *New Mexican*. By 1869 the Chaves group had gained the ascendancy. It is impossible to label the two groups along party lines, because until 1869 both claimed to represent whatever party was in power nationally. But in 1869 the Chaves clique became widely recognized as the leader of the New Mexico Republican party. Early in the 1870s two lawyers, S. B. Elkins and T. B. Catron, joined this group and soon dominated it. This clique, composed of federal officials, prominent Spanish-Americans, and the publishers of the *New Mexican,* became known as the Santa Fe Ring and until around 1898 dominated the Republican party in particular and territorial politics in general.[9]

Although members of the Elkins-Catron group denied there was any Santa Fe clique or ring, most territorial editors strongly maintained that such a group existed. To illustrate, the Las Cruces *Borderer* charged the *New Mexican* with being the mouthpiece of a corrupt clique of political demagogues.[10] The Silver City *Grant County Herald* reprinted a New York *Sun* editorial naming S. B. Elkins and T. B. Catron as leaders of a Santa Fe clique and charged that Elkins expected a senatorship from the impending state of New Mexico as reward.[11] The *Herald* also quoted a St. Louis *Republican* statement that a Republican ring was able to induce the New Mexico legislature to do its bidding with small amounts of cash.[12] After S. M. Ashenfelter became editor of the *Herald,* he confirmed the existence of a Santa Fe Ring, which he held responsible for his dismissal as United States attorney in 1869. He contended that the ring manipulated the legislature by rewarding northern Spanish-American counties as the expense of southern Anglo-American Democratic counties.[13]

Territorial Democrats, following national precedents of the era, sought to imply that the Santa Fe Ring was an organization similar to the St. Louis "whiskey ring" and blamed this organization for all the evils which beset the territory. William Breeden, territorial Republican chairman, countered by asking Democrats for more specific charges upon which territorial officials could take legal action. The Santa Fe *Weekly New Mexican,* insisted there was no ring:

> The word "ring" has of late years grown into very common use, and it is applied very generally and liberally. It is used generally to designate any combination or association of men for any and whatever purpose. It is a favorite word with disappointed aspirants for political favor, sore heads, unsuccessful place seekers, chronic mischief makers and fault finders and noisy demagogues. It is especially a pet word with ambitious outs [*sic*] who are impatient to get in, and above all with fellows who, having lately held office, have been found incompetent or unworthy and been kicked out. It has been the fashion for the classes above named, and even of a more reputable class of Democratic politicians, to talk a great deal of what they term a "Santa Fe Ring" . . . which has no existence except in the distempered brain of fussy demagogues and place hunters.[14]

S. M. Ashenfelter continued to maitnain there was a ring, but believed Democrats in power would act similarly:

> During the last eight or ten years many and grievous complaints have been

made throughout the territory of the acts of oppression by which that combination of individuals known as the Santa Fe ring has maintained its ascendancy. It is generally understood that this ring is made up of government officials whose interests are not identified with those of the Territory, but who have come out from the east, because in the division of political spoils, an office in New Mexico fell their lot. Does anyone doubt that in case the Democratic party won in the next national contest, a new set of cormorants would be foisted upon our people, and that a new ring would be organized in Santa Fe? Does anyone believe that such a ring would hold the welfare of the people in higher esteem than the gratification of their own selfish ends?[15]

Probably the sins of the Santa Fe Ring were exaggerated, for a later Democratic administration secured criminal indictments against many Ring members but convicted few. However, it appears such a group as the Santa Fe Ring existed, if the definition of a political group by modern political scientists is accepted.[16]

When railways came to New Mexico, a large Anglo-American Republican immigration and additional newspapers brought possibilities of change in territorial politics. In 1882 the Ring candidate for delegate to Congress Tranquilino Luna, was challenged for the Republican nomination by L. B. Prince. Only with unfair methods were Ring members able to get the nomination for Luna. As a result, three Republican papers, the Robinson *Black Range,* Las Vegas *Daily Gazette,* and Socorro *Sun* refused to support Luna in the election.[17] In 1884 party dissension brought two Republican candidates into the campaign for congressional delegate, and the Republican press again divided its support. In 1886 and 1888 most Republican papers supported the party nominee. By 1888 T. B. Catron, Ring leader, had regained substantial power in the party.

The *New Mexican* remained faithful to the Santa Fe Ring during the period of political tumult in the 1880s. This foremost spokesman for New Mexico Republicanism, sold by its former owners in 1880, had several owners and managers in the following years. In 1889 Max Frost, who had become a large stockholder in the *New Mexican* Publishing Company, was made editor and publisher of the paper.[18] From 1885 to 1889, while Democrat Grover Cleveland was President, New Mexico was controlled by a Democratic administration. The *New Mexican* then lost the territorial public printing it had monopolized and suffered competition from a series of Democratic papers in Santa Fe. This Democratic administration almost bankrupted the paper; and when Cleveland was re-elected in 1892, Frost was determined to avoid the repetition of such a bleak period. Thus from 1894 until 1897, the *New Mexican* was leased to a combination of Democratic officials headed by Governor W. T. Thornton. It was then merged with the aggressive Democratic Santa Fe *Sun;* and a competitor which would have been tremendously strengthened by Democratic patronage, was eliminated. In 1897 Democrats gladly relinquished the paper to Frost.[19] He then allied himself with the new governor and territorial Republican party leader, M. A. Otero, and again monopolized territorial public printing.[20] In addition, Frost enjoyed patronage as secretary of the Bureau of Immigration.

The Santa Fe newspapers, first the *Weekly Gazette* from 1853 to 1869, and then the *Daily New Mexican* from 1869 to 1912, were a central element of the generally dominant territorial political elites. Before 1880 these papers were the most important media for influencing public opinion. After 1880, when the number of territorial papers increased, the *New Mexican* became a spokesman that many other Republican papers closely followed. Frost continued to lead smaller Republican papers from 1894 to 1897 by writing editorials which were distributed among these papers. Thus, Frost, who also served many years as secretary of the territorial Republican party, used his prestige as a journalist and party leader to help the Santa Fe Ring keep a tight control over a portion of the territorial press.[21] The Santa Fe journalists, for the reward of public printing and offices, became important tools of the dominant and centralized political elites of Santa Fe.

Opposition leaders, lacking the centralized control made possible by political patronage, consisted of the chiefs of various dissident groups. In the 1850s southern New Mexicans became unhappy with the rule of Santa Fe and the northern counties. Anglo-American immigrants, chiefly miners, then led a movement to make southern New Mexico a new territory, Arizona. The Mesilla *Times* became a spokesman for this group, which took Arizona for a short time into the Confederacy.[22] In the post-Civil War era, more Anglo-Americans came to develop mines and ranches, and again there was dissatisfaction with Santa Fe rule. The Bennett brothers, miners and merchants of Las Cruces and Silver City, became the leaders of a Democratic group opposed to Santa Fe domination. Apparently it was to represent this group that N. V. Bennett launched the Las Cruces *Borderer* in 1871. Meanwhile, the followers of J. M. Gallegos reassumed the name Democrat and in 1871 ran him for congressional delegate. The Bennetts, through the *Borderer,* rallied southern New Mexico Democrats to help elect Gallegos.[23] This victory revived the territorial Democratic party, but gave it a divided leadership. As a result, until 1912 party control was vested in strong leaders of dissident groups in various parts of the territory. Under these conditions several newspapers became important to the Democratic chieftains.

The Bennett family, probably because it usually controlled a newspaper, remained leaders of southwestern New Mexico Democrats until 1912. N. V. Bennett suspended the Las Cruces *Borderer* shortly before his death in 1876. However, the Bennetts soon again controlled a paper through S. M. Ashenfelter, son-in-law of Cornelius Bennett. Ashenfelter became editor of the Silver City *Grant County Herald* in 1877 and was connected with this paper until the mid-eighties.[24] In this period he became a leader of southern New Mexico Democrats. E. G. Ross,[25] who as brother-in-law of Cornelius Bennett was a family member, was named governor of New Mexico in 1885 by President Grover Cleveland. At the end of his term in 1889 Ross became editor of the Deming *Headlight,* which had been purchased by Ashenfelter. The *Headlight* then became a spokesman for territorial Democrats until Ross was succeeded in 1893 by W. B. Walton, a son-in-law of Ashenfelter. Walton, later an editor of the Silver City *Independent* and prominent in Grant County politics, was territorial Democratic chairman from 1908 until 1911.[26] The Bennett family thus gained its political power in a large measure by publishing newspapers.

Albert Bacon Fall, another southern New Mexico Democratic leader, also utilized journalism for politics. Fall served several terms in the legislature and as a district judge in the second Cleveland administration. He founded the Las Cruces *Independent Democrat* in 1892 to aid his political career. Although Fall supposedly sold this paper in 1894, some territorial editors believed he still controlled it in 1899.[27] Fall, one of the most influential territorial Democrats of the 1890s, found a newspaper to be an essential element of political power.

On occasion political support was purchased by subsidizing papers or by the outright buying of editorial opinion. These were the methods of Anthony Joseph,[28] the leading territorial Democrat of these decades and at one time a member of the Santa Fe Ring. New Mexico delegate to Congress from 1885 to 1895, Joseph sponsored free campaign weeklies at Santa Fe. Among them were *La Aurora* in 1884, *El Guia* in 1886, and *La Voz del Pueblo* in 1888.[29] According to contemporary observers, Joseph purchased the support of the Republican Las Vegas *Daily Optic* in the campaign of 1886, but lost the allegiance of the Albuquerque *Morning Democrat,* which supported the Republican candidate for a cash reward.[30] J. G. Albright, the politically ambitious publisher of the *Morning Democrat,* believed that a lack of support from Joseph in 1885 had cost him the New Mexico governorship. Until this time Albright had sought to make his paper as important to Democrats as the Santa Fe *New Mexican* was to Republicans. But after his desertion of the party in 1886, the influence of the *Morning Democrat* declined.

Other Democratic leaders acquired newspapers for political use. For example, W. T. Thornton, governor of New Mexico from 1893 to 1897, leased the Santa Fe *New Mexican* and made it the official party paper, hoping to use it to build a political machine. The efforts of the *New*

*Mexican* to increase Thornton's political prestige apparently were futile because after Thornton left office he was never again a figure of political importance, insofar as the press was concerned. And far from having a strong political machine, the territorial Democrats were weak and disorganized. Felix Martinez, later important in Democratic party circles, was a leader of the Union People's party[31] in the 1890s. He purchased the Santa Fe *La Voz del Pueblo* in 1890 and moved it to Las Vegas, where it became a spokesman for the Union People's party. This paper, like Martinez, had become staunchly Democratic by 1900. Also prominent, but less influential than the above, were H. B. Fergusson of Albuquerque and George Curry[32] of Roswell. Curry never controlled a paper, and Fergusson was only briefly a co-owner of the Albuquerque *Tribune-Citizen*. Possibly this partially explains why neither developed a strong, cohesive faction like Fall's.

The Democratic leadership consisted of several strong factions and figures; consequently its press representation followed a similar pattern, with five papers playing key roles. Democrats failed in numerous efforts to sustain a key paper, similar to the *New Mexican,* at the territorial capital. The Republicans depended on one key paper at Santa Fe and a large number of well-established subordinate papers. Republicans, controlling patronage, were able to provide more income for newspaper sustenance, and Republican papers generally outnumbered and were more long-lived than Democratic papers. Thus, for most of the territorial period six papers played key political roles; and several hundred others echoed the key papers in their presentation of the symbols and appeals of the parties.

The important and real issues of New Mexican life rarely were used and never became the chief points in political campaigns, possibly because political leaders held the press in such tight control. These politicos usually neglected education, irrigation, settlement of the titles of Spanish and Mexican land grants, pacification of the Indians and a logical and valid basis for division of the public domain that protected the water and grazing rights of all New Mexicans. Although these points were discussed by some editors between campaigns, the candidates avoided them. Instead, they based their appeals for popular support on false issues or, as Lasswell termed them, "symbols."[33] Prominent among these symbols were appeals for loyalty to Spanish heritage, culture, and religion; loyalty to the United States; and loyalty to the Republican or Democratic party. Other issues which were more valid, but which were not true issues because of the way in which they were used, were free silver and the corruption of opposition partisans. Perhaps the most valid New Mexico campaign issues involved statehood and the tariff on wool.

Few of these issues or symbols called for a program of action by the politicians because these were symbols that appealed to the prejudices of the voters.

The appeal for loyalty to Spanish heritage, which often sought to imply prejudice on the part of the opposition party, was a popular symbol during the entire territorial era. An early example of this appeal provides the strange situation of an Anglo-American candidate for congressional delegate, S. M. Baird,[34] asking for Hispano votes on the Spanish-heritage basis when he unsuccessfully represented the Gallegos faction in 1857.[35] Protest of the use of such an anti-American appeal may be inferred from Santa Fe *Weekly Gazette*:

> We want to demonstrate to Judge Baird and the country that the native citizens of the Territory scorn and repudiate his low appeals to their national prejudices in order to array them against the institutions and government of their adoption.[36]

The appeal to Spanish heritage was resorted to even when both candidates were Spanish-Americans, as happened in 1880. M. A. Otero, Sr., who had defeated Baird in 1857, returned to the territory after a long absence and became a candidate for congressional delegate against Tranquilino Luna. The Santa Fe *New Mexican* and Luna sought to deny Otero Spanish-American votes by labeling him a blue-eyed American, noting his long absence from New Mexico, and referring to his "American" wife. The Las Vegas *Daily Optic* condemned Luna for introducing the ethnic issue into the campaign and asked for votes for Otero as the man who would represent all New Mexicans.[37]

Even as late as 1908 Democratic congressional delegate candidate O. A. Larrazolo used the Spanish-heritage symbol by contending that the Republican party was prejudiced against Spanish-Americans and rarely nominated one as a candidate for congressional delegate. The Santa Fe *New Mexican* replied by citing the long list of Republican Spanish-American congressional delegates and candidates.[38] As these examples show, an appeal to ethnic prejudice carried with it the risk of a counterreaction from the other ethnic group in New Mexico. Nevertheless, the appeal, which had nothing to do with a candidate's qualifications or the protection of the rights of the Hispano, was used repeatedly in the press, enabling the politicos to avoid valid issues.

A counterappeal to the ethnic issue was loyalty to the United States and to the Union. The use of this symbol was increased during the war and Reconstruction period, from 1863 until 1870, but it was seldom used afterward. The item cited concerning S. M. Baird shows an early use of this appeal. In 1865 the *New Mexican* was labeling political opponents "Copperheads,"[39] but in 1867 it was called upon to defend its candidate for congressional delegate, J. F. Chaves, against charges of disloyalty.

> . . . it has been charged by the enemies of Col. Chaves that he is anti-American and anti-military, by which we are to understand that he would be glad, were it in his power, to expel the Americans and the military from the country. . . . These charges are false and absurd in every particular.[40]

Of course, loyalty to the government in which a candidate is seeking office is a first requirement, but in most instances where the use of this charge was noted in the press there was no question of loyalty involved. Hence, again a subterfuge was used and valid issues were avoided.

Equally beside the point were the appeals through the press for party loyalty, which were usually made in the last weeks of the campaign to rally the solid support of party members. This attitude was shown by an 1867 admonition of the Santa Fe *Weekly Gazette*: "Vote for the straight ticket on Monday and nothing but the straight ticket, for such is the kingdom of heaven." In 1884 the Albuquerque *Morning Journal* appealed for party loyalty in the face of party division. "Our best efforts are at the command of the party, in behalf of republican [sic] unity and republican [sic] victory. . . ." Last minute appeals to party loyalty were still common in the 1890s as indicated by a Socorro *Chieftain* demand. "Vote for the entire Republican ticket." The concept of strict party loyalty continued into the twentieth century, particularly among militant southern Democrats of eastern New Mexico. "The Herald has never wavered in its support of the Grand Old Democratic party, and never will so long as there is type to set and a press to run.[41] Since there was so little real difference in the two major parties, such appeals amounted to little more than demands that citizens continue their past voting habits.

Another common campaign maneuver, the charge that an opposition candidate was corrupt, might seem a valid issue since it brought into question the qualifications of the candidate, but for several reasons this monotonously used appeal lacked validity and appeared to have been used principally as a propaganda technique.[42] First, the press of both parties used the technique against the opposition but rarely turned on their own partisans, no matter how guilty they might be of malfeasance. Second, reform was not intended, for editorials on corruption were usually dropped at the end of the campaign and rarely used again until the next campaign. Next, the best territorial administration suffered almost as much abuse as the worst. Finally, editors answered charges against their own partisans not with refutation but with countercharges against opposition leaders or an attack on the paper printing the charge. Newspaper attacks on corruption, however, did prevent a few blatant frauds. In the end, editors and politicians realized that campaigning on an opponent's demerits rather than on their own candidate's merits was a negative approach and began to moderate their attacks.

Democrats, rarely in office and with the example of national party precedents, were the most consistent users of appeals against official corruption. The treatment of the Santa Fe Ring by Democrats was an early example of this approach. However, when Democrats were in office, Republicans used a similar technique. The best example of Republican use of the appeal against official corruption was the treatment of E. G. Ross, who appears to have been the most honest of all the territorial governors. Determined to end many of the evils plaguing the territory, Ross conceived of himself (in the words of Max Frost) as "the man for whom the people of New Mexico had been looking for 300 years."[43] He sought to settle the land title question,[44] to end fraudulent practices in the cashing of territorial warrants,[45] and to have Santa Fe Ring members indicted for past crimes. Ross was hampered in his reform efforts by incumbent Republican officials and a Republican legislature.[46] There were no notable convictions from 300 indictments against Santa Fe Ring members.[47] Perhaps partially as a result of the efforts of Ross, however, Congress established in 1890 a court to settle land grant titles. The legislature acted in 1889 to end the warrant frauds.[48]

Despite the obvious good intentions of Ross, the Santa Fe *New Mexican* editors became his implacable enemies and harangued against him throughout his term. This paper charged Ross with corruption in connection with the construction of the territorial prison and its administration.[49] Many of the charges of the *New Mexican* were echoed by the Albuquerque *Daily Citizen*,[50] and the *Rio Grande Republican* charged the Ross administration with conducting a pardon brokerage.[51] But unlike the Santa Fe Ring, Ross had many defenders among opposition editors. And there apparently was no real question about his honesty, for the succeeding Republican administration made no move to indict him.[52]

Often the territorial editors made no attempt to refute or answer charges against their party leaders and replied by rebuking the other editor or with a countercharge against opposition leaders. For example, the Las Cruces *Independent Democrat* launched what seemed to be a devastating attack on T. B. Catron with this editorial comment.

Looking over the old files of the Territorial newspapers, one discovers that the reputation of Hon. Thomas B. Catron has been besmirched by charges of bribery, subornation of perjury, brutal defiance of law, man made and ethical— charges never disproved. In every campaign, legislative session, criminal trial, land or mining deal that he has been concerned in since he came to New Mexico, that unfortunate reputation has been besmirched with such diligence and painful regularity that it has become like a printing office towel—so dirty that it stands alone.

The Las Vegas *Daily Optic* made no attempt to refute the charges, but instead replied:

Editor Kelly forgot that neither by law, reason or logic is a man to prove a negative. The law presumes every man is innocent until he is proven guilty; hence, the accuser must prove and the accused is not required to disprove.[53]

The Albuquerque *Morning Democrat* also attacked Catron:

Catron's prominence is principally due to the moral obtuseness of our people. . . . We have lacked courage as a people, we have fallen so low that we are satisfied to be filthy. . . . It is bitter to acknowledge it, but none the less true, that the mass of the people of New Mexico care nothing about Catron's moral character and are too languid to sustain those who do care. . . . A few individuals or a few newspapers can only make spasmodic efforts, they must be sustained by popular opinion and popular opinion must express itself unhesitatingly, otherwise the courage and energy of these will flag and expire and we shall all fall into the ditch together.

The Socorro *Chieftain* replied with a countercharge:

It is a pity about our "general moral obtuseness." We think we have heard that before from some of the mongrel college bred Eastern ducks who have fastened themselves upon us.

The editor then began a long diatribe about the corruption of the current Democratic administration of Governor W. T. Thornton.[54] In essence such a reply is no more than the small boy's retort, "you're a bigger one." These charges against Catron, like those against Ross, often had little basis,[55] and they show again that the maligning of political opponents by partisan editors was a political technique rather than a meaningful attempt at reform or a genuine political issue.

Even when the territory was threatened with an open and evident fraud, many newspapers defended, excused, or ignored, the corrupt actions of their fellow partisans. The reaction of Republican papers to an editorial in the Democratic Santa Fe *Daily Sun* furnishes an example. The editorial, headed "CORRUPTION FUND," tells of the discovery of a plot by Abraham Staab, who apparently was a member of the Santa Fe Ring, to gather funds to bribe the legislature to redeem fraudulent warrants:[56]

The following letter was found on the street yesterday where it evidently had been dropped. It was a most fortunate thing for the people of New Mexico as its publication will probably nip in the bud the most gigantic corruption scheme in the history of the legislature.

Dear Sir

It is believed that something can be done [by] this legislature regarding the old militia warrants. The interested parties have come to the understanding that before the matter is taken into hand, all owners of the warrants shall deposit 25 per cent of these outstanding warrants to defray expenses . . . if a funding act is passed converting these warrants into 4 per cent territorial bonds without having to account to the former owner. If no act is passed they shall be returned to their respective owners.

Time is passing and action must at once be taken. If you are willing to go into this in order to ask anything out of your warrants, you may send me the 25 per cent deposit of your holdings and I will send my individual receipt for the same.

Awaiting your reply, I am truly yours

A. Staab.[57]

The Staab letter aroused varied responses from the territorial press, mainly along partisan lines. The Democratic press was general in its denunciation, and Republican papers ranged from condonation to condemnation. The Silver City *Enterprise* held that there was nothing wrong with the Staab letter except that it fell into the wrong hands, and the Santa Fe *New Mexican* took a similar attitude.[58] The Las Vegas *Daily Optic* censured the Santa Fe Ring for this attempt to raid the treasury and maintained that it was merely the latest of many attempts to fund the warrants:

. . . New Mexico has not had a legislative session in years, which has not been disturbed by some effort on the part of the holders of these fraudulent warrants seeking to get good money for their worthless paper.[59]

As the above instances show, press attitude on corruption usually depended on whose party was involved, which must have left the public confused and uncertain of the weight to give such charges. Overuse of this technique probably reduced its effectiveness. At any rate, by 1900 such editorials were rarer, which had the healthful effect of rendering charges of corruption more credible. In addition, politicians and editors were coming to realize that more votes could be won by stating a candidate's qualifications. The Las Cruces *Rio Grande Republican* showed its approval of the new trend by printing an editorial outlining the new technique and heading it "A SOUND ARGUMENT":

The Headlight believes that the newspapers which have the most politicalty [sic] influence are those which seek to win in political elections by presenting the merits of their candidates and principles, rather than by villifying the opposition, which is now considered an admission of weakness. It is no longer possible to convince the members of any one party that all of those who fail to subscribe to their doctrines are necessarily scoundrels, and the newspaper that attempts it will lose prestige.[60]

Since free and unlimited coinage of silver would have helped the economy of New Mexico, this would have seemed a valid basis on which a candidate for delegate to Congress could ask for votes. Neither national party followed a consistent policy with regard to silver coinage until 1896, and territorial political leaders and newspapers of both parties thus were left free to adopt a pro-silver attitude.[61] Republican papers in the mining camps were particularly strong supporters of free silver. For example, the Socorro *Chieftain* reminded its readers that "the agitation for free silver must be kept up," and later maintained that "the remonitization of silver will come when the Republican party returns to power. . . ."[62] The Chloride *Black Range* was equally enthusiastic for the cause of silver, and Republican papers outside the silver mining areas, such as the Albuquerque *Daily Citizen* and the Las Vegas *Daily Optic* were also consistent advocates of free silver.[63] When confronted with their party's gold standard platform in 1896, territorial Republican papers followed three courses: approval, avoidance of the issue in the campaign, and repudiation of the platform. The Albuquerque *Daily Citizen* adopted the first policy and maintained that "if Republicans of this territory cannot endorse the Republican platform, the best ever made by the Republican party in national convention assembled, then the party in this territory will deserve defeat."[64] Republican papers of the silver mining areas chose the second alternative. To illustrate, the Socorro *Chieftain* ignored the silver issue, instead asked for votes for Republican candidates because of the party's tariff policy, and used slogans such as "all law abiding citizens should vote the Republican ticket" and "those who wish progress should vote for Catron."[65] The Las Cruces *Rio Grande Republican* eventually adopted a very similar attitude. Early in 1896 it repeatedly called upon Republicans to support free silver; and when the gold standard was made party policy, it at first refused to endorse that platform. But by September it had changed, agreeing with the *Daily Citizen* that:

> The Republican pledge, to bring about the free coinage of silver by international agreement, is all that the intelligent advocates of bi-metalism ask for. . . . They know the Republican pledge can be counted on and that McKinley will do all that the platform has promised.[66]

Only two Republican papers absolutely refused to support the Republican party in 1896. One of them, the Chloride *Black Range,* called upon all freedom-loving citizens to cast aside partisanship and rally around the silver standard.[67] The other, the *Daily Optic* also bolted the party and supported the Democrats at all levels.[68] Nevertheless, an overwhelming majority of the Republican papers chose to ignore the valid silver issue which they had used earlier and to follow party dictates. In most cases party loyalty seemed to outweigh other considerations as far as editorial stands on the silver question were concerned.

The tariff question presented a case very similar to that of the silver issue. Tariff became an area of party contention in New Mexico between 1883 and 1898 and was important chiefly because of tariff protection for raw wool. The Santa Fe *New Mexican Review* introduced the question in November, 1883, shortly before a Democratic United States House of Representatives was expected to propose tariff reductions. This leading Republican paper set the party policy for other Republican papers with the statement:

> The people of this territory believe in a protective tariff. They demand protection for their wool and stock interests and mineral products.[69]

Tariff did not become an important issue in territorial politics, however, until President Grover Cleveland asked Congress for a general tariff reduction, evidently intending to make this an issue in the campaign of 1888. Democratic proposals for tariff reductions doubtless led the Republican Gallup *Register* to protest that reductions of the tariff on coal would allow Californians to import foreign coal and would cost the Gallup mines their principal outlet. This in turn brought a rebuke from the Republican *Daily Optic* of Las Vegas:

> It is wise policy, and according to the principles on which the government of this country is founded, that the many shall suffer for the benefit of the few, that in order for Gallup to sell her coal at a higher rate than coal can be mined in Australia and then brought to this country, all southern California must be heavily taxed upon this article of prime necessity.[70]

Possibly this was not an honest conviction and was merely a bid for Democratic money by the *Daily Optic,* which in 1886 had supported the Democrats for a monetary reward. Perhaps by mid-summer of 1888 the paper had made satisfactory arrangements with the Republicans—at any rate it had fully adopted their policy and was contending:

> To put iron and coal on the free list would result in closing every iron and coal mine in the country, unless American miners would work for the starvation wages paid such laborers in Great Britain.[71]

In the campaign of 1888 Democratic and Republican papers aligned themselves on opposite sides of the tariff question. Possibly their arguments were based on honest convictions, but it seems more likely that they were rationalizations in defense of party policy. Again the *Daily Optic* furnishes an example. Just before the election in 1888 this paper contended: "Free wool and cheap lead would be the most damaging condition of affairs that could be imagined in New Mexico." A few months later the *Daily Optic* recanted concerning lead, and complained that shutting off cheap Mexican lead ores, which were used as flux in the smelting of silver, would close New Mexico smelters and force New Mexico silver miners to ship their ores to Colorado for smelting.[72]

From 1890 to 1896 the tariff issue was subordinate to the much more important and appealing silver question. But in 1898 it again became important enough that Democrats, courting the votes of sheepmen, chose to oppose national Democratic policy by including in the territorial platform an endorsement of the tariff on wool. Democratic papers, apparently unwilling to recant old arguments in 1898 and adopt them again in 1900 to agree with national party policy, chose to remain almost silent on this issue. To illustrate, in 1893 the Eddy *Current* boldly stated:

What if wool is low? Why should laborers, stockmen and grain farmers pay tariff in the form of high prices for flannels for their little ones to enrich the sheepmen? . . . No other class of men in the United States have made as much money in the past few years as the sheepmen and there is no reason for robbing the poor to give to the rich.[73]

Yet, in the campaign of 1898 the *Current* chose to ignore the tariff issue.[74] It seems, therefore, that in the case of both the tariff and silver issues party loyalty was the primary concern of most territorial editors and that basically their use of these issues was to garner votes for the party rather than to bring about desirable reforms.

For sixty years statehood was an important political question in New Mexico, but like the silver and tariff issues it was often used as a symbol rather than sought as a legitimate goal. For the politicos statehood offered such prizes as senatorships, state offices, and patronage in addition to the prospect of booty from unsettled land grants, fraudulent militia warrants, and graft that could no longer be vetoed by a watchful Congress. The Republicans, usually believing the prizes would be theirs, hid these baser objectives and held out as bait the prospect that statehood would bring new capital and immigration, thus enriching New Mexico. Democrats, on the contrary, rarely hoped to control the new state and usually insisted that statehood had not greatly aided the economy of Nevada and other western states, was besides that too expensive, and that the Republican politicos might realize their true aims. In the rare instances when the prospects of the parties were reversed, their stands also were reversed.

Before 1890 members of the political elite generally ignored the major factor of the statehood question, the unwillingness of the Spanish-

American majority to learn the English language and to accept free, non-sectarian schools. Until this was changed, there seemed scant prospect of congressional and popular approval of New Mexico statehood. Hispano-Catholic objection in 1890 to a constitution providing free, non-sectarian schools increased the reluctance of Congress to grant statehood, stalling for over a decade any serious consideration of the matter. During this interlude, the leaders of both political parties forced on the Hispanos free, non-sectarian schools conducted in English, and the territory attracted a large Anglo-American immigration. Since a great majority of the newcomers were Democrats, that party's chances of controlling a state government were improved. The ever-increasing flood of immigrants were hostile toward the Spanish-Americans, who began to fear that New Mexico might soon have an Anglo-American majority. This led many Hispanos to push for statehood while they still had a majority and would be able to insure that their rights would be protected in the constitution of the new state. Thus, after 1900 the objections of Congress, the Hispanos, and the Democrats began to melt away. Then the politicians and the press began a long drive, with thousands of speeches, maneuvers, and editorials, that ultimately brought statehood in 1912.

Since the statehood question was the most important and valid issue of territorial politics, it most truly reflects the political status of the press. As shown in earlier chapters, the press was relatively free until 1886, and editorial attitudes in this period did not always follow party policy. From 1886 to 1904, the press was held tightly captive; this again was confirmed by editorial policies in the debates over statehood. After 1904 the press was increasingly free; and the nearer statehood approached, the greater the divergence of editorial attitudes from the straight party lines.

The drive to make New Mexico a state began shortly after annexation, when Anglo-American politicians manipulated the native population into a futile bid for statehood. Almost every session of Congress thereafter until 1910 saw a bill or memorial for New Mexican statehood. In the 1860s the question became the subject of editorial debate, with the captive Santa Fe papers echoing the policies of the elites they represented. The *Weekly Gazette* held that few wanted statehood:

> Our information in regard to the state movement is that it meets with a cool reception from the people of the territory. None except those who expect to be rewarded by office, and the immediate friends of such, take any particular interest in the matter.[75]

The *New Mexican* replied that those who opposed statehood did so for selfish reasons:

There are two classes that oppose the state movement. . . . The first of these . . . imagine that any change . . . would be ruinous to their future desires of property. . . . The other class, more numerous than the first, but not so honest, are a set of hungry demagogues, who think that by opposing the state movement, they can establish themselves in the confidence of the people.[76]

Apparently the view of the *Weekly Gazette* was correct, for when delegates to a constitutional convention were elected, only thirty-three of seventy-eight met to write the document, and the effort was abandoned.[77]

In the early 1870s, New Mexicans again showed an unreadiness for statehood. In 1870 the legislature wrote a constitution *sans* convention. When submitted to a popular vote in 1872, it was defeated. Meanwhile, statehood was hotly debated by a few territorial papers. The Albuquerque *Republican Review,* citing the market value of territorial warrants at twenty-five cents on the dollar, maintained New Mexico resources were inadequate to support a state government. N. V. Bennett of the Las Cruces *Borderer* held that a people so poor they could not pay taxes and faced with the necessity of subsidizing railways to come to the area could not afford the luxury of a state government.[78] The Santa Fe *New Mexican,* still a staunch statehood advocate, discussed the question in frequent editorials and concluded that New Mexico needed the political power of a state:

This increased political power will attract attention. We shall become known and the pastoral and mineral resources of the territory will induce new immigration, and this will infuse new enterprise and vigor into our present population. We shall have diversified industry, increased population and greater prosperity. . . .

By becoming a state we shall secure the liberal concessions usually made by the United States in favor of public schools and internal improvements. One hundred and twenty thousand people, an area of 77,000 square miles and settlements and villages more than a century old and not a public school house nor a mile of railroad. Need more be said to indicate our great need in this direction. Let us have a voice in the Senate and the House of Representatives of the United States, with grants for public and normal schools and internal improvements, and there will be an end of this lamentable state of things. By becoming a state we control our own affairs—we shall perhaps make mistakes and blunders. The child falls often in learning to walk, but gains strength and experience by the effort. The best school for liberty is liberty itself.[79]

The attitude of the press reflected the independence of the editors of that era, for of eight papers then being published in New Mexico only the three mentioned in the foregoing took much interest in the matter.[80] The people also were unwilling, for only 5,000 of a usual 12,000 and a potential 30,000 votes were cast in 1872. The maneuvers of the politicians and the editorials of the *New Mexican* had been in vain, and a later generation should have been forewarned to expect a similar result.

Despite defeat in 1872, the skilled politician S. B. Elkins led New Mexicans and Congress to consider statehood seriously in the mid-seventies. Only two editors remained hostile to statehood. Louis Hommel of the Las Vegas *Gazette* predicted tax increases and ring control for such a state, and Bennett of the Las Cruces *Borderer* held the chief objective of the movement was to make Elkins a senator. However, the amiable congressional delegate was more successful with other editors. The Albuquerque *Republican Review* swung into line, and the Mesilla *News* hesitated but soon joined in. The strongest advocate of the cause, other than the captive Santa Fe *New Mexican,* was the Silver City *Mining Life.* It argued that taxes would be only slightly higher. Lack of experience of the native people was not a crippling factor, editor O. L. Scott wrote, for if the federal government could enfranchise four million Negroes, why not New Mexicans. Furthermore, the speediest way to educate people in self-government was to impose upon them its duties and responsibilities.[81] Elkins also was skillful in maneuvering Congress, and at one time its approval seemed assured, which led to premature jubilation on the part of the Mesilla *News:*

Hip! Hurrah! Whoop La!
Hurrah for a State!
Number Thirty-Nine!
Now
RAILROADS!
Telegraphs! Capital!!
Elkins for one Senator
Southern New Mexico should have the other.

The glorious news has reached us that the Senate has passed the enabling act as amended that the House had previously passed. We can enter the Union in time to vote for president in 1876. Now New Mexico will reap the rewards, will no longer be the Rip Van Winkle Territory.[82]

Although Elkins apparently convinced a majority of the editors and Anglo-American population, in view of the defeat of the constitutions in 1872 and later in 1890 it is doubtful that New Mexicans would have accepted statehood in 1876. But near passage of the enabling act aroused among many eastern American editors an active opposition to the admission of backward, Spanish-speaking, Catholic New Mexico as a state. Doubtless this opposition was harmful to later statehood efforts, for as the Silver City *Grant County Herald* editor noted: "The reputation which New Mexico is gaining from the many articles . . . is sadly detrimental to her future welfare."[83]

Further statehood efforts in the 1870s aroused little editorial comment; but with the advent of railways and a tremendously enlarged population, editors renewed their interest in the matter. Most of the new editors, with the enthusiasm of pioneers, favored statehood, but their stands do not appear to have been influenced by political leaders. The opinion of Russell Kistler of the Las Vegas *Daily Optic* was that of many newsmen, "New Mexico must be admitted to the Union within a year—The many newcomers this summer will demand it and our population will more than justify it."[84] While Louis Hommel of the San Lorenzo *Red River Chronicle* dropped an earlier hostility to statehood, J. G. Albright of the Santa Fe *Democrat* gave the movement his active support. Thomas Hughes of the Albuquerque *Daily Journal* at first believed there was no need for haste, but later that year when a bill for New Mexico statehood was introduced in Congress, he wrote, "The JOURNAL favors the idea of a state government for New Mexico."[85] The Raton *New Mexico News and Press,* on the other hand, adopted a hostile attitude, asserting: "No state for us please. We enjoy living in a territory, and so does every man who realizes that our admission as a state means money and glory for three men, increased taxation for all."[86] The Bennetts, Democratic leaders of southern New Mexico, continued their opposition in the 1880s. For example, Cornelius Bennett of the Silver City *Daily Southwest* stated, "few if any voters in New Mexico favor a state movement, except those who expect to divide the loaves and fishes."[87] And S. M. Ashenfelter, who later became editor of the Silver City *New Southwest,* retained the policy of Cornelius Bennett:

> Statehood has been the pet scheme of the Santa Fe Ring for years and that fact alone is sufficient to induce every thinking man in this territory to view it with suspicion.[88]

The Santa Fe Ring, despite the enthusiasm of the new editors, would not for several years be interested in statehood; it was engaged in a fight for control of the territorial Republican party and wanted no state that it could not control. The Albuquerque *Evening Review,* owned by lesser ring members, displayed the ring's attitude toward statehood when it commented that New Mexico was unready for statehood because it could be too easily controlled by corrupt politicians and lacked sufficient taxable property.[89] The attitude of the new Republicans seeking to end ring rule was very similar as was shown by a comment from editor W. S. Burke of the Albuquerque *Morning Journal:* "New Mexico, if made a state, would be run by unscrupulous political charlatans through fraud and bulldozing."[90] Continued ring hostility was reflected in 1884 by a Santa Fe *New Mexican Review* statement that "the people of this territory do not as yet desire [state government]."[91]

While the Santa Fe Ring remained hostile to statehood, Democrats, after winning territorial and national victories, became more interested. Republican intra-party strife had given victory to Democratic congressional delegate candidates in 1882 and 1884. National Democratic victory and the inauguration of a Democratic governor gave further encouragement. In addition, the enthusiasm of the independent new Democratic editors probably moved the party toward the new policy. For example, J. G. Albright of the Albuquerque *Morning Democrat* wrote in 1883: "The State of New Mexico! there's music in the name."[92] In 1885 the Democratic Silver City *Southwest Sentinel* followed the lead of Albright:

> The day when New Mexico will add one more shining star to our national escutcheon is very close at hand. This fossile [sic] and moss covered idea that we are too poor is a "barren ideality." A State! A State! It is bound to come.[93]

By 1886 Democratic leaders, perhaps influenced by these attitudes, had begun to work actively for statehood. The Las Vegas *Daily Optic* held that Governor E. G. Ross did so in hopes of reward:

> It seems to be generally agreed that Governor Ross is doing all in his power to secure admission of New Mexico as a state in the Union, and when the event is accomplished he will be an ardent candidate for the United States Senate.[94]

Ross, however, failed at first to receive the support of the press for his efforts. Even Albright, temporarily alienated from the Democratic party, refused to support the movement.[95] Republican papers also refused to work for statehood. They were by this time coming under the control of the ring, which did not want to create a state in an era of Democratic strength. Again the Santa Fe *New Mexican* displayed the ring attitude:

> New Mexico is not yet prepared for statehood, and the schemes to become a state for the purpose of gratifying the political ambitions of a few small calibred democratic statesmen will die abornin'.[96]

A year later in December, 1887, however, the Santa Fe *New Mexican* began to work for statehood. It sent out questionnaires asking the opinions of prominent citizens of the territory on statehood and, although the opinions were divided, began to support the movement.[97] There appear to be several possible reasons for the changed policy. By this time the Santa Fe Ring had re-established its control of the party, and the party schism was healed. Furthermore, the Ring probably feared national Democratic victory and four more years of Ross rule. Thus, the quickest way to regain full political control was through statehood.

This line of thinking seems to be indicated by a *New Mexican* editorial in March, 1888:

The people of New Mexico are tired of this thing of having a set of irresponsible men sent here to govern them. Under the present system the people have no right which the administration respects. Under Republican administration matters in that line were not so bad, but during the last three years they have simply grown almost unbearable, and the taxpayers and citizens of New Mexico want a change.[98]

The Las Cruces *Rio Grande Republican* quickly accepted the new policy,[99] but the Las Vegas *Daily Optic,* still hostile, held that:

The very strongest argument against statehood is that Santa Fe so earnestly urges it. . . . The members of its ring are crying out that all who oppose New Mexico's admission are enemies of the territory.[100]

In April, 1888, statehood gained almost unanimous press support as the result of a report of the Committee on Territories of the United States House of Representatives. Although the Democratic majority report recommended statehood for New Mexico, the Republican minority report opposed it. The latter report included excerpts from *El Gringo,* written thirty years earlier by a territorial attorney general, which held that Santa Fe inhabitants were of low moral standards, intensely superstitious, and priest-ridden. The minority report acknowledged its source was thirty years old but stated that New Mexico "cannot reasonably be expected to have changed for the better, nor that the most rapid progress will be made in the future."[101]

Almost every territorial paper protested that the minority report was filled with falsehoods and maintained that New Mexico was well qualified for statehood. For example, the Las Vegas *Daily Optic* listed the Republican committee members and stated, "these men should be held in unforgetfulness by every man, woman and child in New Mexico."[102] *El Boletin Popular* of Santa Fe protested, "las escritas son un libelo . . . una calumna, ni mas, ni menos."[103] The Socorro *Chieftain* held it "a gross libel upon the people of this territory and it deserves the censure of every fair minded man regardless of politics." According to the Santa Fe *Herald,* "The newspapers of New Mexico condemn it as an insult and outrage, especially to the native people. . . ."[104] The *Morning Democrat,* which had been fighting statehood, then began to support it, as did almost all other New Mexican newspapers.[105] However, the minority report also raised a storm of objections to New Mexican statehood in the eastern part of the United States, which probably encouraged Senate deletion of New Mexico from the omnibus bill granting statehood to several Western territories in 1889. Thus, statehood was halted apparently by the hostility toward the predominantly Hispano, Catholic,

and illiterate population of New Mexico—a prospect foreseen by some
territorial editors as early as 1876. New Mexicans then began to realize
that external hostility might do more to prevent statehood than internal
division.

Undoubtedly it was to answer the hostile criticism which held that
New Mexicans did not want and had not asked for statehood which led
to the writing of a constitution in 1889. Lincoln County residents
moved to correct this misbelief in January, 1889, by calling for a constitutional convention. The legislature then authorized a convention,
specifying that each county delegation would be twice the number of
its legislative representation. Southern New Mexico counties, which
were Democratic, believed legislative apportionment did not consider
their recent gains in population. Furthermore, Democrats, having elected
their delegate candidate in the last three elections, did not believe the
predominantly Republican legislatures would have been elected if apportionment was fair. Since convention delegates would be elected from
the same districts, Democrats asked for a non-partisan convention. At a
joint meeting of the central committees of the two parties, the Republicans demanded a majority of the convention seats; and Democrats
decided to sabotage the whole affair by neither presenting candidates
nor voting.[106] The oft-repeated admonition of the *Morning Democrat,*
"fairness or no state,"[107] sums up the attitude of the Democratic press.
The Las Vegas *Daily Optic* expressed the general answer of the Republican papers:

> The Democrats, with their usual stupid obstinacy, have forced the fight, and
> the result will be that there will be a straight party issue in the selection of
> delegates to the constitutional convention which meets in Santa Fe in Septem-
> ber. New Mexico is Republican by a decided majority; and there will be a
> majority of Republicans in the constitutional convention.[108]

Since most Democrats did not participate in the election, an almost
solidly Republican convention was elected; but Republican editors
found a new worry. What sort of constitution would be written by a
convention dominated by T. B. Catron and Pedro Perea, who had killed
a public school bill in the legislative session of 1889? Most New Mexico
editors agreed with the ideas expressed editorially by Russell Kistler
when he opposed statehood early in 1886. Kistler believed that education and public schools should come before statehood because New
Mexico had a peculiar case:

> . . . in fact, so peculiar that it cannot be estimated by the general rule. Ac-
> cording to the census of 1880, out of a population of 119,565, 57,156, or nearly
> one half, being those who could not sign their names. Of the other half, being
> those who can sign their names, a very large proportion cannot write, read or

speak the English language. These are a quiet inoffensive people, with as little activity in development and progressive ideas as they have in wrong doing. Ignorant of the English language, they are no more Americanized than the day the country was wrested from Old Mexico. They know not the independence of thought and action common to the American voter. They are led by a few old and wealthy families, and any movement these leaders may agree on will be sure of securing a majority of the votes cast. These few leaders will have the destiny of New Mexico in their hands.[109]

Editorial concern for a desirable constitution increased when Catholic Archbishop Salpointe asked that the constitutional convention not establish a system of public schools. New Mexico Spanish-Americans of the convention under the leadership of M. S. Otero rejected the archbishop's plea and approved a public school system by a unanimous vote. Most editors agreed with the Las Cruces *Rio Grande Republican:*

> Those who oppose the educational clause must necessarily oppose statehood, since it is well known that no [sic] territory that does not favor a non-sectarian school system will ever find sufficient favor among the states to be received into the sisterhood.[110]

Schools, however, became one of the lesser issues in the great debate that began between Democratic and Republican papers. These were the years when the political elites were consolidating their control of the press, and all papers began to follow party policies closely. Territorial Democratic papers led by E. G. Ross, then editor of the Deming *Headlight,* reversed their earlier stands on statehood and asked for its defeat on several bases: present apportionment of the legislature would leave the new state in the hands of the Santa Fe Ring; statehood would increase taxes, and under the control of the Santa Fe Ring, taxation would be ruinous; the Ring leaders would use their power to fund the fraudulent militia warrants, additionally burdening New Mexico taxpayers; although a public school system was included in the constitution, how could New Mexico depend on its implementation by the leadership responsible for the defeat of a public school law in the legislative session of 1889?[111] The editor of the *Headlight* agreed that he would approve statehood under an enabling act which guaranteed a fair legislative apportionment and a thoroughly American public school system.[112]

Republican leadership pushed for ratification of the constitution of 1889, for they believed Congress would grant statehood if presented with a suitable constitution. To meet mounting criticism of the constitution, the convention was recalled and questionable sections were rewritten before its ratification was asked in an election in October, 1890.[113] Republican papers sought to discredit the opposition of Ross as partisan by reminding the public that "not many months ago, Ross of the *Head-light,* was lobbying for statehood. Now he is devoting his paper to defeat the move."[114] To win acceptance of the constitution, Republican editors sought to convince the voters of the desirability of statehood and the hazard of rejecting it. The following statements are representative of their appeals. "If the constitution is defeated it will be many years before New Mexico is a state. Voters which do you prefer?" "Statehood for New Mexico is the battle cry." "Needs of New Mexico: statehood, free schools, and more railroads."[115]

In the election the constitution was rejected overwhelmingly. Apparently the major reason for this Republican defeat was the hostility of Spanish-Americans to the free, non-sectarian school provisions in the constitution.[116] The Republican leaders had ignored for decades the valid issue of free public schools as opposed to sectarian control of schools. Hence, they had failed to convince Spanish-Americans of the necessity of non-sectarian schools conducted in English in order to win general American approval of statehood for New Mexico. The rejection of a constitution incorporating free, non-sectarian schools deepened the hostility of the American public to New Mexican statehood and delayed it for two more decades. Apparently the Republican political leaders realized their error, for in the next legislative session free, public, non-sectarian schools conducted in English were imposed upon the predominantly Spanish-speaking people of New Mexico.[117] The move was too late, however, for ignoring the school question had cost the politicos the grand prizes they might have gained from statehood.

These Republican leaders, however, did not despair, and from 1890 until 1903 the congressional delegates introduced bills for New Mexican statehood at each session of Congress. The territorial press followed these bills with news stories and editorials, but they retained their partisan attitudes. Democrats generally doubted the value of statehood but cheered the efforts of their delegates to achieve it, and Republican editors in each instance usually adopted the opposing attitude. There was less interest in the question than there had been from 1886 to 1891, or would be from 1903 to 1910. Nevertheless, editors paid sufficient attention to statehood so that it was kept before the public as a question of importance to New Mexico.[118]

In addition to using the prospects of self-rule and economic rewards to appeal to New Mexicans to vote for statehood, the politicians and their editorial spokesmen used the statehood issue to appeal for votes in regular campaigns. To illustrate, in 1894 the Republican Socorro *Chieftain* attacked the Democratic candidate for congressional delegate, maintaining that he told "American" voters at Roswell he favored statehood and "Mexican" voters at Abiquiu that he opposed it.[119] Republican candidates for congressional delegate between 1898 and 1908 often asked for votes on the basis that a Republican congressional delegate could best obtain statehood from a Republican president and Congress.[120] Thus we see that in regular and special campaigns from 1850 to 1902 the political leaders used the statehood issue, often appealing to prejudices rather than reason, in asking for votes for congressional delegates.

Despite the importance and apparent validity of the statehood question, it seems that before 1900 it was not a true issue. Before 1900 New Mexico was not ready for statehood, therefore political leaders who held out as bait the territorial economic advancement and self-rule that would result from statehood were not presenting a true issue. Probably they desired statehood because it promised rewards for themselves and ignored the possibility that it might prove disastrous for New Mexico. Statehood was probably impractical for New Mexico before 1900 for several reasons. First, its predominantly Spanish-American population was not ready to accept the conditions Congress would have imposed in granting statehood, as the vote on the constitution in 1890 indicated. Second, the economy of New Mexico was not strong enough to provide sufficient taxable income to support state government, nor were New Mexicans willing to pay the exceptionally high taxes that would have been necessary. Third, the experiences of states such as Nevada showed that statehood did not greatly aid economic development. Furthermore, it appears that many of the territorial political leaders realized that statehood was impractical. For example, the leading territorial Republican in 1901 acknowledged that: "Prior to the advent of the railroads and the introduction and maintenance of a public school system it is an admitted fact that New Mexico was not prepared for statehood."[121] Since the arguments advanced were precisely those used by Democratic leaders such as E. G. Ross, it would seem that the Democrats were presenting the true issue. And this would be so if Democratic leaders had been consistent in their opposition to statehood. But these men favored statehood when it appeared that they would have the opportunity to reap the spoils or when they needed it as an appeal to gain votes. Thus, for the most part, leaders of both parties used statehood as a symbol, as did the editors in presenting their arguments to the public.

By 1903, however, New Mexico was ready for statehood, and it became an important and valid issue, except on a few occasions when facets of the question were used to maneuver the voters not toward statehood but another objective. Statehood seemed assured in 1900 since the platforms of both national political parties included statehood for all the territories. Even Democrats, formerly hostile, sought it because growing Democratic strength improved their chances of controlling that state. In 1903, New Mexico's capable congressional delegate, B. S. Rodey, adopted new tactics. Convinced that the major impediment was the reluctance of eastern seaboard states to give two senators to sparsely populated Arizona and New Mexico, Rodey began to advocate joining the two territories as one state. The idea was well accepted in Congress and by New Mexico Democrats. Since Arizona was heavily Democratic, they anticipated the joint state would be Democratic. Territorial Republican leaders relished neither the prospects of loss of control to Democrats nor the necessity of splitting the spoils with Arizona Republicans. These politicos then sought to scotch the movement by defeating Rodey's bid for renomination in 1904. Congress, however, approved joint statehood, and the two territories were asked to vote on the matter. Defeat in either territory would kill the measure. The plan, overwhelmingly approved in New Mexico, was defeated by Arizona. However, it was only a matter of four years until single statehood was given to each. Then the questions of importance became the constitution and the first elections of officers for the new state.

Naturally, statehood and the constitution were important matters to the press and were in this period the most frequent political topics of its editorials. The journalists, whose interest is shown in thousands of news stories and editorials, created an overwhelming demand for statehood among New Mexicans. This interest not only helped to produce overwhelming acceptance of the joint Arizona-New Mexico state but kept the issue alive past its defeat, strengthening the demands of the political leaders for single statehood. Thus the press, by helping to inspire the popularity of statehood, made a great contribution to its achievement.

At the same time the statehood movement made a significant contribution to the development of territorial journalism. First, newspapers, without regard for their politics, accepted statehood as a desirable goal. This elevated the question above politics, gave the press a somewhat non-partisan attitude in a political matter, and moved most territorial editors nearer to political independence. But more significant, the importance of statehood led journalists to defy political leaders in intra-party disputes. As has been noted, it was in this era that the Albuquerque *Morning Journal* became politically independent, and slowly eastern New Mexico Democratic papers and others began to follow this lead. The trend began with intra-party disputes over joint statehood.

The Albuquerque *Morning Journal* at first took scant notice of the joint statehood plan, but a great many other papers became intensely interested. The Albuquerque *Daily Citizen* was a staunch advocate from the first,[122] and the Santa Fe *New Mexican* was not especially hostile to the plan until September, 1903, when it began to oppose it stren-uously. Most of the smaller Republican weeklies quickly adopted the position of the *New Mexican*,[123] but some of the larger Republican papers remained loyal to joint statehood. For example, the Las Vegas *Daily Optic*, Las Cruces *Rio Grande Republican*, and Silver City *Enter-prise* continued to endorse it in the first months of 1904. The *Morning Journal* also accepted the plan in March, 1904, possibly because it hoped that the more centrally located Albuquerque would be made capital of the joint state.[124] Probably the major reason for the policy of the New Mexican was that Governor M. A. Otero opposed joining the two territories as a state because B. S. Rodey's continued advocacy of the plan threatened Otero's leadership of the Republican party. Then the governor and his henchmen, in a well-concealed but extensive plot, defeated Rodey's bid for renomination as congressional delegate, giving the position instead to W. H. Andrews and having the con-vention endorse single statehood.[125]

The capable and popular Rodey, with the encouragement of the Albuquerque *Morning Journal* and *Daily Citizen,* had entered the cam-paign as an independent candidate for congressional delegate favoring joint statehood.[126] The remainder of the Republican papers fell obedi-ently into line behind the Santa Fe *New Mexican*.[127] Meanwhile, the territorial Democrats endorsed joint statehood, and the Democratic press followed the lead of the Roswell *Daily Record* in accepting this party policy.[128] Thus, most of the territorial press in the campaign of 1904 showed that it was still subservient to the territorial political elites. W. H. Andrews was ultimately the victor in the campaign, and the *New Mexican* hailed it as a victory also for single statehood.[129]

After Congress in June, 1906, authorized a vote on the joint state-hood question, Max Frost, editor of the *New Mexican,* changed his policies. He often had indicated that joint statehood under the right conditions would be acceptable. Doubtless the terms were right, for Frost in an editorial headed "NOW FOR STATEHOOD" enthusiastic-ally approved joining Arizona:

> To refuse the gift, the greatest gift that can be bestowed upon any people, would be nothing short of folly. The New Mexican, which has taken the pa-triotic stand for New Mexico under its present name until the last ditch, is now ready to lend its voice and influence for the acceptance of joint statehood for New Mexico and Arizona under the conditions of the Hamilton Bill just passed. This bill, with its generous provisions, grants New Mexico and Arizona all they have ever asked in connection with statehood and even more.[130]

The Republican satellite weeklies adopted the new policy; and since most other Republican and Democratic papers by this time favored joint statehood, almost the entire territorial press began a campaign for its acceptance. Probably as a result of this intense press effort, victory in New Mexico soon seemed assured. There was, however, an almost equal assurance of defeat in Arizona. Under these conditions the editors began to worry that voter apathy might lead to its defeat also in New Mexico. The Las Vegas *Daily Optic* took a stand that New Mexico should approve joint statehood for even "should the proposition fail in Arizona, the people of New Mexico will be in stronger and better shape than ever to demand recognition of their rights and privileges."[131] Later the *New Mexican* warned of overconfidence: "This is no time to sleep at the oars."[132] The Silver City *Enterprise* also was concerned:

Everywhere in the territory joint statehood papers are sounding a note of warning that is very timely and sensible. . . . Many joint statehood advocates are confident that the current of public opinion will land the joint statehood craft safe in the harbor of victory. But . . . there is a strong under current of feeling against the proposition by the native people who resent the insults flung at them by the unprincipled and hysterical opponents of jointure in Arizona and who hope to retaliate by showing that they no more desire to be joined with Arizona than does Arizona with New Mexico.[133]

Despite these admonitions, editorials diminished as victory was all but assured; however, they were frequent enough to keep the issue alive. The Las Vegas *Daily Optic* sought to convert those still desiring single statehood by contending, "New Mexico can strike no more effective blow at separate statehood than by voting against joint statehood."[134] The Carlsbad *Argus* maintained: "It is well known that New Mexico will vote strongly in favor of [joint] statehood in hopes that Congress may be impressed and give us statehood."[135] The Tucumcari *News* believed that "if Arizona turns it down, then we will be in a position to play our hands alone."[136] In the summer the New Mexico press presented a barrage of editorials for joint statehood. Then, convinced that Arizona would defeat it, New Mexico editors argued in the autumn that approval of joint statehood was the quickest way of obtaining the desired blessing.

Arizona newspapers, waging an intense fight to defeat joint statehood, argued against the plan because of New Mexico's large Hispano population. This quickly brought retaliation from the English-language press[137] of New Mexico, yet did not disturb the steadfast approval of joint statehood by the Spanish-language press. For example, the Albuquerque *Opinion Publica* believed statehood would improve the conditions of all.[138] Las Cruces *El Labrador* thought that it would be wise for Spanish-Americans of New Mexico to vote for joint statehood, for with Spanish-Americans of Arizona they would still have a large enough vote to insure that their rights would be protected by the constitution of the new state. However, if statehood were delayed for a number of years, their rights might be endangered by the Anglo-Americans who were moving into New Mexico so rapidly and who would fully control any constitution written far in the future.[139] Las Vegas *El Independiente* counseled that a great deal of work would be necessary to counter growing opposition in northern New Mexico counties:

> Nos comunican de Rio Arriba y Taos, que esta fuerte la oposicion de la gente alla al estado consolidado, que se necesitara mucho trabaja para hacerla desistir de su hostilidad.[140]

The steadfast and tolerant policy of the Spanish-language papers and the heated defense of Spanish-Americans by the English-language press brought new unity to New Mexicans and improved relations between the two peoples. It contributed to the reconciling of their differences in the constitution that was written in 1910; and in 1906 it helped to return an overwhelming vote, almost two to one, for joint statehood in New Mexico.[141] Although both ethnic groups and both parties strongly favored joint statehood, a great deal of the credit for the large favorable margin must be assigned to the press. Most editors steadfastly advocated statehood; and when combined statehood was offered, they worked diligently for it, advancing innumerable reasons for its approval. The huge majority rolled up for joint statehood in 1906 served to hasten the granting of single statehood. Thus, it seems that the press made a great contribution to the eventual entrance of New Mexico into the Union.

The campaign from 1903 to 1906 for joint statehood had also served to focus the attention of the public and press on this important issue. As a result, many papers, increasingly less dependent on political income, broke sharply with the political elite when it sought to use this important question as a means of political maneuver. The statehood question thus served to free the territorial press from political control. The Albuquerque *Morning Journal,* alienated from the Republican leadership because of its refusal to accept joint statehood in 1904, was the first paper to adopt this policy consistently. Then during the framing of the constitution, its ratification, and the first state elections, more papers rejected the dictates of the political parties and became politically independent.

Political independence was adopted by the Albuquerque *Morning Journal* in 1903, soon after D. A. Macpherson assumed control of its management. He announced that the paper was to be independent Republican and soon launched a fight to end boss rule exercised in Bernalillo County politics by Republican County Chairman F. A. Hubbell.

The real test of this policy, however, came in 1904, when both B. S. Rodey and joint statehood were rejected by the Republican party. The *Morning Journal* editors believed that both had been discarded because they threatened the control of the party by M. A. Otero and his colleagues. As a result this paper then launched a drive to cleanse territorial politics by exposing corruption within the Republican political elite. The awarding of territorial public printing as political patronage was attacked, and the Santa Fe *New Mexican* lost its political subsidy.[142] Congressional delegate W. H. Andrews proved to be a liability to the Republican leaders. His past connections with the Matthew Quay and Bois Penrose political machine in Pennsylvania together with certain earlier indiscretions were so effectively exposed that Andrews was not seriously considered in 1912 for the United States senatorship he so coveted.[143] The charges of the *Morning Journal* were echoed by many of the New Mexico weeklies, and as a partial result Governor M. A. Otero was replaced by Herbert Hagerman. Then the progressive Hagerman, with the support of the *Morning Journal,* began a cleansing of territorial politics.[144] H. O. Bursum, territorial Republican chairman and new leader of the Republican elite, was dismissed as warden of the territorial prison. The *Morning Journal* published a two-page reproduction of an audit of his prison accounts, showing them to be $5,000 short. Free reprints of this audit were offered to New Mexico weeklies for distribution, and at least one paper accepted.[145] Although the Republican politicos secured the removal of Governor Hagerman,[146] the *Morning Journal* continued its effective attack on Bursum and Andrews at every opportunity.[147] The *Morning Journal,* thus, had become a truly independent paper uncontrolled by the politicians.

In the final stages of achieving statehood, other territorial papers began to adopt an editorial position independent of political control. When the enabling act in 1910 authorized the framing of a constitution, the territorial press became very interested. A majority of papers advocated a constitution which reflected the spirit of progressivism, but they were frustrated by the Republican politicos. The weekly press, particularly that of the homestead areas, demanded a liberal constitution. The Estancia *News,* for example, called for the initiative, referendum, and recall.[148] The Las Cruces *Rio Grande Republican* asked for the adoption of the advanced ideas being used in Oregon.[149] The Fort Sumner *Sunnyside Republican* admonished the people that they owed no debt to the old bosses who had brought statehood and should vote for men who would write the best constitution.[150] On the other hand, the Republican dailies, Santa Fe *New Mexican,* Las Vegas *Daily Optic,* and Albuquerque *Morning Journal,* called for a conservative constitution, since President W. H. Taft had indicated that this was the only

kind he and Congress would approve.[151] However, the *Morning Journal*
also advocated that there should be neither political boss nor corporation control of the convention. A Republican convention called for a
conservative constitution, and a Democratic convention called for a
progressive one.[152]

When the constitutional convention met, it soon became apparent
that it was controlled by the politicos and would not write a liberal constitution. Its most prominent members were T. B. Catron, A. B. Fall,
and H. O. Bursum. These men were able to get the Republican majority
of the convention to agree to follow the wishes of a Republican caucus
on all questions. Despite the fact that liberal Democrats and a minority
of liberal Republicans could have controlled the convention, the Republican caucus rule insured that the constitution would be conservative. The liberal weeklies protested. The Tucumcari *Sun* complained
that "the old Republican gang is in the saddle."[153] The Bard City *News*
warned that "a spring housecleaning throughout the country is coming,
let New Mexico prepare for it before she is made to take it." The Albuquerque *Tribune-Citizen,* now a Democratic party organ, campaigned
vigorously for the initiative and referendum,[154] and the Democratic
press followed its lead. Despite the objections by liberals, by the Democratic party, and by a large portion of the territorial press, the Republican majority, with its caucus rule, wrote a conservative document, but
one which apparently was not intolerable. The Silver City *Enterprise*
defended it by quoting an editorial of the *Christian Science Monitor,*
which lauded its protection of the voting and school privileges of Spanish-Americans and concluded that "the constitution of New Mexico
seems to have been framed with intelligence and discretion."[155] Nevertheless, a territorial Democratic convention denounced the constitution's lack of initiative, recall, and the direct primary and asked the
voters to reject it.[156]

At this point the press took another step toward independence; many
Democratic papers defied party policy and supported the ratification of
the constitution. Probably the editors, reviewing more than two decades
of blasted hopes, believed it was wise to seize the opportunity presented.
Over one hundred papers supported ratification, while only about sixteen asked for its defeat.[157] Many liberal Democratic papers remained
silent or adopted the attitude of the Roswell *Daily Record:*

The rejection of statehood by a very narrow margin would be a fatal error
for New Mexico. It would be a setback it would require years to overcome, and
the ground lost would not be regained in time to benefit thousands now living
in this country. . . . The *Record* wants statehood because we want the privilege of minding our own business.[158]

New Mexico voters overwhelmingly approved the constitution in January, 1911; and Democratic leaders, hoping eventually to liberalize it, sought to make it easier to amend.[159] An appeal to congressional Democrats obtained the enactment of the Flood Resolution allowing New Mexico voters to simplify the amending process in the first state elections in November, 1911. Submitted to the voters as a constitutional amendment requiring only the acceptance of a simple majority, it became known as the "Blue Ballot Amendment" from the color of its separate ballot. The Republican state convention, led by T. B. Catron, opposed the amendment. Spanish-Americans, guaranteed equal voting and educational rights in the constitution, opposed any easing of the amendment process.[160]

The press then took a third step toward independence, and this time it was liberal Republican weeklies which defied party policy by supporting or refusing to attack the "Blue Ballot Amendment." The Santa Fe *New Mexican* and the Las Vegas *Daily Optic,* as loyal Republican papers, vigorously attacked the amendment, but the Albuquerque *Morning Journal* adopted a rather non-commital attitude.[161] Spanish-language Republican papers vigorously opposed the blue ballot with editorials and the publication of a letter from the Catholic archbishop recommending its defeat.[162] Democratic papers could now easily follow party policy and most took the position of the Roswell *Daily Record*: "Don't forget that Blue Ballot! Vote yes, and have a constitution that can be made to protect all of the interests of the people, as well as those of the favored few."[163] The significant development, however, was that several Republican weeklies defied party policy and supported the "Blue Ballot Amendment." The Las Cruces *Rio Grande Republican* was notable among the older papers in giving its support, and the Nara Visa *New Mexican and Register* and other homestead area papers also adopted such a position.[164] Thus, with the daily press divided and the weekly press predominantly for the amendment, it was adopted by a safe margin.

The press became increasingly free from political control in these last political campaigns of the territorial era. Having worked hard to inspire the people to demand statehood, many Democratic editors refused to risk its loss by recommending the defeat of the constitution. Whether or not these journalists were justified is less important than the fact that they refused to follow blindly the symbol of party loyalty. The refusal of some Republican editors to ask for defeat of the "Blue Ballot Amendment" was a similar display of independence. Thus, by 1911 a large portion of the territorial press had asserted its political independence.

Another significant development to manifest itself in the campaign of

1911 was the breakdown of the Republican political elite. Political machines are based upon their ability to reward followers with patronage, offices, and spoils. In the election of 1911, H. O. Bursum, leader of the Republican elite and gubernatorial candidate, was defeated, a result to which the Albuquerque *Morning Journal* and its weekly imitators had contributed. The extended efforts of the *Morning Journal* had already undermined the popularity of Bursum, and during the campaign of 1911 it again exposed questionable aspects of Bursum's past record,[165] charges which were echoed in the Democratic weekly press. Despite the election of Republicans to most state offices and to a majority of seats in the legislature,[166] Bursum was defeated. Several things account for Democratic success in this instance, but the attitude of the press was influential. Defeat of Bursum and loss of the governor's office with its control of patronage helped to break down centralized control of the Republican party. The party then divided into several factions following strong leaders who subsequently contested for power within the party.[167] As a result the party which had so long dominated New Mexico was weakened and forced to alternate in power with the Democrats in the first two decades of statehood. Since future elections would be sharply contested, there was a greater prospect that in the new era campaigns would be fought with legitimate issues rather than an appeal to symbols. Thus, the Albuquerque *Morning Journal,* by its efforts to defeat Bursum, made another contribution to freeing the press from political control—particularly by limiting the ability of Republicans to reward the politically faithful papers.

In any evaluation of the political role of the territorial press, journalistic conditions of the area and era must be considered. First of all, political subservience of the rural press was apparently general throughout the United States as late as 1911.[168] Since weekly newspapers could be started with as little as $100 during most of the territorial period, this was an era of intense newspaper competition, robbing editors of profits by which political independence could be attained. The low initial cost of establishing a newspaper made it easier for political leaders to hold editors in line, or bring them in line, by threatening to establish competition which the party faithful would patronize. Economic and cultural conditions in territorial New Mexico, as shown earlier, increased the severity of threats to political independence. Thus, the territorial press, its profits and potential profits curtailed, was even more subject to political inducements and in need of political revenue than the rural press elsewhere.

Under territorial political custom and economic conditions it was relatively easy for groups of political leaders to maintain control over the territorial press. To exercise this control, the Republican political elite allied themselves with the Santa Fe *New Mexican;* and the Democratic political elite established several different newspapers subject to the control of area or factional chiefs. These key papers furnished journalistic example and leadership for the subordinate press, which was held to the party line through patronage, purchase of loyalty, or threats of competition. Through this control of the principal means of communication, the press, the politicos were able to avoid discussion of the true issues of territorial politics and to appeal rather to the prejudice of voters than to their reason.

Near the end of the territorial era, the New Mexico press began to shed its political shackles. Increasing education and prosperity in New Mexico aided its efforts. Almost simultaneously, there arose a commercially, rather than a politically, sustained Democratic weekly press in eastern New Mexico and an independent Republican paper at Albuquerque. The *Morning Journal* provided proof that political independence could be profitable.[169] The editors of many of these papers were not misled by the symbols with which the politicos influenced territorial voters. They refused to be the means by which the symbols were presented to the voters and asked the voters to consider instead the true issues about statehood and the constitution. In addition, a long campaign by the *Morning Journal* helped to break down the cohesion of the dominant Republican political elite, robbing it of control of patronage with which faithful newspapers could be rewarded. Thus, by 1912 the territorial press, freed from monetary dependence on the politicians and more alert to the needs of New Mexico, was moving toward political independence.

# THE TERRITORIAL PRESS AND
# NEW MEXICO'S CONFLICTING
# CULTURES

THREE DISTINCT CULTURES—Indian, Spanish, and Anglo—live peace-fully and cooperatively in modern New Mexico, but behind present peacefulness lie centuries of heated and often bloody conflict. In the early years of the territorial era several nomadic Indian tribes lived in and on the fringes of New Mexico. For centuries these tribes had gained much of their sustenance by predatory raids on the people and property of their more settled neighbors, who often had retaliated with punitive raids. Eventually the civilized people demanded of the American govern-ment that the wild tribes be fully pacified. Conflict between the Spanish and Anglo cultures, on the other hand, was not so harsh. It arose over ethnic differences, desires for political dominance, and conflicting re-ligious views, particularly in the sphere of education.

The role of the press in the reconciliation of these conflicting cultures was that of establishing the bases on which a compromise could be achieved. With regard to the Indians, the editors asked at first for pro-tection and then that the Indians be placed on reservations. When this failed to pacify the Apaches, the journalists demanded either their ex-termination or removal from the Southwest. Eventually all Indians were pacified and forced to abandon their raiding.

In the Spanish and Anglo conflict the contribution of the editors was to reveal the minimum demands of the two ethnic groups in a series of debates over ethnic relations, civil rights, politics, religion, and schools. Once the minimum demands of both sides were known, reasonable men of the two groups could begin to work toward a compromise. This was finally achieved in the constitution of the new state. By its terms Anglo-Americans could look forward to the complete Americanization of the Spanish, and the Spanish-Americans were assured that they would have the right to preserve their language and that their civil and political rights would be protected.

Conflicts with the Indians overshadowed disputes between Spanish and Anglo in the early years of American rule, with the major objective of both being the pacification of the Indians. Before the American conquest, the Spanish in New Mexico had waged war on the Indians for 250 years. Yet the wars had left slight impact on the customs of the nomadic Navajo and Apaches, who had survived for centuries by raiding their more peaceful neighbors; stealing their grain, livestock, and possessions; and enslaving captives. The Spanish were never strong enough to subdue the Indians but sought to restrain them by punitive counter raids in which they regained their possessions and also took slaves. Early American policy was a continuation of the punitive expeditions, but by 1863 it was proposed that the Indian be pacified by placing them on reservations. In the case of the Navajos this policy was successful. But harsher measures were required for the more nomadic and warlike Apaches, and it was not until the 1890s that they were subjugated.

In the first stage of the struggle with the Indians, the editors did not ask for subjugation but simply for protection. Protection from Indians seemed so necessary that when a rumor became prevalent in 1848 that most American troops were to be withdrawn, the Santa Fe *Republican* was provoked into commenting:

> Can it be possible . . . that the troops are to be withdrawn from this territory, with the exception of three companies of regulars? Can it be possible that . . . after paying some fifteen million dollars of money . . . acknowledging the citizens as citizens of the United States [the country] is to be left unprotected [against] . . . *twenty thousand* savage Indians who have never ceased their hostilities during its occupation by a large force of our troops.[1]

When he was placed in command of the military department in 1863, General J. H. Carleton replaced the policy of protection with one of pacification. Carleton proposed that all the territorial Indians be either exterminated or placed on reservations. New Mexico editors hailed this policy enthusiastically, urging fellow citizens to "all go to work with a will to aid his efforts."[2] But when Carleton succeeded in placing most of the Navajos on a reservation at Fort Sumner,[3] the Albuquerque *Rio Abajo Weekly Press* began to question the plan. A few months later the Santa Fe *New Mexican* also began to object to this policy. The Santa Fe *Weekly Gazette,* on the other hand, consistently supported Carleton. The reservation policy soon became an election issue with all three newspapers using it as a point in campaign propaganda. The *New Mexican* editorialized under a heading "THE ELECTION":

> On Monday next is of more significance than many suppose. It involves the

question . . . shall the Navajoes and other tribes foreign to our territory be imported and located here, or shall they be left in their country?

There are two parties in the field asking your suffrages. The ticket at the head of the NEW MEXICAN is composed of men who are in favor of the white man and his rights against the red man. The opposition party favors the benefitting of the lazy thieving Indian at the expense of the honest and industrious white man. . . . We hold that the people, the farmers and stockgrowers should not be crowded off their lands for the benefit of a pack of thieving redskins. . . . We urge the removal of those already at the Bosque Redondo to their own tribe, and believe the interests of the territory demand it.[4]

The Santa Fe *New Mexican* and *Weekly Gazette,* as exponents of opposition groups, battled over Carleton's reservation policy for the next several years, and the groups themselves sought directly to influence federal policy. J. F. Chaves, who was elected territorial delegate to Congress in 1865, used the Fort Sumner reservation as a major campaign issue. In Congress his protests against Carleton's policies led to investigations by the Interior and War departments. Eventually Carleton was transferred, and General W. T. Sherman accepted the petition of the Navajo chiefs that they be allowed to return their tribe to their homeland.[5]

The Navajos evidently were reformed as a result of the affair, for in the years after 1867 they made few warlike moves. There appear to be two major reasons for this change. First, the Navajo, thoroughly defeated and held captive 400 miles from their homeland in the strange plains country, did not care to risk such punishment again. Secondly, the New Mexicans were forced to halt slave raids on the Navajo.[6] After the Navajo surrendered in 1864, General Carleton ordered the governor to publish a proclamation forbidding further raids on the Navajo to take slaves. In 1867 Senator Charles Sumner, who had been interested in the question of Indian slavery since 1864, inspired a Senate Judiciary Committee investigation of peonage and Indian slavery in New Mexico. A resultant congressional act of 1867 forbade the practice of peonage, and the territorial administration began to enforce this act along with the Thirteenth Amendment.[7] Thus, the Navajo not only feared the consequences of resuming their earlier practice of raiding the New Mexicans, but they no longer had the motive of retaliating for slave raids carried on by the New Mexicans against them.

Press contribution to the pacification of the Navajo took two forms, encouragement of the reservation policy and exposure of the practice of Indian slavery. The Santa Fe *Weekly Gazette* consistently supported the reservation policy. The Santa Fe *New Mexican* did not oppose reservations but only the policy of relocating the Navajo in New Mexico— as the following editorial excerpt illustrates:

While we believe the reservation policy the correct one, and the only one outside of extermination that will give us permanent peace, we further believe that each tribe should be permanently located upon its own Territory . . . and we doubt the wisdom, however good the intention, that would take the fairest portion of our land and make it an asylum for Indians.[8]

The Santa Fe *New Mexican* and *Weekly Gazette* helped to curtail Indian slavery by identifying prominent opposition party members as slave owners. The *Weekly Gazette* noted that delegate Chaves himself was involved in the practice:

His immediate family—that of his mother, with whom he stays while in the territory—has beyond the shadow of a doubt, the most numerous lot of Mexican peons and Indian slaves of any one family in New Mexico.

The Santa Fe *New Mexican* countered by identifying as slave owners several members of the political faction represented by the Santa Fe *Weekly Gazette*.[9] Thus, as a part of the political struggles in New Mexico the contending newspapers held up to light the practitioners of Indian slavery, made public the penalties for slave ownership, and therefore helped to bring an end to the practice. While the primary intent of these newspapers was the advancement of their own political interests, their editorial comments encouraged the subjugation of the Navajo, their confinement to a reservation, and the removal of the irritation of slave raids—all of which contributed to an almost permanent peace with that tribe.[10]

After the subjugation of the Navajo, General Carleton began forcing other Indian tribes into reservations. Although the Apaches located in southwestern New Mexico and eastern Arizona were placed on reservations, they were still very troublesome; while most of the tribes remained on the reservations, small war parties from 1870 to 1890 intermittently maurauded civilized New Mexicans. In these years an extensive silver mining and cattle industry grew up near these reservations, providing loot which encouraged the Apaches to revert to the centuries-old practice of robbing and killing weaker neighbors.

During these periods of hostilities, the territorial editors asked for extermination of the Apaches or their removal from the Southwest. In times of war the editors were bitterly critical of both pacifists and the army for not quickly subduing the Indians. In times of peace the editors asked that the Indian be subject to the white man's rules of justice but that he be properly fed. Otherwise, the journalists took scant interest in integrating the Indians into New Mexican society.

When Indian wars raged and atrocities were freshly in mind, the expanding territorial press of the 1880s was less interested in accommodation than annihilation and thus adopted a harsh and uncompromising

attitude toward all Indians. Under such conditions their minimum demand was "war, relentless, merciless war, till the savage devils are
content to promise good behavior [and] abide by their promises."[11] As
conditions became worse, editors became more extreme in their demands: "exterminate them from branch to root as you would rattle-
snakes."[12] When United States Army efforts were not immediately successful, the editors encouraged the use of other methods. "The citizens
of Silver City have subscribed $2,000 which they will cheerfully pay out
at the rate of $100 per head for every Indian killed and brought in.
There is a royalty for wolf scalps and why not for Indian scalps," asked
the Las Vegas *Daily Optic*.[13] Under warlike conditions these editors
often recommended extermination as an economy measure, for as they
pointed out, "a live Indian cost the government twenty dollars a head
per annum; a dead one nothing. Sabe?"[14] When Geronimo was per-
petrating his harshest acts, most territorial editors believed "it would
be justice to slaughter all of the bucks in Geronimo's little band of
Apaches, when they are captured. The Indian tribes must be abolished
and this is an opportunity to get rid of them."[15] Even after hostilities
had abated, some territorial editors demanded death for the Apaches:
"let them be hunted to death. . . . We kill mad dogs and mountain
lions on sight. Of the beast and the Indian which is the worst?"[16] Other
New Mexicans believed there was little hope for any policy but extermination, for as one wrote: "the experience of the last ten years proves
conclusively that the only sure way to civilize the average Indian is to
shoot his system full of holes. A dead Indian can always be counted as
reliably good."[17] While these editors recognized that their attitude was
unhumanitarian, they believed they were justified, maintaining that
"New Mexico has had quite enough of simpering philanthrophy. Let
the cloistered humanitarian exchange places with the ranchmen in the
valleys and the miners in the mountains in the neighborhood of the
Apache reservation."[18] Thus, in periods of Indian war, most editors
usually were ready to recommend extermination of the Indians rather
than reconciliation with them.

A less drastic proposal, which most territorial editors also supported,
was the removal of the Apaches from the Southwest. Since the Southwest
was a sparsely populated area with rugged terrain, with which the
Apache was more familiar than the intruding peoples, it was easy for
the Indian to remain at large after he fled the reservation. The Santa Fe
*New Mexican* sought to show the validity of such a suggestion:

It is unreasonable to expect that they will adapt themselves to civilized
customs so long as they are permitted to live in their own wild country, and
retain their arms and horses. The temptation is before them every day of their
lives to indulge in their natural pastimes of hunting, stealing, murdering and

scalping.—But place them where they will be surrounded by civilization, deprive them of their arms, and then the process of civilization can go on uninterruptedly and with some effect. Set them down on a small reservation in New England and the middle states, and give the sentimentalists of the Indian question of these sections a chance to labor for their reformation and the salvation of their souls.—and while they are educating and civilizing these barbarians, the Indian philanthropists of the East will necessarily become educated themselves as to the true character of these people. . . .[19]

Suggestions that the Apaches be transplanted to eastern areas delighted the territorial editors, and they reacted with jeers when those areas rejected such plans. One editor suggested that the government "establish a reservation somewhere near classic Boston. . . . There would be another Boston massacre, and all sentimental ideas would vanish with the last red devil on the reservation."[20] New Mexico editors gleefully reported that "the governor of North Carolina objects to the placing of Geronimo's band within that state. . . . [and] suggests that Vermont would be a good place for the Apaches." At other times the editors started and promoted petitions asking for the removal of the Apaches, and when the dreaded Chiricahua Apaches were removed they wrote: "at last the 'great father' at Washington has answered the prayers of the long suffering and persecuted people of the far West."[21] The desire for the removal of the Apaches from the Southwest was general among the territorial editors; like the suggestion that the Indians be exterminated, this approach demanded elimination of the tribes rather than reconciliation with them.

Territorial editors had a more reasonable attitude in the intervals between the spasmodic Indian wars and were among the first to object when the government did not provide sufficient funds to feed its Indian charges properly. An example of this attitude was shown by the editor of the Santa Fe *New Mexican* who, after noting that the recently pacified Navajo were in need of help, wrote:

. . . we therefore urge upon Congress the absolute necessity of an immediate appropriation of money for providing food for the Navajoes. They are in a starving condition, in a country where there is but little game, and no wild fruits or berries.[22]

While the territorial editors thus demanded justice for the Indians who had lost some of their ability to sustain themselves when they were placed on reservations, at the same time editors asked for justice of another type, one that the Indians found less appealing. In the aftermath of Indian wars the editors asked that known Indian murderers be arrested and that New Mexico grand juries bring criminal indictments against such criminals. Thus, while the territorial press in time of war asked for extermination or exile for the Indians, in time of peace they asked for fair treatment of them and that they be placed under a system of justice with which they must abide if there ever was to be a reconciliation of the two cultures.

The territorial press was generally hostile toward anyone who would stop short of the subjugation of Indians and the imposition of white standards of justice upon them. Since a great many of the Indian agents were so inclined, the press was generally antagonistic toward them. The Silver City *Grant County Herald* voiced the general sentiment: "we will publish the death notices of sanctimonious Indian agents free of charge."[23] A similar attitude was reflected when Vincent Colyer, the pacifist Quaker, resigned from the Indian Peace Commission: "New Mexico and Arizona can well spare him."[24] Since most of these agents were employees of the Interior Department which reflected the more lenient attitude of the pacifists, the territorial press generally endorsed the proposal that the Indians be placed under the control of the War Department. The usual attitude among editors was that "the Interior Department has had a fair trial in the management of the war-like Indian tribes of New Mexico—let us see the result of placing them in the hands of the War Department."[25]

The army, on the other hand, did not escape the wrath of the territorial editors when, as so often happened, it failed promptly to subdue the Apaches. From 1879 until 1883, New Mexico was almost constantly harrassed by small bands of raiding Apaches; and Colonel Edward Hatch, in command of the military department of New Mexico, was continually censured by most editors.[26] During most of these years Hatch was defended only by the Santa Fe *Weekly New Mexican* and the Albuquerque *Golden Gate*.[27] In this period Hatch and his subordinates were repeatedly accused of cowardice,[28] incompetence,[29] and lying to their superiors about the situation in New Mexico.[30] As Indian atrocities mounted, the editors continued a campaign of denunciation and exaggeration. For example, one claimed that "Victorio has Hatch on the reservation."[31] Another suggested, "Let us ask Victorio what terms he will give."[32] And the Las Vegas *Daily Optic* contended: "The government would gain a chip or two by discharging Hatch and hiring Victorio to command the troops in New Mexico. Anything for economy."[33]

Editorial discontent with the army was tremendously increased by the fact that the troublesome Apache bands were small, usually numbering only 50 to 100 warriors. The editors did not appreciate the difficulty of capturing the slippery Apache in desert and mountainous country with which he was more familiar than the army. The territorial press, exerting its utmost energies to advance New Mexico, was disgusted with the course of events; as the editor of the Silver City *Daily Southwest* commented: "We are dreaming of a golden age and a future empire—and fifty dirty, lousy Indians have us in a state of siege."[34] Nor had the high-ranking military officers, who were unfamiliar with the area, a much better concept of the problem. General Philip Sheridan was sent to New Mexico to investigate Hatch's campaign and was reported by one editor to have stated that if the troops at hand had done their duty the Apaches would have been squelched.[35] On the other hand, the Santa Fe *New Mexican,* a consistent supporter of Hatch, contended:

> General Hatch should be reinforced with four times the amount of troops now commanded by him. The most brilliant military maneuvers and well studied strategical movements must fail of their effect when not sufficiently supported by numbers.[36]

Eventually other editors supported the contention of the Santa Fe *New Mexican* and spearheaded drives for petitions asking more federal troops for New Mexico.[37] At the same time, however, they asked that local strength be utilized, and governors Lew Wallace and Lionel Sheldon were repeatedly asked to organize volunteers and militia units to combat the Indians. The War Department doubted the efficiency of volunteers. In an effort to prove the contrary, the Silver City *Daily Southwest* joined other papers in citing instances of successful of volunteers in New Mexico:

> Those people who cheapen the effectiveness of volunteers evidently do not know the history of Indian wars in New Mexico.
> In 1851 the Utes . . . [and] about a year later the Mescaleros made war . . . volunteers soon reduced them.
> During the Rebellion, the Navajos commenced . . . war, and . . . volunteers, in a short time conquered a peace that has endured to this day.
> In point of fact there have been no successful wars against the New Mexico Indians except where volunteers were employed. This is history. No one can gainsay it.[38]

In 1881 the pleas of the New Mexico editors were answered. Colonel Hatch was replaced with Colonel Ranald S. Mackenzie, famous conquerer of the Comanches; a large number of militia companies were organized; and federal reinforcements were brought into the territory.[39] Very probably the clamor of the territorial editors had aided in bringing about all these changes, which in turn contributed to a sharp decline in Apache raids in New Mexico.[40] Thus, the territorial editors quite possibly were responsible in part for the subjugation of the Apaches—a necessary first step in the reconciliation of the conflicting cultures.

By 1890 the pacification of the New Mexico Indians was completed, but even before this a few editors had interested themselves in efforts to help the Indian adapt himself to a new way of life. The Las Cruces

*Rio Grande Republican* favored the plan introduced in Congress in 1884 to give each Indian 160 acres of land and implements for farming.[41] However, this paper and the Santa Fe *New Mexican* were intrigued chiefly by the fact that a great deal of reservation land would thus be opened to white settlement.[42] On the other hand, the *New Mexican,* more than any other paper, interested itself in efforts to teach the Indians ways to improve themselves. This paper noted with pleasure Navajo reception of a sawmill, looms, and spinning wheels, commenting:

> Surely this is educating the Indian to some purpose and is in addition to the building of acequias [irrigation works] and bringing of land under cultivation and other pursuits of which we have heretofore taken occasion to speak. . . . We are always glad to notice such efficiency and progress in the treatment of the Indian as affording something of substantial benefit to him. . . .[43]

In addition, the Santa Fe *New Mexican* praised the progress of the territorial Indian schools and supported efforts to secure more money to educate Indian children. Although on rare occasions other editors praised such efforts, the *New Mexican* was a much more consistent supporter and in this way contributed to the reconciliation of the Indian and European cultures.[44]

Early in the twentieth century some New Mexicans saw the value of preserving some of the picturesque Indian customs as tourist attractions. D. K. B. Sellers, editor of the Farmington *Hustler,* took some Navajo to Albuquerque to perform some of their colorful tribal dances, and an Albuquerque *Morning Journal* news story indicated the tourist values of such performances:

> . . . as in former years four blocks of the street were roped off and great bonfires built at intervals along the Avenue which lit up the buildings and great throngs of people with a fitful and lurid glare. The Indians dressed in fanciful and fantastic barbaric costumes gathered around the leaping flames and made the strange monotonous movements of the fire dance accompanying it with the peculiar intoning chant, varied by shrieks and groans which never fail to send at least a few chills over the paleface observer, even him who has heard the blood curdling sounds before.

> The mounted Indians went through various evolutions. . . . and the blanket fight especially created a sensation. The Indians try to unhorse each other by swiping each other in a forcible manner with blankets, making a scene of pandemonium and dust and confusion which is hard to describe. There was some wild riding when the whole mob of Navajos rushed at top speed down the length of the four blocks, each one straining every nerve to reach goal ahead of his dusky companions. All of which of course was accompanied by shrieks and war whoops, such as only an Indian from the southwest can give utterance to.

The long street was lined with crowds of people, faces illuminated by the blazing bonfires, the wild yelling Indians, the furious riding pell mell back and forth and the dances all combined to make a scene which was the most novel and picturesque sight which the delayed Santa Fe tourists have seen in many a day.[45]

This event was probably an ancestor of the present-day Inter-Tribal Indian Ceremonial held annually at Gallup and foreshadowed the future role the New Mexico press would play in encouraging the presentation of the native culture as a tourist attraction to the common advantage of all New Mexicans.

Since the efforts of the press to improve the lot of the subjugated Indians was rather feeble, its chief contribution appears to have been that of the removal of a threat to the other two cultures of New Mexico, hastening the development of the territory. Removal of the Indian menace was a common desire of all New Mexicans. The press, however, provided the necessary leadership and amplified the voices of New Mexicans until removal of the Indian menace became a matter of national concern, and the federal government was then compelled to take the necessary steps to subdue the Indians.

The press took an active interest in all matters concerning the relations of the varied peoples of New Mexico and by its presentation of the demands of the conflicting groups hastened progress and harmony. Reconciliation of Spanish and Anglo cultures was more rapid and extensive than that of the Indian and European cultures. Nevertheless, complete reconciliation of Spanish and Anglo cultures was difficult for a variety of reasons arising from conflicts over ethnic differences, economic advantages, religion, educational practices, language, disputes over political preferment, political rights, and civil rights. In the instances when the press became involved in these conflicts it was divided roughly into three groups: papers representing predominantly Anglo-American areas or interests, the Spanish-language press, and journals serving both groups. In general the papers of the first two groups became advocates of the Anglo and Spanish peoples, respectively, while the last group of papers urged a course of moderation. Usually Anglo editors were most hostile toward the Hispanos when those editors first came to the territory, but they became more tolerant as time passed. Most Hispano editors, on the other hand, were moderate in their demands and often apologetic when questions of ethnic differences were raised.

The integration of Spanish-Americans was eased by their quick acceptance of United States citizenship and the American political system. But their final assimilation was slowed because their numerical superiority in New Mexico encouraged their continued use of Spanish and the old customs. Had this small number of Hispanos been scattered out over the United States, assimilation would have been rapid. In any case, there was then little evidence of the bitterness of a conquered minority such as manifested itself in the case of the Poles or the people of Alsace-Lorraine.

Despite general progress in reconciliation of the conflicting cultures, Spanish and Anglo[46] relations became intermittently worse until the final territorial years. Evidence of the good relations between the two peoples in the 1850s and 1860s was the large number of mixed marriages —considering the small number of Anglo-Americans in New Mexico.[47] With the influx of Anglo-American miners into southwestern New Mexico in the 1870s an element hostile to the Spanish-Americans was introduced, but here again there were a great many mixed marriages.[48] A new and larger wave of Anglo-Americans came with the construction of the railways. As a result, both their predominance in the territorial southwest and their numbers in the larger towns greatly increased. Then in the next few years ethnic conflict also increased but had declined again by the 1890s in most of these areas. During the '90s and in the early twentieth century, however, a new Anglo-American group came to New Mexico, settling principally in its southeastern portion. This group, largely from the South, was more hostile toward the Hispanos than prior Anglo immigrants, and the clash between the two cultures became more heated than at any period of the territorial years. Yet, in the aftermath of these attacks and the counterattacks of the Spanish-language and English-language press of the older towns, an understanding was reached and incorporated in the constitution and in early laws of the state of New Mexico so that relations between the two ethnic groups began to improve in the new state.

Editorial attitudes toward ethnic relations usually reflected the attitude of the majority of the people of their section of the territory. This seemed to be the case of the Silver City *Grant County Herald,* which supported an effort of the people of Grant County to annex that county to Arizona on the basis that they would be better represented by an "American" legislature.[49] This movement of the 1870s was unsuccessful, but in 1886 continued hostility toward Spanish-Americans by the people of this area was shown by the attitude of the Hillsboro *Sierra County Advocate* with this statement: "It is a pity if the Republican party is still afraid to put forward a white man [as a candidate for congressional delegate]."[50] In 1889 the effort to join southwestern New Mexico to Arizona was renewed, and again the motive appeared to be to escape the domination of the northern New Mexico Spanish-American counties.[51]

Meanwhile, beginning in 1879 a large number of Anglo-Americans began moving into many northern New Mexico counties. Although this element was initially hostile toward Spanish-Americans, the attitudes of the editors of this area were divided. This division was shown in press reaction to one of the few instances of inter-cultural violence in New Mexico. The incident began with the murder of A. M. Conklin, editor of the Socorro *Sun,* by three Baca brothers. Anglo-Americans at Socorro demanded that the Spanish-American sheriff arrest the Bacas. Upon his refusal to do so, Anglo-American vigilantes seized eight Spanish-Americans as hostages, offering to exchange them for the Baca brothers. The Spanish-Americans at Socorro then formed a group and threatened counter violence. As a result the out-numbered Anglo-Americans telegraphed for help, and Anglo-Americans of nearby towns rushed to Socorro. At the same time federal troops were sent to the town and required the sheriff to arrest the Bacas. Subsequently they escaped from the Socorro jail. One was killed in the jail break; another was quickly recaptured and hanged by the vigilantes, while the third was recaptured months later and brought to trial. At this trial important witnesses were absent, and a Spanish-American jury freed Baca, who quickly fled Socorro before the Anglo-American vigilantes could act. The vigilantes then escorted prosecuting attorney J. F. Chaves to the train and forbade him ever to return to Socorro. The Anglo-American press reported these episodes, including the mutual hostility of Hispano and Anglo groups, but was reluctant to comment editorially on that hostility.[52] The Albuquerque *Daily Journal,* however, was an exception, and concerning the mob treatment of Chaves its editor wrote: "The people of Socorro may think they are doing wisely, but we wish to tell them they are disgracing their town and rendering the name American obnoxious."[53] The Las Vegas *Daily Optic* then began a defense of the Socorro mob. Although this paper did not openly approve of the antagonism toward Spanish-Americans that the mob displayed, such would seem to be implied:

> The people of Socorro . . . found their only safety in the organization of a committee of safety to protect themselves and their families. They carry with them the sympathy of the good citizens of New Mexico, and should they ever need assistance and protection against paid assassins or others, they will find their ranks increased by thousands of good citizens, ever ready to afford protection to this good community. . . .[54]

Editorial comments of the Socorro *Miner* and the Socorro *Sun* also expressed approval of the actions of the vigilantes but ignored the ethnic element of these clashes. Although the fact was ignored editorially, complete approval of vigilante actions implied hostility toward Hispanos on the part of an element of the Anglo-American press, since the action of the Anglo-American mob was directed against a Spanish-American sheriff, prosecuting attorney, and community.[55]

This hostility by some editors in the counties of mixed populations continued for several years in the 1880s. The attitude of the Las Vegas *Daily Optic* provides an example of this hostility. In 1879 this paper asserted that the Anglo-American "East Las Vegas is an American town and will be governed by Americans only!"[56] This hostile attitude of the *Daily Optic* continued; for example, in 1884 this comment appeared: "It is hoped that San Miguel County will elect an American sheriff this fall."[57] The Las Cruces *Rio Grande Republican* also showed hostility toward the Hispanos with comments such as this one: "A Mexican jury! Ye Gods! Our court is doing its utmost to strengthen the hands of Judge Lynch."[58] On the other hand, the Albuquerque *Daily Journal* criticized the hostility of the newcomers toward Spanish-Americans:

> There is a disposition in this territory on the part of a few, to stir up discord between the American and Mexican population. . . . If you do not like the Mexicans, there is room in a hundred lands where you will never see them.[59]

While it is apparent that many Anglo-American editors were hostile toward the Hispanos, this attitude changed sharply in the late 1880s as a result of external attacks on the Spanish-Americans. The minority report of the Committee on Territories of the United States House of Representatives attacked the fitness of New Mexico to become a state because of its predominantly Spanish-American population. This report charged the Hispanos with low morals, religious bigotry, and backwardness. As a result the entire territorial press sprang to the defense of the Spanish-Americans.[60] Newspapers in the eastern United States also opposed the admission of New Mexico because of its predominantly Spanish-American population. For example, the Chicago *Tribune* maintained that since "A Mexican Aztec Indian is not now and never has been eligible to American citizenship by process of naturalization, . . . it would be preposterous to allow 125,000 of them to come in and constitute a state on the level with the more prosperous and enlightened commonwealths." To this the Las Vegas *Daily Optic,* now a militant defender of the Hispanos, answered that these people were not Indians and that they had been granted full United States citizenship by the Treaty of Guadalupe Hidalgo.[61] In subsequent years the attacks of eastern American papers continued, and Spanish-Americans were defended by most of the territorial press.[62] The result of these external attacks was that in seeking to defend New Mexico the editors found the many admirable qualities of the Hispanos to cite in their defense, which led to an improvement in relations between the two cultures in a large portion of the territory.

This new attitude of the press was fortunate, for after 1889 there was a new outbreak of violence with an ethnic background. In this period Spanish-Americans rebelled against the loss of ancient rights as the result of injustices perpetrated by some land grant owners[63] and by the Anglo-American cattlemen's fencing of the public domain. Under a name borrowed from a secret society active in the eastern United States, the White Caps, the Hispanos sought to halt these abuses. This organization became quite strong in San Miguel County, where 300 hooded White Caps once openly paraded on the Las Vegas streets. Less successful efforts were made to organize White Cap groups in Santa Fe, Bernalillo, and Dona Ana counties. When fences put up by land grant owners or by cattlemen on the public domain barred the right of way or access to wood or water, the White Caps cut them. This secret society also took action to help strikers in a strike by Spanish-American railway track workers and destroyed ties purchased by the Santa Fe railway after it had reduced the pay of Spanish-American tie cutters per tie.[64] While most territorial papers were hostile toward the White Caps, two disapproved of their methods but admitted the justice of their cause. The Las Cruces *Rio Grande Republican* reflected the attitude of most papers: "White Caps . . . are entirely out of place in the progressive West."[65] In an editorial headed "Citizen 'White Caps' Let Us Reason Together" the *Daily Optic* called for them to work for their ends openly:

We are all American citizens now no matter what our former place of birth or prior or present race origin. We are all amenable to the same laws and alike subject to punishment for their violation. Upon a proper observance of the law and a compliance with its mandates, you and we must alike depend for the safety of life, the protection of property and the security of our homes. Some of the laws are bad but we must repeal them by the same methods by which they were enacted. It will not do to trample even a bad law underfoot simply because it is bad. . . . The OPTIC knows, and as many of our citizens know, you are among the worthy and well meaning citizens of this county. You should go about the streets in broad daylight, disseminate your doctrines under the midday sun, circulate your documents in the ordinary manner of men in a holy and worthy cause, and this will secure for you the respect and esteem of your neighbors and other citizens, and aid you in getting their sympathy to help right any real wrong of which you may complain. Besides, you and the people whose suffering you are working to relieve are largely in the majority. . . . How easy to remedy your wrongs through the peaceful and honorable channel of the ballot box.[66]

Yet the Las Vegas *Daily Optic* left little doubt that it favored the ends if not the means of the White Caps: "Land grabbers who have fenced miles and miles, to which they have no early color of title . . . need not look to the OPTIC for sympathy and help in their grabbing schemes."[67] Ultimately, however, the *Daily Optic,* as did most New Mexico papers, concluded that, "The White Cap way of settling things is worse than the original wrong."[68] Spanish-language papers appeared to be divided on the question, for the Mesilla *Defensor del Pueblo* congratulated the White Caps for effecting a successful organization in San Miguel County, while the Les Vegas *Sol de Mayo* held that in the end the White Caps would prove to be the enemies of the people.[69] The only English-language paper to defend them fully was the Gallup *Gleaner* which contended: "The White Caps, as they are called in New Mexico, are the progressive men in the territory, . . . men who are opposed to allowing a gang of 'land grabbers' to control the affairs of New Mexico."[70] Thus, most territorial editors, whether Anglo or Hispano, disapproved of violent methods, but some recognized the justice of the ends of the White Caps and sought to persuade them to use methods that would lead to reconciliation rather than conflict between the ethnic groups.

However, the White Cap movement also represented a new leadership element among Spanish-Americans. Until this period most Spanish-Americans had been content to follow the lead of the richer members of their group such as J. F. Chaves, M. S. Otero, Pedro Perea, and Tranquilino Luna, who were generally large land grant owners and had allied themselves with the Republican Santa Fe Ring. After 1879, however, the White Caps and the Partido Pueblo Unido arose to contest these older leaders. In addition, the increased education of Spanish-Americans encouraged the founding of Spanish-language newspapers by Spanish-Americans, and these papers also assumed a leadership role. One of their foremost demands was for an increase in political rewards for Spanish-Americans. For example, the Mora *Mosquito* in 1892 endorsed statehood on the basis that native sons instead of "carpetbaggers" would command the higher political offices of New Mexico,[71] and in 1894 Las Vegas *El Independiente* complained of the lack of federal appointments for Spanish-Americans.[72] Apparently the demands of this new leadership influenced territorial Republican policies, for in 1897 M. A. Otero, Jr. was appointed territorial governor and soon gained control of the New Mexico Republican party. *El Independiente* hailed Otero's appointment as a turning point in New Mexico politics.[73]

Soon after the Hispanos had achieved greater political power, however, *El Independiente* recognized a new threat to Spanish-Americans from the flow of Anglo-American settlers into eastern New Mexico. In 1903 *El Independiente* noted that Spanish-Americans had welcomed all immigrants to the territory, believing that the newcomers would hasten the development of the territory to the benefit of all. But the editor warned that despite this excellent attitude of the Spanish-Americans:

Poco a poco los enimigos del pueblo nativo de Nuevo Mexico lo van despojando de todo sus derechos y subjetandolo a una especie de esclavitud semejante a lo que sufriron los isrealites en Egipto.[74]

A large percentage of the newcomers, whom *El Independiente* feared, were from the South, introducing a fourth cultural element into the already confused New Mexican population. These southerners, often from Texas, brought with them a prejudice that was to further complicate ethnic relations in New Mexico. The editor of the Santa Fe *New Mexican* contended: "It has been demonstrated repeatedly that the Democrats of southeastern New Mexico, like their brethern [sic] in Texas, hate the early white settlers of Spanish descent in New Mexico."[75] The press of the territorial southeast readily confirmed this hostility. For example, the Hagerman *Messenger* asserted:

> The "greaser" is doomed; he is too lazy to keep up; and smells too badly to be endured. You should take a trip to other parts of New Mexico. Dilapidated old adobe buildings, chili and the smell of garlic were everywhere very much in evidence. How different in the towns of the Pecos Valley! Everything is new here, neat and trim. The magic wand of the Anglo-Saxon is over it, and that means development, enlightenment, progress and power.[76]

Evidence of the attitudes of other editors of this area was shown by the Portales *Times,* which referred to the southeast as the "whiteman's [sic] division of New Mexico,"[77] and the Artesia *Advocate,* which displayed a venomous type of prejudice:

> Among the intelligent people of this valley he [the Spanish American] falls into the niche that God Almighty intended when he put on the impress of color. It was Texas men and Texas money that brought forth the gushing fountains and made this the fairest vale in New Mexico. If a single native has ever spent a dollar in developing this great work, we have never heard of it.[78]

The press of southeastern New Mexico, deeming their culture progressive, energetic, and generally superior, seemed determined to end Spanish-American dominance of politics—at least as far as their area was concerned. At first, as the Anglo-Americans of southwestern New Mexico had done earlier, they hoped to annex themselves to a nearby Anglo-dominated area, in this instance Texas.[79] Later they sought to use southern methods to disfranchise Spanish-Americans. In an attempt to warn native New Mexicans that their voting rights were in danger, Las Vegas *El Independiente* cited the example of south Texas counties, which had eliminated the Hispano vote with the all-white primary.[80] Then, in 1906 the Eddy County Democratic Central Committee instituted this type of primary in their county. *El Independiente* denounced this policy but maintained that it was only natural for the party of slavery to seek to deprive Spanish-American citizens of their rights and to seek to put upon them the stigma of inferiority.[81] Clayton *El Fenix* labeled this "un-American, unprincipled and cowardly! Without doubt such action has resulted from the prejudice of some of the floating, no account

Texans, who drift hither and thither and everywhere distinguishing themselves for their hatred of everything Mexican."[82] The only southeastern New Mexico Democratic paper to oppose the action of the Eddy County Democratic Central Committee was the Carlsbad *Sun,* but only on the basis that it would invite retaliation from the Spanish-American-dominated areas.[83] Democratic papers in other parts of the territory disapproved of the all-white primary. For example, the Alamogordo *Otero County Advertiser* maintained that: "this is un-American, poor politics and unwarranted by any possible condition that may exist."[84] While the Santa Fe *New Mexican* appeared to be consistently in favor of preserving the rights of Spanish-Americans, this journalistic spokesman for Republicanism did not hesitate to use the incident to alienate Spanish-American voters from the Democratic party:

> The Roswell Daily Record, the Carlsbad Current, the Carlsbad Sun, the Artesia Advocate, the Hagerman Messenger and other Democratic papers of the Pecos Valley do not like the stand the Daily New Mexican is taking in defense of the native citizens of the Territory. The Democratic leaders and papers in the southeastern part of New Mexico are determined to disfranchise the native people because the majority of them are wise enough to be Republicans, although there is nevertheless a minority of 14,000 of them who vote the Democratic ticket.[85]

Apparently because of the tremendous furor raised throughout the territory, the Eddy County Democratic Convention overruled its central committee and discarded its all-white primary. Meanwhile, southeastern New Mexico editors had explored other means of curtailing the votes of Spanish-Americans. The Roswell *Tribune* asked for a poll tax law similar to that in effect in Texas,[86] and the Roswell *Record* maintained that educational qualification for voting should be imposed.[87] The *New Mexican* held that although the schools needed the poll tax revenue, the tax at the moment should not be made a prerequisite for voting. Concerning educational qualifications, the *New Mexican* maintained that this was a southern practice which should not be imposed on New Mexico.[88] These challenges to their voting rights doubtless left the Spanish-Americans ill at ease. Apparently for this reason Las Cruces *El Labrador* favored the joint statehood proposal, submitted to New Mexico and Arizona voters that year, on the basis that it would be better to accept the joint state while Spanish-Americans had enough strength to insist upon clauses in the constitution protecting their rights. At current rates of Anglo-American immigration, *El Labrador* maintained, they would soon be outnumbered and might lose their rights.[89]

During these same years Spanish-Americans were fearful of the loss of another right because of their lack of proficiency in English. In 1905 a proposed congressional act excluded anyone from jury duty in the United States courts who was not proficient in English. The Hillsboro *Sierra County Advocate* favored the bill, believing that if it were enacted it would rapidly advance education in New Mexico.[90] The Las Vegas *Daily Optic* claimed that this practice was already in effect in some New Mexico courts but maintained that the time had not yet come when such a practice should be extended throughout the territory. The *New Mexican* did not recommend that the policy be adopted but held that if it should be there were enough Spanish-Americans proficient in English in every county so that no jury need be formed without a Spanish-American member.[91]

Perhaps even more disturbing to Spanish-Americans was the stigma of separate schools, the establishment of which apparently became a practice in some predominantly Anglo-American communities in the twentieth century. Las Vegas *El Independiente* stated that such a policy was in effect in 1903 at Cerrillos, Silver City, Roswell, Carlsbad, and Raton, and resented the implication that the Spanish-American students were not good enough to rub elbows with the Anglo-American children.[92] In 1906 the *New Mexican* noted this practice at Carlsbad and maintained that:

> All Mexican children can attend the regular schools if they so desire. Under the New Mexico statutes there is absolutely no distinction provided, expected or recognized and none should be had; if the present statutes in this respect are not strong enough, they should be made so.[93]

Concerning separate schools the Carlsbad *Current* wrote:

> No power, no government on earth can enforce racial association against the desires of either race in question. The whole power of the greatest government on earth was once bent toward that end and failed utterly.[94]

Although the Spanish-Americans at Carlsbad and Deming were reported to prefer separate schools for their children,[95] such trends as this and the threat to voting rights evidently alerted most Hispanos to a potential danger. Thus, when the New Mexico Constitution was written in 1910 it provided guarantees against ethnic discrimination in voting and education. The congressional enabling act stipulated that the constitution must provide that all state business be conducted in English. Although the convention honored this stipulation, it also provided that this portion of the constitution could be changed by a simple legislative act, and the first state legislature placed the Spanish and English languages on an equal basis for the conduct of the State's business.[96] While it appears that the Spanish language and many Spanish customs will survive for several generations, their forced curtailment envisioned by the enabling act might have kept them alive indefinitely, as examples in central Europe show. On the other hand, the meeting of the children of the two cultures in public schools from early ages will serve to increase mutual respect and understanding. Thus, the editorial comments and demands helped to alert the Spanish-Americans to dangers to their rights and shaped public opinion for the acceptance of a constitution which dealt justly with each of these conflicting cultures.

Although conflicts between Spanish and Anglo cultures based on ethnical antagonism and the struggle for the preservation of the Spanish-American's civil and political rights raged until 1912, conflict over religious differences of the two cultures had subsided much earlier. In fact, as far as the press reveals there was little conflict over religious doctrine directly, but a great deal over the question of public non-sectarian schools. This question became prominent in the 1870s, but no final decision was reached. Then in 1890 militant Spanish-American Catholics defeated a proposed constitution which had incorporated the principle of non-sectarian public schools. The legislature, which met in 1891 shortly after the defeat of this constitution, was hounded by the entire territorial press to enact a law providing adequate public non-sectarian schools. Such a law was enacted and for the next three years the editors campaigned successfully for the voting of bonds to erect school buildings. Most of the press then lost interest in the schools as a newsworthy subject for discussion. The provisions of the law of 1891 that the schools be non-sectarian and be conducted only in English were major steps toward the reconciliation of the two conflicting cultures.

Initially the Spanish-Americans of New Mexico were led to expect difficulty with the Anglo-Americans in religious matters, but after one brief flurry in 1848 this topic was generally avoided by the press until the 1870s. Mexican officials had predicted that New Mexicans' freedom of worship would be endangered under American rule—propaganda which was probably very effective because of the centuries of conflict between Anglo Protestants and Spanish Catholics.[97] Thus, the Anglo-American press first sought to allay the suspicions of Spanish-Americans that their new government would tamper with their religion. In January, 1848, a letter, probably written by the editor or an official of the military government, appeared in the Santa Fe *Republican,* explaining that there was religious freedom in the United States. However, this same letter asked that the legislature enact a law legalizing civil marriage, which would tend to loosen the hold of the Catholic church on the people.[98] Two weeks later an editorial in the same paper bitterly attacked the Catholic priesthood in New Mexico and intimated that conditions would improve rapidly when the New Mexico clergy came under the control of American Catholic officials.[99] After this early display of

ill will, the press retained good relations with the Catholic clergy until
the 1870s—despite the fact that the editors were predominantly Anglo-
American Protestants.

These Protestant editors noted with pleasure the establishment of
Protestant churches.[100] For example, the founding of a Presbyterian con-
gregation at Santa Fe brought this comment from the *Weekly Gazette*:
"All who love the welfare of Santa Fe, will rejoice that another church
is added to those already in place." Similarly, at Silver City the *Mining
Life* noted that the town was several years old and had no churches.
Evidently this editorial provoked action, for soon three Protestant de-
nominations were petitioned to establish churches at Silver City. The
Methodists were the first to take action, which led the *Mining Life* to
comment: "We congratulate our citizens upon this expected addition to
our society."[101]

Despite their approval of the founding of churches, the editors did
not hesitate to criticize any overzealous Protestant churchman who was
believed to have exaggerated about conditions of New Mexico life in
order to obtain funds for his church work in the territory. Thus, when
a Santa Fe minister was reported to have told a national Presbyterian
conference that his congregation did not dare to attend evening services
without a guard of soldiers to protect them from Catholics, the Santa Fe
*New Mexican* stated: "The effect which such a speech must have on
people cannot for a moment be doubted, and we publish it more in sor-
row than in anger, though abundant reason exists for gross indigna-
tion."[102] Similar incidents at later dates also aroused the ire of the territorial press.[103] It thus appears that the New Mexico press generally
adopted an impartial attitude in most religious matters, for it welcomed
all churches while remaining very critical of the actions of any sect that
threatened harm to New Mexico.

Since the Anglo-American press was not hostile toward Catholic doctrine, the chief area of conflict was the dispute between Spanish-American Catholics and Anglo-American Protestants over public schools. In
the 1870s there were few public schools in the territory, and the press
fought two battles—to gain funds for public schools and to keep public
education free from sectarian control. New Mexico's educational shortcomings were graphically revealed by the census of 1870. Of a population of 51,000 over ten years of age, 49,000 could not write and 48,000
could not read. There were only 5,000 school pupils out of 30,000 of
school age.[104] The press made efforts to correct this poor showing in several ways. For example, the Santa Fe *Post* called upon the legislature of
1872 to enact a comprehensive school law. The legislature, however,
merely authorized counties to levy only a very small tax for schools.[105]
Thus, in 1873 public taxation provided but $792.71 for schools in Grant

County. In order that Silver City might have public schools, the *Mining Life* sponsored a public subscription to add to this tax money.[106] A year later the *New Mexican* aided a drive to raise funds to build a public schoolhouse at Santa Fe. The efforts of the public, the press, and the churches had by 1875 brought a small improvement, for it was reported that New Mexico had 131 public and 28 private schools with a total enrollment of 6,578.[107]

The growing school enrollment led to the first major conflicts about sectarian influence in public schools. In 1875 the Jesuit order sought to sell to territorial public schools the text books it was printing for church schools. The Jesuit paper, Las Vegas *Revista Catolica*, and the Albuquerque *Republican Review*, edited by the Irish-Catholic William McGuiness, strongly supported this proposal, while the Santa Fe *New Mexican* editor W. H. Manderfield, also a Catholic, joined other territorial editors in opposing it. Nevertheless, such books were used in some public schools.[108] Defeat in this matter was probably responsible for the appeal of the *New Mexican* to the legislature to enact a school law which increased tax support and safeguarded the schools against sectarian influence. When such a bill was introduced, the *Republican Review* and *Revista Catolica* immediately opposed it, charging that its intent was to destroy the influence of the Catholic church in New Mexico. These papers asked instead that tax money be divided on the basis of church membership, allowing each sect to control its own schools.[109] The answer of the *New Mexican,* recommending the American system as the best means of protecting Spanish-American rights, foretold the ultimate course of events in New Mexico:

> The *Review* says ninety-nine of a hundred of the children of this territory are Roman Catholics. Suppose it was the reverse, would the Catholics desire, even if they were but one in a hundred, that their children should be taught the New England Catechism? Is it honorable because you are powerful to force your peculiar religious dogmas upon the weak? If the minority pay taxes shall they not be protected in enjoying equal rights? There are some districts now in this Territory where the Protestants outnumber the Catholics ten to one; would it not be prudent as well as just for the Catholics now in power in the whole Territory to provide in all cases no sectarianism shall be taught! So that in case they should ever be in the minority they can point with pride to the fact that in the day of their power they were both just and liberal. Besides this is according to the Constitution of the United States which is binding upon us all. . . . Let us unite in good faith to establish the doctrine and practice of religious toleration. . . .[110]

Those in favor of sectarian control were strong enough to defeat this bill, but the two papers debated the question for months and even introduced it into the political campaign of 1876. The Santa Fe *New Mexican* stated that territorial Republicans favored free, non-sectarian public schools, and the Albuquerque *Republican Review* challenged that party to put such a plank into its platform. The *New Mexican* retorted that the Republicans had done so. But, in fact, the party had neatly straddled the issue by declaring for freedom of conscience in one plank and free public schools in another—but said nothing about non-sectarian schools.[111] Meanwhile, New Mexico public schools made little progress, and there was a growing hostility between Anglo-American Protestant and Spanish-American Catholic partisans.

In the legislative session of 1878 new fire was added to this partisan hostility over religion. In this session Donato Gasparri, a Jesuit leader in New Mexico, succeeded in lobbying a bill through the legislature chartering the Jesuit order in New Mexico as a tax-free corporation. Governor S. B. Axtell vetoed the bill, and the legislature promptly over-rode his veto. All New Mexico papers except the Albuquerque *Republican Review* and Las Vegas *Revista Catolica* approved of the veto of the governor.[112] The Mesilla *Valley Independent* immediately began a campaign against the Jesuits which lasted several months. At length the Silver City *Grant County Herald* condemned the *Valley Independent*, stating that it had extended its attack so far that it had become an attack on Catholics in general.[113] However, the high point of the Jesuit controversy was an editorial in *Revista Catolica* admonishing Spanish-American legislators to combine as a solid Spanish-American party in order to control territorial politics:

Let old quarrels then disappear. What is there about Democrats and Republicans? BE MEXICANS! ***** But we say be MEXICANS; that is to say let your policy be union in all that which may be necessary for the preservation and development of the inherent interests of the country. So long as you shall be united you will govern; divided you will be governed; and governed not alone by the American portion in the territory, but also by a few adventurers that over you and over the Americans will extend their usurping hand.[114]

This attempt to unite native New Mexicans into an ethnocentric block was attacked by the *New Mexican* in a bellicose and flag-waving editorial addressed to the Jesuits:

The attempt of the Italian *refugees,* who have sought and obtained shelter under our flag, to create disturbances between the citizens of the United States resident in New Mexico on account of nationality . . . deserves a severe reprimand. . . . We call ourselves, for want of a better term, Americans, the citizens of Mexico call themselves Mexicans. Under which flag, cunning priests, do you desire to live? Not Mexico, for they would not permit you to live there an hour; they have had too bitter a taste of your mischievous teachings. Then if you intend to become a citizen of the United States by adoption, why do you teach these young men to sink all party ties and bind themselves together as Mexicans against Americans? Whose flag floats over the building in which they sit? Whose money pays for their valuable services? Whose Army guards your seditious heads from violence? and New Mexico from border raids and Indian massacres? Mexico? Bah! Treacherous Jesuit, this is America, United States—Uncle Sam's country—Yankeeland. If you don't like it you can leave it. We came to stay—to introduce for our use and benefit our common schools, our railroads, and our laws and language.[115]

The chief influence of the Jesuit incorporation bill (which Congress annulled in 1879) and the Jesuit attempt to form an ethnic party was to unite most of the territorial press against the Jesuits in a demand for free, non-sectarian public schools. Of fifteen papers being published in the territory in February, 1879, thirteen favored non-sectarian free public schools. Two of these papers were edited by Spanish-Americans, indicating that the Jesuits had been unable to form a solid block of Spanish-Americans. The Las Cruces *Thirty-Four* enthusiastically hailed this wide approval of public schools and predicted it would continue to grow:

It is a sign of better times when Mexican editors, who have been bred under the old regime, come gallantly forward to combat the old ideas. By the time the next legislature meets, there will be such a demand for a good public school law . . . that body will hardly dare return to its constituency with that duty neglected.[116]

Despite the optimistic prediction of *Thirty-Four*, the next legislature passed no such law, presaging bleak years for education in New Mexico throughout the 1880s. With the advent of railways in 1879, the press became deeply intersted in the economic development of New Mexico and lost some of its concern over schools. This new attitude was reflected by the Santa Fe *New Mexican* in February, 1880:

The NEW MEXICAN is sorry for nothing in its past attitude toward the Jesuits, and has nothing to retract. It neither attacks or defends the Jesuits at the present time, for the reason that the time has come when a newspaper can devote itself with more profit to the material advancement of our territory than to religious discussion.[117]

Editorial interest in the economic rather than the cultural development of New Mexico continued during most of the 1880s. In 1884 the legislature passed a new school bill which raised school taxes from two-and-one-half to three mills per dollar of assessed valuation, but there was practically no newspaper agitation for an increase in school taxes at this time.[118] An 1887 law requiring three months of school attendance annually for all children was also preceded by little editorial effort to inspire such a law. Since assessed valuations for all the territory were but $11,363,406 in 1885, school taxes from this source for that year

amounted to only about $34,000. And the territorial poll tax dedicated
to schools returned a very small revenue, for the payment of the tax was
not a voting prerequisite. The Las Vegas *Daily Optic* called the attention of New Mexicans to the fact that they were lagging far behind in
educational matters. Yet only three months before it had boasted that
taxation was lower in New Mexico than in any western territory, for the
rates in the most heavily taxed county were only one-and-one-fourth per
cent. In Arizona, on the other hand, tax rates were as high as four per
cent of assessed valuation. Doubtless the low income of the schools derived from tax revenue was responsible for there being no schools operating at all in Socorro or Rio Arriba counties in 1883, or for the fact
that in 1886 there was only one month of school in Sierra County.[119]
Despite the appalling condition of education in the face of the increased
wealth and population of the territory in the 1880s, until 1889 there was
little agitation by the press for improvements in education.

The increased demand for schools in 1889 came as a by-product of
the demand for statehood. In 1888 it seemed possible that Congress
would grant statehood to New Mexico along with most of the other western territories. Then the strong attack contained in the minority report
by the Committee on Territories of the United States House of Representatives probably made many Anglo-American editors realize that the
territory must be made more acceptable to the American public before
it could gain admission as a state.[120] Thus, in 1889 the Anglo-American
editors seized upon the desire of the native New Mexicans for statehood
to demand as a prior or concurrent condition an amply supported public, non-sectarian school system. By way of illustration, the San Marcial
*Reporter* opposed statehood unless the legislature of 1889 provided a
better school system, and the Chloride *Black Range* commented: "New
Mexico needs school houses and teachers and fewer statehood 'blather-
skites.'" The Albuquerque *Daily Citizen* supported a measure introduced by W. D. Kistler which provided for a general school levy of ten
mills and allowed any district to vote an additional mill for building
purposes.[121] When the Kistler school bill was defeated, the territorial
press in general held T. B. Catron responsible. While the record showed
that Catron had voted for the bill, his critics claimed he really opposed
it. These critics believed Catron opposed the bill because he was one of
the largest property owners in the territory and was an attorney for other
large property owners. These editors then contended that although
Catron had kept his record clean, he had killed the bill by appealing to
the prejudices of the Spanish-American majority in the legislature.[122]
In addition, the Las Vegas *Daily Optic* and others noted the hostility
shown to the bill by the Spanish-American political leaders and large
land grant owners, Pedro Perea and J. F. Chaves. In the final votes on

the measure Spanish-Americans had opposed and Anglo-Americans had favored it almost unanimously.[123] Thus, the efforts of the Anglo-American editors to assure amply supported public, non-sectarian schools were defeated, but the matter was soon to be revived in conjunction with efforts to obtain statehood for New Mexico.

The same legislative session that brought defeat of the Kistler school bill authorized the calling of a constitutional convention. When this body met in September, 1889, it was dominated by T. B. Catron, J. F. Chaves, and Pedro Perea, and some editors were concerned about the attitude that the convention would take toward public schools. The prospect that the constitution might provide for sectarianism in schools arose when Archbishop J. B. Salpointe asked that any system of public education provided by the constitution authorize religious instruction for students by the church selected by their parents. The convention rejected the plea of the archbishop and provided for non-sectarian schools supported by a mandatory tax of two-and-one-half mills per dollar of assessed valuation. In addition, voters of each county were to be allowed to impose an additional two-and-one-half mills to support schools. However, implementation of both provisions was to be dependent on the legislature of the new state.[124] It thus appears that the agitation of the editors for improvements in education and the establishment of non-sectarian schools was instrumental in wringing some concessions from the men who had defeated the Kistler school bill.

Meanwhile, other efforts were being made to secure better schools for New Mexico. Almost as soon as the legislature defeated the Kistler bill, some editors asked that Congress be petitioned to enact a school law for the territory. In 1890 such a bill, almost an exact duplicate of the Kistler school bill, was introduced in Congress. At the instigation of the *Daily Optic* a mass meeting was called in Las Vegas to express approval of this proposed legislation. The Albuquerque *Morning Democrat,* Raton *Range,* and Kingston *Shaft* approved the proposed act, but the Santa Fe *New Mexican,* then closely aligned with T. B. Catron, opposed it.[125] Perhaps as much to forestall action by Congress as to answer complaints of Democrats and school proponents that the constitution did not provide enough tax support for schools, the constitutional convention reconvened and changed the school section to allow counties to vote school levies as high as five per cent of the assessed valuation.[126] Thus, ardent opposition to the constitution by the Democratic press and the demands of the Republican press apparently forced the territorial political leaders to make another concession concerning schools. However, in an election on October 7, 1890, the constitution was soundly defeated, indicating that while the press might induce the convention to place a non-sectarian school provision in the constitution, it could not force the predominantly Spanish-American Catholic voters of New Mexico to accept it.

The religious background of Spanish-American hostility to the constitution was revealed through the press. When the convention rejected the suggestion of the archbishop concerning public schools, the Las Vegas *Daily Optic* foresaw active Catholic opposition to the adoption of the constitution:

> Archbishop Salpoint, although he failed to convince the late constitutional convention that his views on the school question were good, will by no means consider himself a defeated man on the main issue . . . when the constitution is submitted to the people for ratification.[127]

A few weeks later the *Daily Optic* reported that the Santa Fe clergy had started denouncing the constitution.[128] In the post-election period the *New Mexican* began a denunciation of the Catholic church for its work in defeating the constitution. The church denied an official policy of opposition to the constitution, and the Las Vegas *Revista Catolica,* the Spanish-language Jesuit paper, gently reminded the *New Mexican* that priests enjoyed freedom of speech under United States laws and that numerous non-Catholics had contributed to constitutional defeat. At the same time the *Revista Catholica* implied that Spanish-Americans had defied their old political leaders of their own ethnic group to defeat the constitution.[129]

The lack of an official church policy opposing the constitution seems to be indicated by a Silver City *Enterprise* report that "at Las Cruces where the priest addressed the people in favor of statehood, the people walked off and left him with jeers and laughter."[130] A Spanish-American element, uncontrolled by ecclesiastic leaders, defied Spanish-American political leaders such as M. S. Otero and J. F. Chaves and defeated the constitution in the name of Catholicism. This group showered the territory with pamphlets printed in Spanish and English, directed especially toward "Mexican" voters.

> It is the intention of some to incorporate in the organic law of the new state [that] which will deny your children all kinds of education except that of the world. You will be required by law to support with taxation public schools [to] which you cannot conscientiously send your children. No faithful son of the church or of the Mexican caste will submit to this. . . . What they call progress is progress to perdition.[131]

Although there were several causes for the defeat of the constitution, the hostility of Spanish-American Catholics seems to have been the decisive factor. From the foregoing, it appears that the constitution was neither opposed nor favored officially by the archbishop. His hostility toward its school provisions, however, probably induced many Catholics to vote against the constitution. Perhaps even more conducive was the unofficial Catholic group, whose pamphlet was cited above. The weight of these two influences probably was sufficient to convince Spanish-American Catholics to vote against the constitution despite the fact that prominent Catholics and Spanish-American political leaders favored it.[132]

The defeat of the constitution in 1890 apparently brought a greater disunity to Spanish-Americans. Although Spanish-American legislators of both parties had united to defeat a non-sectarian public school proposal in 1889, a similar measure was passed two years later by a predominantly Spanish-American legislature. Perhaps ardent advocates of statehood believed Catholic hostility toward non-sectarian schools responsible for defeat of the constitution and vengefully retaliated by supporting enactment of a law creating such schools. Doubtless some of the richer Spanish-American leaders, who had strongly supported the constitution, resented the challenge to their leadership of Spanish-American Republicans. Possibly these same men, most of them large property owners, believed it was wiser to enact a territorial school law with lower tax rates than to risk a congressionally imposed school system with higher tax rates. Probably the ardent proponents of statehood believed that only after the enactment of such a law would New Mexico again be considered for statehood. Evidently all these things contributed to break the front of the Spanish-Americans, for although this group still controlled a majority of legislative seats in the session of 1891, a comprehensive non-sectarian public school law was enacted. As had been the case in 1889, the press in 1891 closely followed legislative action with regard to schools and constantly urged enactment of an improved school law. For example, the Santa Fe *Sun* reminded these who had "murdered the Kistler bill" that the public eye was upon them,[133] and the Las Vegas *Daily Optic* reminded T. B. Catron that "no man will ever reach the Senate of the United States from this Territory who stands in the way of enactment of an efficient school law opening our schools nine months of the year."[134] The Las Cruces *Rio Grande Republican* urged action: ". . . a good school law is the crying need of this territory and should be passed at once. . . . Don't waste any more time gentlemen introducing new bills, but pass something."[135] The chief contribution of the press was that of making it clear that a large majority of the Anglo-American Protestant population of New Mexico and the nation demanded a substantially supported public, non-sectarian school system. In the face of this clear demand and dissension in their ranks, enough of the Spanish-American legislators supported the Paulin school law of 1891 to secure its enactment.

This law provided for large tax increases to support non-sectarian public schools conducted in English. A general tax levy of three mills per dollar of valuation was made mandatory, and school districts were authorized to levy an additional five mills. In addition, the Paulin law allowed school districts to vote bonds for school construction and made the payment of a poll tax a requirement for voting, allocating to schools revenue derived from it. Moreover, by this date fines for violation of liquor and gambling laws had been assigned to schools.[136] The provisions of this law presented several threats to the efforts of the Spanish-Americans to preserve their culture. The poll tax threatened to curtail their political influence,[137] the English-language provision assured that the assimilation of their children into the Anglo-American culture would be hastened, and the non-sectarian provision threatened to curtail the influence of the Catholic Church on their children. The emphatic demand of the English-language press for such a law, presented at a time of Spanish-American disunity, helped to secure this victory for the Anglo-American culture.

In order to make effective their victory, the next step of the press was to demand the construction of public school buildings under the bonding provisions of the law. There was great need for action, for there were practically no public schoolhouses in the territory.[138] Almost as soon as the Paulin law was passed, the Albuquerque *Daily Citizen* demanded that bonds be voted immediately in order that a schoolhouse would be ready for the fall session.[139] The *Rio Grande Republican* asked for similar action at Las Cruces: "If Albuquerque can vote $60,-000, Las Vegas $15,000, Socorro $15,000, Deming $12,500, Springer $10,000, it would seem Las Cruces possessing every natural and many material advantages ought to do at least as well as Springer."[140] Here again the press was influential in insuring the ultimate domination of the Anglo-American culture.

Despite the fact that the Paulin law and the school building era provided only a minimum basis for school progress, the interest of the press in schools sagged back to the level of the early 1880s.[141] Since New Mexico lagged far behind most western states and territories in school development, there was a great need for a continuing campaign by the press for school improvement. The complacency of the editors tends to confirm the belief that one of the chief interests of the press from 1889 to 1892 was the imposition of a school system that would assure the eventual dominance of the Anglo-American culture. In this the press was reasonably successful. The question of sectarian control of public schools was never again important in the territorial era. In addition, most Spanish-American leaders soon began to advocate that native New Mexicans learn the English language. In illustration of this, Amado Chaves and J. F. Chaves who served as territorial superintendents of public schools constantly urged local school boards to hire as teachers only those who were competent in the English language.[142] O. A. Larrazolo, a Spanish-American political leader, also urged Spanish-Americans to learn the English language.[143] The Spanish-language press, for the most part, also urged this course. *El Combate* of Wagon Mound urged that local school boards hire only those teachers competent in English; and even that militant defender of the Spanish-American culture, *El Independiente* of Las Vegas, maintained that while Spanish-Americans should retain their Spanish language they should also learn English—the language of government, law, and business.[144]

Apparently prejudices concerning the ethnic differences are inherent, for it is a natural trait for men to prefer the familiar and dislike the strange. Thus, when contrasting cultures are drawn into close proximity, conflict is inevitable. The role of the press in conciliating the different cultures in New Mexico was that of presenting repeatedly a few basic and minimum demands, and thus establishing a basis from which a gradual movement toward full reconciliation could begin. The territorial ethnic conflicts reached peaks of intensity in three instances, the first coming during the series of Indian wars which culminated in the 1880s. The continual and insistent demand of the press that the southwestern Indians be rendered peaceful helped to arouse the people of the territory and the nation, and their petitions forced the federal government to act. The second high point of dissension concerned the reconciliation of the Spanish and Anglo cultures and was reached about 1890. It appeared then that the religion, language, and ethnic backgrounds of a majority of New Mexicans were unsatisfactory to the general American public, which delayed statehood for two decades. To counter this animosity, the press waged a successful campaign for free, public non-sectarian schools, which would hasten the Americanization of the native peoples. Such schools when inaugurated sped the reconciliation of the two cultures. The final peak of conflict came about 1906, after a heavy immigration of Anglo-Americans presaged their future predominance in New Mexico. The editors representing the newcomers showed their hostility to the Spanish culture, which was defended by the Spanish-language press and by Anglo-American editors who, after years of residence in New Mexico, had come to admire and were tolerant concerning the Spanish-Americans. Alerted by this hostility, the Spanish-Americans with the help of Anglo-Americans of good will and good sense insured that the rights of both ethnic groups would be protected under the constitution and laws of the new state. In each of the three instances cited, the press by revealing the minimum demands of the conflicting groups had hastened progress toward ultimate reconciliation.

# VI

# THE CONTRIBUTION OF
# THE PRESS TO TERRITORIAL
# ECONOMIC DEVELOPMENT

WHEN NEW MEXICO BECAME a United States Territory, it was a depressed area and underdeveloped economically. Most of its farms were very small, and its farmers, using the very crudest of equipment, raised little more than enough to feed their families. Although the territorial grasslands supported large herds of sheep, sheep raising was relatively unprofitable because of the continuing Indian raids and the poor quality of the animals. Furthermore, strenuous efforts to improve agricultural methods and livestock seemed pointless since New Mexico was so remote from any market. Thus, one of the first concerns of the territorial editors was the inducement of railway construction, which became the most important economic topic throughout the whole territorial era. Agitation for railways continued for years, for New Mexico was so vast that many railways were needed for its development. Consequently the editors appeared insatiable in their appetite for railroads. Once rail connections to markets were obtained, the press devoted more attention to the promotion of mining, irrigation, dry farming, and the livestock industry as a means of increasing New Mexican prosperity and population. With the characteristic enthusiasm and optimism of the frontiersman, the editors often exaggerated the prospects of New Mexico industries. Doubtless some persons who were led to make investments or to immigrate to New Mexico were harmed by this, but the press, on the whole, provided a worthwhile service with its attempt to improve the territorial economy.

New Mexico editors began promotion of the territorial economy in the 1850s by hopefully hailing plans for a Pacific railway. Such a railway was sure to come through New Mexico, they thought, since it had advantages of more population, milder winters, and lower mountain ranges than other proposed routes. However, the Pacific railroad was to be influenced more by political developments than these considerations, and New Mexico waited until December, 1878, for its first railway. Then others quickly followed until in 1882 there were four major railroads: the Santa Fe, extending from Raton to El Paso and Deming; the Southern Pacific, crossing the southwestern corner of the territory; the Atlantic and Pacific, joining Albuquerque to California; and the Denver and Rio Grande, stretching out from Colorado to Espanola. New Mexico gained no new lines until 1888 when the Fort Worth and Denver City crossed the northeastern corner of the territory. More railway construction followed in the 1890s, and before 1912 New Mexico had four new major lines. The Pecos Valley Northeastern was completed from Pecos, Texas, to Amarillo, via the Pecos Valley. The El Paso Northeastern was built from El Paso to Tucumcari and from there north to Dawson. In addition, other lines were constructed from Dalhart and Amarillo, Texas, to Tucumcari. The Santa Fe Central was built south from Santa Fe to Torrance via Estancia, and a new Atchison, Topeka and Santa Fe line extended from Belen to Texico. By 1912 New Mexico had an adequate, if not complete, rail network.

The territorial press was intensely concerned about all these railways and dozens more that were never built. Press interest went through three stages. First, there was anticipation. The press followed each railway from the first rumors of it until actual construction began or the route was abandoned. Second, there was encouragement. In this stage the press aided in the selling of stock and the raising of bonuses to insure that a line was launched and came by the editor's town. Finally, there were editorial complaints about high rates and bad practices that threatened to rob New Mexico of part of the fruits of the golden dreams these newspapers had nourished.

These golden dreams first became credible in 1857 with the chartering of the Atchison, Topeka and Santa Fe Railroad by the Kansas legislature. In subsequent years they were fed by the advance of this and other lines toward New Mexico. Hopes were quickened by a congressional act of 1863 granting the state of Kansas twenty sections of public lands for each mile of track completed by the Santa Fe railway.[1] Although construction of the Santa Fe line was delayed, editorial dreams were renewed by the interest of the Union Pacific in New Mexico. This company surveyed a route south from Wyoming to New Mexico and from there along the thirty-fifth and thirty-second parallels to the Pacific coast.[2] Simultaneously a Union Pacific official came to New Mexico to talk to territorial leaders and to secure information about resources that could be exploited with rail transportation, which would provide revnues for such a route.[3] At about this same time the Kansas Pacific contemplated a road to New Mexico, and the Texas Pacific was organized and planned to build its lines across southern New Mexico. The press noted these developments, and their collective attitude was seemingly in accord with that of the Santa Fe *New Mexican*:

> With these inspiring prospects in view, so far as our railroad prospects are concerned, we think we will discover a splendid career for New Mexico in the near future.[4]

Prospects for a rail connection seemed even brighter in the early seventies. The Santa Fe began construction of the eastern portion of its lines. The Denver and Rio Grande and the Atlantic and Pacific both planned lines which would pass through New Mexico. The Albuquerque *Republican Review* noted the anxiety of Missourians and Californians for the completion of the latter line and commented:

> If the people of the cities at the ends of the line are anxious for its completion, we are certain that they are no more so than the people of Arizona and New Mexico.[5]

Southern New Mexicans also had high hopes when first work began on the Texas and Pacific in 1873. At this time the Silver City *Mining Life,* noting the presence of strangers in the area who were seeking ways to profit from this new transportation, predicted: "It is evident from these 'signs of the times' that this frontier is about to wake from its lethargy and bound forward in the career of progress. Let the car roll on."[6] However, the national depression which began in 1873 forced New Mexicans to wait for several years for the realization of their dreams, and not until 1878 did the anticipations of twenty years become realities. In that year the first rails crossed the New Mexico border and brought forth an enthusiastic greeting from the Mesilla *News*: "HOOP-LA! Railroad in New Mexico. We are joined to the world by Iron Rails. Three cheers and a 'Tiger.' "[7]

Once the railways reached New Mexico, the editors began to dream of more lines. They had ample precedent for this, for most other western editors had done the same. And having seen as a result of promotional efforts that some towns grew miraculously, editorial pens projected branches in every direction, with each editor hoping that his town would become a rail and trading center. The Albuquerque *Daily Journal* looked forward to the time when Albuquerque would gain its third railway, the Denver and Rio Grande.[8] In 1882 the Albuquerque *Daily Democrat* predicted four new rail lines would soon enter the city from the east. This optimistic building of paper railways by the territorial editors continued for many years. The claims of the Albuquerque editors became so extreme that a nearby newspaper jested: "According to the Albuquerque Democrat, that city is about to experience the greatest railroad boom of modern times. Seven new roads are now being built on paper into the home of Munchausen's worthy successor."[9] The *New Mexican* was almost as bad, for that paper boasted in 1886 that "Santa Fe is destined to be a railroad center. Nearly all of the projected north and south lines take in this city as one of the points to be considered."[10] Later editorials in a similar vein apparently led the Albuquerque *Daily Citizen* to remark: "THE NEW MEXICAN has the happy faculty of corralling all of the railroads and running them right into Santa Fe and deserves the gratitude of everybody at the capital."[11] These claims led the Las Vegas *Daily Optic* to counterclaim that despite:

the boom in railroad making by our sister cities . . . we make this prediction and let our friends and enemies mark it: Las Vegas will be the first city in the territory to have a railroad connection to the east.[12]

This paper railway building continued until the end of the territorial era as a Tucumcari *Times* editorial shows:

Railroads continue to be built in New Mexico on paper. Several have sprung up in the past week and if the newspapers could only build the railroads as they map them out every town in New Mexico would have a dozen or more.[13]

Along with their anticipation of more railways the editors painted bright pictures of the rewards to be gained from them. From first to last we find optimistic claims that the railways would "swell our population, increase our wealth, and develop our vast internal resources."[14] One editor noted benefits accruing to Colorado from railroads:

Capital, labor, machinery knock at her door for admittance, manufactories are being established, . . . almost daily pleasure seekers spend their time and money at her springs. . . . With railroads our future prosperity is assured, without them all our efforts will be failures.[15]

Editors continued to make similar predictions until the twentieth century. For example, the Silver City *Grant County Herald* predicted: "If the Texas Pacific railroad bill passes the people of Silver City will advance the price of their real estate about 500 per cent. . . ."[16] The Albuquerque *Review* contended: "There will be such a rush to the territory as was only witnessed during the flush times in California, . . . [with] Albuquerque being the center of the territory and the junction of three railroads . . . is not the future bright for our flourishing little city."[17] Even in the twentieth century this expectation that prosperity followed the building of railways can be seen, for in 1900 the Santa Fe *New Mexican* predicted: "When all of these projected railroads are built in New Mexico the territory will soon catch up to Colorado, and some day to Texas as far as population and wealth are concerned."[18]

Such editorial anticipations of railways to be built and a resultant expansion of the New Mexican economy whetted the appetite of the territorial public for these developments and prepared it for the next stage, direct aid and inducement to railways.

The main forms of aid and inducement encouraged by the editors were bonuses to the railways to insure that the lines would pass through or send branches to the established towns. As early as 1878 the people of Santa Fe learned that they might have to pay heavily to be on the railway lines. That year the Denver and Rio Grande sent officials to Santa Fe to demand of the town a $200,000 cash bonus, right of way across Santa Fe County, and twenty acres in the city for a station and yard site. The city countered with an offer of $92,000 in 8 per cent bonds—all that it could legally give them under federal statutes. Perhaps the attitude of the officials of Santa Fe was stiffened by the promise of an officer of the Atchison, Topeka and Santa Fe, then present in the capital city, that within a year his railway would run its tracks into the town. The *New Mexican* believed that the offer of $92,000 was ample but apparently hoped that negotiations would not be broken off, for it added:

> The citizens of Santa Fe are prudent for long years of adversity have made them so, but we feel satisfied that they will not be outdone in liberality; and if these railroads pursue a noble and generous course toward them, they will respond in like spirit.[19]

The Denver and Rio Grande never built into Santa Fe, and the people of that town soon realized what would be required of them to enjoy rail connections, for the Santa Fe railway gave them an example with its treatment of Las Vegas. Before coming to Las Vegas the railway demanded of the town a bonus of $10,000, right of way through the Las Vegas grant, 20 acres for a depot and yards, and 400 acres for a townsite. The Las Vegas *Gazette* objected to the plan: "We favor giving the company all asked for except the last proposition. That is the dead fly in the ointment. It is suicidal to the town."[20] The *New Mexican* also was hostile to the proposal:

> The exorbitant demands of the Atchison, Topeka and Santa Fe road upon the people of Las Vegas as a condition of establishing a depot near the town, is denounced generally by the territorial press, and will result in the outgrowth of feeling not at all favorable to the road and its managers. The propostion smacks too much of the highwayman's "stand and deliver," to meet with favor anywhere; and the citizens of Las Vegas we think are hardly the kind to be bullied into improverishing themselves for the benefit of a grasping corporation.[21]

The people of Las Vegas gave the railway most of the concessions demanded, so that the new town of Las Vegas grew up on the stipulated townsite between the original town and the railway station. Other New Mexico towns, therefore, knew well in advance what might be required of them to enjoy rail connections.[22] Santa Fe, however, had an even more difficult problem with which to deal. Because of the steep grades into the capital city, the railroad decided to pass by the town. Realizing that this might mean the ultimate extinction of Santa Fe, the *New Mexican* sought to induce the citizens to vote for bonds with which to pay part of the cost of building a branch line into Santa Fe:

> The extra cost of making Santa Fe a station is indeed a proper subject of consideration; and no doubt there is justice in Santa Fe considering the equity of bearing a portion of the extra cost. As Santa Fe interests would be specifically benefitted . . . there would be good business sense in fairly meeting the logic of the situation.[23]

Other territorial editors, realizing the danger to Santa Fe, also approved of the bond issue:

> The 4th day of October next will decide whether Santa Fe will have a railroad or not. Only $150,000 in bonds are required for the building of the road and assuring the prosperity of the Holy City. It is hinted, however, that the bonds will meet considerable opposition, but we can hardly give credence to such a report. The people are too intelligent to commit such a fault knowing it would be the destruction of the city.[24]

Even before this branch line was completed, Santa Fe learned that it was not to be on the line of the Denver and Rio Grande, for that line had made an agreement with the Atchison, Topeka and Santa Fe to build no farther south in New Mexico than Espanola. However, the citizens of Santa Fe, undaunted by this began the organization of a company—the Texas, Santa Fe, and Northern—to build a line to connect their city with the Denver and Rio Grande and hoped eventually to extend this line south to Laredo, Texas. Santa Fe County was again asked to vote bonds, but this time the measure was defeated. The *New Mexican* opposed the bond issue, probably because the paper was now the property of major stockholders of the Santa Fe Railway. Later, however, the *New Mexican Review,* under a new ownership, endorsed the issuance of $250,000 in bonds for this project, and the voters approved.[25] Albuquerque was the next objective of the Texas, Santa Fe, and Northern, and the Albuquerque papers endorsed the raising of money and voting of bonds to aid in construction of the line.[26]

Throughout the territorial era newspapers continued to support bond issues and subsidies for railroads to induce them to come to their towns. For example, in 1909, when a line from Fort Worth to Albuquerque was planned, Lubbock, Hereford, and Roswell offered $100,000 each to the railway to build through their towns. The Portales *Roosevelt County*

*Herald* asked fellow townsmen to make a similar offer: ". . . why may not Portales have the new road? We can do it if we will, but will we? Other towns are acting, shall we not do something and do it now?"[27] Thus, it can be seen that the territorial press quickly turned from dreams of railway-induced prosperity to the practical reality of insuring that this prosperity would flow into their towns. In so doing the editors were wise, for the railroads, knowing that they had the power to destroy or insure the prosperity of these small towns, sought to gain for themselves or their stockholders part of the increased real estate values accruing to rail centers. Consequently the editors realistically fought for the railway bonuses, for the alternative was eventual ruin for their towns.

While the territorial press cooperated fully in securing bonuses for railway construction, it was an unrelenting critic of other unjust railway practices. For example, when the legislature in 1878 sought to encourage the building of railroads into New Mexico by establishing maximum rates of ten cents per mile for passengers and fifteen cents per mile per ton of freight, some papers immediately attacked the policy. The Mesilla *Valley Independent* commented that this rate was exceptionally high since in most states maximum passenger rates were three cents a mile.[28] In 1882 the Santa Fe *Democrat* urged the legislature to lower these rates to: "rid the Territory of the monopoly, thraldom, and unjust discrimination of our railroads."[29] Passenger rates were evidently lowered to six cents per mile at this time, for two years later efforts were made to further reduce them to three cents. The Las Vegas *Daily Optic* approved: "We think the Santa Fe company can now afford to carry passengers for three cents a mile."[30] The legislature never approved of the three-cent rate, but one railway had not yet complied with the six-cent rate several years later. In 1888 the *Daily Optic* noted: "The Southern Pacific Railroad pays no attention to the Territorial statute but continues to charge 10 cents per mile in New Mexico. The road ought to be compelled to observe the requirements of the law."[31] At length the Santa Fe voluntarily reduced its rates to four cents per passenger mile, and the *New Mexican* called on the other carriers serving the territory to follow suit.[32] Press criticism here appears to have been of some aid in reducing unjust rail rates.

Other unfair practices, such as higher rates for short hauls than for long hauls, also were attacked by the territorial press. The Lordsburg *Advance* noted this policy of the Southern Pacific and told its readers that they could have freight from the east consigned to someone in California and reshipped to them for less than the rate from the east into Lordsburg.[33] Because three lines competed for freight shipments to El Paso, it cost less to ship to that point than to New Mexico towns. The Las Cruces *Rio Grande Republican* called attention to this and conducted a campaign to lower the rate between Las Cruces and El Paso. At length this paper boasted: "Truly the RIO GRANDE REPUBLICAN is accomplishing much for shippers here. It is but a short time since we had the rates from El Paso reduced 800 per cent (from $2.70 to 33¢). . . ."[34] Other New Mexico papers noted the much higher cost of shipping freight east than west. As an illustration, the Albuquerque *Morning Journal* reported that: "It cost $33 a ton to ship hay to Albuquerque from Las Cruces, while it can be brought from Kansas for $12."[35] Although a few unfair practices of the Santa Fe railway may have been corrected, there were still abuses on some lines as late as 1908. In that year, for example, the Santa Rosa *Sun* cited instances of lower rates from Chicago to El Paso than for the shorter distance from Chicago to Santa Rosa.[36] Since discriminatory rates still prevailed in 1908, apparently the the chief contribution of the territorial press was that of adding its voice to the general clamor of the American press, which led to the strengthening of the Interstate Commerce Commission to combat such practices.

Other editorial criticism affecting the railways voiced the objection of some editors to the special tax advantages extended to railroads in 1878. The legislature in that year voted to exempt railways from taxation for the first six years after they were completed, apparently hoping to induce lines to build into New Mexico. The Mesilla *Valley Independent* noted that this bill was being considered and admonished the legislature to reject it, contending that if railways could not make a profit in New Mexico they should not come.[37] The Silver City *Grant County Herald* agreed with this and maintained also that such legislation would not induce a railway to build into New Mexico that had not already intended to do so. This paper also charged that a railroad lobby must have secured the enactment of the law, but this proved to be only partially true.[38]

In 1883 and 1884 Santa Fe and Grant counties sought, despite the law, to collect taxes from the railways, maintaining that the act of 1878 was void because a congressional act of 1867 forbade territories to give railways special privileges. The papers of both counties thoroughly approved of this action of the county officials, but the territorial courts upheld the act of 1878 on the basis that it was a contract and that tax exemption was not a special privilege.[39] Despite the protests of the press, consequently, the railroads were given the benefit of the law of 1878. This law was repealed in 1887 at the instigation of the press, but a similar act was passed in 1893 and evidently remained in effect until statehood.[40]

The Santa Fe *New Mexican* strongly favored the re-enactment of the law, and there was little apparent objection from the rest of the territorial press.[41] Since New Mexico was in a period of economic depression in 1893, the editors probably were ready to agree to any move that might bring a measure of economic relief to the territory. Possibly the *New Mexican* was right in favoring this, since three large railways were subsequently built by promoters who had very little capital.[42] This act may have helped them to acquire needed capital and hastened railway construction in New Mexico. Perhaps the editors were right in both cases, for it does not appear that the special tax advantage induced the Santa Fe, the Southern Pacific, and the Atlantic and Pacific to build in New Mexico—other considerations had motivated them more and earlier. On the other hand, since most of the railways constructed after 1893 were started by small independent companies, this law may have been instrumental in speeding their construction.

The contribution of the press to this phase of the economic development of New Mexico appears to have been significant, for railways gave a great impetus to territorial growth. Thus, any aid the press could give toward obtaining them was worthwhile. Similarly, in favoring bonuses for railroads for putting the stations near the established towns, the press took a realistic attitude, preventing the extinction of these towns and great losses to their citizens. Finally, editorial criticism of unjust rates and practices probably helped to bring some immediate relief to New Mexicans and became a part of the general clamor of the American press and thus served to impress the federal government with the necessity of action. While press action concerning railways may not always have been beneficial to the whole public, it did help to speed the economic development of New Mexico which benefitted all the public.

The introduction of rail transportation hastened the development of mining, one of New Mexico's major industries in the territorial years. The lure of mineral wealth has played an important part in the history of New Mexico, bringing first, Spanish explorers, and finally in 1598, its first permanent settlers. Mining operations in the Spanish and Mexican periods failed to produce great riches, but there was enough evidence of precious metals that the earliest Anglo-American inhabitants saw this as the principal route for the development of New Mexico.

The first mining camp opened in the American era apparently was that at Pinos Altos, on the Gila River northwest of present-day Silver City. While mining there was halted by the Civil War and the Indian wars that followed, territorial mining was rapidly expanded in the postwar period. Operations were resumed at Pinos Altos, and in 1866 a gold strike in the Moreno Valley led to the founding of Elizabethtown. A few years later silver was discovered in southwestern New Mexico, which led to the founding of towns at Ralston, 1869, Silver City, 1870, and Georgetown, 1874. When railways came to the territory, a large number of new miners came into this area. As a result, intensive development of mines near Socorro began in 1880, and before 1884 new discoveries had led to the opening of camps at Robinson, Lake Valley, Kingston, Chloride, and Hillsboro. Although this area, the Chloride district, produced a great deal of silver throughout the territorial era, its greatest production came before the decline in silver prices. Meanwhile, gold mines were discovered at White Oaks. After the initial discovery there in 1879, the camp soon attracted over 2,000 people. During these same years following the construction of the railways, many other discoveries were made in northern New Mexico at Hell's Canyon, Cerrillos, San Pedro, Wallace, Golden, Amizett, Labelle, Red River, and Tecolote.

While these discoveries of precious metals were being exploited, minerals of a different type were being developed. The need of the railways for coal led to the exploitation of New Mexico's ample resources, first at Raton, then at Cerrillos, Gallup, and Carthage, southeast of Socorro. Late in the territorial era the people of the San Juan Valley expected the huge coal resources of their area to be developed, but a lack of transportation prevented this. However, the needs of Arizona copper mines for coking coal led to the opening of mines at Capitan and Dawson. Evidences of another common fuel, oil, were discovered quite early, for in 1882 newsmen noted its presence in small quantities at Coolidge. However, lack of markets held back the development of this resource in northwestern New Mexico, and the first extensive oil development began near Artesia only in 1909. Meanwhile, the mining of precious metals had almost come to an end without New Mexico's ever having enjoyed a great boom such as that which had brought a flood of population into California and Colorado. Nevertheless, New Mexicans in 1912 were optimistic that the development of the mineral fuels would provide the major industry which the state needed for prosperity.

The role of the press in aiding the growth of the territorial mining industry took three forms. The first, and earliest, was the effort to induce prospectors and investors to come into New Mexico to open mines. The second stage was the announcement of exciting mineral discoveries, which, through the system of newspaper exchanges, spread the news far and wide and brought a rush of miners into New Mexico. Finally, the press encouraged importation of capital for the full development of the mines. This took the form of routine reporting of the general mining news of their areas to induce capitalists to invest in New Mexico mines, and the encouragement of the building of smelters, exhibits at mineral fairs, and government geological surveys, all of which would aid the mining industry. It was in this last stage that the press made its most valuable contribution, and at some sacrifice, for where the first two stages presented news copy of great and general interest, the last stage included a great deal of dull and routine reporting uninteresting to the general reader.

The first stage of press participation in the development of territorial mineral resources began with the initial issue of the first English-language newspaper of New Mexico. The editor of the Santa Fe *Republican* held out the prospect of a rapid advance for New Mexico from mining development:

It is admitted by all that this country is rich in mineral wealth, and it is an equally admitted fact that large districts, rich not only in the precious metals, but iron, coal and other productions, have been neglected and suffered to retain their hidden treasures on account of the Indian tribes that infest the country.—Let peace be restored . . . then the wealth of New Mexico can begin to show itself. . . . Obtain scientific miners from the United States, let some old miners come here and but make a commencement, and we will soon have more prosperity in New Mexico than in any state subject to the rule of Santa Ana.[43]

Almost twenty years later the Santa Fe *New Mexican* noted that extensive prospecting for minerals had begun, and as a result the immigration which all territorial editors desired would begin and miners and others would pour into New Mexico, for:

New discoveries of mineral wealth during the past year . . . when fully developed will almost surpass human credibility. A new empire of wealth west of the Rio Grande is springing into the knowledge of the people and will add an additional encouragement to an enterprising imigration to settle in New Mexico. . . . These mines are equally, if not more, valuable than the mines of California and Colorado, and far more easily worked.[44]

In 1866 mining also began at Elizabethtown, although the great impetus to territorial mining actually came in southwestern New Mexico. With the dissemination of the news of the rich mines at Silver Cty, the long-awaited immigration to the territory began. The enthusiastic reports of the Silver City mines in the Las Cruces *Borderer* probably helped to spread this news. This paper used three-quarters of its first page in one issue to describe the mines and listed assays of the ores being produced, most of which were from $1,000 to $8,000 per ton.[45] Thus, editorial desires for mineral development, with the expected surge in immigration that would accompany it, led the press to make repeated optimistic predictions about impending discoveries or real discoveries of mines in New Mexico. Such stories encouraged hardy prospectors to come to New Mexico and to persevere in their efforts to find mineral wealth.

The discoveries at Silver City led the press into the second stage of encouragement to the mining industry, the announcement of the exciting discoveries. Editors often resorted to extravagant claims to hasten the growth of their towns. For example, the San Pedro *Golden 9 Nine* claimed:

> When a man buys a San Pedro town lot at a nominal figure, washes about $1,000 in placer gold in his back yard, and strikes a lead in his cellar he isn't taking long chances. . . .
> People planning to move to San Pedro, bring a tent or wagon cover etc. with which to improvise a tent to live in . . . no for let signs here.[46]

The general public was always eager to believe such stories, as was shown by an incident at Las Vegas in 1883. Here workmen digging a foundation for a new courthouse in West Las Vegas quit work and filed a mining claim on the lot on which the courthouse was being constructed.[47] Apparently this was nothing more than a plot of East Las Vegas citizens to halt the construction of the courthouse until they could have it moved to their town. However, more than 600 of the people of Las Vegas rushed into the nearby hills to file mining claims and gold rushees flocked into town. The *Daily Optic* was apparently torn between a desire to stop the foolishness and a hope that gold would be found and bring a tremendous growth to the town:

> It has arrived at the point where it behooves the people of Las Vegas to bestir themselves to find a foundation for the mining boom that is upon us. Every train brings a score or more of men into our city—men who have read the glowing accounts of the recent gold strikes in newspapers far and near, and it will not do to sit idly in our offices and residences and be surprised to see them come. Let us give evidence of the faith that is in us by rolling up our sleeves and going into the mountains with these men.[48]

The attitude of the Las Vegas *Daily Optic* was characteristic of most territorial editors; they hesitated to report less than the best estimate of any new discovery, fearing that they would be blamed for retarding the growth of their town and its mines. Nevertheless, editors occasionally recognized that they had a duty to avoid exaggeration. For example, the Santa Fe *New Mexican* wrote: "Newspapers which believed that by lying extravagantly about the mines of a district nearby they are benefitting it make a great mistake." This provoked the Silver City *Daily Southwest* to reply: "Why then do you keep up the practice?"[49] The Las Cruces *Rio Grande Republican* held that such exaggeration was not only harmful but futile:

> The bare assertion so often made by the newspapers of this Territory . . . that New Mexico is "the gold seekers goal"; that it "contains more gold and silver than Colorado and Nevada," &c. is not helping the mining interests of the territory. Capital seeking a field for investment is not attracted by such state-

ments as these. They are naturally regarded as an attempt to puff life into
something that has no existence in fact. These papers can do more good by
looking up the news and stating the facts of the discoveries and developments
leaving capitalists to draw their own conclusions.[50]

To make matters worse, some papers published news stories which
clearly exaggerated the value of some mines, apparently in the hope of
luring prospective purchasers. This service was a form of advertising
for which the mine owner paid, and was used in the 1880s by the Albuquerque *Morning Democrat,* the Albuquerque *Morning Journal,* the
Santa Fe *New Mexican,*[51] and possibly others.

Thus, in this stage of press interest in mining, editors freely indulged
in exaggeration and sometimes published paid propaganda as news
stories to hasten population growth and induce the importation of
capital for the development of territorial mineral resources. At length,
however, they realized that territorial mineral development would be
aided best by factual stories about New Mexico mines. This change of
attitude ushered in the third stage of press interest in mines, their encouragement of capital investment for full mineral development.

By the mid-eighties most New Mexico papers had begun a routine
factual coverage of the development of the mining camps, often devoting a large portion of their space to this practice. Their intent was to
advertise the camp to attract both capital and new miners. Considering
the widespread use of exchanged papers as news sources, their stories
were often spread far beyond their towns. A quotation from the Chicago
*Mining Review* illustrates the influence of their efforts:

> The chief factor of the development of the mining industry in any locality
> is the unappreciated and usually poorly sustained local paper. The true value
> of the mining claims, the advantages to capitalists, the rich strikes of well con-
> ducted properties all fail of their legitimate influence if the fact is not made
> known outside the narrow circle of isolated localities.[52]

Another way in which the territorial press sought to aid miners lay in
its efforts to induce local businessmen to build smelters or custom mills,
which would enable the smaller mines with low-grade ores to operate
profitably. The papers at Silver City, Las Cruces, and Albuquerque apparently helped to raise capital to erect such facilities.[53] In addition,
newspapers provided leadership for efforts to obtain aid in the form
of mineral surveys, the promotion of territorial mining by the preparation of entries in mineral fairs,[54] and by their long fight for free silver.[55]

On the whole, it appears that the territorial press made a substantial
contribution to the advancement of the New Mexico mining industry.
This was done first by encouraging the patient prospectors to come and
make the initial discoveries, then by reporting accurate factual details

which led capitalists to invest funds to fully develop the mines, and finally by asking for government and private aid to miners. Even though New Mexico never experienced a boom such as those of California and Colorado, mining was one of its chief industries during most of the territorial period, and the press had aided the territorial economy by helping to make mining a major New Mexico industry.

Although the livestock industry of New Mexico provided a very large portion of the territorial income throughout this era, the press had a great deal less interest in livestock production than in the mining industry. Perhaps this was true because the chance of sudden wealth from mining and the resultant great immigration into the territory made the editors more eager to encourage it. What interest the press had for the livestock industry was in four areas. First there was the effort to encourage the development of better sheep breeds. Next, came an invitation from the press to cattlemen to take advantage of the vast unoccupied ranges in New Mexico. Following this, there was an attempt to improve cattle breeds and to foster the organization of a cattlemen's association, which was encouraged to defend the interests of the New Mexico cattle industry. Finally, the editors became concerned with the manner in which the ranchers used the public domain—offering both criticism and a defense of the ranchers. Nevertheless, throughout this period the general territorial press devoted a relatively small amount of its space to the livestock industry.

When New Mexico was annexed to the United States, sheep raising was its principal industry. These sheep were generally of poor quality, raised more for mutton than wool. Although there had been some cattle raising in New Mexico from the days of the earliest Spanish settlements, cattle ranching did not become important until the 1870s. Then Texas cattlemen, who had driven cattle into New Mexico in the 1860s to sell to mining camps, military posts, and Indian reservations, began to establish ranches. However, until the 1880s the territorial cattle industry lagged far behind that of many western states because of a shortage of water and the distance from markets. But with the advent of the railways and the pre-emption of the free range in many other areas, New Mexican grassland became well stocked with cattle.

By 1882 the large cattle companies were seeking to crowd out the small rancher and sheep raiser by fencing large areas of the public domain. The territorial cattle industry continued to grow in the following years, despite declining prices in 1884 and the severe winters of 1886 and 1887 that had discouraged ranchers elsewhere.[56] By 1893, however, New Mexico ranges were understocked and remained so until the early years of the twentieth century. Nevertheless, in this decade territorial livestock growers were confronted with new difficulties. Laws forbidding fencing of the public domain, which had been enacted in 1885, were at length enforced by the national government, and an advancing wave of homesteaders into eastern New Mexico pre-empted some of the best range. In addition, ranchers faced the prospect of a federal law to force them to lease the public domain they had long used free of charge. All of these seemed to indicate a sharp curtailment of the livestock industry in the final territorial years. By this time, however, the press had lost much of its interest in the livestock industry and had turned to the more fascinating subject of dry farming, which the editors hoped would make the ranges into farms and triple the population of the territory.

The earliest display of interest in the livestock industry by the territorial editors was their effort to improve the quality of New Mexico sheep. To illustrate, the Santa Fe *New Mexican* in 1870 urged the importation of rams which would improve the wool production of territorial sheep.[57] Later this paper took note when sheepmen imported such rams, which also encouraged increased wool production.[58] The Las Vegas *Daily Optic* became interested in sheep culture for a short time and cited examples of profits of 100 per cent or more made possible with the better breeds of sheep available.[59] Otherwise, the sheep industry elicited few comments from the general press from 1880 until 1890, and only then because the wool tariff had become a political issue. However, sheep raising remained important, for a report of the territorial government in 1900 noted that sheep outnumbered cattle in New Mexico 4,000,000 to 1,000,000. Furthermore, in 1907 the *New Mexican* estimated that the territorial per capita income from sheep was almost $40 annually.[60]

Despite the predominance of sheep in numbers and apparently as providers of income, the territorial press after 1880 made cattle the subject of most of their news stories and editorials about the livestock industry. For example, the Cimarron *News and Press* in January, 1880, published an extensive editorial which invited cattlemen to take advantage of the excellent grasslands nearby and described the profits that could be made from cattle production—profits of over 250 per cent during a five-year period.[61] The Albuquerque *Daily Journal* in scattered editorials in 1881 and 1882 reported the rise of the cattle industry in New Mexico, predicting annual profits of almost 200 per cent once the rancher was well established. In addition, this paper pointed to the advantages of the mild New Mexico winters.[62] The Las Cruces *Rio Grande Republican* stated that cattle, which were being forced out of Texas, Kansas, and California by an increase in farming in those states, would be welcomed in New Mexico and would never be molested by farmers. Furthermore, the editor optimistically predicted that the cattle would "by their natural increase compel [the cattleman] to become wealthy in spite of himself."[63] The Las Vegas *Daily Optic* also extended such an invitation in 1884 and denied that New Mexico ranges were over-stocked—such deceiving statements were by stockmen who wanted all the range to themselves. But even then territorial ranges were apparently well stocked, for in 1887 the *Daily Optic* contended that the New Mexico ranges were fully occupied.[64] Since ranges throughout the West were overstocked by 1887, probably the growth of the New Mexico cattle industry was more the result of a national trend than the efforts of these editors. Nevertheless it may be concluded that by their invitation the editors had helped to bring cattlemen to New Mexico.

Almost simultaneously with their enticements to new cattlemen the editors began to recommend the importation of better cattle for breeding purposes. The Cimarron *News and Press* in 1880 noted the prospect of overstocking the range and recommended that ranchers buy more pro-ductive cattle which would return the same profits on less land.[65] Subse-quently other editors noted with praise the importation of high-quality range bulls, and thus fostered breeding improvements.[66] The press retained its interest in better breeding; for example, in 1899 the Silver City *Independent* reminded cattlemen that the surest way to increase cattle profits was to improve cattle breeds.[67] The editors made a worth-while contribution, for the improvement of cattle breeds provided in-creased profits while the earlier encouragement of cattle raising had led to a disastrous overstocking.

Another contribution of the press to the cattle industry was its sup-port of efforts to organize local and territorial associations of cattle-men.[68] Later the editors asked these associations to oppose the move-ment of Texas cattle into New Mexico by asking for rigid enforcement of the territorial cattle-quarantine law. Apparently this was wise, since herds had infected New Mexico cattle with Texas fever.[69] When the editors learned, as the result of a congressional investigation, that a combination of meat packers was conspiring to reduce the price of cattle, they asked for federal action against the packers. Here again the press sought to alert the cattlemen to dangers threatening their in-dustry and to arouse public support for governmental policies favor-able to ranchers.[70]

On the other hand, a few editors did not hesitate to criticize unjust actions of some cattlemen. The San Lorenzo *Red River Chronicle*, for example, censured the larger cattle companies for illegal homesteading which took away water rights from smaller ranchers. This paper also noted the consolidation of the range by these large cattle companies and suggested a cooperative system to protect the rights of the small ranchers.[71] Few editors approved of another bad practice, the illegal fencing of public lands. The *Red River Chronicle*, for one, condemned this and contended that "no man has a right to take what is not his own."[72] The Silver City *Enterprise* also objected to this practice and held that small cattlemen had "the same right to grass and water as the larger cattlemen who have the means to fence."[73] Many editors, on the other hand, sympathized with the building of drift fences, which prevented cattle from drifting and made roundups easier.[74] However, in the end the editors asked a vigorous enforcement of the law against fencing the public domain because such fences retarded the settlement of the much more desirable homesteaders.[75] In this instance the press probably had little influence on the ranchers, but it did contribute to the general clamor of the American press which led the federal government to forbid the fencing of the public lands and much later to the enforcement of the law.

Another controversial issue concerning the public lands was the prospect that the federal government would charge a rental for their use. When Texas began to lease public range, the *New Mexican* held that the application of this policy in New Mexico would retard immigration since it was having that effect in Texas.[76] The Socorro *Chieftain* vigorously opposed the lease plan. Its main objection was that under such a plan larger ranchers would be able to force out the smaller ones.[77] The Silver City *Enterprise,* on the other hand, favored such a law since it legalized fencing. With fenced ranges, ranchers would reduce operating costs, conserve grass, develop better watering facilities, and purchase better breeding stock, since they had the assurance they would be the chief beneficiaries of that breeding stock.[78] The Hillsboro *Sierra County Advocate,* which had already noted the advantages cited by the *Enterprise,* held that they did not offset other disadvantages of the lease law. It maintained that such a law would be harmful to small ranchers, would discourage homesteaders, and that the fencing, which in many cases would cost more than the value of the land, would impose a heavy tax burden on the ranchers.[79] In general, the editors opposed the enactment of a federal lease law until it became apparent that such a law was inevitable.[80] Since the lease law eventually enacted provided a very low rental and favored the small over the large rancher, apparently the attitude of the territorial press, again as a part of the general western press, had helped to guide the federal government toward a policy favorable to the livestock industry.

Thus, it appears that the territorial press had been an able champion and protector of the New Mexican livestock industry. It had first invited the ranchmen to exploit the vast territorial public domain. Then it had asked for justice for small ranchers in the use of these public lands, encouraged improvement of livestock breeds, endorsed the forming of cattlemen's associations, and urged these groups to act against threats to their industry. Finally, it became their advocate before the federal government, aiding the ranchers' efforts either to defeat range lease laws or at least to obtain very low rates.

The territorial press always found irrigation a more engrossing subject than the livestock industry. Perhaps this was true because the overly optimistic editors foresaw millions upon millions of acres being farmed through irrigation with a consequently large territorial population. To illustrate, in 1905 the Santa Fe *New Mexican* wrote that if New Mexico river valleys had a population density of one-half that of the valley of the Nile, the population of the territory would exceed 12,500,000.[81] Naturally, with such population growth would come statehood and increasing wealth for all New Mexicans. Other pioneer editors shared this optimistic view and consequently were irrigation enthusiasts.

When the Anglo-American editors arrived in New Mexico, they found irrigation already extensively practiced. Irrigation was very old in New Mexico, for evidence exists of prehistoric civilizations that used extensive systems of ditches to bring water from the mountains to the plains of southern New Mexico. The Pueblo Indians were farming with irrigation when the Spanish arrived, although the Spanish friars, through knowledge gained from the Moors in Spain, helped the Indians to improve their practices. Furthermore, many of the Spanish settlers who came to the area established small irrigated farms. The first Anglo-American editor noted this relatively widespread practice and told of an extensive grape culture along the Rio Grande between El Paso and Santa Fe.[82] At this time exploitation of the Rio Grande waters for irrigation of the Mesilla Valley began.[83] In the Pecos Valley, on the other hand, irrigation apparently was limited to small plots near Anton Chico, San Miguel, and Las Vegas. Then in the 1870s the waters of the Pecos began to be used at Puerto de Luna and by L. B. Maxwell, who had purchased the lands cleared by the Navajo at Fort Sumner. Even earlier irrigated farms had been established on the Bonito, Ruidoso, and Hondo rivers. Through the 1880s new lands were placed under irrigation on the Mimbres River, in the Maxwell Land Grant, and in the San Juan River Valley. By 1889, the irrigated areas of New Mexico were still relatively small, probably between 25,000 and 35,000 acres in all.[84] All irrigation up to this time was by means of ditches leading out of the rivers to water the lands at lower levels. It was in 1889 that there came the first large projects using reservoirs for storing flood waters for irrigation.

After 1889 there was a tremendous increase in irrigation acreages cultivated with waters made available through the construction of large reservoirs. The first project was started on the lower Pecos by Charles W. Greene, Pat Garrett, and C. B. Eddy. This group successfully interested prominent capitalists in their projects, which included a canal from the Rio Hondo to water lands south of Roswell and storage reservoirs near Eddy on the Pecos and Black rivers. Altogether, these projects irrigated 200,000 acres.

While these projects were being developed in the 1890s, there was an extensive exploration for artesian waters. The success of this search made irrigation water available for another large block of land on the lower Pecos.[85] Elsewhere in the territory there was only a slight increase in irrigated lands. Thus, by 1900 there were probably 250,000 acres under irrigation, but after 1900 the pace of development quickened. The Maxwell Land Grant Company soon placed 12,000 acres under irrigation, irrigated acreages in the San Juan Valley became extensive, and several thousand acres were placed under irrigation near Tularosa. The artesian water district near Roswell was found to extend beneath 200 square miles of land, and a great deal of the surface of this land came under irrigation before 1912. In addition, in the last territorial years the extensive use of pumps to extract water from strata of ground water near the surface made possible irrigation at Deming, Portales, and in the Pecos and Rio Grande valleys. Finally, storage reservoirs under construction or approved for the Mesilla Valley and on the Gallinas at Las Vegas promised to add over 120,000 acres of irrigated land after 1912. Thus, by 1912 New Mexico had made a great start toward developing the 650,000 acres of irrigated lands that it would have by mid-century.

The territorial press played a leading part in encouraging the development of irrigation in New Mexico. First of all, the press aroused and sustained territorial interest in the irrigation prospects of New Mexico. At the same time it cooperated with the national irrigation movement in its studies and efforts to secure federal government aid for irrigation. In addition, the press worked very hard to promote specific projects in New Mexico. When stream water was unavailable or in short supply, the editors encouraged efforts to develop ground waters from both deep artesian strata and strata nearer the surface. Throughout the territorial era the press exerted a consistent effort to encourage full development of the territorial irrigation potential.

In their efforts to advance the area, the Anglo-American editors from the first pointed out the value of irrigation. For example, the Santa Fe *Republican* in its earliest editorials noted the advantage of irrigation over ordinary farming, for with irrigation "every man, with the least possible trouble, makes his own season, and never fails, either by too much or too little rain, to have a liberal crop."[86] Later editors continued to ask for exploitation of the irrigation potential of New Mexico. The Santa Fe *New Mexican* in 1868 pointed out: "There are thousands on thousands of acres of the public domain in this territory, which, if Congress would but foster irrigation, might in a few years become fruitful and rich; the homes of thousands of thriving and hardy farmers."[87] A few years later the Albuquerque *Republican Review* asked for local action:

There is a place in front of La Joyita, in this county, where with little trouble half the water of the Rio Grande could be taken off, or at least enough to irrigate the whole of the western half of the valley from Alamillo down to . . . Fort Craig.[88]

Throughout the remaining territorial years the interest of the press in irrigation continued to grow. In 1885 the Santa Fe *New Mexican* sought to introduce it into a political campaign: "Works pertaining to irrigation as carried on in Colorado and California are in great demand throughout New Mexico at this time. The prospective candidates for the legislature are studying up on the subject."[89] Another editor foresaw that through irrigation New Mexico could gain wealth and population: "The Rio Grande Valley alone, within the limits of the territory, properly irrigated is capable of sustaining a population of half a million people."[90] Allowing precious water to flow unused down to sea seemed a crime to these editors: "If the water that annually goes to waste in this territory was saved, it would be sufficient to irrigate thousands of acres more of land."[91] In addition, the editors often published articles from national publications or by national irrigation authorities to increase interest in irrigation.[92] The pace of irrigation development after 1900 became more rapid; however, the editors did not assume that their job was completed but continued to push for more irrigation. For example, in 1904 the *New Mexican* denied that there were no further opportunities for private irrigation investment in the territory but asserted that there were more such opportunities in New Mexico than anywhere else in the world. Later the Las Cruces *Rio Grande Republican* noted:

The engineer who a decade ago declared that the available water in New Mexico would reclaim only 250,000 acres, should read the first biennial report of Territorial Irrigation Engineer Vernon L. Sullivan. During the past two years he has approved irrigation projects to cover 800,000 acres and there are applications for water rights pending to cover more than a million acres in addition.[93]

Although the press was an enthusiastic supporter of irrigation, it retained a practical attitude, warning against the possibility of fraud in some projects. As an illustration, the *Daily Optic* of Las Vegas stated:

There are quite a number of mammoth irrigation schemes projected and underway in New Mexico. . . . This system of enterprise, like nearly all others, presents opportunities for combinations of adventurers to perpetrate frauds and work up wildcat schemes which, if not exposed, will do much injury to legitimate irrigation enterprises. . . . It should be the duty of the press to watch combinations of this character and ruthlessly expose them when detected in crooked methods.[94]

Editors also showed their practicality by recognizing that new crops would be required to provide ample rewards for the high expense of irrigation farming. As early as 1866 the Santa Fe *Weekly Gazette* foresaw that railways would import the cheaper grain of the plains into New Mexico and argued that territorials should anticipate this by a wider adoption of grape culture and wine making.[95] The Santa Fe *New Mexican* continued this campaign for grape culture,[96] and in 1894 the Socorro *Chieftain* maintained: "Fruit will make New Mexico as it has California."[97] In 1904 the *New Mexican* encouraged efforts to raise cotton in the lower Pecos Valley;[98] and in 1910 the Portales *Roosevelt County Herald,* anticipating an irrigation project nearby, sought to sign up sugar beet growers to induce a sugar refinery to locate at that town.[99]

The territorial press did not confine its efforts to the encouragement of private irrigation projects alone but sought to promote cooperation with other western states and territories to obtain federal aid for irrigation. One of the first movements of this type, the formation of a committee of western territorial congressional delegates to work for irrigation, was praised by the Santa Fe *New Mexican.*[100] This paper also became very interested in two irrigation meetings of the western territories called by Colorado in 1873. The *New Mexican* maintained that since:

New Mexico is as much, and we think more, interested in the subject of irrigation than any other state or territory, and certainly has a larger practical experience in this direction than any other portion of the United States, it becomes generally important to the general question, that she should have not only an intelligent delegation, but the convention should have the benefit of the experience of all parts of the territory.[101]

When the series of national irrigation congresses began, the territorial press enthusiastically supported them. For example, the editors called the territorial press convention to meet on the same date as the territorial irrigation congress and then endorsed its actions, as the following quotation shows:

THE OPTIC heartily approves of the stand taken by the irrigation convention, in asking for the cession of the arid lands. . . . The cry of the opposition that the plan conceals a gigantic scheme for theft has no terror for our ears. . . . THE OPTIC doubts the settlement of New Mexico under the 160 acre tract law. Water cannot be developed that way, and without water the land is next to worthless.[102]

Throughout the years the press continued to follow the activities of the territorial and national irrigation meetings, for the editors believed, as the Santa Fe *New Mexican* declared in 1906:

New Mexico is more vitally interested in the irrigation congress than ever before. It owes to it indirectly the eight million dollars which the reclamation service is expending and will expend on the irrigation projects on the lower Hondo, the lower Pecos, the Rio Grande and elsewhere in the territory. . . . How important, therefore, that New Mexico send a large and strong delegation to the congress at Boise this year! It is a business proposition.[103]

While the press was offering a general encouragement to the development of irrigation projects along the New Mexico rivers, some papers were making vigorous fights in behalf of projects to serve their own areas. The best examples of editorial efforts to promote irrigation in a specific area were those made by the Mesilla Valley papers. In the Mesilla Valley there was a large acreage of rich, irrigable lands, but efforts to expand the irrigated area were blocked by an inefficient system and resistance to change by some landowners of the valley. Meanwhile, there was an almost constant threat that others lower down the river might gain a prior right to the water and prevent full development of the Mesilla Valley. The Mesilla *Valley Independent* began in 1877 a fight to improve irrigation in the valley, noting its inefficient ditch system and suggesting that a reservoir be built a few miles upstream.[104] After the Las Cruces *Rio Grande Republican* was founded, it took up this fight for irrigation improvement: "The valley needs a more extended and better regulated system by which water may be provided for irrigation purposes." This paper also suggested that a reservoir be built on the river north of the valley and warned that if the people of the valley did not act, farmers of the El Paso area might pre-empt the water needed for irrigation expansion.[105] A few years later a company was formed to build a reservoir, but those who held prior water rights in the valley objected that the plan would increase their costs and require a large new investment by them. The objectors then requested an investigation of the project by the Interior Department. Years of delay followed, and the capitalists abandoned the proposal, despite approval of the project and assurances of its feasibility by the Interior Department. In this period the *Rio Grande Republican* argued, reasoned, and pled for the removal of all obstructions to the plan.[106]

While the obstructionists were defeating plans for a dam north of Las Cruces, farmers south of El Paso, Texas, and Juarez, Mexico, began the promotion of an international dam to be built just north of El Paso. Had the dam been built there, Mesilla Valley irrigation would have been limited to the small acreage then under cultivation.[107] The

Las Cruces *Rio Grande Republican* agreed to the principle of an international dam, but asked that it be built farther north in order that it would provide water for the Mesilla Valley.[108] At length an English company with ample capital proposed to build a dam at Elephant Butte which would furnish water for both areas. However, the people of El Paso and Juarez then sought to forestall the plan—apparently because if the dam were built just north of El Paso it would mean more water for irrigation in that area. The Mexican government then intervened on grounds that the Treaty of Guadalupe Hidalgo had guaranteed that no impediments to navigation would be constructed on the Rio Grande. Then the Justice Department, at the request of the State Department, sought an injunction to halt construction of the dam, appealing finally to the United States Supreme Court. The case was twice remanded by the Supreme Court to the lower courts, but on the third appeal to the Supreme Court an injunction was granted. During all these years the *Rio Grande Republican* fought valiantly for the water rights of the Mesilla Valley and invoked the aid of both the press and officials of the territory to prevent the passage of a congressional act to construct an international dam at El Paso.[109] At length the Interior Department was empowered to build the reservoir at the Elephant Butte site. However, the *Rio Grande Republican* did not halt its campaign at this point but urged Mesilla Valley landowners to sign pledges to purchase irrigation waters on completion of the dam. Eventually 110,000 acres were pledged, and the future prosperity of the Mesilla Valley and Las Cruces was assured.[110] That prosperity was due in great part to the *Rio Grande Republican,* for it had led a twenty-year fight to preserve the water rights of the valley. In the course of its battle this paper had secured the aid of the press and officials of the territory to add to its strength, for it required the combined efforts of them all to prevent the diversion of New Mexico flood waters to Texas and Mexican lands.

Even when there was no prospect of irrigation from a stream, as was possible in the Mesilla Valley, the editors continued to work for irrigation in their areas by urging searches for artesian water. The Silver City *Enterprise* became interested in such a project in 1883 and, noting the success of such wells in Colorado and Arizona, asked that one be drilled near its town.[111] The Santa Fe *New Mexican* became enthralled with the subject and broached it from time to time for the remainder of the territorial era, maintaining: "Artesian wells in abundance will determine the future of this section as a fruit growing and agricultural section." In 1887 it supported a proposal to irrigate 200,000 acres near Santa Fe and admonished the public to "push the artesian well scheme."[112] Many other territorial editors praised efforts to drill artesian wells,[113] but perhaps the papers at Portales waged the longest fight in support of such an effort. The Portales *Times,* for example, conducted a two-year campaign in behalf of artesian wells. During this time it urged a test, helped gather funds for that test, closely followed its drilling and failure, and then urged the voting of bonds for a second test. All the while the *Times* predicted success for the tests and resultant prosperity for Portales.[114] Although most of the artesian test wells promoted by the editors were failures, the tests often revealed water strata near the surface from which irrigation waters could be pumped.

The Las Cruces *Daily News* was one of the first territorial papers to note successful pump irrigation projects in other areas and to suggest that the system be tried in New Mexico.[115] The Socorro *Chieftain* became interested in such a system to bring additional nearby valley lands under irrigation and for many years waged a campaign to interest local farmers.[116] The *New Mexican* believed pump irrigation practical for many sections of the territory and particularly pushed for a trial in the Santa Fe Valley.[117] Large acreages were irrigated from such ground water strata near Deming and Portales in the last territorial years, and the Portales papers took a most active interest in the matter. For example, the *Times* on several occasions noted the testing of such a system at Portales and recommended its use.[118] By 1909 the system seemed practical to many Portales Valley farmers, and both the *Times* and the *Roosevelt County Herald* then became active advocates of a proposed project. They conducted extensive campaigns to secure farmers' pledges to install pumps in order that capitalists would build a plant to generate electricity to power those pumps.[119] Success at Deming and Portales encouraged pump irrigation at other points. Thus, once again the efforts of the press had aided irrigation development in the territory.

Throughout the territorial era the press aided and encouraged irrigation. The editors did this by continually calling attention to the irrigation potential of the territory; at the same time they encouraged private projects and supported the efforts of the irrigation congresses to secure federal aid for irrigation. Furthermore, the editors were not just dreamers but practical men who realized that expensive irrigation farming called for exceptionally profitable crops and that private irrigation projects might contain possibilities of fraud. Meanwhile, other editors went beyond these general efforts to conduct extended campaigns in behalf of local projects. Thus, in addition to its general encouragement of irrigation, the press became the active leader without which some irrigation projects would not have been undertaken during the territorial era.

In many areas of New Mexico, irrigation of any type was impossible, but as the advancing frontier line of farmers from the Great Plains reached the Rocky Mountain states large numbers of these pioneers moved into eastern New Mexico to farm without irrigation. The earliest such movement was in the late 1880s when many farmers poured into the northeastern corner of New Mexico. This overflow of the western Kansas and eastern Colorado frontiers followed the Fort Worth and Denver City railroad lines into the territory. Since the 1880s were years of ample rainfall, the pioneers did well for a few years, but the droughts of the nineties led many of them to abandon their farms—just as farmers in western Kansas did in those years. After 1900 a wet cycle began and the westward migration of the farmers was resumed. This time they came from Oklahoma and Texas, the advance guard of west-ward-marching Southerners, who leaped over the large ranches of west Texas to claim some of the last free farming lands in the United States. Many who today see the bleak plains of eastern New Mexico cannot understand the homesteaders' belief that this was a farming country. But let it rain two inches in the late spring, and the prairie looks like a lush green lawn, only awaiting the plow to become productive fields. Since the first decade of the twentieth century was a wet cycle and a net-work of railways was being built across these prairies to provide access to markets, eastern New Mexico became very attractive to homesteaders.

The territorial press welcomed this new immigration, which prom-ised to add sufficient population to win statehood and held out the prospect of opening large areas to agriculture with the new dry farm-ing methods. In relation to this new immigration the press played sev-eral roles. The role of the general press was that of offering an invitation to the new pioneers. With the homesteaders came a new group of news-men who played a more active part in the development of the dry farm-ing area. The new editors not only continued the invitation to the homesteaders but helped them to adapt themselves to this area by urging on them proper crops and dry farming methods. Finally, these editors sought to help the homesteaders convert the forage crops that grew best in this area into greater profits through dairying, hog raising, and poultry production. Probably the over-optimism of the pioneer editors of eastern New Mexico encouraged the cultivation of a great deal of land that should have remained in pastures, but the intervening years have sus-tained the editors in their beliefs that profitable farming was possible over a large part of eastern New Mexico.

One of the earliest editors to extend an invitation to dry-farmer immi-grants and to boast of the agricultural potential of eastern New Mexico was J. E. Curren of the Folsom *Idea*. In 1889 he wrote: "If you poor clodhoppers back east want a good farm for nothing in the finest country under the sun, you had better come to Folsom, New Mexico, right now, just now. Now is the accepted time. . . ."[120] As the second wave of dry-farmer immigration began, the Santa Fe *New Mexican* noted the fact with pleasure: "Eastern New Mexico is making a record in the direction of homestead entries."[121] This paper reported from time to time the increasing flow of homesteaders to eastern New Mexico and encouraged others to come and fill the remaining 52,000,000 acres of public lands in the territory. In 1905 the *New Mexican* predicted that at the current rate of immigration into New Mexico the 1910 census would show a population growth of 50 to 60 per cent.[122] Optimistic editors believed dry farming possible throughout the territory and urged that it be tried everywhere. For example, the Alamogordo *News* asserted that local farmers had raised sorghum grain that grew to fourteen feet, and invited homesteaders to Otero County. The Aztec *San Juan Democrat* contended that dry farming was being conducted successfully even in the arid San Juan Valley,[123] and the Albuquerque *Morning Journal* approved of a dry-farming project planned near its town.[124] It can be seen, thus, that the entire territorial press invited this new immigration, welcomed it when it came to New Mexico, and anticipated that the homesteaders would magically convert millions of arid acres to valuable farm lands.

The eastern New Mexico editors, even more than the general press, were enthusiastic about the agricultural potential of New Mexico and their area in particular. The Portales *Roosevelt County Herald* offers a good example of their appeal: "Land is selling for $8.00 an acre in Texas and for 10 cents an acre in New Mexico." Later the editor stated that the American people soon would discover the wonders of New Mexico and "will be sad because of the fact this veritable Eden has lain unnoticed and undeveloped before their eyes."[125] With such encouragement as this by the press along with that of the railways and the New Mexico Bureau of Immigration, thousands homesteaded on the free lands of eastern New Mexico.[126]

The new immigrants reaped bountiful harvests for a few years before the wet cycle became a dry one; then the editors sought to help the farmers adjust to this climatic change. This was done with countless columns explaining the Campbell dry-farming system. In addition, the press urged farmers to attend farmers' institutes conducted by the territorial agricultural college or to visit exhibits sent into the country by the railways. Some editors quoted success stories from other arid areas, while others clipped articles from *Campbell's Soil Culture* or other agricultural journals.[127] There was great distress among the homesteaders, but many of them, helped by the advice of the editors, succeeded as dry farmers.

The editors' advocacy of crops adapted to the arid New Mexico climate was an equally important contribution in helping the homesteaders adjust to the new area. To illustrate, the San Jon *Quay County Times* stated in 1909 that kafir corn and milo maize should have been planted instead of a great deal of the corn that had been planted, for with the little moisture and the insect infestation corn production was uncertain.[128] The Santa Rosa *Sun* also urged the planting of acclimated crops, and the Fort Sumner *Review* suggested broomcorn as a possible crop for eastern New Mexico.[129] This crop also appealed to the Grady *Record,* for it maintained that "broomcorn is king in eastern New Mexico," and boasted that farmers who had followed the advice of the editor to plant it were harvesting an ample reward.[130] On the other hand, the Cuervo *Clipper* suggested winter wheat as a suitable crop for the area.[131] To help convince the farmers of the profits to be obtained from planting these crops, the editors used the success-story technique. For example, the Fort Sumner *Review* stated that fifty-eight acres of broomcorn had yielded $4,000.[132] Thus, the eastern New Mexico press by reason and example convinced many of the homesteaders of the importance of planting crops suited to that arid area.

On the other hand, there was a very poor market for the forage crops which thrived best in this area. A letter to the Portales *Roosevelt County Herald* amply illustrates this point:

Mr. Editor:—Perhaps a few dots from this part of "The Moral Vineyard" will be of interest to some of your readers.

Emigration to the eastern cotton fields has about ceased and we are so lonesome since our wives have taken the children, wagon and team and yellow dog and pulled for the cotton fields four hundred miles away and left us at home to hold down the claim, for such is life in New Mexico in the fall of the year and so our life is one of solitude. Wish those Portales merchants would devise some plan to utilize our produce so we could keep our wives and children at home and then we would be happy.

What is the matter with the business men of Portales? Guess they have not gotten over their summer knap [sic] yet. Has Texas still to keep up Mexico? We nestors have worked hard this year in hopes of a home market for our produce, but alas our fondest hopes are banished, our home left desolate and the cook gone.

Hello, there goes old "Brindy" over the fence into my field of corn, maise, cane, melons—let her eat it, they say you can't get anything for it in Portales, let her rip, plenty of it.

The old woman and children can pick enough cotton to pay the Portales merchants anyway. Give us another drink, who cares for expenses, I will pay you when the old woman and children send me some money. Now for the kaffir corn.

                    More anon, Old Nestor.[133]

The townsmen, however, had already begun to anticipate the demands of those such as the "Old Nestor." At Portales, for example, the merchants and newspapers had encouraged the growing of cotton by offering prizes for the first bale grown. Once the experiment had proved a success, the Portales *Times* led the movement for the establishment of a cotton gin at Portales to process the cotton and to provide a market for it.[134] The editorial advocacy of growing broomcorn was also an attempt to answer the marketing problem, for like cotton it provided a cash crop. In addition, the editors began to advocate diversified farming as a solution to the marketing problem. The Portales *Roosevelt County Herald,* for instance, proposed that the easily grown forage grain crops be fed to dairy cattle, hogs, and poultry.[135] Other editors also turned to this system as a means of making the eastern New Mexico farms more profitable. The Portales *Times* reported a dairy farmer's profits from the sale of cream and asked that others try it.[136] The Tucumcari *News* advanced the prospect of potential gains to be made from raising poultry, and the Logan *Leader* asked that a creamery be established in its town to provide a market for dairy production.[137] The Nara Visa *New Mexican and Register* also became interested in dairying and conducted a campaign lasting several months in 1911 to convince local farmers they should become dairymen.[138] In these last proposals the editors helped to set the homesteaders on the road to a prosperous farm economy. Dairying and the raising of hogs and poultry became very prevalent and were the chief means by which many homesteader families survived as farmers.[139]

In evaluating the contribution of the press to the dry-farming frontier, one must first consider the possibility that the editors did the homesteaders a disservice in urging them to come and to stay in New Mexico. Certainly this appears to be true of editors who urged homesteading west of the Pecos River, and doubtless a great deal of the land east of the Pecos should have been left as grassland. The "dust bowl" of the 1930s and the great number of Soil Bank farm leases in eastern New Mexico today tend to confirm this opinion. Nevertheless, there are many prosperous farms in the area; and with the continuing improvements in farm equipment and drought-resistant crops, this will remain a prosperous farming area. In any case, thousands would have come to New Mexico lured by the free land. The great contribution of the press, then, was in helping those who came to adapt themselves to the conditions in New Mexico, and in this they apparently succeeded very well.

Doubtless railways, mines, ranches, irrigation, and dryland farms would have been developed in New Mexico without the aid of the territorial press. Thus, to measure editorial influence on the development of New Mexico, one must look for the ways in which the press aided these economic advancements. One contribution of the press was its invitation to the capitalist and to the immigrant to come and to invest his money and himself in New Mexico. Here again, no doubt, many of them would have come and would have invested without this invitation.

But since the invitation represented a favorable public attitude toward both capital and immigrants, it hastened their flow into New Mexico. The next contribution of the press was that of furnishing information about the territorial resources, which further interested and encouraged the investor and the homeseeker. In addition, the editors furnished information and encouragement to aid various industries to adapt to changing conditions and the climate of New Mexico. In this connection, the press urged ranchers to improve breeds to enable them to maintain profits despite the diminishing public domain. Their effort also included information and persuasion of dry farmers to adopt crops and practices which would make farming in this semi-arid area more profitable. Finally, the press aided territorial economic development by becoming the voice of protest against economic injustices. The press protested against unfair railway rates and practices which were detrimental to the New Mexico economy. It protested against range grabbing and illegal fencing which discouraged the small rancher and homesteader. It protested against the attempt to steal the irrigation waters needed to develop fully the Mesilla Valley. In these various ways the editors hastened the flow of capital into the territory, smoothed the path into New Mexico for immigrants, and sought to aid newcomers in adjusting themselves to life in the territory. And in doing these things the territorial press became the inviting, encouraging, protesting voice of New Mexican society. All the economic developments discussed might have come without the aid of newspapers, but newspapers eased and sped the process.

# VII

# EDITORIAL AID
# IN THE CURTAILMENT OF
# VIOLENCE AND VICE

VIOLENCE, OUTLAWRY, AND VICE were common in the territory during the first forty years of rule by the United States. After this time conditions gradually improved, and by 1912 New Mexico had become a rather placid area with the conservative mores of an agrarian society. Although much of the early violence was between the people of the Indian and European cultures, violent conflicts between Anglo groups were also common. Apparently the predominance of Spanish-Americans in New Mexico was not responsible for the high incidence of violence, for the peak of lawlessness was between 1870 and 1885 and came mainly from members of the vanguard of the westward-moving American frontier.[1] An editorial of 1876 illustrates the prevalence of violence in this era, noting that in a period of two months mob violence had occurred in Rio Arriba, Mora, San Miguel, Colfax, and Santa Fe counties and had led to six deaths plus the destruction of a store and a newspaper plant. Meanwhile, there had been a riot in Dona Ana County in which six persons were killed or wounded.[2]

A major part of the violence of the 1870s grew out of struggles between organized groups which did not hesitate to use violence to gain wealth and power. In the 1880s, on the other hand, violence was more the result of a general lawlessness. Killings were so common in Las Vegas in 1880, for example, that the Santa Fe *New Mexican* reported that the common breakfast comment was: "Well, who was killed last night?"[3] Since ordinary law enforcement agencies were unable to cope with the lawless elements, the public approved the use of extraordinary measures such as vigilante groups and the territorial militia until in the mid-eighties the Indian wars were ended and most of the lawless element

175

was subdued. Nevertheless, impromptu pistol duels were still common and moral laxity was prevalent. Territorial society then sought to stop the open wearing of arms that easily led to deadly exchanges of fire. At the same time there was a general demand that the legally constituted agencies be upheld. As a result, by 1900 New Mexico had become a relatively peaceful area.

After 1900 the territory began to feel the influence of the national reform movements which led to the suppression of public gambling, openly conducted houses of prostitution, and the free operation of saloons. In a few instances saloons were closed by local option laws. Thus, by 1912 the territory had become a placid area with a rural or small-town morality.

The attitude of territorial editors toward the suppression of crime and violence varied with the conditions of that period. Before the 1870s the press generally ignored crime and violence. During that decade, however, editors not only became interested in the Lincoln and Colfax County wars, but often became partisan supporters of one of the competing factions. With the beginning of a new wave of violence in the early 1880s the editors supported almost unanimously vigilante mobs which acted to end an era of outlaw terror. Later in the 1880s the press turned against similar groups fighting against the unpopular Maxwell Land Grant, holding in this instance that the use of violence against legal authorities and court orders could not be condoned. Meanwhile, the editors asked that the almost universal practice of wearing pistols be discontinued, and in the 1890s the press clearly showed its support for orderly legal processes by denouncing Oliver Lee for his resistance to a posse seeking to arrest him on a charge of murdering A. J. Fountain. In the last territorial years the editors, probably hoping to aid the statehood movement, worked to eradicate the old image of New Mexico as the home of the badman and the land of violence and vice.

Before 1875 the territorial editors were rarely interested in the suppression of violence, crime, and immorality and, in fact, were not very interested in even reporting such incidents. For example, in 1866 the Santa Fe *Weekly Gazette* reported: "One man was killed and several wounded in a row which took place in this city at the southwest corner of the plaza on Monday night. We did not learn any of the particulars." This paper was published five days after the event described, yet the editor was so disinterested that he had not concerned himself to learn names or further details.[4] The Albuquerque *Review* noted in 1879 that over a period of time six men had been lynched at a place near the newspaper office. Again, these lynchings apparently were not considered newsworthy enough to be reported in the paper.[5] Sometimes editors gave a humorous twist to violent crimes.[6] The Silver City *Grant County Herald* published this story in 1875:

We learn that on Friday, Jose Garcia, who lives at the Chino copper mines, caught his wife in flagarante delicto—we leave the reader to guess the crime— Jose, then and there, gave her the quietus with an axe. She's dead—deadest sort of dead, and it is said that Jose did not run away and intends to face the music.[7]

Since there apparently was no lack of violence and violent crimes in New Mexico in this era, it must be concluded that the editors often ignored them through a lack of interest. However, after 1875 there were two series of violent incidents, the Lincoln and Colfax County wars, in which the press became very interested, principally because they were struggles for power and wealth and because the Santa Fe Ring[8] was involved. The involvement of this political clique in the Colfax County war is more apparent than in the case of the Lincoln County war, for the Colfax County war seemed to grow out of a letter by a Cimarron Methodist minister, F. J. Tolby, to the New York *Sun* exposing the activities of the Santa Fe Ring. When subsequently Tolby was found murdered, with his personal possessions unmolested, O. P. McMains, a fellow Methodist minister, assumed that Tolby had been murdered because he had written the letter. McMains then led a mob which lynched two Spanish-Americans believed to have been hired to commit the murder. One of these men had claimed that he had been paid by Cimarron supporters of the Santa Fe Ring to murder Tolby. After the lynching, the mob remained active in Cimarron, and there was such general disorder that federal troops were brought in to suppress it. During this period an editor who had leased the Cimarron *News and Press* severely criticized the mob, which then retaliated by having Clay Allison's men throw the plant of the paper into the Cimarron River. Such violence provided an excuse for the Ring-dominated legislature to take away the courts of Colfax County and to attach them to Taos County for judicial purposes. Later at Taos a grand jury held there was insufficient evidence to indict the Cimarron supporters of the Santa Fe Ring for the Tolby murder, but Parson McMains, the only known member of the lynch mob, was indicted for murder.[9]

Newspaper interest in the Colfax County war was concerned principally with the responsibility of the Santa Fe Ring for the Tolby murder and subsequent Ring actions with regard to Colfax County. Ring interest in the Tolby murder was shown in letters from both contending factions to the Pueblo (Colorado) *Chieftain*. In both cases unidentified correspondents connected the Ring or its supporters with the Colfax County troubles.[10] A revived Cimarron *News and Press*, edited by its true owners, excused the mob for destroying the newspaper plant and asked for a resumption of the popular support it had enjoyed as an exponent of the people "as against the abuses . . . by a servile and corrupt legislature." This editorial was reprinted in the Silver City *Grant County Herald,* which also believed that the legislature was controlled by the Santa Fe Ring—"the political monster which lives by oppression of the people."[11] When the legislature took away Colfax County courts, this paper pointed out that mob action and a riot in five other counties in the same period had not moved the legislature to take away the courts of those counties.[12] The Santa Fe *New Mexican,* which immediately took the opposite stand, ignored the possibility that there was a Santa Fe Ring, but defended the supporters of the Ring at Cimarron, congratulated them on their exoneration by the Taos grand jury, and attacked the *News and Press* for its defense of the mob which had destroyed its plant.[13] When McMains was later tried for murder, the *Chieftain, News and Press,* and Albuquerque *Review* again implicated the Santa Fe Ring, contending that it was persecuting McMains.[14]

With regard to the Colfax County war, a majority of the territorial papers was willing to condone violence and lawlessness directed against a corrupt political clique—apparently in the belief that those opposed to the Santa Fe Ring could obtain justice in no other way. With regard to the Lincoln County war, on the other hand, a majority of papers refused to support either faction, although they devoted more space to reporting Lincoln County violence than they formerly used for this type of news. A minority of papers, however, took stands on the Lincoln County disputes, which were based mainly on prior prejudices rather than on the merits of the cause of either faction. The Santa Fe *New Mexican* supported the group allied with the Santa Fe Ring, and the Cimarron *News and Press* chose the opposite side. The Mesilla *Valley Independent* sought to maintain an unbiased position but often favored the views of the faction opposed to the Ring members. The Mesilla *News,* on the contrary, opposed the stands of its local competitor. In addition, these papers published letters from the contending Lincoln County factions, becoming a means by which the factions appealed for public support.

At heart the Lincoln County war was a struggle for power and wealth between two factions which soon resorted to violence. The firm of L. G. Murphy, J. J. Dolan, and J. H. Riley, merchants, ranchers, and freighters, had a monopolistic hold on a large segment of the Lincoln County economy, while A. A. McSween, a Lincoln lawyer, and his friends sought to break that hold. The Lincoln County troubles began over a dispute about the receipts from a $10,000 insurance policy on the life of Emil Fritz, a former partner of Murphy in the Lincoln firm. The com-

pany which had issued the insurance policy was bankrupt, and the heirs
of Fritz turned the policy over to McSween for collection. He collected
most of the money due on the policy, but apparently proposed to keep
the larger part of it for his fee and expenses. In any case, McSween rejected the request of the administrators of the Fritz estate that he turn
the money over to them or to the court. The administrators then employed T. B. Catron, territorial attorney general, and W. L. Rynerson,
district attorney, to recover the insurance funds from McSween. After
McSween was brought into court he still refused to turn over the receipts from the insurance policy, and the court then ordered that his
property at Lincoln be attached as bond. By this time McSween and J. H.
Tunstall had launched a mercantile establishment at Lincoln to compete with the Murphy firm. Both this store and Tunstall's ranch were
attached by the court; and in the process of attaching by the officers,
Tunstall was killed. As a result open warfare began between the two factions, both of which at various times secured legal authorizations for the
arrest of the leaders of the other side. The actions of the territorial governor, S. B. Axtell, appeared to favor the Murphy-Dolan faction in this
struggle, in which many lost their lives—including McSween himself.
The apparent partiality of Axtell motivated Secretary of the Interior
Carl Shurz to send a special investigator to the territory, and as a result
Axtell, Catron, and Rynerson were removed from their positions. At
this point Lew Wallace was appointed territorial governor and he
helped bring the Lincoln County war to an end.[15]

Several months before the Lincoln County war began, A. J. Fountain,
editor of the Mesilla *Valley Independent,* charged that there was extensive lawlessness and thievery in Dona Ana County and promised to
expose the criminals along with the businessmen who were helping
them to dispose of stolen property.[16] When the Mesilla *News* immediately sought to refute this editorial, the Santa Fe *New Mexican* noted
the fact and added:

> We have labored all along to keep out of the inky fight between the Inde-
> pendent and its contemporary, the News, for bread and butter, thinking all
> the time the News would come out ahead in defending the character of its
> citizens, wantonly and uncertainly assailed by the uncertain lawyer Fountain.
> In this we have not been mistaken; Fountain has not only proved himself a
> very poor subject for a martyr, but has placed the Independent and the citizens
> of his county in an unenviable light before the public, in which he has no ex-
> cuse, except perhaps of making for himself a certain kind of notoriety.[17]

The Cimarron *News and Press,* hostile toward the Santa Fe *New Mexican* because of their conflict over the Colfax County war, immediately
sided with the Mesilla *Valley Independent* and commented: "with the

advent of that able and fearless sheet the INDEPENDENT, we have learned the truth in regard to these matters."[18]

Even before the Lincoln County violence began, therefore, it can be seen that these newspapers had aligned themselves into mutually hostile camps. This being true it was almost inevitable that they would become involved in the Lincoln County conflict since the Santa Fe *New Mexican* was already strongly attached to one faction. When T. B. Catron, a leader of the Santa Fe Ring, became an exponent of the Murphy-Dolan faction, the *New Mexican,* allied with the Ring, was almost automatically to be found in that camp. In addition, W. H. Manderfield, of the *New Mexican,* and J. H. Riley, a partner in the Murphy firm, apparently had a close friendship since they joined each other in fishing and business trips.[19] The Mesilla *Valley Independent,* on the other hand, continued to attack the lawless element of Dona Ana County, noting later that part of it had joined the Murphy-Dolan faction and that some of its members were in the posse which had killed J. H. Tunstall.[20] Because of this, the *Valley Independent* was often hostile toward the Murphy group.

The course of events had thus made available propaganda vehicles for the use of the warring factions of Lincoln County. This propaganda was in the form of letters from participants in the war and editorials in which the Santa Fe *New Mexican* and Mesilla *News* attacked the McSween faction and supported Murphy's group,[21] while the Mesilla *Valley Independent* and the Cimarron *News and Press* usually held the opposite views.[22] Other territorial papers generally limited themselves to reporting the incidents of the war and rarely took sides. It would appear that these latter papers, uninvolved by prior prejudices or proximity to the scene of the war, should have been first to ask for impartial outside intervention to end this blood bath, but such was not the case. On the other hand, the *Valley Independent,* despite its bias for the McSween forces, asked for such impartial intervention and for reasonable actions by Lincoln County residents. For example, after the death of J. H. Tunstall it noted the conditions in Lincoln County and expressed a hope that despite the actions of the posse:

the law will be permitted to take its course, and that the good citizens of Lincoln County will not permit themselves to become violators of the law by aiding or abetting any unlawful act.[23]

When it was revealed that known outlaws, some of them men whom the Mesilla *Valley Independent* considered it had hounded out of Dona Ana County, were in the posse which had killed J. H. Tunstall, the *Valley Independent* asked that the sheriff explain why known criminals were made members of the posse.[24] After a sheriff appointed by the

Lincoln County commissioners was removed because he appeared to be a McSween partisan and was replaced by a Murphy partisan, the *Valley Independent* predicted that this action would only lead to further bloodshed.[25] The prediction was ignored, and as a result the Lincoln County war entered its bloodiest phase, with more than a dozen men losing their lives. Again the *Valley Independent* protested and asked that peace be restored, not by those already involved in these troubles but by:

unprejudiced minds—and if the governor of New Mexico cannot do it—if he cannot devise a plan by which these troubles can be ended, Uncle Sam should interfere. The management of this whole affair is not only wrong but disgraceful, and shows that a want of ability somewhere exists to properly handle difficulties of this kind.[26]

Unlike the Santa Fe *New Mexican* and the Mesilla *News* the Mesilla *Valley Independent* was not consistent in its support of the faction which it seemed to have chosen. For example, when Robert A. Weiderman, the deputy United States marshal who was friendly with the McSween faction, appeared to have acted illegally, the *Valley Independent* commented:

We hope he will be able to present a satisfactory explanation of his alleged friendly association with thieves and murderers at the time he had in his pockets a warrant for their arrest. If it appears that he has made use of his official position as Deputy U. S. Marshal to conciliate outlaws in the interest of one or the other party of men whose rancorous feuds have thrown Lincoln County in disorder, he will not be held free from responsibility for the death of Mr. Tunstall. All that we desire is to have the matter thoroughly ventilated, and then—"Let justice be done tho' the Heavens fall."[27]

The Mesilla *Valley Independent* was initially favorable toward McSween's supporters when they formed a group known as the Regulators for the alleged purpose of protecting their lives and property from the known outlaws of the Murphy-Dolan faction. That paper, however, soon lost sympathy for the Regulators when their vengeful and illegal actions were revealed.[28] Thus, despite its somewhat restrained partisanship for the McSween men, the *Valley Independent* apparently has the best record of any territorial paper with regard to the Lincoln County struggle. Where other papers were merely impartial reporters or consistently supported their chosen side editorially, the *Valley Independent* was editorially critical of both sides at times, consistently asked for just and impartial solutions, and maintained in the end that there were two wrong sides rather than one right side.[29]

Whereas few of the editors of the 1870s were willing to campaign vigorously for law and order, those of the 1880s were very devoted to ending the reign of crime and terror that beset New Mexico. These editors of the 1880s were almost entirely a new group, part of the large wave of Anglo-American immigrants that accompanied railway construction into the territory. The newcomers were of two types: those who were adventurous but industrious and wished to build a peaceful, prosperous society; and those who were the adventurous but lawless men ever present in frontier areas. The addition of this last group to a similar element already in the territory made the years from 1880 to 1884 the period of greatest civil violence in New Mexican history. Inefficient territorial law enforcement agencies could not cope with the situation; as a result the territorial editors, belonging to the group desiring peace and justice, sanctioned extraordinary measures to end this era of criminal violence. To bring peace within the towns, the editors advocated the use of vigilantes and lynch mobs. To bring order to the open range, most editors approved the use of territorial militia to hunt down large gangs of cattle thieves. In the case of the legal but unjust Maxwell Land Grant, however, the editors were reluctant to condemn extra-legal violence that might lead to just ends. But as the decade wore on, the editors lost patience with this futile fight and asked that the laws and court decisions be respected. Thus, in each instance the press advocated and recognized the necessity of a peaceful and orderly but just society. Considering that a long interlude of lawlessness and violence came to an end very quickly, their sanction of the extra-legal action of the vigilantes appears to have been justified.

In two instances in the early '80s territorial officials efficiently suppressed criminal violence. In both cases these officials were called on to break up gangs engaged in cattle thefts. These two gangs were led by hired gunmen who had fought on opposite sides in the Lincoln County war. One gang leader, W. H. (Billy, the Kid) Bonney, established his headquarters at Los Portales in eastern New Mexico and levied upon the herds of ranchers in that area until he was hunted down by Pat Garrett, New Mexico's most noted lawman. Bonney escaped from captivity and Garrett again hunted him down, this time killing him. Territorial editors would have had little understanding of the tendency to glamorize Billy the Kid. To them he was similar to a rattlesnake, something to be ruthlessly exterminated. For example, the Cimarron *News and Press* maintained:

> We can all unite in the sentiment expressed in the verdict of the coroner's jury that Garrett has earned the gratitude of the whole territory by ridding it of this dangerous outlaw.[30]

The Las Cruces *Rio Grande Republican* adopted a similar attitude and urged everyone to contribute to funds being raised to reward Garrett for his feat:

> Since he entered the killing business two years ago Kid has been a terror to honest law loving people and hence the general satisfaction at his decease, and deep seated gratitude to the man who marked him for burial. . . . The people certainly owe him much and nearly every town in the territory is moving to show a cash appreciation of its gratitude. All are equally interested and each should come up with its mite. . . . The fund cannot be swelled beyond desserts.[31]

By its efforts to raise rewards for Garrett, the press showed its appreciation of brave and effective conventional law enforcement. However, monetary rewards failed to inspire similar performance from other territorial lawmen and even Garrett soon left his position.

The other gang of cattle thieves was led by John Kinney, also a hired gunman in the Lincoln County war. Territorial society used different means to suppress this group, which was active in southwestern New Mexico. Cattle losses became so great in that area by 1883 that ranchers appealed to the territorial governor for aid. He in turn asked the crusading former editor of the Mesilla *Valley Independent,* A. J. Fountain, to investigate. Fountain had earlier helped to organize militia companies at Mesilla and in 1883 was a major in command of them. After his investigation confirmed excessive cattle theft, Major Fountain was ordered to take the field against the "rustlers." Subsequently a large part of the Kinney gang was captured and placed in jail at Mesilla. They were then so closely guarded by the militia that no one was able to storm the jail and release them as had frequently happened in the past when outlaws had been captured. The militant Fountain, who was also a lawyer, then gathered evidence and helped the prosecution convict John Kinney.[32] But Fountain's actions were not supported by all the territorial press. The Santa Fe *New Mexican* sharply questioned his report of large-scale "rustling" in Dona Ana County.[33] The Silver City *Southwest Sentinel* was hostile to the use of militia to hunt criminals, deeming this martial law.[34] The paper continued its hostility toward Fountain during the trial of Kinney. For this it was rebuked by the Silver City *Enterprise,* which maintained that "instead of censure Major Fountain and Governor Sheldon deserve praise for so speedily ridding the country of this part of its rustler element."[35] The Las Cruces *Rio Grande Republican* generally supported Fountain, confirming his findings about cattle theft and endorsing his efforts.[36] The Silver City *Enterprise* did maintain, however, that the use of militia gave too much advance warning to rustlers and was therefore impractical. Further use of the militia in the summer of 1883 seemed to sustain this conclusion, and the use of militia was abandoned.[37] Nevertheless, it had been successful in halting large-scale open operations of the type Kinney had been conducting and had helped to bring law and order to the ranges of southwestern New Mexico. In general the efforts of Fountain and Garrett to bring law and order to the range met with public approval; the chief contribution of the press was that of giving a voice to the general desire for an orderly society.

Fearless men such as Sheriff Pat Garrett and Major A. J. Fountain were exceptional, consequently other areas resorted to mob action when regular law enforcement agencies were ineffective. Such appeared to be the case at Las Vegas in 1880 when three men rode into town bearing arms, contrary to the laws of both the territory and Las Vegas. The marshal, who asked this trio to disarm, was shot down for his pains. The next issue of the *Daily Optic* revealed that these men had stopped at nearby Mora, after fleeing Las Vegas; the paper asked that a posse be formed to bring them to trial. This was soon accomplished and the men were placed in the San Miguel County jail. Apparently motivated by fear that the trio might escape, a masked mob took them from the jail and executed them without benefit of trial. The next edition of the *Daily Optic* recounted the story under a heading of "THE LYNCH-ING," and displays the barbarism often involved in such incidents as well as the journalistic styles then currently in use for reporting such events:

The hanging yesterday morning was certainly a deplorable affair and one which has been viewed in many lights by citizens. One thing is certain; if these men had by any chance escaped from the clutches of the law, they were of the right cut and calibre to wreak vengeance upon the town that they hated with a deadly hatred.

## THE VIGILANTES

. . . demanded the keys, and as the jailor was under the cover of several guns he had no other alternative but to give them up. The men were taken out each with a rope around his neck and conducted toward the plaza. West, alias Lowe, was so badly wounded that he had to be carried. He pleaded most pitifully but still refused to give his history or where he came from. Tom Henry says "Jim, be still and die like a man." The poor fellow was shivering with cold and said "Boys, you are hanging a mighty good man."

Tom Henry died game 'though he weakened a little when first taken out of the cell. When asked if he had any friend that he wished written to, he said he had an old father and mother living in Pueblo, Colorado, by the name of House. His right name was Thomas Jefferson House, and when asked if he had anything to say replied, "Boys, its pretty rough to be hung, but I wish someone would write to my father and mother. I will stand the consequences and die like a man." Henry, alias House, though only twenty one years of age was cool and self possessed to the last. Dorsey said that he hadn't a friend in the world, and would not tell where he was from or give any information in regard to his previous history.

### AT THE SCAFFOLD

It is understood that West was jerked up first and the last words he said were, "please button up my pants."

### THE HANGING

was apparently a failure and the mob, fearing someone would come to protect the prisoners, commenced shooting. Henry, alias House, fell at the first shot, but crawling to the side of the platform said, "Boys, for God's sake shoot me again! Shoot me in the head!" Dorsey said not a word but hardly a second after the first shot was fired both men fell pierced with bullets.[38]

On his editorial page the Las Vegas *Daily Optic* editor held that the lynching was fully justified:

SPEEDY trials and swift punishment are two things needful. If such were the case our citizens would never take the law into their own hands. . . .

We are not an advocate of mob law; neither do we believe that wild reckless drunken men should be permitted to come into town and ruin the place, shooting down in cold blood any parties who may chance to interfere and endeavor to stop them in their bloody work.

The killing of Joe Carson was cold blooded. They had not the least provocation in the world for committing the deed which in the end cost them their lives. . . . The day when roughs can run towns has passed. Public sentiment will not tolerate such conduct. Men who rob and kill and laugh at the law must remember that a new era has dawned upon New Mexico.

The lesson taught by the awful spectacle in the plaza Sabbath morning will not soon be forgotten. No man could look upon it without being overcome with feelings of inexpressible horror. However, it must be remembered that these men were desperate characters who regarded human life as worth nothing when standing between them and the accomplishment of any evil design. They had been terrors to our people. They acknowledged the killing of Joe Carson, could offer no palliating circumstances, and their own lawyer said no court under heaven would acquit them. The only hope was to delay a trial, permitting the evidence to scatter.[39]

Most editors agreed with the Las Vegas *Daily Optic* that immediate action by the populace was necessary to put an end to the terroristic violence of this era, for the regular legal processes were too slow and uncertain. The Albuquerque *Daily Journal* contended:

As long as we have no prisons where lawbreakers can be confined with any degree of certainty that they will remain until brought to justice as prescribed by law, we may expect lynching.[40]

The Las Cruces *Rio Grande Republican* maintained: "Speedy trials and sure punishments would do a little toward making judge lynch [sic] unpopular."[41] A similar argument was used by the Manzano *Gringo and Greaser* which condoned lynching on the basis that: "nothing deters the commission of crime as much as the swift and certain vengeance of the people visited upon the criminals."[42]

A few editors, on the other hand, held that it was always better to "allow the law to take its course without regard to the consequences."[43] The Albuquerque *Evening Review,* for example, was consistently opposed to vigilante law and once recommended that law officers discover the identity of lynchers and bring them to justice. When a Socorro man confessed that he had raped an eight-year-old girl and given her a venereal disease, the editor of the *Evening Review* held that while this lynching was more justified than one for simple murder, in no circumstances was lynching justifiable.[44] Frontier New Mexico soon became more placid and law enforcement improved to the extent that in 1886 one editor reported: "Lynch law is more popular in the states than in New Mexico. Mob law has ceased in this territory."[45]

Certainly many things contributed to the decline of lawlessness in New Mexico, and among them was the quick reaction of an outraged populace. The editors contributed to bringing law and order by encouraging the outraged people to use extra-legal methods to eliminate or intimidate those who disturbed or threatened to disturb the peace of the territory.[46] Yet at the same time many editors showed themselves ready to allow the peace to be disturbed by sanctioning violent resistance to what most editors considered a gigantic fraud, the Maxwell Land Grant. When the territory became more placid, the editors were to regret their advocacy of mob action, for they were forced to recant and to call upon the anti-grant group to accept injustice in order that peace and order might be preserved.

The Maxwell Land Grant Company purchased and then extended a large Mexican land grant. The original grant, about 90,000 acres (and larger than allowed by Mexican law), was extended enormously when the grant was confirmed by the United States Congress. Some have charged that surveyors made it larger than the area Congress had confirmed. At any rate, eventually it consisted of about 1,800,000 acres and extended from Elizabethtown and Cimarron into southern Colorado. Meanwhile, many small ranchers, believing themselves upon the public domain, had begun ranching on the fertile grasslands of the grant and had made valuable improvements on their ranches. When the Maxwell Company sought to expel these "squatters" from its lands, a leader arose to direct them in a resistance movement. This leader was O. P. McMains, the Methodist minister who led the mob involved in the

Colfax County war, a man already known as a fearless leader against large-scale corruption. Expelled from the ministry for his leadership of the lynch mob, McMains had become a rancher on Maxwell grant lands and was thus bound to the other ranchers with a common tie. The so-called squatters furnished money for McMains to conduct law suits and make innumerable trips to Washington where he appealed to the Justice Department, Interior Department, Supreme Court, Congress, and the President to set aside the fraudulent grant. While making these appeals, he again and again advocated violence to prevent the Maxwell Company from seizing the squatters' lands before they could set aside the grant by legal means. Ultimately, the Maxwell Company gained undisputed possession of the grant.[47]

In the early stages of the struggle, the press was hostile toward the Maxwell Company and sympathetic toward the squatters. For example the Las Cruces *Rio Grande Republican* maintained:

McMains is a man who is bravely fighting an alleged corrupt and fraudulent land grant in Colfax County, and all who are opposed to robbery and corruption should side with him.[48]

The Raton *Independent* adopted a similar attitude:

The leading members of the law profession in Santa Fe say there is no chance for the settlers to get the Maxwell land grant set aside. No doubt it will be a hard task and one that will require a vast amount of time to accomplish, but it does not seem like the vast amount of allegations and proofs will be wholly ignored by the government. Right will triumph in the end. . . .[49]

The Las Vegas *Daily Optic* also openly favored the small ranchers: "We are body and soul in sympathy with the Maxwell squatters. . . ."[50] While some editors expressed only sympathetic encouragement, others urged a more active program on the squatters. The Raton *Guard,* for example, advocated that the squatters oppose unjust court orders:

We do believe that when the court is prostituted from its high position to serve the ends of a corrupt corporation, the people are not so much to blame for rising up in a body and protesting against injustice. . . . It is their privilege to organize so as to afford self protection.[51]

The San Hilario *Red River Chronicle* believed violence was justified but hesitated to advise its use:

We advise our friends in Colfax County to go slow. If Judge Prince, Tom Catron, Bill Breeden, Frank Springer and a lot of other hell hounds and land grant swindlers would have to serve the writ [to expel the squatters from Maxwell lands] in person, we might advise the Raton folks to take good aim and kill every mothers son of them; but such is not the case. Innocent tools will be called in to execute the law.[52]

When in the last years of the 1880s the press became more interested in peace, law, and order, the editors lost sympathy for a fight which could be won neither in a court nor against the armed might of the United States government. Under these circumstances the entire editorial corps lost sympathy for McMains and those squatters who were inclined to resort to violence. The changed attitude of the territorial press is shown in the advice of the Raton *Range* to the squatters:

> We hope these people will consider the consequences of any further attempts in violation of the law. Let them consult their own best interests, advise with those entitled to their confidence and respect, and they certainly will not attempt to bring on a conflict that can only result in disaster for themselves.[53]

The efforts of McMains to continue the struggle when any reasonable man would have concluded it was futile eventually led many editors to conclude that he did so to continue to draw funds and subsidies from the squatters:

> The settlers would do well, alike for themselves and the man, to help McMains to a back seat. His day of usefulness, if it ever dawned, is ended, and his championship of any movement is a certain death blow to it. He has lived off the poor settlers long enough.[54]

Thus, by 1890 the press no longer considered a just cause sufficient excuse for resorting to violence. This desire for peace, law, and order reflects the more even tenor of territorial life and the desire of a large majority of citizens to preserve these conditions. In this new era instances of large-scale violence by outlaw gangs or mobs were rare. However, violence between ordinarily peaceful citizens continued. To eliminate exchanges of gunfire growing out of hasty impulses, the editors sought to curtail the frontier custom of men habitually carrying weapons. This movement to curtail the carrying of pistols had begun much earlier as a part of the effort to halt violence in New Mexico. It culminated in a legislative act of the 1870s prohibiting the wearing of guns. By 1880 the Las Vegas *Daily Optic* was calling for the enforcement of this law and in 1881 renewed its campaign with an editorial, the "WAR ON WEAPONS":

> The officials of this precinct will rigidly enforce the law prohibiting the carrying of deadly weapons. Printed notices to this effect will be posted up conspicuously where they cannot fail to reach the eyes of the public. Every good citizen is expected to observe this injunction without further notice and the other classes will be compelled to do so. . . . A new era has dawned in the local history of Las Vegas.[55]

Although at various times in the 1880s territorial editors called for the enforcement of this act,[56] it was never rigorously enforced in those

years. Another act providing heavy fines for carrying arms was praised by
the Las Vegas *Daily Optic* in 1887.[57] With the advent of the more peaceful era of the late 1880s, the press seized upon tragic accidents to remind
New Mexicans of the dangers that came from being constantly armed.
For example, in 1888 when a pistol fell from a man's coat and killed his
wife, the *Daily Optic* stated:

> There is no more useless and senseless custom than that of carrying loaded
> pistols. The laws of New Mexico look upon the practice in this light, and have
> fixed upon the custom one of the heaviest financial penalties. Yet men will
> constantly violate the law in this particular. Especially is it done by parties
> coming to the territory, evidently looking upon New Mexico as a land of
> violence, where every man's life is carried in his hand. Still the fact remains
> there is no more need for a man to carry a pistol in Las Vegas, Albuquerque,
> Santa Fe or any of the towns and villages of New Mexico than there would be
> for the same man to go armed in New York, Washington City or Boston.[58]

The wearing of weapons declined in the 1890s, perhaps as a result of
the editorial admonitions, but "gun totin' " continued to be the habit of
many. When in 1902 an armed cowboy shot a practical joker for sprin-
kling water on his boots, the San Marcial *Bee* again called for a halt to
the carrying of arms.[59] In fact, with the movement of homesteaders into
eastern New Mexico in the first decade of the twentieth century the practice again became prevalent, and again the press cited tragic incidents to
illustrate the result of carrying arms.[60]

From the foregoing it can be seen that the practice of ordinary citizens
carrying arms in public had not been eliminated completely by the end
of the territorial era. Nevertheless, the editorial pleas for disarmament
were probably not without effect; and it would seem a safe assumption
that, as general frontier violence declined, the editorial reminders
helped to curtail gun wearing by their stress on disarmament as a wise
and accepted practice.

There were only sporadic instances of violence in New Mexico after
1890; and the attitude of both public and press was remarkably different,
as the editorial views expressed about the famous Fountain murder
case clearly show. A. J. Fountain, who during most of his adult life
remained a vigorous advocate of law enforcement, in 1895 was employed
by the New Mexico Cattleman's Association to uncover evidence of
extensive cattle thievery in southern New Mexico. Fountain told friends
that he had sufficient evidence to indict for cattle theft a Dona Ana
County rancher and former deputy sheriff, Oliver Lee, and some of his
associates. Shortly after this Fountain disappeared while driving from
Tularosa to Las Cruces. Evidence found along this route, which was
near the Lee ranch, indicated that he had been murdered, but his body
was never found. Subsequently when Pat Garrett, then Dona Ana

County sheriff, sought to arrest him, Lee and his followers resisted and a deputy sheriff was killed. Lee in a letter to the Las Cruces *Independent Democrat* defended his actions on grounds that members of the posse were his enemies and that he feared for his life. Eventually he surrendered to another sheriff, employed A. B. Fall as his lawyer, and won acquittal.

The press closely followed the Fountain-Lee case and clearly showed its attitude by its rejection of Lee's contention in his letter that he would not have been given fair treatment after arrest. Only the Las Cruces *Independent Democrat* was sympathetic to Lee.[61] The common editorial view is shown by the following quotations: "Oliver Lee is not improving his side of the case by the course he has adopted, and is rapidly losing what little sympathy he has gained."[62] "There is nothing whatever in Lee's conduct to entitle him to further recognition as anything else than an outlaw. When Garrett's posse came up, he should have given up and not tried to dictate terms to the law."[63] "Oliver Lee's letter will not do him any good. His record is against him and his actions give the lie to his words."[64] "No matter at what time or place the curtain is rung down on this drama of blood, the law's supremacy will be recorded."[65] This last contention seemed to reflect the stand of most of the territorial press —uphold the supremacy of the law and live by rules of law and order or take the consequences. Thus, by 1898 the territorial press had lost the traditional impatience of the frontiersman for the fine points of the law and called for strict adherence to the law and legal procedures.

However, past lawlessness had given New Mexico a bad reputation which some territorial editors were eager to remove, as the following editorial excerpt reveals:

The bulletin of the New Mexico Publicity Association recently announced the inauguration of a campaign to work for the abolition of the "bad man" cartoon of New Mexico in eastern newspapers. The movement is a most necessary one and should have the support of every booster in New Mexico.[66]

The changing attitude of the territorial press toward bringing law and order reflects the general trend among American frontiersmen, except where certain peculiarities of New Mexico gave it a different bent. In most western areas the time from the founding of the first newspapers to the arrival of an era of law and order was relatively short, but in New Mexico it extended from 1847 to about 1884. Accustomed to violence by centuries of frontier life, isolated New Mexicans from 1847 to 1880 were most interested in eliminating the violence of Indian wars. In this early period the only significant effort to bring law and order was that of editor A. J. Fountain of the Mesilla *Valley Independent*. The ending of New Mexican isolation by railways, the subsequent mining boom, and the influx of Anglo-American frontiersmen brought a period very similar to that which occurred in other frontier regions. The press, as it apparently did in other western areas, at first encouraged vigilantes to combat lawless elements but soon demanded the preservation of law and order and the following of regular legal procedures in every case. In this latter phase the territorial press made its greatest contribution toward bringing law and order. In some instances the editors became the leaders of the movement; in others the press became the means of communication between the leaders and the people. Although the suppression of lawlessness and violence was not solely the work of the journalists, it must be recognized that their efforts helped to attain that goal.

The press made less of a contribution to the elimination of vice in New Mexico than it did to the emergence of law and order. National and local reform movements, which reached their peak effectiveness after 1900,[67] were responsible for curtailing vice. Nevertheless, some newspapers did aid in this work, and the Santa Fe *New Mexican* became a rather ardent advocate of these reforms. Most editors favored the closing of saloons on Sundays and the elimination of public gambling. On the other hand, they almost completely ignored the battle to eliminate open prostitution, possibly because they belived this not to be a fit topic for a public newspaper. Few of the editors became exponents of the prohibition movement, apparently believing it sufficient to curb the bad practices of the saloonkeepers.

Although for years there had been attempts to restrict saloons with their accompanying prostitution and gambling, such efforts were intensified after 1900 as a result of the influence of local and national prohibition groups and the increasing maturity of New Mexico. The first important action of the reformers was the attempt to close the saloons on Sundays. The territorial legislature in 1876 had ordered Sunday closing for all but essential businesses. The Santa Fe *New Mexican* immediately held that the law was a good one. The Silver City *Grant County Herald,* on the other hand, was very hostile toward the law, believing it impractical and unenforceable.[68] In subsequent years the law was enforced only intermittently. Even this, however, was apparently more an effort of law enforcement officers to impress moralistic citizens near election times than genuine reform, for the normal Sunday practices were soon resumed.[69] Although the newspapers usually supported the occasional enforcements of the law, until after 1900 no paper made strenuous efforts to have the law rigidly enforced; then the editors gradually swung over to the point of view of the reformers. In September, 1900, all merchants at Silver City agreed to close on Sunday. The Silver City *Independent* praised their action and predicted approval by the general public.[70]

When in 1902 the law was invoked at Socorro, the *Chieftain* expressed surprise and predicted that the law would prove so unpopular that it would be repealed.[71] However, it was enforced and the *Chieftain* soon complained because it was not being enforced also at Albuquerque.

It was during this period that the Santa Fe *New Mexican* became convinced that the law should be enforced throughout the territory and waged a campaign lasting several years to bring this about.[72] The law was enforced after 1902 in Santa Fe and after 1903 in Las Vegas, Deming, Raton, and many other towns. In 1904 the *New Mexican* noted that Albuquerque saloons generally violated the law and agreed with the Albuquerque *Daily Citizen* that the law should either be enforced or repealed.[73] Finally, in 1905, the *New Mexican* jubilantly reported:

> Hurrah for Judge Abbott, and bully for Sheriff Perfecto Armijo! What was deemed impossible six months ago is coming to pass. Sheriff Perfecto Armijo of Bernalillo County, last Sunday, saw to it that the saloons of the Duke City were closed tight, in front as well as back doors. When the New Mexican began its campaign for equal enforcement of the Sunday law throughout the territory and supported Judge John R. McFie in enforcing it in Santa Fe, not only the press and people of Albuquerque, but many people in Santa Fe insisted that this enforcement would never come to pass. . . . That this . . . [enforcement of the law] . . . will redound to the benefit of the Duke City and its people in general goes without saying for no town ever gained permanent prosperity by countenancing law breaking or encouraging gambling.[74]

Although the press did not join the movement to end public gambling until the twentieth century, editors often noted gambling and public action concerning it. For example, in 1876 the Silver City *Grant County Herald* maintained that it was all right for the legislature to empower Grant County to license gambling despite an earlier territorial law prohibiting it. The editor explained that the anti-gambling law was never meant to be enforced, but that the territory took this method of taxing gambling through fines at each term of court.[75] When in 1887 the legislature legalized gambling, the Las Vegas *Daily Optic* approved, holding that the previous subterfuge had been wrong:

> Our legislators took the proper view of the subject by putting a tax upon it, by giving it a legal existence, it would be controlled, restrained, and deprived of many of its most objectionable features. Put a tax on gambling, let it be conducted only in properly licensed houses, and . . . minors will no longer be enticed into dives to be made drunk, robbed of their money, and then thrown into the lascivious embraces of the most degraded of the female sex.[76]

Later efforts to repeal this law led the Deming *Headlight* to state that should they succeed it would "prove to our people the necessity of selecting for legislators citizens of a little above rather than a little below the average in intelligence."[77] However, not all papers approved of legal gambling. The Cerrillos *Rustler,* for example, called for a repeal of this law and the Las Cruces *Rio Grande Republican* endorsed its stand.[78] Nevertheless, there was no serious effort to curtail gambling until the reform movement of the twentieth century included gambling among the vices it was attacking. Probably the press was without deep convictions in the matter and only actively opposed gambling when it appeared that the public was demanding its end.

Artesia apparently was the first town to respond by outlawing gambling in 1905 through a local ordinance.[79] This same year the Santa Fe *New Mexican* began a campaign against legal gambling, citing as an argument the lower criminal rates and mounting savings accounts in towns in which gambling had been outlawed. As other papers joined the fight, the *New Mexican* applauded and republished their editorial comments. Roswell was congratulated for its decision in 1906 to prohibit gambling. Under the leadership of the *New Mexican,* the territorial press became almost unanimous in its attack on legalized gambling. Possibly this encouraged the legislature to enact a law that ended legalized gambling in New Mexico as of December 31, 1907.[80]

While the press was of great assistance to the reform movement in the fight against gambling, it did very little to aid in the elimination of open prostitution. The earliest paper to suggest curtailing prostitution was the Albuquerque *Evening Review.* This paper noted in 1882 that a legislative act of 1860 forbade the practice and lamented that despite this prostitutes still sold their wares in seven houses in the midst of the Albuquerque business district. The *Evening Review* then published scattered brief editorial squibs in the succeeding days asking the city to "remove the prostitutes from Railroad Avenue" and others demanding that the city "have a respectable business street." An Albuquerque minister called the attention of the public to the fact that the editor did not propose to exclude prostitution from the city, but only to relegate it to obscure places. The editor did not answer this criticism but continued his editorial briefs for some time thereafter.[81] The Albuquerque *Morning Democrat* adopted a similar position in 1889, predicting that an attempt of the city to curtail prostitutes would meet with failure. This paper stated that efforts to close "red light districts" in other cities had merely driven prostitutes into respectable neighborhoods and had led to the molestation and contamination of many decent people.[82] When in 1900 Carlsbad passed ordinances prohibiting public prostitution, the Santa Fe *New Mexican* maintained that it would be impossible to enforce this law properly. But in 1903 the same paper noted a death in Tucumcari which occurred as a result of a dispute at a "bawdy house" and asked that district attorneys close such places. The *New Mexican,*

however, retained some of its former attitude, for in 1906 it held that if
such licensed immorality was to be tolerated in Santa Fe it should be
confined to a "red light district" in an obscure part of the city.[83] The
Albuquerque *Morning Journal,* on the other hand, reprinted a 1905
Las Vegas *Daily Optic* editorial telling of an Albuquerque police policy
of licensing prostitutes at $10 each per month, a practice which netted
the city about $800 monthly. Subsequently the *Morning Journal* asked
for the elimination of licensed prostitution. After a brief campaign,
however, the paper halted its efforts, and the practice apparently continued throughout the territorial era.[84]

On the other hand, open prostitution was ended in most of the small
eastern New Mexico towns in this period. For example, in 1908 the
Carlsbad *Argus* noted that every town in the lower Pecos Valley had an
ordinance similar to that of Carlsbad's prohibiting prostitution. Unlike
Carlsbad, however, the other towns enforced their ordinances.[85] An
example of editorial reluctance to discuss prostitution can be seen in
the Portales papers. In their town a citizens' committee expelled the
prostitutes,[86] yet neither Portales paper mentioned the movement. On
the whole, it is evident that the press contributed very little to this
reform.

Despite its lack of an active policy to eliminate prostitution, the press
probably helped indirectly by working with the movement to close
saloons in New Mexico. The press supported the first effective effort to
regulate saloons by endorsing a legislative act of 1891 which raised the
license fees so sharply that the number of saloons was reduced almost 60
per cent by 1893.[87] It was not until the twentieth century, however, that
prohibition sentiment became strong in New Mexico. With the advent
of southern immigrants into the eastern section of the territory, a movement was launched for local option prohibition in that area. The Santa
Fe *New Mexican* was heartily in sympathy with this movement and became one of its chief leaders—at least, this was the contention of the
Roswell *Baptist Workman* in 1906.[88] Editor Max Frost of the *New
Mexican* maintained also that prohibition sentiment was strong among
Spanish-Americans. He believed that the women of this group, having
suffered impoverishment because of liquor, were responsible for this attitude. In the same editorial Frost predicted that 1909 "will bring New
Mexico its two greatest gifts since the American conquest, that of statehood and that of prohibition, or at least complete local option."[89] Frost,
however, was only partially right. Local prohibition was put into effect
by city ordinance in Portales in 1909 and Roswell in 1910. Such an
ordinance was enacted in Santa Fe in 1909, but an election called to
measure public acceptance defeated the move.[90] Although the efforts of
the press in behalf of local option prohibition were not as extensive as

those to eliminate legal gambling, several papers supported the attempt to dry up communities by local option. In the post-territorial era the press became a better supporter of prohibition so that New Mexico voted in 1917 to approve a national prohibition amendment.

It cannot be said, however, that the curtailment of alcoholic beverage sales in New Mexico was the work of the press, for it was mainly the result of the efforts of the prohibition movement. Similarly, it must be said that all of the efforts to make the territory a more civilized community reflected the desires of a majority of New Mexicans, for even the best of leaders can accomplish little without popular support. Nevertheless, at times some editors did provide the necessary leadership to bring these reforms. Probably the greatest contribution of the editors was their demand for an end to the era of criminal violence, and their later demand for respect of law which ultimately helped bring order and peace to New Mexico. Other editors exercised leadership in the movements to close saloons on Sundays and to end legal gambling. On the other hand, the efforts to halt open prostitution and to bring prohibition of the sale of alcoholic beverages were supported by only a few of the editors. Thus, in summing up the contribution of the press to the whole movement to civilize New Mexico it is to be noted that the movement was supported by a majority of New Mexicans and led by the reform movement, with the press more a follower than a leader.

# THE CONTRIBUTIONS OF
# THE TERRITORIAL PRESS

THE DEVELOPMENT OF New Mexico journalism was very similar to that of all rural American journalism, particularly in the West, but territorial journalism consistently lagged behind the general progress because of the isolation, mixed population, and poverty of New Mexico. When New Mexico became a possession of the United States, it was on the far frontier, hundreds of miles to the west of the line of westward-marching pioneer farmers. Thirty years passed before this isolation was ended, and it was fifty years until the frontier farmers reached New Mexico in any considerable numbers. Until 1878 the press of New Mexico, largely run by Anglo-Americans, was forced to serve two cultural groups and thus was handicapped by the necessity of dividing its already limited space between two languages. With the advent of railways in 1878 the first large Anglo-American immigration began. With the newcomers came a great many Anglo-American journalists who largely ignored the Spanish cultural element and published newspapers almost exclusively in English. In this they were practical because the lack of schools in poverty-ridden New Mexico had left the native people illiterate, and it was wise to publish papers for the literate immigrants. However, the new journalists did not ignore the poverty of New Mexico because it threatened to slow population growth and business prosperity, limiting circulation and advertising incomes. Because territorial isolation, poverty, and the problems of a bilingual population reduced profits, the elimination of these handicaps became of great interest to territorial editors.

The most significant contribution of the press of New Mexico was the aid it gave to solving the problems of isolation, poverty, and the Americanization of New Mexico's Spanish-speaking people. One of the first concerns of the editors became that of ending isolation, and for more than two decades the editors extolled the advantages of railways and encouraged others to invite, and make New Mexico attractive to, railroad builders. Once the first rail line arrived, the editors did not cease their efforts but intensified them, continually inviting new railroads to come and open more and more of the territory. They made and urged other New Mexicans to make the sacrifices that would induce railroad construction, and by 1912 New Mexico was well served by a network of railways. While this was not the work of the editors alone, they had played a significant part.

The ending of isolation caused the press to intensify its efforts to hasten the economic development of New Mexico and to combat the evil of poverty. The journalists encouraged the development of mining by announcing the rich strikes and printing detailed information of the mineral deposits and discoveries that would induce capitalists and prospectors to come and exploit these resources. At the same time they continued to urge the development of irrigation as a means of bringing a better life to New Mexicans already farming and inducing a new immigration of farmers who would promote territorial growth. The press kept the public informed of the new irrigation techniques, encouraged efforts to find new sources of water, and battled to preserve territorial water rights; when eventually the advancing line of frontier farmers reached New Mexico, they were welcomed by the editors, who soon saw the necessity of helping these farmers adapt themselves to the conditions of New Mexico. The newcomers were urged to adopt the dry-farming system and to diversify crops in order that they might obtain the maximum revenues from their farms. The press, on the other hand, was less interested in the development of the livestock industry, perhaps because in ranching only a few people were needed to work on a range that might consist of thousands of acres. Therefore, development of the livestock industry would never encourage the large immigration so desired by the journalists. Nevertheless, the editors also offered this industry aid, encouraging ranchers to improve breeds and to form cattlemen's associations to protect their interests. Altogether the press did a great deal to relieve the poverty of New Mexico by inviting and encouraging the railroads, the miners, the farmers, and the ranchers to come and exploit New Mexican resources.

A problem equally as important to the editors as the isolation and poverty of New Mexico was that of reconciling its conflicting cultures. The first step was that of eliminating the Indian menace, a problem which of course was common to all the American West. In this matter the editors echoed the demands of the public and often led the public to make those demands. Such efforts coupled with those of other western areas brought the matter to the attention of the nation, and the federal

government was forced to act. Meanwhile, the press had already turned
to the problem of Anglicizing New Mexico's Spanish-speaking people.
Reconciliation of the differences between Anglos and Spanish in religion posed no particular problem, despite the fact that most of the
Anglo-American editors were Protestants. These tolerant frontier journalists generally cited the American Bill of Rights with its guarantee of
freedom of religion and vigorously rebuked any who adopted a bigoted
point of view. Ethnic differences presented more of a problem, but its
severity was reduced because of the docility and general good will of the
Spanish-Americans. As a result, after a few years' residence in New
Mexico, the editors usually defended the Hispanos against the more
aggressive Anglos. Education, on the other hand, became more of a
problem, for the native New Mexicans desired parochial schools supported by public funds in which the language, culture, and religion of
their ethnic group would be taught. Ultimately the newsmen won their
campaign for free, public non-sectarian schools taught in the English
language. Such schools held out the prospect of a more rapid Americanization of the native New Mexicans by promising to eliminate the language barrier and to remove ethnic prejudices through close association
of the two peoples from early childhood.

Almost equally as pressing as the problem of reconciling conflicting
cultures was the necessity of taming frontier violence and immorality—
another problem common to most western areas. With the arrival of the
large number of Anglo-Americans and a growing press to serve them, the
editors made a determined attack on criminal violence. Usually with
the encouragement of the journalists, and sometimes under their leadership, vigilance committees ended extreme lawlessness and violence in
the towns. In subsequent years the editors pressed for strict adherence to
law and order, aiding in the pacification of all of New Mexico. Then in
the final territorial decade the press helped local and national reform
movements to close saloons in some towns and to provide for closer
supervision of them in others. Public gambling was also eliminated with
the aid of the press in this period. As a result, by 1912 New Mexico had
been transformed into a rather placid rural area.

The decline of violence, vice, and moral laxity more closely aligned
New Mexico with the American nation and consequently hastened the
coming of statehood. This was a topic to which the journalists dedicated
thousands of editorial comments. Until about 1900 the editors advanced
views on the question of statehood generally in line with the policies of
their political parties. Soon after 1900, almost all the newsmen united
on the desirability of statehood and conducted a sustained drive to
achieve it.

In addition to efforts to solve the problems resulting from isolation, poverty, and the mixed population of New Mexico, the press made the normal contribution of newspapers to public information in general. The press provided news and information about national and local events in political, cultural, and economic affairs. Such information extends the awareness of readers, allowing them to learn relatively quickly of events which may in future affect their lives. The territorial press through its news stories and editorials speculated about or predicted the effect of some of these events on the lives of New Mexicans, rendering to them a valuable service.

Although the territorial journalists made significant contributions to the development of New Mexico, they did not always use their positions to the best advantage of the territory. Among the most notable faults of the press were its failure to push for continued improvements in schools after 1894 and its somewhat reluctant support of the reform movement's efforts to curtail vice. The editors also failed to offer or support plans that were proposed to help the Indians integrate themselves into territorial life as useful, productive, and self-sufficient citizens. The demands of the editors of southeastern New Mexico for the curtailment of the civil and political rights of Spanish-Americans displayed a bigotry and a shortsightedness that were among the more lamentable failures of the press.

Perhaps the greatest shortcoming of the New Mexico press was its failure to establish its independence from political control until very late in the territorial era. However, this was not unique, for small newspapers all over America were in a similar condition of political dependence. Only the newspapers of the large cities had much prospect of developing sufficient revenue to remain outside the control of the politicians. And it should be noted to the credit of the territorial press that when the economy of some towns did develop sufficiently to support independent newspapers several publishers took the opportunity to assert their independence.

It was not alone the poverty of New Mexico but also harsh and incessant newspaper competition that forced the editors to submit to the will of the politicians. Since in these years only a small capital investment was required to launch a paper, political leaders could easily found or sponsor a paper that would follow their dictates, thereby providing a rival to drain away part of the revenues of the journalists who dared to challenge them. The blasted hopes and careers of such able publishers as J. G. Albright of the Albuquerque *Morning Democrat* or Russell Kistler of the Las Vegas *Daily Optic* provide examples of those who dared to follow independent political policies.[1] Thus, harsh and almost continuous competition seems to have been a significant facet of territorial journalism, crippling the efforts of some journalists to improve their papers and forcing others to seek political subsidy and submit to political control.

Newspaper rivalry varied from town to town but was generally more hectic in the booming mining camps and rapidly growing towns. While there was less competition in the quiet agricultural towns of eastern New Mexico, even here there were usually two papers in towns which provided insufficient revenue to support one. Rivalries of the types described earlier apparently were common among small rural newspapers throughout the United States, but the period of hectic competition began to decline about the time New Mexico became a state.[2] Thus, intense journalistic competition and the beginning of its decline apparently were characteristic of all rural American journalism in these years.

Competition is not inherently bad, for under the impetus of rivalry men are inspired to greater diligence and effort from which society in general can benefit. Journalistic rivalry might lead to lower subscription and advertising prices, better reporting, more extensive news coverage, and serve as the means of presenting contrasting views to the public. In territorial New Mexico, however, improvements in journalism resulting from competitive struggles appeared to be very limited. As has been shown earlier the chief competitive method of weeklies was to begin daily publication, while dailies bought and sometimes tried to monopolize Associated Press services. In some instances rivalry provided a town with a daily newspaper and the Associated Press services years earlier than would have occurred without such contests. Nevertheless, in most instances daily publication was soon abandoned, and in other instances the Associated Press was quickly abandoned or monopolized to withhold it from rivals. Newspaper competition probably advanced the dates of the beginning of daily papers and the Associated Press service at Santa Fe, Albuquerque, Las Vegas, and Roswell, and thus provided some limited benefits to the territorial public.

Among the other prospective gains from newspaper competition are lower advertising and subscription prices. But in New Mexico, while subscription prices were lowered gradually throughout the territorial era, this trend appears to have been more the result of reductions in newsprint prices and freight costs than in benefits derived from competitive battles between newspapers. After 1900 there was a deliberate effort to reduce subscription rates to gain circulation and, as a result, higher advertising rates. These lower prices were not brought about primarily by competition. On the other hand, advertising rates probably were reduced as a result of rivalry, although there is little positive evidence because most advertising rates apparently were set by private bargaining. It does not seem, however, that all advertisers benefited from this practice because before 1900 most advertisers patronized the paper which had their party's endorsement, and it is probable that such advertisers received no preferential rate. Other merchants, interested in advertising as a sales tool, really received little benefit from the lower rates resulting from rivalry. Instead of providing lower advertising costs per reader, competition, by dividing the newspaper subscriptions, actually made advertising costs higher.[3] On the whole, it appears that newspaper rivalry did not produce substantially lower subscription prices and advertising costs.

As shown, competing papers divided the available income that might have been derived from advertising and subscriptions. This reduced publishing to a struggle for existence, forcing many newsmen to hold other jobs in order to maintain their papers. Such publishers could ill afford to hire more and better reporters, to improve news coverage, and to publish the larger papers necessary to print this news. Because competition so limited income, it seems to be a fact that journalists more often produced worse rather than better newspapers as a result of rivalry.

A possible asset of newspaper rivalry is the prospect that the public will be presented with contrasting views on vital public issues. This certainly appeared to be a possibility in New Mexico where many towns had both a Democratic and Republican paper, and in the larger towns other partisan groups were represented. The low cost of establishing and sustaining newspapers made such diversity possible. Despite newspaper potential for representation of diverse partisan groups, it seems doubtful, because of the customs of that day, that the general public was well informed on the various views. Most of the subscribers attracted by the partisan papers were those who wished to read the views of their own partisan groups. And in most instances editorial policies were controlled by political leaders who used these means to present political propaganda to their followers. As has been shown earlier, this propaganda appealed to the prejudices of the voters and avoided the true issues of territorial life. For the most part, before 1900, newspaper subscribers in New Mexico were neither reading the diverse views available to them nor being presented the true issues. Thus, it appears that before 1900 New Mexicans received few of the expected benefits of rivalry such as better newspapers, lower prices, and the presentation of diverse views.

By 1900 a new type of journalism was possible. Improved composition and printing machinery made possible expanded newspapers and circulations. Retail merchants, following new merchandising concepts, began to buy more and larger advertisements. In these same years the influence of the progressive movement encouraged New Mexicans to appear independent and to subscribe to an independent newspaper. Publishers more and more began to cater to the wishes of this group because they were being freed from dependence on political leaders by the increased revenue from retailer advertising. Part of these profits was invested in the production of better newspapers, and many new subscribers were attracted who had not in the past been avid partisans and had not sub-scribed to newspapers. As a result, by 1912 a great many papers, nomi-nally affiliated with one of the parties but no longer controlled by politi-cal leaders, were adopting an increasingly independent position.[4] The trend toward newspaper monopoly was the result of  major forces in American life such as industrialization, improved business techniques for selling mass-produced merchandise, and the progressive movement. On the whole, it brought a much better journalism than had been produced by the harsh competition so prevalent before 1900.

  With the advent of independent newspapers, publishers became more important in the territorial political power structure. Editors were free to analyze and to point out the needs of the territory so that the poli-ticians could no longer so easily appeal to the voters on the basis of the old prejudices. Political officeholders now faced the prospect of sharp inquiries about their conduct in office from the independent editors. Newspaper criticism was more often based on facts and provided valu-able information for the guidance of the citizens.[5] On the whole, the freeing of the territorial editors from political control had a wholesome effect on New Mexico politics, and, as has been pointed out earlier, aided the reform movements to cleanse the politics of the new state.

  The various factors such as the new printing machinery, the profitable new advertising, and the progressive reform movement began to be of influence in New Mexico about 1900, and that year seems to have been a turning point in territorial journalism. Journalists who began and served most of their careers before 1900 were quite different from the new breed of journalists who became prominent after 1900. Perhaps the two best illustrations of this were the careers of Max Frost and D. A. Macpherson. However, to evaluate the contributions of the territorial journalists of either era one should consider the peculiar handicaps and advantages of each group.

  Frost of the Santa Fe *New Mexican* displays best the good and bad traits apparent in New Mexico journalism before 1900. Certainly in politics the record was very bad for both Frost and the *New Mexican*. From first to last, the *New Mexican* and Frost supported a corrupt clique of politicians who often used their positions for personal advantages. Furthermore, since the *New Mexican* was one of the leading territorial papers, and particularly influential with Republicans, its editorial policies were followed by many smaller papers, extending this harmful bias. On the other hand, outside of partisan politics Frost and the *New Mexican* usually adopted a course that was beneficial to the territory.

To illustrate, the *New Mexican* was the most consistent and strongest advocate of statehood throughout the period. This paper was also a constant defender of the political and civil rights of Spanish-Americans. It interested itself in all facets of the economic development of New Mexico and consistently advocated, with thousands of editorials, policies to aid that development. In addition, the *New Mexican* more than any other single paper became the spokesman for the reform movement in New Mexico after 1900 and was particularly effective in helping to end legal gambling and in closing saloons on Sundays. Finally, no other territorial paper was a more consistent advocate of improving education in the territory. The conclusion seems warranted that Frost and the *New Mexican* despite their records in politics made a significant contribution to the development of New Mexico.

It is difficult to reconcile the divergent attitudes with regard to reform and politics. But the answer lies in part in the inability of Santa Fe to provide proper support for a daily newspaper of the quality of the *New Mexican*.[6] Under these conditions the *New Mexican* was made a captive of the politicians because of its dependence on public printing contracts. While this does not excuse the poor political record of Frost and the *New Mexican,* it does explain how he and the paper could follow divergent policies In appraising the true position of Frost in territorial journalism, the ideas of a contemporary editor seem particularly apt. The opinion of W. B. Walton, editor of the Silver City *Independent,* is significant because at one time Walton was a vigorous opponent of Frost.[7] Perhaps this was a family attitude gained from his father-in-law, S. M. Ashenfelter, and another relative, Governor E. G. Ross, under both of whom Walton began his journalistic career. Eventually, however, Walton changed his opinion of Frost as his editorial of 1905 indicates:

> When writing and speaking of Colonel Frost, the student of New Mexico affairs immediately thinks of the Santa Fe New Mexican, for the New Mexican is Colonel Frost and Colonel Frost has been the New Mexican for thirty years. He is the Nestor of journalists in the territory, and his individuality has been accentuated by his activity as a newspaper writer, and yet the man is so much more than his newspaper and he has taken such an active hand in the formation of the political and industrial life of New Mexico today that the historian of the future must study the deeds and aims of this leader if he would form a clear idea of what the territory is at the present day in every respect. . . . The man is terribly misjudged by those he is called upon to oppose in political life, but whose work New Mexico will approve more highly on some future day.[8]

The career of Frost represents the extremes of good and bad in territorial journalism, and the careers of most territorial journalists of the years before 1900 reflect to a lesser degree these same extremes.

As the career of Frost displays best the good and bad traits of territorial journalism before 1900, so does the career of D. A. Macpherson best reflect the new trend in the territorial journalism of the years after 1900. Macpherson accepted the new printing techniques and adopted the tactics of yellow journalism to increase the circulation of his Albuquerque *Morning Journal*. With increased circulation came the profitable new retail advertising and financial independence. The financially independent *Morning Journal* had to answer only to its subscribers, and as long as they continued to buy the paper its editors could freely embrace the unpopular but worthy causes, defy political and economic leaders, and develop the leadership that is an essential component of newspaper greatness. Macpherson is significant for New Mexico journalism because he first pointed out the route to truly independent journalism in New Mexico; and in following his example, the press became increasingly freed from political and economic control in the new state of New Mexico.

# NOTES

## CHAPTER I

[1] In contrast, during the first twelve years of the booming California mining camps more than 600 different papers were published. See Edward C. Kemble, *A History of California Newspapers, 1846-1858,* ed. Helen Harding Bretnor, (Los Gatos, California, 1962); hereafter cited as Kemble, *History of California Newspapers.*

[2] Henry R. Wagner, "New Mexico Spanish Press," *New Mexico Historical Review,* XII (January, 1937), pp. 1-12; hereafter cited as Wagner, *New Mexico Historical Review,* XII. A possible fourth paper, unlisted above, is Padre Jose Antonio Martinez' Taos *El Crepusculo.* This paper has been listed by several New Mexico historians, but Wagner compiles circumstantial evidence that casts serious doubt upon its existence in Taos.

[3] Santa Fe *Republican,* January 1, 1847. A prospectus was a sample issue from which subscriptions and future advertising could be sold. This was a common practice in this period.

[4] *Ibid.,* September 10, 1847.

[5] *Ibid.,* January 15, 1848; Albuquerque *Rio Abajo Weekly Press,* January 20, 1863; Santa Fe *New Mexican,* November 28, 1849. See Oliver La Farge, *Santa Fe: The Autobiography of a Southwestern Town* (Norman, Oklahoma, 1959), pp. 3-8; hereafter cited as La Farge, *Santa Fe.*

[6] Santa Fe *Weekly Gazette,* December 17, 1864, February 19, 1853. From the numbering of the latter issue it can be deduced that the paper was founded early in June, 1851, if no publication dates were missed. Since missing publication dates was rather usual, possibly the *Gazette* started earlier in 1851.

[7] James L. Collins, a native of Kentucky and former resident of Missouri, first came to New Mexico in the Santa Fe trade in which he engaged from 1826 until the Mexican War. During the war, he joined the United States Army, and after the war he established his home in Santa Fe. He was the founder of the *Gazette* and was its editor and publisher several times. At other times he occupied various offices in the Indian Agency and the territorial government. Collins fought in the battles of Valverde and Apache Canyon as a member of the Union forces. While serving as United States Depositary in June, 1869, he was murdered during a robbery of his office.

[8] Albuquerque *Rio Abajo Weekly Press,* January 20, 1863.

[9] Mesilla *Times,* October 18, 1860, to January 15, 1862; Las Cruces *Rio Grande Republican,* April 8, 1882, January 20, 1899; United States Census Office, *Population of the United States in 1860: The Eighth Census* (Washington, 1864), pp. 566-73; hereafter cited as *Eighth Census.*

[10] Albuquerque *Rio Abajo Weekly Press,* January 20, 1863.

[11] *Ibid.,* January 20, August 4, 11, 1863, May 10, 1864; Santa Fe *New Mexican,* November 7, 1863, May 27, 1864.

[12] Santa Fe *Daily New Mexican,* June 9, 1868.

[13] Santa Fe *Weekly Gazette,* September 11, 25, 1869; Santa Fe *Weekly Post,* October 16, 1869.

[14] Albuquerque *Republican Review,* June 17, 1871; Santa Fe *Weekly New Mexican,* March 4, July 23, 1872.

[15] Santa Fe *Weekly New Mexican,* August 27, 1872, February 17, 1874; Albuquerque *Daily Journal,* March 1, 1881.

[16] Silver City *Mining Life,* October 31, 1874; Albuquerque *Republican Review,* October 16, 1875.

[17] Albuquerque *Republican Review,* September 5, November 14, 1875.

[18] Santa Fe *Weekly New Mexican,* August 31, September 14, 1878.

[19] Silver City *Grant County Herald,* January 19, 1878, March 29, 1879; Santa Fe *Rocky Mountain Sentinel,* November 7, 1878; Albuquerque *Review,* July 17, 1879.

[20] Albuquerque *Review,* December 31, 1879; Albuquerque *Daily Journal,* March 1, 1881.

[21] Santa Fe *Weekly New Mexican,* July 18, 1876, March 20, 1878; Albuquerque *Daily Journal,* March 1, 1881; N. W. *Ayer and Son's American Newspaper Annual* (Philadelphia, 1880), p. 224; hereafter cited as *Ayer, American Newspaper Annual* (with year of publication).

[22] Santa Fe *Daily New Mexican,* December 31, 1877.

[23] H. S. Johnson, a native of Pennsylvania, came to New Mexico in 1849 following an older brother, H. C. Johnson, who was a political appointee in the territorial administration. In 1853 H. S. Johnson became an apprentice printer on the Santa Fe *Weekly Gazette* and for a short time in 1859 edited this paper. In 1863 he was elected to the territorial legislature, and in 1869 he was appointed judge in the Second Judicial District and continued in this position until his death in 1876.

[24] Albuquerque *Rio Abajo Weekly Press,* January 20, 1863; *Eighth Census,* pp. 566-73.

[25] Albuquerque *Republican Review,* March 16, 1870; Albuquerque *Review,* April 29, 1876, December 31, 1880.

[26] Santa Fe *Weekly Gazette,* July 20, 1867; Mesilla *Weekly Times,* July 21, 1867; Santa Fe *New Mexican,* August 24, 1867.

[27] Las Cruces *Rio Grande Republican,* April 8, 1882; Santa Fe *Weekly New Mexican,* October 19, 1869.

[28] United States Census Office, *Ninth Census, Vol. I. Statistics of the Population of the United States, 1870* (Washington, 1872), pp. 204-06; hereafter cited as *Ninth Census.* See also Las Cruces *Borderer,* March 16, 1871.

[29] Silver City *Grant County Herald,* February 27, 1876. N. V. Bennett was a native of New York and had taught school in Louisiana and Texas. Several years before he came to New Mexico for his health, Bennett had edited the Red Wing, Minnesota, *Argus.* In New Mexico he became a leader in the Democratic party and was believed to have been the best potential candidate of that party for congressional delegate in 1875. However, he rejected the nomination because of illness.

[30] Santa Fe *Daily New Mexican,* October 12, 1873; Mesilla *News,* March 14, August 27, 1874; Santa Fe *Weekly New Mexican,* March 30, 1878.

[31] Mesilla *Valley Independent,* June 23, 1877, July 26, 1879. The latter date is the last issue of extant copies; and since no further mention of the *Valley Independent* was found in any other territorial paper, this is preseumed to be the final issue.

[32] Mesilla *El Democrata,* September 14 to November 2, 1878; Hillsboro *Sierra County Advocate,* May 5, 1911. S. H. Newman earlier had been editor-publisher of the *Mail* at Las Vegas, but he lost this paper when he was convicted of libeling T. B. Catron, territorial attorney general. Unable to pay a fine for his conviction for criminal libel, Newman sought to edit the *Mail* from the Las Vegas jail but failed. Las Cruces *Thirty-Four* remained at Las Cruces until 1882 and then was moved to El Paso and renamed the *Lone Star.* Newman edited this paper intermittently as a daily and weekly until the mid-eighties. Eventually he moved to Albuquerque where he became a successful insurance man.

[33] Las Vegas *Acorn,* May 25, 1875; Santa Fe *Weekly New Mexican,* January 25, 1870; see also Santa Fe *New Mexico Advertiser* above. A. V. Aoy, a native of Spain had lived

in Cuba and Mexico before coming to the United States. After being involved in newspaper publication for over ten years at Las Vegas, Santa Fe, Wallace, and Cerrillos, Aoy lived for a short time at Salt Lake City, Utah. Later he founded a school at El Paso, Texas, to teach English to Spanish-American children. This school was a part of the public school system at El Paso, and El Pasoans have honored Aoy by giving his name to one of their city schools. See Dolores P. Lugo, "Aoy's Gift to El Paso," *The Junior Historian of the Texas State Historical Association*, XXV (September, 1964), pp. 10-15; population of Las Vegas, *Ninth Census*, pp. 204-06.

[34] Albuquerque *Republican Review*, July 22, 1871, September 21, 1872; Las Cruces *Borderer*, August 31, 1872; Albuquerque *Daily Journal*, March 1, 1881.

[35] Albuquerque *Republican Review*, October 13, 1873; Silver City *Mining Life*, April 11, 1874; Santa Fe *Weekly New Mexican*, March 23, 1875. J. H. Koogler, an Iowan and a graduate of one of that state's normal schools, had earlier edited the Cimarron *News*. After selling the *Daily Gazette* in 1883, Koogler remained at Las Vegas, becoming a lawyer. His brother, W. G. Koogler, who also worked for the *Gazette*, later served as San Miguel County superintendent of schools.

[36] Santa Fe *Weekly New Mexican*, January 5, 1875; *Ayer, American Newspaper Annual*, 1880-1912 (New Mexico pages).

[37] Albuquerque *Daily Journal*, March 1, 1881; Santa Fe *Weekly New Mexican*, October 6, 13, 1869.

[38] Albuquerque *Daily Journal*, March 1, 1881; Albuquerque *Republican Review*, September 9, 1871, February 3, 1872.

[39] Santa Fe *Weekly New Mexican*, October 11, 1870, December 22, 1874; Albuquerque *Evening Review*, November 2, 1882.

[40] Silver City *Mining Life*, May 17, 1873. Editors of this era usually headed the first editorial of the first issue of their paper "Salutatory." This was usually a long statement of the aims of the paper. Correspondingly when a paper suspended, it often published a "Valedictory," explaining why it was necessary to suspend publication.

[41] Silver City *Grant County Herald*, March 6-23, 1875. The *Herald's* profitableness can be deduced by the fact that it had the highest advertising rate of any territorial paper of this era and consistently had the largest percentage of advertising.

[42] Among the editors, publishers, and directors of this paper were Dav. J. Miller and S. M. Yost, Indian Agency; C. P. Clever, adjutant general and other positions; J. L. Collins, Indian Agency and United States Depositary; J. T. Russell, Indian Agency and adjutant general.

[43] W. H. Manderfield, a Pennsylvanian, came to New Mexico from Pueblo, Colorado, to become the shop foreman of the Santa Fe *New Mexican* in 1863. Thomas Tucker, an Ohioan, had worked on Kansas and Denver papers as a printer and in Colorado and New Mexico mines. When he first came to Santa Fe, Tucker was a printer on the Santa Fe *Weekly Gazette*. See Chapter IV for the political activities of Manderfield and Tucker.

[44] A. J. Fountain came to New Mexico with the California Volunteers and immediately after the Civil War, as a resident of El Paso County, Texas, served two terms in the Reconstruction era Texas Senate. Later he returned to New Mexico and established himself as a lawyer. He became a co-publisher and editor of the Mesilla *Valley Independent*, and later was a stockholder of the Las Cruces *Rio Grande Republican*. He served several terms in the New Mexico legislature, was an assistant district attorney, and as a colonel of New Mexico militia led troops against Indians and rustlers. While representing the New Mexico Cattlemen's Association, he was murdered in 1896. His body was never found, creating one of the most famous and controversial mysteries in New Mexico's past. A gold miner, printer, journalist, and fledgling lawyer while in California, Fountain is believed by a recent biographer to have been a native of New York. See A. M. Gibson, *The Life and Death of Colonel Albert Jennings Fountain* (Norman, Oklahoma, 1965), pp. 5-9; hereafter cited as Gibson, *Life and Death of Colonel Albert Jennings Fountain*.

[45] Albuquerque *Rio Abajo Weekly Press*, January 20, 1863.

[46] Albuquerque *Republican Review*, April 23, 1870.

[47] Santa Fe *Weekly Gazette*, May 22, 1958.

⁴⁸ S. M. Ashenfelter, a native of Pennsylvania, was appointed a territorial district attorney by a Republican administration in 1869. Dismissed from this position, he began the practice of law at Las Cruces, where he met and married the daughter of a prominent Democrat, Cornelius Bennett, and became a Democrat. In 1877 he became editor-publisher of the Silver City *Grant County Herald* and retained a connection with this paper and its successors until the mid-eighties. At the same time, he continued to practice law and became one of the most prominent lawyers in southwestern New Mexico. See also Chapter IV.

⁴⁹ San Lorenzo *Red River Chronicle*, May 3, 1882.

⁵⁰ Albuquerque *Review*, March 9, 1878. McGuiness apparently was well educated, having spent three years in a Dublin, Ireland, collegiate seminary. He came to America in the 1850's and joined the American army. During his service he was stationed on the frontier in Utah and in New Mexico. Louis Hommel was in the same army unit with McGuiness, and both of the men took Spanish-American wives in New Mexico and remained in the territory. Hommel also apparently was well educated and was literate in three languages. Before becoming editor of the Las Vegas *Gazette*, Hommel conducted a school at Trinidad, Colorado, teaching Anglo-Americans and Spanish-Americans to speak Spanish and English, respectively.

⁵¹ In common terminology in this era, editors "ascended the tripod" upon becoming an editor. *Webster's International Dictionary* defines tripod as a three-legged stool upon which early nineteenth-century aspirants for college degrees were seated during their final oral examinations. Thus, editors, like the candidates, were expected to be able to answer all questions. Another term used by the editors of this era was "sanctum," which was the editor's office. Dictionaries define sanctum as a secluded place for deep concentration and study. Thus, the editors' terminology reveals their self-estimate as men of erudition and intellect.

⁵² Silver City *New Southwest*, April 23, 1881.

⁵³ Silver City *Grant County Herald*, January 20, 1877.

⁵⁴ Santa Fe *Weekly New Mexican*, March 30, 1875.

⁵⁵ Albuquerque *Rio Abajo Weekly Press*, May 10, 1864.

⁵⁶ Silver City *Grant County Herald*, September 1, 1877.

⁵⁷ Albuquerque *Rio Abajo Weekly Press*, January 20, 1863.

⁵⁸ Santa Fe *Weekly New Mexican*, April 9, 1872.

⁵⁹ Silver City *Mining Life*, October 25, 1873, November 14, 1874; Mesilla *News*, September 5 to December 5, 1874, *passim*.

⁶⁰ Frank Luther Mott, *American Journalism: A History, 1690-1960* (New York, 1962), p. 313; hereafter cited as Mott, *American journalism*.

⁶¹ *Ibid.* Judging by Mott's description of American rural journalists in general, New Mexico editors, considering their handicaps, were above the average. At the same time American papers were generally better than comparable papers of the 1880's in New Mexico. Albuquerque *Review*, July 15, 1876.

⁶² Albuquerque *Rio Abajo Weekly Press*, May 5, June 30, July 7, 1863, July 19, 1864, provides an example of an unsuccessful effort to publish separate Spanish- and English-language newspapers at the same plant. The origin of the term Spanish-American is given in Chapter V, footnote 46.

⁶³ Santa Fe *Weekly New Mexican*, April 20, 1875; Las Cruces *Eco del Rio Grande*, February 12, 1876.

⁶⁴ Editors occasionally signified a willingness to print letters with news or information on economic development from anyone in any part of the territory. For examples, see Santa Fe *Weekly Gazette*, February 5, 1859; Albuquerque *Rio Abajo Weekly Press*, September 1, 1863. As a result of this practice, the early territorial newspapers sometimes provide poor sources for historical facts unless several papers and other sources are compared. However, the familiarity of the editors with the motives, backgrounds, and interests of the leading personalities of the lightly populated territory provided them with an insight which is valuable in understanding territorial history.

⁶⁵ Apparently the only motive for such a wasteful feature was to impart information. Although uncommon in New Mexico in this era, it was more widely used elsewhere.

For examples, see William J. Peterscn, *The Pageant of the Press: A Survey of 125 Years of Iowa Journalism, 1836-1961* (Iowa City, 1962), pp. 65, 71, 94.

⁶⁶ Albuquerque *Rio Abajo Weekly Press,* February 17 to May 12, 1863.

⁶⁷ Albuquerque *Republican Review,* May 31, 1874, *passim.*

⁶⁸ Albuquerque *Rio Abajo Weekly Press,* October 10, 1863.

⁶⁹ Silver City *Grant County Herald,* July 1, 1876.

⁷⁰ Silver City *Grant County Herald,* September 17, 1877.

⁷¹ Silver City *Grant County Herald,* November 5, 1876.

⁷² Silver City *Grant County Herald,* December 8, 1877, and Mesilla *News,* March 13, 1875, both provide examples of multi-tiered headlines.

⁷³ Wagner, *New Mexico Historical Review,* XII, pp. 1-3; Kemble, *History of California Newspapers,* pp. 50-52.

⁷⁴ Comments of contemporary journalists indicate that the press and material of the Santa Fe *Republican* belonged to the United States Army, and the army had a small hand press capable of printing the three- and four-column tabloid page that was being used in this period. Such a press was later used to launch the *Daily Optic* at Las Vegas. Albuquerque *Rio Abajo Weekly Press,* January 20, 1863; Santa Fe *Republican,* March 11, 1848; Las Vegas *Daily Optic,* October 2, 1882.

⁷⁵ Willi Mengel, *Ottmar Mergenthaler and the Printing Revolution* (Brooklyn, 1954), pp. 1-13.

⁷⁶ Albuquerque *Republican Review,* August 21, 1875. At this press speed it would require 32 to 40 hours to print a four-page newspaper with 4,000 subscribers.

⁷⁷ Occasionally the fastest printers of several papers or towns would hold contests in which the best printers would set twelve to fifteen column inches of the body type of the paper per hour. If the best printers working under the impetus of a contest did no better than this, the average journeyman printer probably set less than ten inches per hour. For an example of such a contest, see Las Vegas *Daily Optic,* April 20, 1882.

⁷⁸ Albuquerque *Rio Abajo Weekly Press,* April 14, 1863.

⁷⁹ This appears to be true; previous to Tucker's co-publishership, territorial Supreme Court Justice Kirby Benedict was believed to have been writing editorials for the *New Mexican.* In any case, after this date editorials seem to be more consistent in style and form.

⁸⁰ Albuquerque *Republican Review,* March 16, 1872.

⁸¹ Albuquerque *Review,* March 15, 1879.

⁸² Santa Fe *Republican,* January 1, 1847. Probably the true rates of most territorial papers of this era were known only to the advertisers and publishers, except for the rare non-local advertiser who paid the published rates. It was for such unwary ones that the rates were published; other rates probably were reached by negotiation.

⁸³ Santa Fe *Weekly Gazette,* February 19, 1853.

⁸⁴ Albuquerque *Rio Abajo Weekly Press,* January 20, 1863.

⁸⁵ Santa Fe *Daily New Mexican,* July 9, 1868.

⁸⁶ Silver City *Grant County Herald,* March 6, 1875; see also Weiss, A. E. (ed.), *Editor and Publisher International Yearbook* (New York, 1964), p. 168.

⁸⁷ Mott, *American Journalism,* pp. 397-98.

⁸⁸ For example, see Albuquerque *Republican Review,* December 16, 1871. The *Review* had as its agent Geo. P. Rowell & Company, the advertising representative of a majority of American weeklies of this era.

⁸⁹ Mesilla *Times,* October 18, 1860 to January 15, 1862; Mott, *American Journalism,* pp. 299-397, describes eastern American advertising practices of this era. Frequent copy changes provide more interesting advertising. Hence it is better read, produces more results, and advertisers are encouraged to advertise more. Thus, publishers benefit from more revenue and a more interesting paper.

⁹⁰ For example, see Albuquerque *Republican Review,* March 26, 1870.

⁹¹ Santa Fe *New Mexican,* November 24, 1849; Santa Fe *Daily New Mexican,* July 9, 1868.

⁹² Albuquerque *Rio Abajo Weekly Press,* January 20, 1863.

⁹³ Mott, *American Journalism,* p. 396, states that the average American country

weekly of this time had a circulation of less than 1,000; considering New Mexican illiteracy and the high prices of newspaper subscriptions in New Mexico, the figure 500 appears reasonable for New Mexico weeklies.

⁹⁴ For example, see Albuquerque *Review*, January 13, 1877.

⁹⁵ Silver City *Grant County Herald*, July 6, 1878.

⁹⁶ For more detailed information on the connection between politics, territorial public printing, and the Santa Fe *New Mexican*, see Chapter IV.

⁹⁷ The editors were Louis Hommel, Ira M. Bond, and S. M. Ashenfelter. The two surviving newspapers were the Santa Fe *New Mexican Review*, a combination of the *New Mexican* and Albuquerque *Evening Review*, and the Silver City *Grant County Herald*, which after numerous changes in name became the Silver City *Press and Independent* and survives today, as does the *New Mexican*.

⁹⁸ Albuquerque *Review*, December 31, 1879.

⁹⁹ Santa Fe *Weekly New Mexican*, March 24, 1874.

## CHAPTER II

¹ Later a company of Santa Fe townsmen built a line to Espanola, leasing it to the Denver and Rio Grande in order that Santa Fe could have a direct connection with Denver. See Chapter VI.

² Santa Fe *Weekly New Mexican*, January 3, 1884; Albuquerque *Daily Journal*, March 1, 1881. The bilingual Las Vegas *New Mexico Herald* was established by R. W. Webb, formerly of Little Rock, Arkansas, and Miguel Salazar. Webb later published the Santa Fe *Era Southwestern*, Golden *Retort*, and in 1884 briefly edited the *Daily Gazette* at Las Vegas. U.S. Bureau of the Census, *Thirteenth Census of the United States: Vol. III, Population, 1910* (Washington, 1913), pp. 161-83; hereafter cited as *Thirteenth Census*.

³ Russell Kistler and W. J. Turpen founded the Otero *Optic* May 22, 1879. In July, 1879, the *Optic* was moved from the railway construction-camp town of Otero to Las Vegas. Turpen later sold his equity in the paper to Kistler shortly before it became the *Daily Optic*. Kistler, a native of Ohio, had worked on papers in Indiana, South Dakota, and Montana. W. D. Kistler, brother of Russell, was associated with the management of the paper until his death in 1890. The Kistler brothers were sons of a Methodist minister; despite this background, Russell Kistler in his adult years apparently became an alcoholic. Las Vegas *Daily Optic*, November 5-20, 1879, November 21, 1881, October 2, 1882, July 3, 1884, November 5, 1898.

⁴ *Ibid.*, December 18, 1879, February 5, 1880.

⁵ Silver City *Enterprise*, April 1, 1883.

⁶ Las Vegas *Daily Optic*, April 4, 1883, March 7, May 29, September 10, 1884, February 16-21, September 8, 1885.

⁷ See Chapter IV for complete details and documentation.

⁸ Santa Fe *Weekly New Mexican*, October 18, 1880; Las Vegas *Daily Optic*, October 8, 1886; Las Vegas *San Miguel County Republican*, October 16-30, 1886, Las Vegas *Cachiporra*, October 19, 1888, Las Vegas *Cachiporrita*, October 8, 1890.

⁹ Albuquerque *Daily Journal*, March 1, 1881; *Ayer, American Newspaper Annual*, 1881, p. 293, 1886, p. 370. W. C. Hadley, original editor and publisher of *Mining World*, was educated at Haverford College and the University of Chicago as a mining engineer. Hadley, a native of Indiana, also edited the Las Vegas *Daily Gazette*, was the first president of the New Mexico Press Association, and later made a fortune from Lake Valley, New Mexico, mines before his death in 1896. Hadley was the son of a distinguished New Mexico educator, Hiram Hadley, who was first president of the present-day New Mexico State University, president of the University of New Mexico, and territorial superintendent of education.

¹⁰ San Lorenzo *Red River Chronicle*, July 1, 1882; Las Cruces *Rio Grande Republi-*

*can,* April 29, 1883, February 29, 1884. In January, 1886, the *New Mexico* portion of its title was dropped and it became *The Stock Grower.*

[11] Santa Fe *Weekly New Mexican Review,* September 11, 1884; Silver City *Enterprise,* November 27, 1886; Las Cruces *Rio Grande Republican,* May 2, 1887, January 7, 1888, January 5, 1900; Las Vegas *Sunday Courier,* July 8, 1888; Las Vegas *Sunday Morning Review,* June 25, December 24, 1899.

[12] Las Vegas *Daily Optic,* October 14, 1884, July 10, 1886; Las Vegas *Chronicle,* December 14, 1884. In this campaign two Republicans and a Democrat sought election as delegates to Congress. The *Daily Optic* and the *Daily Chronicle* each supported one of the Republicans, and the *Daily Gazette* supported the Democratic candidate. Louis Hommel, editor of the *Chronicle,* was one of the most colorful of the editors of the territorial era. A native of Germany, Hommel was literate in three languages. Hommel was the founder of the Las Vegas *Gazette* and while a co-owner of this paper was charged with assault. After his release on bond, he was arrested again and charged with stealing a horse. During this arrest he struggled with a deputy sheriff and killed him. Hommel was then convicted of murder but was later pardoned by Governor Lew Wallace. Soon after his pardon, Hommel in June, 1880, launched the San Lorenzo *Red River Chronicle.* San Lorenzo was a small village on the upper Canadian River. Later the *Chronicle* was moved to nearby San Hilario, and in 1884 to Las Vegas. Hommel's last paper was *La Cronica de Mora,* which he was publishing at the time of his death in 1890. (See also Chapter I, footnote 50.)

[13] White Oaks *New Mexico Interpreter,* March 13, 1891; Deming *Headlight,* December 19, 1881; Las Cruces *Rio Grande Republican,* November 25, 1892.

[14] Las Cruces *Rio Grande Republican,* June 7, 1895; Las Vegas *Stock Grower and Farmer,* January 2, 1897; *Ayer, American Newspaper Annual,* 1896, p. 505, 1898, p. 529; Las Vegas *Daily Optic,* February 9-28, 1898. Among the major stockholders of the company which acquired the *Optic* in 1898 were Felix Martinez, Union People's party leader and later prominent as a Democrat; A. A. Jones, future Democratic United States Senator from New Mexico; and F. A. Manzanares, Democratic delegate to Congress from New Mexico, 1883-85. George T. Gould, a doctor of divinity and former Methodist minister, was a native of Kentucky. He later published newspapers at El Paso and Albuquerque and was prominent in territorial Democratic circles.

[15] Santa Fe *New Mexican,* October 17, 1900.

[16] Santa Fe *Sun,* June 6, 1890; Santa Fe *Voz del Pueblo,* October 20, 1888, February 2, 1889, June 7, 1890; Las Vegas *Voz del Pueblo,* June 14, 1890; Las Vegas *Independiente,* March 24, 1894. Felix Martinez, leader of the Union People's party at Las Vegas, became publisher of *La Voz del Pueblo,* which had originally been launched as a Democratic campaign paper.

[17] *Thirteenth Census,* pp. 161-83.

[18] Santa Fe *Daily New Mexican,* February 27, 1880; Santa Fe *Weekly New Mexican,* March 15, 1880; Santa Fe *Era Southwestern,* September 30, 1880.

[19] J. G. Albright, a native of Ohio, had been engaged in newspaper publication in Missouri and Kansas before he came to New Mexico in 1880. Later he founded the Albuquerque *Daily Democrat,* which he continued to publish until 1895. Albright then was engaged in newspaper publication at El Paso, and in 1910 he founded the Albuquerque weekly *New Mexico State Democrat,* which he published for the remainder of the territorial era.

[20] Santa Fe *Daily Democrat,* October 7, 1880, January 31, August 1, 1882; Santa Fe *Weekly Democrat,* January 6, 1881; Albuquerque *Evening Review,* August 25, 1882.

[21] Santa Fe *Daily New Mexican,* February 27, March 1, 1880, February 19, 1881, May 27, 1883; Santa Fe *New Mexican,* February 21, 1906; Albuquerque *Daily Journal,* March 1, 1881; Silver City *Southwest Sentinel,* January 7, 1882, June 13, 1883. The railway officials also owned the Topeka *Capitol.*

[22] See Chapter IV for information concerning the Santa Fe Ring and Max Frost's connection with it.

[23] Territorial officials, appointed by the President, rotated in office as national administrations changed. Thus, the inauguration of Democratic President Grover Cleveland in 1885 and 1893 and of Republican presidents Benjamin Harrison and

William McKinley in 1889 and 1897 changed the control of New Mexico administrations.

²⁴ Santa Fe *New Mexican Review,* July 19, August 6, September 11, 1883; Santa Fe *New Mexican,* February 20, 1905, December 27, 1889. Frost later claimed to have gained control of the paper both in 1883 and in 1885, but after 1885 the masthead listed two others as publishers of the paper. In any case, after the death of James A. Spradling, Frost assumed control of the paper, and comments of other editors indicate that from 1885 he was active in its management. However, it appears that Frost never owned all of the paper at any time. Democratic papers at Santa Fe in this decade are listed in Appendix I.

²⁵ The *Sun* was published as a weekly from 1890 to 1894 and briefly in 1891 as a daily.

²⁶ J. H. Crist, owner and editor of the *Sun,* was rewarded with a political appointment rather than a printing contract.

²⁷ Santa Fe *New Mexican,* January 31, 1893, February 16-20, 1905; Socorro *Chieftain,* September 15, December 1, 1893; Las Cruces *Rio Grande Republican,* December 9, 1893; Las Vegas *Daily Optic,* January 23-29, 1897.

²⁸ *Thirteenth Census,* pp. 161-83.

²⁹ Albuquerque *Review,* February 14, 1880.

³⁰ Albuquerque *Daily Journal,* October 14, 1880, March 1, 1881. Officers of the Albuquerque Publishing Company included Franz Huning, A. Grunsfeld, W. C. Hazeldine, and W. P. K. Wilson.

³¹ Albuquerque *Review,* June 5, July 15, 1880; Albuquerque *Daily Journal,* March 1, 1881. J. A. Spradling, a native of Missouri, came to Albuquerque from the staff of the Santa Fe *Daily New Mexican.* After establishing the Albuquerque *Daily Journal,* he moved to Las Cruces where he founded the *Rio Grande Republican* in 1881. However, he soon sold his equity in this paper and returned to Missouri. In 1886 he returned to New Mexico as the editor-publisher of the Santa Fe *New Mexican,* a post which he held until his death in 1889.

³² Albuquerque *Daily Journal,* February 8, 9, March 2, 1881, February 4, 1882. Thomas Hughes, reared and trained as a printer in Missouri, established a paper at Marysville, Kansas, in 1872. After selling this paper in 1881 he became a co-owner of the Albuquerque *Daily Journal.* He left this paper to accept the Albuquerque postmastership in 1882, but retained an interest in the paper until 1885 when he once more briefly edited it. In 1886 Hughes published the weekly Albuquerque *Opinion* and was a co-owner and editor of the Albuquerque *Daily Citizen* from 1887 until his death in 1905. Hughes was also active in territorial politics and served four terms in the territorial Council.

³³ Albuquerque *Daily Journal,* March 15, 1881; Albuquerque *Evening Review,* February 20, 1882; Santa Fe *New Mexican,* March 22, 1905. W. H. Bailhache, a native of Ohio, served in the Union army quartermaster corps during the Civil War. After the war he was connected with a Springfield, Illinois, printing establishment. He came to Albuquerque in 1881, briefly managed the *Daily Journal,* and then purchased the *Review.* Later he was appointed to a position in the land office in Santa Fe. There he became friendly with Max Frost, also employed there. Together they launched the Albuquerque *Evening Review* and later moved it to Santa Fe. In 1886 Bailhache left New Mexico for San Diego, California, where he lived until his death in 1905. W. F. Saunders, editor of the *Evening Review* and a former Denver *Tribune* reporter, had been city editor of the Santa Fe *New Mexican* in 1881. He returned to Denver in 1883 and eventually moved to Saint Louis, Missouri, where he was employed in newspaper and public relations work.

³⁴ Albuquerque *Morning Journal,* October 10, 1881; Albuquerque *Evening Review,* November 7, 1882.

³⁵ The most interesting of *Journal* editors of this era was W. S. Burke, a native of West Virginia, who had moved to Iowa as a lad. He became an apprentice printer at fifteen and later an editor. After Union army service, he was discharged, disabled, as a captain. He then edited Iowa and Kansas newspapers before coming to New Mexico as superintendent of the Pacific Coal Company. Burke was appointed United States collector of revenue in 1883 but held that position and his editorship simultaneously.

Elected county superintendent of Bernalillo County schools in 1884, he left the *Journal*. He returned to journalism in 1889 and worked for an Albuquerque paper until his death in 1910.

[36] Santa Fe *Weekly New Mexican Review*, June 12, 1884; Santa Fe *Weekly New Mexican*, March 11, June 24, 1886, January 7, 1887; Silver City *Enterprise*, June 27, 1884, September 18, 1885; Las Vegas *Daily Optic*, May 7, September 3, November 11, December 1, 1884, April 9, June 22, 1885; Albuquerque *Journal*, July 7, 1933. J. G. Albright purchased the plant and assets of the *Morning Journal* at a sheriff's auction and *Morning Journal* was then added in small letters to the flag of the *Morning Democrat*.

[37] Albuquerque *Daily Citizen*, October 8, 1886, May 31, 1890; Las Vegas *Daily Optic*, June 1, 1887. W. T. McCreight, a native of Kentucky, came to Albuquerque to work on the *Daily Journal* in 1880. He helped organize the first Albuquerque printer's union and later published papers at Socorro and Albuquerque. McCreight was a co-publisher of the *Daily Citizen* until its sale in 1905, but he remained in Albuquerque until the 1930s.

[38] Socorro *Bullion*, January 3, 1886; Santa Fe *Leader*, January 23, 1886; Santa Fe *Weekly Sun*, November 28, 1891; Albuquerque *Times*, April 23, 1892; Albuquerque *Evening Citizen*, January 4, April 6, 1893, and as quoted in Las Cruces *Independent Democrat*, April 25, 1894.

[39] Albuquerque *Journal*, July 7, 1933; Las Vegas *Daily Optic*, April 17, 1895. In 1899 A. A. Grant changed the political policy of the paper to Republican and its name to the *Journal-Democrat*.

[40] Las Cruces *Rio Grande Republican*, May 21, July 30, September 10, December 10, 1881. Officers of the local company included W. L. Rynerson, S. B. Newcomb, William Dessauer, Aaron Shutz, and, later, A. J. Fountain.

[41] *Ibid.*, July 14, 1882, November 29, 1884, July 17, 1886, December 6, 27, 1890, March 18, 1892, April 12, August 11, 18, 1893, March 10, November 3, 1894, January 5, 1895. A rapid change of owners and managers indicates a troubled career, for profitable papers are more stable.

[42] Las Cruces *Daily Times*, May 4, 14, 1889; Kingston *Shaft*, June 1, 1889; Las Cruces *Daily News*, March 5, October 14, November 23, 1889.

[43] Las Cruces *Mesilla Valley Democrat*, September 28, October 1, November 5, 1886, October 28, 1890; *Ayer, American Newspaper Annual*, 1890, p. 469, 1891, p. 468; Las Cruces *Independent Democrat*, February 3, March 2, 1892; Las Cruces *Democrat*, November 8, 1899; Socorro *Chieftain*, April 28, 1899. Albert Bacon Fall, formerly of Kentucky and Texas, first lived in New Mexico at Kingston and later at Las Cruces, where he became a Democratic leader. As a Democrat he served two terms as territorial councilman, district judge, and solicitor general. During the Spanish-American War, Fall was an officer in the army, and early in the twentieth century he became a Republican. As a member of this party he was appointed territorial attorney general, served as a member of the constitutional convention, and was elected United States senator in 1912. During the administration of President W. G. Harding he served as secretary of interior and became widely known for his involvement in the "Teapot Dome" scandals.

[44] Las Cruces *El Tiempo*, November 9, 1882; Las Cruces *El Labrador*, September 8, 1896, November 23, 1900.

[45] Silver City population in 1880 was 1,800. United States Census Office, *Statistics of the Population of the United States at the Tenth Census, 1880* (Washington, 1883), p. 263; hereafter cited as *Tenth Census*.

[46] Silver City *Daily Southwest*, March 1, 15, August 31, 1880; Santa Fe *Weekly New Mexican*, April 13, 1880; Albuquerque *Daily Journal*, January 1, 1882; Silver City *New Southwest and Grant County Herald*, April 23, 1881, April 22, 1882; Las Cruces *Rio Grande Republican*, September 10, 1881. *Tenth Census*, p. 263.

[47] Las Cruces *Rio Grande Republican*, June 6, August 19, December 30, 1882; Silver City *Southwest Sentinel*, March 10, 24, 1883; Silver City *Enterprise*, November 16, 1882.

[48] Las Cruces *Rio Grande Republican*, July 7, September 9, 1883; Silver City *Enterprise*, January 25, August 2, October 26, 1894.

[49] W. A. Leonard from 1882 to 1893, and J. E. Sheridan from 1893 to 1899.

[50] Silver City *Daily Southwest*, March 1, 1880; Silver City *Grant County Herald*, January 29, 1881; Silver City *Southwest Sentinel*, May 12, November 3, 1882, September 20, 1884; Silver City *Enterprise*, December 19, 1884, June 4, 1886, June 7, 14, 1888; Las Cruces *Rio Grande Republican*, October 1, 1886, April 26, October 1, 1890; Las Vegas *Daily Optic*, October 15, 1891; Silver City *Independent*, July 6, 1897, December 31, 1911.

[51] Las Vegas *Daily Gazette*, June 14, 1881; Albuquerque *Daily Journal*, July 6, 1881. J. E. Curren was an unusual figure in New Mexico journalism. It was common for small publishers to own several different papers before keeping one or leaving journalism. Curren, however, published fourteen different New Mexico papers in addition to five in Colorado and Texas. Curren apparently loved the excitement and boom times of new towns, for he established or bought newspapers in many such towns in New Mexico from 1881 until 1911, in both the miners' and homesteaders' areas.

[52] Las Cruces *Rio Grande Republican*, September 22, 1883; Silver City *Enterprise*, October 5, 1883. Charles W. Greene, publisher of the Anthony (Kansas) *Journal* became manager and editor of the Santa Fe *Daily New Mexican* in February, 1880. After a year he left the *New Mexican* and launched the Lake Valley *Herald* and Kingston *Tribune*. These papers were moved to Deming as the Deming *Tribune*. In December, 1885, Greene moved this plant to El Paso, Texas, to launch the El Paso *Tribune*. He was very successful with this paper and sold it for $15,000. Greene then tried mining at Kingston but lost his profits. Later he became involved in the promotion of Pecos Valley irrigation.

[53] Las Cruces *Rio Grande Republican*, August 23, September 20, November 15, 1884; Silver City *Enterprise*, December 11, 1885; Santa Fe *Weekly New Mexican*, June 6, 1886; Deming *Headlight*, September 7, 1889.

[54] Albuquerque *Daily Citizen*, March 27, 1893; Silver City *Enterprise*, August 12, 1898. W. B. Walton, a native of Pennsylvania, was graduated from the South Jersey Institute at Bridgetown, New Jersey. After a few weeks experience on an Altoona, Pennsylvania, paper he moved to New Mexico as the business manager of the Deming *Headlight* in 1891. In 1893 he succeeded Ross as editor of the *Headlight*, a post he held until 1898. While acting as business manager, he also read law in the offices of S. M. Ashenfelter and soon married one of his daughters. Walton was admitted to the bar and gained reputation as a lawyer. He also became involved in politics, winning the Grant County clerkship, a seat in the legislature, a seat in the constitutional convention, and became territorial Democratic chairman. During all this time he continued as editor and publisher of either the Deming *Headlight* or the Silver City *Independent*.

[55] Chloride *Black Range*, November 14, December 12, 1884, July 16, 1885; Kingston *Sierra County Advocate*, January 10, March 7, 1885; Hillsboro *Sierra County Advocate*, February 11, March 11, April 29, 1887; Las Cruces *Rio Grande Republican*, March 14, 1885, April 17, May 22, July 31, 1886, May 21, 1887; Las Vegas *Daily Optic*, July 30, 1886, November 30, 1889.

[56] Las Vegas *Daily Optic*, March 12, 1889; Lordsburg *Western Liberal* as quoted in Las Cruces *Independent Democrat*, January 3, 1894; Rincon *Weekly*, February 20, 1896. John O'Connor, postmaster at Marysville, Missouri, anticipating a discovery of his misuse of postal funds, fled to New Mexico in 1882 and took the name John P. Hyland. He became prominent in G.A.R. and Republican circles and led a volunteer cavalry troop against Geronimo. Recognized by a Missouri acquaintance in 1895, he fled again and was finally arrested in Kansas City, Missouri.

[57] The *Black Range* was launched by V. B. Beckett in 1882 at Robinson and moved to Chloride in 1883.

[58] Hillsboro *Sierra County Advocate*, April 24, 1891, April 27, 1900; Albuquerque *Evening Review*, March 26, 1882; Robinson *Black Range*, October 6, 1882; Silver City *Enterprise*, January 18, 1883; Chloride *Black Range*, June 5, 19, 1885, August 6, 1897.

[59] Albuquerque *Daily Journal*, March 1, 1881; White Oaks *Golden Era*, September

29, 1881; Las Vegas *Daily Optic,* December 19, 1881; Santa Fe *Weekly New Mexican,* July 31, 1884.

⁶⁰ J. J. Dolan, who earlier had been a leading figure in the Lincoln County war, bought the paper and soon renamed it the Lincoln *Independent.* This weekly was published intermittently after 1888 and lapsed early in the 1890s.

⁶¹ Las Cruces *Rio Grande Republican,* October 28, 1882, January 27, 1883; Socorro *Chieftain,* December 15, 1893.

⁶² J. E. Sligh came to White Oaks in 1881 and was one of the early editor-publishers of the *Golden Era.* Later, he was pastor of the Congregational church at White Oaks, but he again became a publisher with the launching of the *New Mexico Interpreter.* After he sold this paper in 1887, he founded the Nogal *Nugget,* which later was sold to the Lincoln County Farmers' Alliance and was renamed the *Liberty Banner.*

⁶³ William Watson, White Oaks realtor, lawyer, and miner, as well as journalist, was a co-owner of the rich Old Abe gold mine at that town. Other co-owners of the White Oaks *New Mexico Interpreter* or its successors and the Old Abe mine were the Hoyle brothers (A. B. and M. W.) and John Y. Hewitt.

⁶⁴ Hillsboro *Sierra County Advocate,* July 25, 1885; Las Vegas *Daily Optic,* May 5, 1887; White Oaks *New Mexico Interpreter,* May 27, 1887, September 14, 28, 1888, January 2, March 27, June 21, 1891; Kingston *Shaft,* October 5, 1889; White Oaks *Old Abe Eagle,* November 27, 1891, October 13, 1892; White Oaks *Eagle,* January 5, May 4, 1899.

⁶⁵ Las Vegas *Daily Optic,* January 17, June 6, 1881; Raton *Guard,* November 25, 1881.

⁶⁶ Cimarron *News and Press,* September 12, 26, October 22, 1881; Raton *New Mexico News and Press,* October 29, 1881, May 6, 1882; Raton *Guard,* May 12, July 7, 1882; Raton *Comet,* July 14, 1882; Albuquerque *Evening Review,* November 2, 1882. O. P. McMains was the leader of a group that was opposed to the confirmation of the Maxwell Land Grant, a tremendous acreage in Colfax County upon which many of Mc-Mains' followers had established ranches. McMains wished to be elected to Congress to fight the Maxwell grant in Washington. Thus, many of the people in and near Raton ardently supported his candidacy, and Canis became rather unpopular. For more information on McMains and the Maxwell Land Grant, see Chapter VII.

⁶⁷ Raton *Comet,* November 10, 1882, June 1, 1883, February 20, August 29, 1884, February 26, 1886; Santa Fe *Weekly New Mexican,* March 11, December 23, 1886; Raton *Range,* January 21, 1887, May 1, 1891, April 26, 1900. T. W. Collier, an Ohio journalist who had been a Union army captain in the Civil War, leased the Santa Fe *New Mexican* in 1885 and 1886. In February, 1888, he became a co-publisher of the *Range* and in 1891 acquired all of it. In 1897 he was appointed postmaster at Raton.

⁶⁸ Raton *Daily Independent,* July 7, 1884; Raton *Weekly Independent,* November 16, 1886; Las Vegas *Daily Optic,* September 2, 9, 1889.

⁶⁹ Raton *Reporter,* April 22, 1890, June 7, 1894, June 23, 1897, January 18, 1899.

⁷⁰ Santa Fe *New Mexican Review,* May 12, 1898, Las Cruces *Rio Grande Republican,* January 2, 1891, May 20, 1898; Santa Fe *Sun,* July 25, 1891; Raton *Union,* February 26, September 10, 1898; *Ayer, American Newspaper Annual,* 1890-1901 (New Mexico pages).

⁷¹ San Lorenzo *Red River Chronicle,* May 6, 1882; Santa Fe *Weekly New Mexican Review,* June 18, 1885; Las Vegas *Daily Optic,* January 19, 1891; Springer *Colfax County Stockman,* September 23, 1893, May 4, 1895.

⁷² Silver City *Enterprise,* October 10, 1887; Las Vegas *Daily Optic,* January 14, February 15, 1888, May 5, 1890; Gallup *Register,* July 10, 1888; Gallup *Gleaner,* August 11, 1888; Cerrillos *Rustler,* November 30, 1888; Las Cruces *Rio Grande Republican,* December 22, 1888; Gallup *News-Register,* April 15, 1889, February 4, 1890; Kingston *Shaft,* February 15, 1890; *Ayer, American Newspaper Annual,* 1889, p. 554, 1901, p. 555.

⁷³ Albuquerque *Daily Citizen,* March 13, 1893; Las Cruces *Rio Grande Republican,* June 16, 1894; Farmington *San Juan Times,* May 17, 1895, January 6, May 5, 1899; *Ayer, American Newspaper Annual,* 1889-1901 (New Mexico pages).

[74] Roswell *Pecos Valley Register,* November 29, 1888; White Oaks *New Mexico Interpreter,* January 16, 1891; Roswell *Register,* August 26, October 30, 1895, January 15, 1896; July 2, 1897, August 12, 1898; Las Vegas *Stock Grower and Farmer,* August 17, 1895; Las Vegas *Daily Optic,* November 23, 1899; Santa Fe *New Mexican Review,* August 25, 1898; Roswell *Record,* January 6, February 24, 1899.

[75] Eddy *Argus,* November 16, 1889, October 31, 1891; Las Cruces *Rio Grande Republican,* November 25, December 20, 1895, January 3, 1896; Santa Fe *New Mexican,* May 25, 1901. L. O. Fullen, who with his brother-in-law, J. A. Erwin, was a co-publisher of the Roswell *Pecos Valley Register* and the Roswell *Herald,* became the shop foreman of the Eddy *Argus* in its early years and in 1895 became its editor and publisher. In 1897 he was appointed postmaster at Eddy (which later became Carlsbad), a position which he held until 1905. Meanwhile, he had read law and was admitted to the bar in 1905, becoming a law partner of A. H. Freeman. In 1907 he accepted a position as district attorney and resigned his editorship. In later years Fullen had a distinguished career as a lawyer at Roswell.

[76] Kingston *Shaft,* October 15, 1892; Eddy *Current,* December 31, 1898, December 8, 1900; Silver City *Enterprise,* December 11, 1891, July 14, 1893; *Ayer, American Newspaper Annual,* 1894, p. 500, 1895, p. 504, 1899, p. 554. W. H. Mullane published papers at Eddy, Hagerman, and Roswell, for most of the years from 1892 until 1912. During this period Mullane became a leader in the Democratic party in southeastern New Mexico.

[77] Clayton *Enterprise,* May 17, 1888; Hillsboro *Sierra County Advocate,* July 28, 1888; Folsom *Idea,* February 9, 1889; Las Vegas *Daily Optic,* July 1, 1890; Clayton *Union County Democrat,* July 7, 1894; Santa Fe *Weekly New Mexican Review,* February 1, 1894; *Ayer, American Newspaper Annual,* 1889-1901 (New Mexico pages).

[78] Arthur E. Curren, "Pioneer Editor," *New Mexico Magazine,* XXXII (November, 1954), p. 37; cited hereafter as Curren, *New Mexico Magazine,* XXXII.

[79] White Oaks *Golden Era,* April 24, 1884; Albuquerque *Morning Journal,* October 28, 1882; Santa Fe *New Mexican,* April 27, 1900, May 25, 1901; Las Vegas *Daily Optic,* March 31, 1894, February 9, 1898; San Marcial *Bee,* June 10, 1893.

[80] Las Vegas *Independiente,* February 15, 1900; Socorro *Chieftain,* February 5, 1897; both show the rewards for county printing and the contests for it.

[81] The only Republican paper that became Democratic because of the silver issue was the Chloride *Black Range.* While the change in ratio in favor of the Democrats was largely the result of political subsidy, the appearance of the Populists' papers was more the result of the political turmoil of the 1890s than subsidy.

[82] Will Irwin, "The Voice of a Generation," *Collier's,* July 29, 1911, reprinted under the title "How far have we come? A view from 1911," *Columbia Journalism Review,* II (Summer, 1963), p. 42; hereafter cited as Irwin, *Columbia Journalism Review,* II.

[83] The small number of journalists whose origins are known and have been considered is inconclusive evidence of the origins of almost 500 newsmen of this period. To check fully the influence of the sectional origin of journalists on New Mexico journalism, factors other than origin need also to be considered: for instance, the importance and influence of the journalists and the length of time in which they engaged in journalism. Considering these factors and believing that the sampling indicates a general trend, the writer contends that the cultural influence, attitudes, and ideology of the majority of journalists in this era were those of people from the northern Midwest.

[84] *Ayer, American Newspaper Annual,* 1898, p. 528.

[85] Concerning E. H. Salazar, see Santa Fe *New Mexican,* February 11, August 6, 1902, January 23, 1903. Martinez was an influential political leader in both the Democratic and Union People's parties, and E. Cabeza de Baca later became the second governor of the state of New Mexico.

[86] Las Vegas *Daily Optic,* February 12, 1881, May 27, 1889.

[87] Kingston *Shaft,* January 25, 1890; see also Las Cruces *Rio Grande Republican* editorial, "Prune the Profession," November 25, 1881.

[88] Albuquerque *Daily Journal,* March 1, 1881; Silver City *Southwest Sentinel,* April 7, 1883; Las Vegas *Daily Optic,* October 10, 1883, March 4, April 16, September 15,

October 1, 1889, January 17-20, 1890, January 13, 1891, January 20-25, 1892, January 18, September 3, 1893, January 16, 1897; Santa Fe *Sun*, January 13, 1891; Albuquerque *Morning Democrat*, October 5, 1886; Hillsboro *Sierra County Advocate*, August 25, 1888, March 9, 1889; Santa Fe *New Mexican*, March 4, 1886, January 18, 1890.

[89] Las Vegas *Daily Optic*, July 27, 29, 1887.

[90] Gallup *Gleaner*, May 1, 1889; Gallup *News-Register* as quoted in Kingston *Shaft*, May 11, 1889.

[91] Chloride *Black Range*, January 29, 1886.

[92] Albuquerque *Daily Citizen*, January 6, 1893; Santa Fe *New Mexican*, April 21, 1898.

[93] Mott, *American Journalism*, p. 312, notes that personal journalism began to decline in the 1850s among the New York papers.

[94] Las Vegas *Daily Optic*, June 25, 1889. The Albuquerque *Daily Citizen*, July 12, 1890, charged the *Morning Democrat* with reprinting editorials from the Louisville *Courier-Journal*. The Albuquerque *Morning Democrat*, June 20, 1889, editorial, "Local vs. General Interests," provides an example of an editorial worthy of perhaps one-fourth the space devoted to it. For other illustrations of this practice, see Las Cruces *Independent Democrat*, February 17, May 18, 1892; Silver City *Enterprise*, June 29, 1888; Las Cruces *Rio Grande Republican*, August 13, 1881.

[95] Albuquerque *Evening Review*, February 20 to March 29, 1882, June 21, 1882.

[96] Las Cruces *Rio Grande Republican*, June 10, October 20, 1882, March 10, 1883.

[97] Manzano *Gringo and Greaser*, February 15, 1884.

[98] Las Vegas *Daily Optic*, January 9, 1893.

[99] *Ibid.*, January 8, March 7, 1880, *passim*.

[100] *Ibid.*, January 1, 1884 to March 1, 1884; Albuquerque *Morning Democrat*, September 10 to October 20, 1889.

[101] Albuquerque *Review*, July 8, 1876. Pre-printed pages and boiler-plate copy was not necessarily uninteresting; it was like the modern syndicated feature story. However, such copy seemed a great waste of space in the small New Mexico papers which were unable to publish all the local news and many important territorial news stories. For examples of this practice, see Las Cruces *Rio Grande Republican* in 1892 and Magdalena *Mountain Mail*, October and November, 1888.

[102] Socorro *Industrial Advertiser*, August 17, 1889; Socorro *Chieftain*, June 14, 1895.

[103] Mott, *American Journalism*, pp. 470-78.

[104] Las Vegas *Daily Optic*, May 4, October 2, 1882; Albuquerque *Evening Review*, November 7, 1882.

[105] C. M. Chase, *The Editor's Run in New Mexico and Colorado* (Lyndon, Vermont, 1882), pp. 126-27; Las Cruces *Rio Grande Republican*, February 4, 1882.

[106] Santa Fe *New Mexican*, July 14, 1887, December 20, 1900; Las Cruces *Rio Grande Republican*, July 3, 1896.

[107] Albuquerque *Evening Review*, May 6, 7, 1882; Albuquerque *Morning Journal*, October 22, 1882; Las Vegas *Daily Optic*, April 7, 1882, May 24, 1884; Mott, *American Journalism*, p. 478.

[108] Cattle-brand advertisements pictured a cow with the advertiser's brand placed upon it and usually required from one to one-and-one-half column inches of space.

[109] A legal notice, published three times, was required of a person who wished to file a claim on a mining claim that had been abandoned. Homesteaders were required to publish a notice of filing of a claim with a description of the land, and at the end of the residence period they were required to publish an affidavit that they had complied with the residence requirements.

[110] For examples of some large advertisements in this period, see Las Vegas *Daily Optic*, October 18, 1882; Silver City *Southwest Sentinel*, November 8, 1884.

[111] Las Cruces *Newman's Semi-Weekly*, April 20, 1881; Silver City *Southwest Sentinel*, March 10, 1883; Kingston *Shaft*, January 25, 1890.

[112] *Ayer, American Newspaper Annual*, 1889-1899 (New Mexico pages).

[113] Las Vegas *Daily Optic*, December 31, 1891; Silver City *Southwest Sentinel*, November 14, 1883; Las Cruces *Rio Grande Republican*, July 20, 1889; Mott, *American Journalism*, p. 48.

[114] United States census estimate as reported in Hillsboro *Sierra County Advocate*, September 12, 1885. A further indication of the rapid rise and fall of the population of Socorro is shown by the census figures of 1,272 in 1880 and 2,295 in 1890, United States Census Office, *Compendium of the Eleventh Census, 1890, Part I—Population* (Washington, 1892), p. 464. Compare this with population figures for Albuquerque, old town and new town, which were both 2,315 in 1880 and 5,118 in 1890; see *Tenth Census*, p. 263; *Thirteenth Census*, p. 161.

[115] Las Cruces *Rio Grande Republican*, July 20, 1889; Socorro *Industrial Advertiser*, January 30, November 30, 1889, September 23, 1899.

[116] Las Vegas *Daily Optic*, February 1 to April 2, 1885, January 9, 1893; Albuquerque *Evening Citizen*, November 30, 1892.

[117] Las Cruces *Rio Grande Republican*, June 16, 1883. By his term "American town" the editor meant a town predominantly Anglo-American. Hence, he blamed Spanish-Americans for his lack of advertisements.

[118] *Ibid.*, March 4, 1882.

[119] *Ayer, American Newspaper Annual*, 1880-1901 (New Mexico pages).

[120] Pueblo (Colorado) *Merry World* as quoted in Kingston *Shaft*, December 17, 1889.

[121] Las Vegas *Daily Optic*, January 24, 30, 1889.

[122] *Ibid.*, January 25, 28, 30, 1889; Chloride *Black Range*, February 22, 1889. Most territorial papers believed T. B. Catron responsible for the libel law as he was reputedly able to control the legislature. Significantly, perhaps, Catron was not in the legislature in 1893 when it was repealed.

[123] Siver City *Enterprise*, February 8, 1889; Socorro *Chieftain*, Deming *Headlight*, and Lordsburg *Western Liberal* as quoted in the Silver City *Enterprise*, February 15, 1889. The American common-law rule on libel was of English derivation; and the English common-law rule, the greater the truth the greater the libel, held until the Fox Libel Act was passed by Parliament in 1792. This act provided that the truth was a defense against the charge of libel, according to R. F. T. Plucknett, *Taswell-Langmead's English Constitutional History* (Boston, 1960), pp. 110, 666-68. The Fox Libel Act passed in 1792, thus, would have no effect on the American common law. Mott, *American Journalism*, p. 38, confirms this and states that despite the decision of the *Zenger* case in the colonial era, American states, and presumably territories, in the absence of any libel law used the old common-law rule that the truth was no defense against the charge of libel.

[124] Las Vegas *Daily Optic*, February 9, 1891.

[125] *Ibid.*, August 30, 31, December 29, 1898; Las Cruces *Rio Grande Republican*, September 30, 1898.

## CHAPTER III

[1] Many papers were launched at towns which no longer exist, such as Knowles, Lakewood, Lalande, Dayton, Obar, and Bard City. Others were founded at towns which have remained only small crossroads villages, such as Grady, House, Tolar, Taiban, Penasco, Moriarty, and Willard.

[2] Portales *Progress*, August 1, 1901; letter of C. M. Dobbs, printer's devil on the Portales *Times*, to the Portales *Daily News*, September 21, 1952.

[3] Portales *Herald*, May 7, 1904; Portales *Times*, February 7, 1903.

[4] Munsey Bull, a native of Texas, spent his youth in Oregon where he became a printer. He then worked on California and other Western papers before coming to New Mexico in 1886. Bull, an excellent printer who did all the mechanical and editorial work of the *Times*, represented a type of printer-publisher who would soon become extinct by the advances in printing mechanics. Bull earlier had published the Roswell *Pecos Valley Stockman*.

[5] W. C. Hawkins came to New Mexico from Oklahoma where he was publisher of

a weekly. Later he owned New Mexico weeklies at Cuervo, Montoya, and Tucumcari.

⁶ E. P. Alldredge, a Dallas, Texas, Baptist minister and Doctor of Divinity, came to New Mexico for his health. He was a Portales Baptist pastor who became a newspaper editor to supplement his meager church salary. Under his managment the *Herald* developed one of the largest weekly circulations in New Mexico. Alldredge left the *Herald* in 1909 to devote his full time to Baptist church work throughout New Mexico.

⁷ Portales *Herald*, March 19, April 16, 1904.

⁸ J. E. Curren, founder of the Deming *Headlight*, as well as Sierra County and Union County papers, returned to the territory in 1903 after journalistic ventures in the Texas Panhandle.

⁹ Hillsboro *Sierra County Advocate*, February 28, 1902; Tucumcari *Quay County Democrat*, April 11, 1903; Tucumcari *Actual Settler*, January 7, July 19, 1905; Tucumcari *Times*, December 17, 1903. The *Times* was founded in April, 1903.

¹⁰ Santa Fe *New Mexican*, July 28, 1905.

¹¹ Tucumcari *News*, October 28, 1905. S. M. Wharton, S. R. May, and J. A. Haley were at various times owners of the White Oaks *Eagle*. It was discontinued in 1903; its circulation was then given to the Capitan *Progress*, which the partners also owned; then the plant of the *Eagle* was moved to Alamogordo to found the weekly and daily *Journal*. Unable to win in the competitive battle at Alamogordo, the plant was moved to Tucumcari to found the *News*.

¹² Tucumcari *News*, January 19, 1907, January 4, 1912; Tucumcari *Sun*, December 20, 1907, January 5, 1912.

¹³ Santa Rosa *Voz Publica*, founded at Puerta de Luna in 1898, was the oldest paper at Santa Rosa. The Santa Rosa *Sun* was established in 1904 by F. D. Morse, who earlier had published the Raton *Range*.

¹⁴ Curren, *New Mexico Magazine*, XXXII, p. 37; Santa Rosa *Sun*, June 19, 1908; Fort Sumner *Review*, July 17, 1909. Clausen was a former co-publisher of both the Raton *Range* and *Reporter*.

¹⁵ Santa Fe *New Mexican*, September 9, 1906; Portales *Times*, April 22, 1909. Curren's first territorial paper was the Deming *Headlight*, founded in 1882.

¹⁶ Arthur E. Curren article in the Clovis *News-Journal*, April 1, 1954; Portales *Times*, May 18, 1907, April 22, August 22, 1909; Clovis *News*, May 7, 28, 1909, January 4, July 11, 18, 1912; Portales *Roosevelt County Herald*, November 9, 1909. H. O. Norris, personal interview with the writer at Fort Sumner, New Mexico, August 30, 1963; hereafter cited as Norris interview, 1963.

¹⁷ Thomas J. Mabry served as a member of the New Mexico Constitutional Convention and was later a distinguished attorney, chief justice of the New Mexico Supreme Court, and governor of New Mexico from 1947 to 1951.

¹⁸ Estancia *News*, July 22, 1910; Estancia *Morning News*, April 5, 1911, January 22, 1912; Estancia *Daily Herald*, April 1, June 10, 1911; Santa Rosa *Sun*, November 3, 1907; Santa Fe *New Mexican*, January 23, December 8, 1910. The population of Estancia in 1910 was 517, *Thirteenth Census*, pp. 161-83.

¹⁹ Capitan *Progress*, December 28, 1900; Capitan *News*, August 14, 1903; Carrizozo *News*, June 12, 1908.

²⁰ White Oaks *Outlook*, December 20, 1906; Santa Fe *New Mexican*, October 21, 1904; *Ayer, American Newspaper Annual*, 1912, p. 589. The White Oaks *Outlook* was founded in 1904, about one year after the suspension of the White Oaks *Eagle*. Lee H. Ruidisille, founder of the *Outlook*, had also established the White Oaks *Lincoln County Leader* in 1882.

²¹ *Ayer, American Newspaper Annual*, 1901, pp. 554-55, 1904, pp. 555-56, 1905, pp. 559-60, 1912, pp. 588-89; Alamogordo *Nueva Epoca*, December 30, 1911; Tularosa *Valley Tribune*, January 6, 1912.

²² To illustrate the importance of railroads and homesteaders to town growth, consider that neither Tucumcari nor Clovis existed in 1900, but by 1910 their populations were 2,526 and 3,255, respectively; *Thirteenth Census*, pp. 161-83.

²³ Clayton *Citizen*, October 5, 1906; Clayton *Enterprise*, August 3, 1910; *Ayer, American Newspaper Annual*, 1912, p. 589.

[24] Cimarron *News and Press,* January 10, 1907; Raton *Range,* October 22, 1908.

[25] Springer *Colfax County Stockman,* January 6, 1900, December 20, 1911; Springer *Sentinel,* February 8, 1901; San Jon *Sentinel,* May 6, 1910; Estancia *Daily Herald,* May 2, 1911; *Ayer, American Newspaper Annual,* 1912, p. 590.

[26] C. E. Mason and H. F. M. Bear were brothers-in-law who came to New Mexico from Kansas. Bear was a University of Kansas graduate and had served as Wellington, Kansas, city superintendent of schools for eleven years. Later he became Chaves County superintendent of schools. After Bear's death in 1905, Mason assumed full control of the *Record* and served as its editor from 1909 until the late 1930s.

[27] Socorro *Chieftain,* August 30, 1903; Santa Fe *New Mexican,* January 16, March 17, July 25, 1903; Roswell *Daily Record,* October 14, 28, 1903, October 3, 1938; Roswell *Register,* March 20, 1903. Roswell's population grew from 2,049 in 1900 to 6,172 in 1910; *Thirteenth Census,* pp. 161-83.

[28] Will Robinson became one of the best known southeastern New Mexico journalists. He first worked on the Las Cruces *Democrat* and then on the Roswell *Record,* the Carlsbad *Argus,* and the Carlsbad *Current.* During many of these years he wrote a humorous editorial column, "Impressions of a Tenderfoot," which appeared in many New Mexico weeklies. Robinson remained at Roswell as an editor until the 1940s and then moved to Albuquerque.

[29] Leaders of this group were L. K. McGaffey, J. W. Stockard, J. W. Poe, and J. P. White.

[30] Roswell *Tribune,* January 11 to February 22, 1906; Roswell *Register-Tribune,* March 6, 1906, August 4, 1911; Roswell *Morning News,* August 15, 27, 30, December 30, 1911.

[31] Included in this group were the Dexter *News,* the Hagerman *Messenger,* the Lake Arthur *Times,* and the Kenna *Record.*

[32] Artesia *Advocate,* August 29, 1903; Artesia *Pecos Valley News,* September 13, 1906; *Ayer, American Newspaper Annual,* 1912, p. 589.

[33] Santa Fe *New Mexican,* May 18, 1905; Carlsbad *New Mexico Sun,* January 5, December 28, 1906; Carlsbad *Current and New Mexico Sun,* August 28, 1907; Carlsbad *Argus,* January 2, 1903; Santa Fe *New Mexican,* February 9, 1910; *Ayer, American Newspaper Annual,* 1912, p. 589; *Thirteenth Census,* pp. 161-83.

[34] D. K. B. Sellers, editor of the *Hustler,* was a realtor, and the name *Hustler* typifies his journalism. A man of great vigor, Sellers later moved to Albuquerque where he became a very successful realtor.

[35] Frank Staplin, a former publisher of the Taos *Cresset* and a territorial legislator, while publisher of the *Enterprise* was also a United States court commissioner.

[36] Farmington *Hustler,* January 17, 24, 1901; Farmington *Times-Hustler,* September 10, 1903; Santa Fe *New Mexican,* May 24, 1905; Aztec *San Juan Democrat,* September 9, 1906; Las Cruces *Rio Grande Republican,* January 5, 1912; *Ayer, American Newspaper Annual,* 1912, p. 589; *Thirteenth Census,* pp. 161-83.

[37] Santa Fe *New Mexican,* January 24, 1907; *Ayer, American Newspaper Annual,* 1912, p. 589.

[38] Las Cruces *Progress,* February 22, 1902, January 4, 1904; Las Cruces *Rio Grande Republican,* January 15, 1904; February 24, September 12, 1911; the Fosters published the Raton *Range* from 1905 to 1910 and during that time owned papers at Clayton, Maxwell, and Cimarron; Las Cruces *Citizen,* April 5, 1902, February 5, 1910.

[39] *Thirteenth Census,* pp. 161-83. Four Las Cruces Spanish-language weeklies will be discussed later.

[40] Deming *Headlight,* January 5, 1911; Deming *Herald,* April 4, 1901, February 24, 1903; Deming *Graphic,* March 24, 1903, January 5, 1912; *Thirteenth Census,* pp. 161-83.

[41] Raton *Reporter,* July 2, 1901; Fort Sumner *Republican* as quoted by the Vaughn *News,* October 7, 1910; *Ayer, American Newspaper Annual,* 1912, p. 593; *Thirteenth Census,* pp. 161-83.

[42] Farmington *Hustler,* January 23, 1902; Silver City *Enterprise,* September 26, 1902; Gallup *Independent,* October 31, 1912; *Thirteenth Census,* pp. 161-83. There was less demand for the low-grade Gallup coal than for the coking coal mined at Raton.

⁴³ Socorro *Chieftain*, December 1, 8, 1900, January 6, 1912; Santa Fe *New Mexican*, October 15, 1904; *Ayer, American Newspaper Annual*, 1905, p. 562, 1912, p. 593; *Thirteenth Census*, pp. 161-83.

⁴⁴ W. B. Walton became very active politically in this period; he was a member of the legislature in 1901, a probate clerk of Grant County from 1903 to 1907, a member of the New Mexico Constitutional Convention, and a territorial Democratic chairman from 1908 to 1911. In addition, he became a prominent attorney in these years.

⁴⁵ Silver City *Independent*, March 4, 1899, December 31, 1911; Silver City *Enterprise*, July 19, 1901, January 4, 1912.

⁴⁶ W. O. Thompson published the Chloride *Black Range* from 1885 until 1897. Hillsboro *Sierra County Advocate*, April 13, 1900, December 12, 1911; Hillsboro *Sierra Free Press*, April 27, 1911, January 8, 1912.

⁴⁷ Evidence of conflict between Spanish and Anglo cultures and the attitudes of the Spanish-language press are described in Chapter V.

⁴⁸ Santa Fe *New Mexican*, December 12, 1901, June 26, 1902; Wagon Mound *Combate*, December 6, 1902; Wagon Mound *Mora County Sentinel and El Combate*, May 26, 1911; *Ayer, American Newspaper Annual*, 1901, p. 556, 1907, p. 575, 1908, p. 561, 1909, p. 560, 1910, p. 568, 1911, p. 593, 1912, p. 593.

⁴⁹ Las Vegas *Voz del Pueblo*, April 22, 1905; Las Vegas *Independiente*, August 22, 1901, September 8, 15, 1910; *Ayer, American Newspaper Annual*, 1912, p. 591.

⁵⁰ Isadoro Armijo, Jr., earlier had edited the short-lived Las Cruces *Flor del Valle* in 1894 and had worked on a Trinidad, Colorado, paper. Armijo, a graduate of New Mexico College of Agriculture and Mechanic Arts now New Mexico State University, was prominent in Republican politics, serving as a legislator, probate clerk of Dona Ana County, and member of the New Mexico Constitutional Convention.

⁵¹ Las Cruces *Tiempo*, July 8, 1911; Las Cruces *Eco del Valle*, November 18, 1905, May 12, 1910; Santa Fe *New Mexican*, July 15, 1911; Las Cruces *Labrador*, March 29, 1901; *Ayer, American Newspaper Annual*, 1911, p. 590.

⁵² Nestor Montoya and E. H. Salazar were the original publishers of La *Voz del Pueblo*, when it was launched at Santa Fe in 1888.

⁵³ Elfego Baca, former Socorro County sheriff and New Mexico attorney, was later immortalized by a Walt Disney Studios television series and Kyle S. Crichton's *Law and Order Limited, the Life of Elfego Baca* (Santa Fe, 1928).

⁵⁴ *Thirteenth Census*, pp. 161-83. A. J. Loomis was editor and publisher of the Deming *Daily Headlight* in 1885 and 1886, the Silver City *Daily Southwest Sentinel* in 1887 and 1888, and the Silver City *Eagle* from 1894 to 1897 when it was suspended. The *Eagle* was revived briefly in 1900 by Loomis. From 1897 until 1900 Loomis served as a United States customs official.

⁵⁵ Socorro *Chieftain*, March 24, 1906; Santa Fe *Eagle*, December 7, 1912; *Ayer, American Newspaper Annual*, 1908, p. 561, 1909, p. 560, 1910, p. 568, 1911, p. 593.

⁵⁶ Santa Fe *New Mexican*, January 21, 1909, January 5, 1912.

⁵⁷ Las Vegas *Daily Optic*, March 18, May 4, 18, 1903; Farmington *Hustler*, May 5, 1903; *Thirteenth Census*, pp. 161-83.

⁵⁸ Las Vegas *Advertiser*, March 22, October 9, 1903; Las Vegas *Daily Advertiser*, May 3, June 19, 1903. The weekly *Advertiser* lapsed in October, 1903.

⁵⁹ Hillsboro *Sierra County Advocate*, April 15, 1905; Las Vegas *Daily Star and Homesteader*, March 7, April 22, 1910; *Ayer, American Newspaper Annual*, 1906, p. 565, 1909, p. 559.

⁶⁰ *Thirteenth Census*, pp. 161-83.

⁶¹ Albuquerque *Daily Citizen*, March 29, 1905. Thomas Hughes died in June, 1905, following the sale of the paper the previous March. The Albuquerque *Tribune* was established with the plant of the defunct El Paso *News* on September 1, 1909. Felix Martinez, of Las Vegas *La Voz del Pueblo*, who had published the *News*, was a shareholder in the concern along with prominent territorial Democrats A. A. Jones of Las Vegas, O. N. Marron and H. B. Fergusson both from Albuquerque.

⁶² Albuquerque *Tribune-Citizen*, January 3, March 6, 1911; Albuquerque *Evening Herald*, March 7, 1911; Artesia *Advocate*, March 11, 1911; Las Cruces *Rio Grande Republican*, June 23, 1911. F. A. Hubbell, Bernalillo County Republican Chairman,

was one of the principal owners of the paper as well as co-owner of the Albuquerque *La Bandera Americana.*

⁶³ *Ayer, American Newspaper Annual,* 1903, p. 561, 1912, p. 589; Albuquerque *Journal-Democrat,* March 6, 31, 1903; Albuquerque *Morning Journal,* October 7, 1903. Associate editors of the *Morning Journal* in this period were such noted New Mexicans as E. Dana Johnson and William A. Keleher.

⁶⁴ The new twentieth-century concepts of advertising and circulation and the use that territorial papers made of them will be discussed later.

⁶⁵ A. A. Jones later became a United States senator; H. B. Fergusson was a former Democratic territorial delegate to Congress and a future New Mexico congressman; Felix Martinez and O. N. Marron were territorial Democratic leaders.

⁶⁶ Editor and publisher C. E. Mason apparently was suspect, for he had edited the Republican Roswell *Register* for a time and refused to follow all territorial Democratic policies. W. H. Hutchinson in *A Bar Cross Man: The Life and Personal Writings of Eugene Manlove Rhodes* (Norman, Oklahoma, 1956), says that Roswell Democrats sought to have Rhodes made editor of the *Daily Record* so that the paper might have a truly Democratic editor. Rhodes, however, was turned down by Mason, *ibid.,* pp. 79, 88, 90. In January, 1911, the *Daily Record* refused to support the territorial Democratic convention demand for defeat of the proposed constitution, which probably was the reason for the launching of the *Morning News.*

⁶⁷ The Republican Tucumcari *Times* and Tucumcari *Quay County Democrat* and the Republican Clovis *News* and *Democrat* were owned by Curren and his son.

⁶⁸ Notices were required to be published in newspapers of general circulation, and the Republican land officials arranged for them to be published in papers loyal to the Republican party.

⁶⁹ Portales *Times,* April 15, 1909; Santa Fe *New Mexican,* December 3, 1901; Lovington *Leader,* January 5, 1912; Fort Sumner *Review,* February 25, 1911; Montoya *Republican,* February 14, 1908; Farmington *Enterprise,* May 17, 1907.

⁷⁰ This compilation was made from the listings in *Ayer, American Newspaper Annual,* 1901-1912 (New Mexico pages) and from the newspapers themselves; it reflects changes of political affiliation under different owners.

⁷¹ This development is covered in detail in Chapter IV.

⁷² No effort was made to check the origins and backgrounds of all journalists. However, from the facts which came readily to hand, the conditions outlined appear to be true. The editorials and attitudes of the various journalists, particularly those of importance, tend to confirm this opinion.

⁷³ Portales *Times,* February 3, 1904.

⁷⁴ Albuquerque *Morning Journal,* November 7, 1909.

⁷⁵ *Ibid.,* September 23, 1910.

⁷⁶ Deming *Headlight,* January 1 to October 12, 1911.

⁷⁷ Albuquerque *Morning Journal,* April 20 to July 1, 1910.

⁷⁸ Las Cruces *Eco del Valle,* September 23, 1911; Roswell *Daily Record,* February 1, 1905; Portales *Roosevelt County Herald,* December 19, 1908, February 26, June 18, 1909; Carlsbad *Argus* as quoted in Socorro *Chieftain,* January 26, 1900; Portales *Daily News,* September 21, 1952. McBride left Portales to become president of a college at Canadian, Texas.

⁷⁹ Las Vegas *Daily Optic,* September 27, 1900; Santa Fe *New Mexican,* February 22, 1901, August 20, 1908; Norris interview, 1963.

⁸⁰ Portales *Herald,* August 28, 1907. Subsequent Pecos Valley Press Association presidents are listed in Appendix II.

⁸¹ Santa Fe *Sun* as quoted in Mora *Mosquito,* February 18, 1892; Las Cruces *Flor del Valle,* March 24, 1894; Las Vegas *Independiente,* September 21, 1911.

⁸² Norris interview, 1963.

⁸³ Albuquerque *Morning Journal,* September 8, 1908; Santa Fe *New Mexican,* June 15, 1906. Plunderbund was the name given one group of Republican leaders by the Albuquerque *Morning Journal.*

⁸⁴ Albuquerque *Daily Citizen* as quoted in Socorro *Chieftain,* March 15, 1902.

⁸⁵ The Linotype so simplified and reduced the time and cost of composition that

many publishers enlarged their papers. In New Mexico, for example, in 1903 the regular four page daily was replaced with an eight-page daily in each of the dailies at Albuquerque, Santa Fe, and Las Vegas. Since it was no longer necessary to conserve space, publishers were free to use space to make their papers more attractive.

[86] Mott, *American Journalism*, pp. 573-77; Curtis D. McDougal, *Newsroom Problems and Policies* (New York, 1947), pp. 438-39; John K. Winkler, *William Randolph Hearst: A New Appraisal* (New York, 1956), pp. 1-5; John Tebel, *The Life and Good Times of William Randolph Hearst* (New York, 1952), pp. 78-79; Albuquerque *Morning Journal*, January 9, 1909, illustrates the usage of a lead paragraph in this era.

[87] Las Vegas *Advertiser*, March 22 to October 1, 1903; Las Vegas *Daily Advertiser*, May 1 to June 16, 1903. Although Lyons might appear to have sacrificed valuable financial backing for his principles, in reality he had little to lose and more to gain by continued sensationalism. He had practically no capital investment and no plant; his paper was printed in the shop of *El Independiente* at Las Vegas. Lyons probably foresaw that without sensationalism he would never successfully compete with the established Las Vegas *Daily Optic*, and a successful paper without financial backing is better than an unsuccessful one with financial backing. In addition, one may judge that Lyons' sensationalism was distorted because the further his paper pursued these tactics, the greater his loss of advertising—even among the merchants of the older town. The asylum incident furnishes a further example. A bipartisan commission of prominent territorial doctors investigated the asylum and cleared its officials of anything other than excessive scientific zeal in taking a skeleton from a body relatives would not claim. Yet Lyons refused to accept this, claiming it was merely a "whitewash."

[88] Albuquerque *Morning Journal*, March 1, 1903 to January 1, 1912, *passim*. See also Chapter IV; Mott, *American Journalism*, pp. 573-75, notes that crusades were a tactic of the yellow journalists and a recognized tactic of newspaper promotion.

[89] Santa Fe *New Mexican*, September 6, 13, 1901, June 20, 1910.

[90] These trends can be seen by scanning the front pages of the Albuquerque *Morning Journal* from 1903 to 1912, the *Daily Optic* at Las Vegas during 1908, the Albuquerque *Tribune-Citizen* from 1909 until 1911, and the Albuquerque *Evening Herald* in 1911.

[91] The Santa Fe *New Mexican* had not fully eliminated front-page advertising by 1912, but it began to move toward this practice in 1910 and 1911; for weeklies which continued the use of front-page advertising, see Fort Sumner *Review* throughout 1909; Socorro *Chieftain* from 1908 to 1912. Mott, *American Journalism*, p. 594, states that front-page advertising was still common in U.S. weeklies in 1914.

[92] Max Frost of the Santa Fe *New Mexican* published photos and flattering biographies of legislators as one of his tactics to capture territorial public printing. He also published photographs of buildings at various territorial towns. However, these engravings and copy had first been used by the New Mexican Publishing Company to print pamphlets for the New Mexico Bureau of Immigration. Thus, the use of photography in this instance was not truly representative of the new journalism.

[93] Albuquerque *Morning Journal*, October 1, 1906; Santa Fe *New Mexican*, January 1, 1906.

[94] The use that the Cuervo *Clipper* made of community correspondents from 1909 to 1912 is one of the better examples of this practice.

[95] The dailies often exchanged with the better territorial weeklies which might provide them with good sources of territorial news. Max Frost of the Santa Fe *New Mexican*, on the other hand, courted country publishers, particularly Republicans, and exchanged with all territorial weeklies. For more amplification of the practice of Frost, see Chapter IV.

[96] Hillsboro *Sierra County Advocate*, February 22, 1907.

[97] For an example, see Santa Rosa *Sun*, October 22, 1909.

[98] The Albuquerque *Morning Journal* contrary to the general trend, had an editorial page very similar to the style the *Journal* uses today. Mott, *American Journalism*, pp. 580-83, shows national trends in editorial pages and styles.

[99] The Santa Fe *New Mexican* did publish general feature stories on territorial towns from 1900 to 1907. It did this, however, by using type composed by its commercial department to print pamphlets for the New Mexico Bureau of Immigration, hence they cannot be considered true feature stories; see also footnote 92 of this chapter.

[100] Mott, *American Journalism*, pp. 569-99, says that between 1892 and 1914 advertising in American newspapers increased two-and-one-half times. The advertising of retail merchants, particularly department stores, was chiefly responsible. Such advertising was very interesting to readers and helped to increase newspaper readers and subscribers, adding to the general increase brought by the new journalism. Robert D. Leigh (ed.), *A Free and Responsible Press* (Chicago, 1947), pp. 80-85, states that the number of American newspapers has steadily decreased since 1910; hereafter cited as Leigh, *Free and Responsible Press*.

[101] Roswell *Daily Record*, October 10, 1903; House *Plains News*, March 26, 1909; Santa Fe *New Mexican*, May 3, 1906, April 22, July 1, 1909; Farmington *Hustler*, January 23, 1902; Obar *Progress* as quoted in Tucumcari *News*, June 12, 1909; Socorro *Chieftain*, July 5, 1902, September 1, 1906.

[102] Fort Sumner *Review*, July 17, 1909. In this paper a Western Newspaper Union advertisement offered newspaper plants on the installment-payment plan. See also Mott, *American Journalism*, p. 589.

[103] Mott, *American Journalism*, p. 601.

[104] Tucumcari *News*, October 1, 1906, to May 1, 1907.

[105] Silver City *Enterprise*, October 31, 1902; Tucumcari *News*, February 16, 1909; San Jon *Quay County Times*, April 3, 1908; Nara Visa *New Mexican*, January 3, 1908; Vaughn *News*, April 22, 1910. While few papers in the older areas published rates for advertising, most papers in the newer areas did so—probably hoping to encourage advertising with their low rates. The rates of the older towns encouraged small, standing advertisements. This lowered production costs but reduced advertising effectiveness and advertising sales. Thus, ultimate net profits were reduced by the system.

[106] Fort Sumner *Review*, July 17, 1909; Artesia *Advocate*, January 23, 1904; Santa Fe *New Mexican*, March 14, 1901, April 20, 1906; Portales *Times*, March 16, 1907; Taos *Cresset*, June 14, 1900; Mott, *American Journalism*, p. 589.

[107] Santa Fe *New Mexican*, August 1, 1903; Las Vegas *Daily Optic*, June 27, 1903; Albuquerque *Morning Journal*, December 1, 1903.

[108] Farmington *Enterprise*, December 28, 1906.

[109] By 1912 the circulation rates of the Las Vegas *Daily Optic* had been advanced to to 65 cents per month by carrier and $7.50 annually by mail.

[110] Albuquerque *Morning Journal*, March 3, 1903; Las Vegas *Daily Optic*, October 11, 1904, October 12, 1911; Santa Fe *New Mexican*, March 25, 1907; *Ayer, American Newspaper Annual*, 1904, pp. 555-57, 1909, pp. 560-61, 1912, pp. 589-95.

[111] San Jon is the correct spelling of this town name. T. M. Pearce, in his *New Mexico Place Names*, says the name may have been derived from the Spanish *zanjon*, "deep gully."

[112] Portales *Daily News*, September 21, 1952; Clovis *News*, February 24, 1910; Tucumcari *News*, June 19, 1909; Roswell *Register-Tribune*, January 11, 1906; *Ayer, American Newspaper Annual*, 1912, pp. 589-94. All circulation claims must be discounted. Nevertheless, the figures offer some measure of the circulations of these papers.

[113] Albuquerque *Morning Journal*, March 10, 1908; Tucumcari *Sun*, March 26, 1909; Fort Sumner *Review*, October 23, 1909.

[114] Mott, *American Journalism*, pp. 600-01.

[115] Albuquerque *Morning Journal*, September 11, 1910.

[116] Portales *Times*, August 24, 1907; Clovis *News*, May 7-28, 1909; Portales *Roosevelt County Herald*, November 9, 1909; Alamogordo *Daily Journal*, July 7, 1904, March 6, 1905. In 1910 the population of Texico was 409; *Thirteenth Census*, pp. 161-83. Other examples of the small populations of these towns and other competitive struggles have been given earlier in the chapter.

[117] Portales, Artesia, and Carrizozo are examples of this. In other towns after a brief

flurry of competition, two competing papers of opposite parties were left; Tucumcari, Alamogordo, and Estancia are examples.

[118] Roswell *Pecos Valley Stockman,* November 11, 1902.

[119] Portales *Times,* February 13, 1904.

[120] Santa Fe *New Mexican,* March 1-30, May 15, 1903, July 22, 1905, August 27, 1907; Las Cruces *Rio Grande Republican,* June 25, 1909. Governor Hagerman was generally believed to be a member of the progressive wing of the Republican party and made a determined effort to clean up New Mexico politics.

[121] Aztec *San Juan County Index,* March 7-28, 1907; Farmington *Enterprise,* August 10, 1906.

[122] Albuquerque *Morning Journal,* February 15, 16, 1905, March 1-31, 1906, July 24-31, 1907, August 1-31, 1908; Santa Fe *New Mexican,* February 17, 20, March 22, April 3, 1906, August 18, 1908. A small fine and light damage awards seem to be indicated by the absence of a news story about these cases and their disposition in either the *Morning Journal* or the *New Mexican.* An acquittal or heavy fines would have been newsworthy, but light fines and light damage awards are neither victory nor defeat, and both sides might simply ignore them. Apparently the *Morning Journal* seemed assured of no more than light fines or damages, for it continued its attacks. See also Chapter IV.

CHAPTER IV

[1] The term "political elites" is borrowed from Harold D. Lasswell, *POLITICS: Who Gets What, When, How* (Cleveland, 1958), p. 13, *passim;* hereafter cited as Lasswell, *Politics.* Lasswell defines the political elite as the group most influential in politics and as the group receiving for their political participation most of the basic values—deference, safety, and income. Other terms used to describe political leadership groups, such as "politicos," are intended to be roughly synonymous with the term political elite as used by Lasswell. The writer has borrowed heavily from the ideas in Lasswell's book in an effort to analyze the political role of the territorial press.

[2] Arthur Thomas Hannett, *Sagebrush Lawyer* (New York, 1964), p. 46. Hannett, governor of New Mexico (1925-1927), notes this characteristic as late as 1912.

[3] Las Vegas *Daily Optic,* January 20, 1890.

[4] *Ibid.,* September 9, 1890.

[5] Journalists obtained postmasterships at Albuquerque, Santa Fe, Las Vegas, Carlsbad, Lordsburg, Gallup, and in a host of other towns as political patronage. Often they continued to be editors as well as postmasters. See Chapters II and III. The Socorro *Chieftain,* February 5, 1897, provides an example of the rewards and competition for county printing contracts. The Portales *Herald,* May 14, 1904, furnishes an example of the use of homesteader legal notices in politics.

[6] Las Vegas *Voz del Pueblo* was an example of a campaign paper that lasted for many years, as was the Las Cruces *Thirty-Four.* The purchase of the Las Vegas *Daily Optic* in 1898 by such men as Felix Martinez; A. A. Jones, later a United States senator; and F. A. Manzanares, a former territorial congressional delegate, was for political purposes. These men changed the political affiliation of the paper from Republican to Democratic. Later the Albuquerque *Tribune* was founded by Felix Martinez; A. A. Jones; H. B. Fergusson, a former congressional delegate and future congressman; and O. N. Marron, prominent Albuquerque Democrat.

[7] Purchase of editorial opinion was frequent in the 1880s according to the Albuquerque *Daily Citizen,* October 30, 1886. The Las Vegas *Daily Optic* changed sides in political campaigns at least twice for monetary awards according to current observers who have been cited.

[8] Las Vegas *Daily Optic,* October 28, 1886, February 9, 10, 11, 17, 1898; Albuquerque *Morning Journal,* October 23, 1886; Las Cruces *Rio Grande Republican,* October 16,

1886; Santa Fe *New Mexican*, October 17, 1900, March 14, 1901; Farmington *Hustler*, May 5, 1903.

⁹ Santa Fe *Weekly Gazette*, April 4, 1857, May 22, 1858, February 18, March 4, August 5, September 16, November 25, 1865, February 2, 14, June 15, September 7, 1867; Santa Fe *New Mexican*, February 25, April 21, 1865, January 11, 1870, July 23, 1873; Cimarron *News and Press*, November 20, 27, 1879; Silver City *Independent*, January 23, May 22, 1900.

¹⁰ Las Cruces *Borderer*, February 28, 1872.

¹¹ Silver City *Grant County Herald*, April 1, 1876.

¹² *Ibid.*, October 26, 1878.

¹³ *Ibid.*, March 8, 1879.

¹⁴ Santa Fe *Weekly New Mexican*, October 17, 1876. For the statement of William Breeden, see issue of September 14, 1878.

¹⁵ Silver City *Grant County Herald*, September 21, 1878.

¹⁶ The behavioralist school of political science defines a political group as those with shared attitudes or activities. Arthur F. Bentley, *The Process of Government* (Bloomington, Illinois, 1908), p. 211; David B. Truman, *The Governmental Process* (New York, 1951), pp. 23-26. A recent book, Victor Westphall, *The Public Domain in New Mexico* (Albuquerque, 1965), pp. 21, 52-54, 60, 106, identifies the Santa Fe Ring and discusses its manipulation of private land grants and the public domain, confirming the existence of a Santa Fe Ring and some of the territorial editors' estimates of this group. Howard Roberts Lamar, *The Far Southwest, 1846-1912: A Territorial History* (New Haven, 1966), pp. 136-70, 179-80, 182, 185-86, 193, 196, 549, 595-96, identifies the Santa Fe Ring and traces its activities and those of succeeding Republican political groups down to 1912.

¹⁷ Albuquerque *Morning Journal*, October 6, 1882; Las Vegas *Daily Optic*, October 11, 12, 31, November 18, 1882.

¹⁸ Max Frost, a native of Vienna, Austria, at first gave as his origin New York (Santa Fe *Weekly New Mexican*, September 19, 1876) and later claimed New Orleans as his birthplace. Frost came to New Mexico as a sergeant in the Army Signal Service; and in this period he traveled extensively over the territory, making friends in all parts of New Mexico. With the aid of his friends he was appointed to a position in the territorial land office. As a territorial official, Frost soon became a member of the Santa Fe Ring and secretary of the territorial Republican party. A free-lance journalist when he came to New Mexico, Frost became a stockholder in the Albuquerque *Evening Review* in 1882. The *Evening Review* replaced the Santa Fe *New Mexican* in 1883. From time to time Frost evidently increased his holdings in the publishing company and in 1889 assumed complete direction of the paper.

¹⁹ Santa Fe *Daily New Mexican*, December 31, 1893, January 1, 1894, February 16, 20, 1905; Las Cruces *Rio Grande Republican*, December 9, 1892; Las Vegas *Daily Optic*, January 23, 25, 29, 1897.

²⁰ Silver City *Independent*, January 23, May 22, 1900.

²¹ Marion Dargan, "New Mexico's Fight for Statehood (1895-1912)," *New Mexico Historical Review*, XIV (1939), p. 130; hereafter cited as Dargan, *New Mexico Historical Review*, with volume and year. See also Las Vegas *Daily Optic*, January 26, 1897.

²² Mesilla *Times*, October 18, 1860, to January 15, 1862, *passim*; see also Chapter I.

²³ Las Cruces *Borderer*, March 16, 1871, to September 20, 1871; Silver City *Grant County Herald*, February 27, 1876; Las Cruces *Rio Grande Republican*, April 8, 1882.

²⁴ Silver City *Grant County Herald*, February 27, 1876, August 25, 1877; Las Cruces *Borderer*, December 21, 1872; Silver City *Southwest Sentinel*, September 20, 1884.

²⁵ Edmund Gibson Ross, born in Ashland, Ohio, in 1826, entered a printshop as a lad of eleven and worked in his youth on Ohio and Wisconsin papers. In 1855 Ross moved to Kansas and obtained his first editorial position on the Lawrence *Tribune*. Later he founded the *Kansas State Record*. After three years' Union army service, Major Ross was appointed United States senator from Kansas. Senator Ross was one of the few Republicans who refused to vote to convict President Andrew Johnson when he was tried under impeachment charges by the Senate. As a result he lost his

senatorship and was expelled from the Republican party. Ross then became an ardent Democrat and leader of that party in Kansas. He remained a newspaperman, and in 1882 he came to Albuquerque where he worked on the *Daily Democrat* and the *Morning Journal* until 1885. Ross was governor of New Mexico from 1885 to 1889 and held a minor territorial governmental position from 1893 to 1897. He then lived at Albuquerque until his death in 1907.

[26] Deming *Headlight*, September 7, 1889; Albuquerque *Daily Citizen*, March 27, 1893; Santa Fe *New Mexican*, March 13, 1893; Silver City *Independent*, October 14, November 11, 1902, December 31, 1911.

[27] See footnote 43, Chapter II, for a brief background of Albert Bacon Fall.

[28] Born Antonio Joseph de Treviz and of Portuguese extraction, his father was a "mountain man" and trapper—friend of Kit Carson and Ceran St. Vrain. Joseph was educated in the school of Padre J. A. Martinez at Taos, St. Michael's College at Santa Fe, and a St. Louis, Missouri, business college. Joseph apparently Anglicized his name to appeal to Anglo-American voters. His five terms as Democratic congressional delegate from a predominantly Republican territory indicate his skill as a politician. However, Joseph was aided by Republican internal dissension in 1884 and 1886, national Republican rejection in 1888 of New Mexican statehood because of its predominantly Spanish-American population, silverite and Populist dissatisfaction in 1890 and 1892. He was beaten in 1894 by T. B. Catron when silverites and Populists turned away from the Democratic party. See Las Vegas *Daily Optic*, June 9, 1886; Albuquerque *Morning Democrat* as quoted in Santa Fe *Weekly New Mexican Review*, October 21, 1886; Dargan, *New Mexico Historical Review*, XV (1940), p. 136.

[29] Albuquerque *Morning Journal*, October 23, 1886.

[30] Albuquerque *Daily Citizen*, October 30, 1886, July 16, 1890; Santa Fe *Aurora*, August 9 to November 11, 1884; Santa Fe *La Voz del Pueblo*, October 20, 1888, February 2, 1889.

[31] This was a Spanish-American party active in northeastern New Mexico, principally in San Miguel and Mora counties. It consistently supported Democratic candidates for congressional delegate. Despite the similarity of names, it had no connection with the Populist party.

[32] George Curry left the Democratic party about 1900 and was soon appointed sheriff for the recently organized Otero County. In 1908 he was appointed governor of New Mexico and in 1911 was elected as a Republican to the United States House of Representatives from New Mexico.

[33] Lasswell, *Politics*, pp. 13-20, maintains that the basic values for which the political elites contend are deference, safety, and income. Deference, safety, and income are involved in the true issues listed above. Lasswell contends, however, that the political elites do not appeal on the basic values but use symbols, violence, goods, and practices to manipulate the masses to gain the basic values for themselves. Since the use of newspapers is the only propaganda medium considered, this study seeks to identify and illustrate the symbols presented through the press to win the adherence of the masses.

[34] Spruce M. Baird came to New Mexico in 1848 as the representative of the state of Texas to claim the area east of the Rio Grande and to incorporate it into Texas as Santa Fe County. Despite his failure in this mission, Baird elected to remain in New Mexico where he established a law practice. During the Civil War, Baird sought to take New Mexico into the Confederacy. Failing in this, he left New Mexico when the Confederate troops retreated from the territory in 1862. In the post-Civil War era, Baird practiced law at Trinidad, Colorado, until his death in 1872 at Cimarron, where he was attending court.

[35] Jose Manuel Gallegos was a Catholic priest at Albuquerque until unfrocked by Archbishop Lamy in 1852. Gallegos then turned to politics, appealing to the loyalty of Spanish-Americans to the old regime both in religion and politics. Gallegos was elected delegate to Congress in 1853 and 1871. He was an unsuccessful candidate in 1855, 1863, and 1873.

[36] Santa Fe *Weekly Gazette*, May 22, 1858. Although there is no direct evidence of Baird's appeal to the loyalty of Spanish-Americans to their heritage, it appears likely

that the charge is true, for Baird was the candidate of the Gallegos faction, which was Anti-American.

[37] Las Vegas *Daily Optic*, August 21, 1880.

[38] Santa Fe *New Mexican* as quoted in Las Vegas *Daily Optic*, September 25, 1908.

[39] Santa Fe *Weekly Gazette*, June 3, 1865.

[40] Santa Fe *New Mexican*, June 8, 1867.

[41] Santa Fe *Weekly Gazette*, August 31, 1867; Albuquerque *Morning Journal*, August 29, 1884; Socorro *Chieftain*, October 26, 1894; Portales *Herald*, June 21, 1907.

[42] Lasswell, pp. 13-20. The ethics of candidates are valid issues by Lasswell's standards because treasury raiding by a corrupt official may cause an increase in taxes, taking the income of citizens; or the corrupt official may lower the standards of public services and protection, endangering the safety of citizens.

[43] Santa Fe *Weekly New Mexican*, November 26, 1885; Santa Fe *New Mexican*, January 22, 1906.

[44] Many Spanish land grants in New Mexico had been made by the provincial governors, with varying restrictions and often with vague boundaries. Under the early primitive conditions there were no clearly defined surveys, deed records, etc., as we know them today. While the Treaty of Guadalupe Hidalgo provided that valid Spanish or Mexican titles would be upheld, there was ample room for fraud or chicanery in proving the validity of a title. Ring speculators and others could buy the rights of one heir and manipulate matters to acquire the whole; grants could be enlarged far beyond their original size; and there were opportunities for political influence on those grants that were to be approved by a special act of Congress in faraway Washington. Old grants that had lost their validity through abandonment or by violation of their original terms were resurrected and validated; documents sometimes were forged. The malpractices were not limited to Anglos.

[45] Santa Fe Ring members and treasury officials had an arrangement under which some ring members were notified when there were funds in the teirritorial treasury to redeem territorial warrants. Warrants then were redeemed and the treasury was drained so that other warrant holders on presenting their warrants found that the treasury had no funds. Ring members then bought these warrants at about 65 cents on the dollar. Consequently all bids on goods and services for the territory were increased proportionately and territorial expenses were tremendously increased. See Las Vegas *Daily Optic*, October 20, 26, November 26, December 5, 1887.

[46] The territorial attorney general, district attorneys, treasurer, and other officials had been appointed for four-year terms the year before Governor Ross took office, and they refused to comply with his order to vacate their offices. The territorial courts upheld them. But S. M. Ashenfelter, whom Ross had appointed a district attorney, appealed to the United States Supreme Court, and the territorial courts were reversed late in the Ross term.

[47] Max Frost's trial aroused great public interest. He reputedly had made a fortune through land office graft while he was an official in the land office. He was charged with accepting a $30 extra fee from Abraham Staab to register a mining entry. Frost contended the $30 was given to R. E. Twitchell, noted New Mexico historian, to retain him as an attorney for Staab in connection with the entry. In the first Frost trial the jury divided eleven to one for acquittal; his second trial resulted in a conviction, with Frost receiving a one-year prison sentence. On appeal, the territorial Supreme Court ordered a new trial. Before the third trial, part of the evidence was lost or destroyed, and Frost was acquitted. During much of this time the Republican prosecution officials were still in office. See Albuquerque *Daily Citizen* as quoted in Gallup *Register*, August 28, 1888; Silver City *Enterprise*, August 24, 1888; San Marcial *Reporter* as quoted in Santa Fe *New Mexican Review*, September 6, 1888; Santa Fe *New Mexican Review*, October 11, 1894.

[48] R. E. Twitchell, *The Leading Facts of New Mexican History*, II (Cedar Rapids, Iowa, 1912), p. 501, note 420; hereafter cited as Twitchell, *Facts of New Mexican History*.

[49] Santa Fe *Weekly New Mexican*, December 3, 1885, January 7, 1886; Las Vegas *Daily Optic*, March 5, 1886.

[50] Las Vegas *Daily Optic*, May 4, October 12, 1887; Albuquerque *Daily Citizen* as quoted in Santa Fe *New Mexican Review*, April 21, 1887.

[51] Las Cruces *Rio Grande Republican* as quoted in Santa Fe *New Mexican Review*, August 30, 1888.

[52] Socorro *Chieftain* as quoted in Santa Fe *New Mexican Review*, December 13, 1888, March 3, 1887; Las Vegas *Daily Optic*, April 8, 11, July 25, 1889. Years later Max Frost, implacable enemy of Ross while he was governor, wrote of Ross, "he was personally honest," Santa Fe *New Mexican*, February 16, 1905.

[53] Las Cruces *Independent Democrat* as quoted and answered in Las Vegas *Daily Optic*, September 9, 1895. The editor of the *Optic* was right that by law and by logic Catron had to prove nothing. Nevertheless, failure to refute, or at least deny, such charges was damaging, for it is a widely held American concept that public officials should be above reproach.

[54] Albuquerque *Morning Democrat* as quoted and answered in Socorro *Chieftain*, November 1, 1895.

[55] T. B. Catron, as far as the press reveals, was convicted on only one of the many charges leveled against him. In a civil suit he was made to pay for a large quantity of brick he had ordered from the territorial prison, and in this case there was no clear intent to defraud. Thus, though Catron was much maligned there was no clear evidence of his guilt. It should, however, be noted that Ross, unlike Catron, had many defenders among opposition party papers. The incident which provoked the editorials cited was a charge of professional misconduct as a lawyer. Catron was acquitted; and while the trial was in progress, he was elected president of the New Mexico Bar Association. See Albuquerque *Daily Citizen*, October 1 to November 8, 1895, *passim;* Las Vegas *Daily Optic*, October 1 to November 8, 1895, *passim.*

[56] These warrants were issued under authority of an act of the territorial legislature of 1867 and were to pay for the services of territorial militiamen called into federal service to fight Indians in New Mexico. Impoverished New Mexico was too poor to pay the militiamen, and the legislative act specified that New Mexico was never to pay them. The warrants were given in hopes that the federal government might be induced to redeem them, but Congress refused to do so. Territorial officials issued many warrants illegally, it was charged, in addition to those given in lieu of military pay so that about $600,000 in warrants were issued. One source considered $60,000 and another $250,000 legitimate. Speculators purchased the warrants at a fraction of their face value, hoping that a territorial or state legislature might be induced to redeem them in interest-bearing bonds. Efforts were still being made to redeem warrants as late as 1912. The implication of the Staab letter was that a bribery fund by assessment of more than $5,000 a legislator was to be raised to induce passage of a funding act. See Santa Fe *New Mexican*, July 24, 1906; Santa Fe *New Mexican Review*, February 2, 1893; Las Vegas *Daily Optic*, January 9, 1891; see also Dargan, *New Mexico Historical Review*, XV, 1940, p. 175.

[57] Santa Fe *Daily Sun*, January 1, 1891.

[58] *Ibid.*, January 11, 1891, and as quoted in Las Vegas *Daily Optic*, January 14, 1891.

[59] Las Vegas *Daily Optic*, January 7, 8, 9, 1891.

[60] Las Cruces *Rio Grande Republican*, April 24, 1896.

[61] Before 1896 the Albuquerque *Morning Democrat* was the only territorial paper consistently to oppose free coinage of silver, according to the Las Cruces *Indenpendent Democrat*, August 23, 1893. The Las Cruces *Rio Grande Republican* for a few months opposed free silver, maintaining it was inflationary. However, the owners of the paper forced the editor-lessee to relinquish his lease and changed this editorial policy. *Rio Grande Republican*, February 3, 24, May 19, August 4, 11, 1893.

[62] Socorro *Chieftain*, September 1, 1893, April 19, 1895.

[63] For editorial attitudes of these papers, see Chloride *Black Range*, May 20, June 3, July 22, 1892, August 9, 1895; Las Vegas *Daily Optic*, June 23, September 1, 1891; Albuquerque *Daily Citizen* as quoted in Las Cruces *Independent Democrat*, August 23, 1893.

[64] Albuquerque *Daily Citizen* as quoted in Las Vegas *Daily Optic*, August 8, 1896.

[65] Socorro *Chieftain*, October 30, 1896.

[66] For the attitude of the Las Cruces *Rio Grande Republican* early in 1896, see issues of May 29, June 5, 12, July 24, 1896; for the changed attitude of this paper, see issue of September 4, 1896.

[67] Chloride *Black Range,* June 26, 1896.

[68] Las Vegas *Daily Optic,* September 30 to November 1, 1896.

[69] Santa Fe *Weekly New Mexican Review,* November 22, 1883.

[70] Gallup *Register* as quoted and answered by the Las Vegas *Daily Optic,* March 10, 1888.

[71] Las Vegas *Daily Optic,* November 1, 1888.

[72] *Ibid.,* September 28, 1889.

[73] Eddy *Current* as quoted in Santa Fe *New Mexican Review,* July 29, 1893.

[74] Eddy *Current,* July 1 to October 29, 1898. A survey of other Democratic papers with extant files for this period reveals also the attitude of avoiding the tariff issue. See Springer *Colfax County Stockman,* Silver City *Independent,* Roswell *Record.*

[75] Santa Fe *Weekly Gazette,* February 17, 1866.

[76] Santa Fe *New Mexican,* March 2, 1866.

[77] *Ibid.,* May 4, 1866.

[78] Albuquerque *Republican Review,* December 31, 1870; Las Cruces *Borderer,* March 23, 1871.

[79] Santa Fe *Weekly New Mexican,* April 16, 1872.

[80] There are no extant copies of the other five territorial papers published in this period, but a lack of interest may be deduced because none of the papers whose files are available quote them concerning statehood. And, on the other hand, they often cited them in relation to other matters.

[81] Silver City *Mining Life,* April 11, 18, May 2, 1874; Mesilla *News,* November 14, 24, December 6, 1874.

[82] Mesilla *News,* March 13, 1875. The House of Representatives did not pass the bill as amended by the Senate in either 1875 or 1876. The astute Elkins had at first won the friendship of southern and western Democrats. They aided his efforts until he congratulated Michigan Representative J. C. Burrows at the end of a bitter partisan speech supporting the Force Bill. Elkins, who had just come onto the floor of the House, was unaware of the nature of the speech and joined others in congratulating Burrows. Southerners, in revenge then delayed action on the New Mexico enabling act in 1875 and prevented its passage in 1876. See Silver City *Grant County Herald,* May 5, 1876; Twitchell, *Facts of New Mexican History,* p. 403.

[83] Silver City *Grant County Herald,* April 22, 1876. See also Warren A. Beck, *New Mexico: A History of Four Centuries* (Norman, Oklahoma, 1962), pp. 230-31; hereafter cited as Beck, *New Mexico.*

[84] Las Vegas *Daily Optic,* April 27, 1880.

[85] Albuquerque *Daily Journal,* May 4, December 2, 13, 1881.

[86] Raton *New Mexico News and Press,* December 17, 1881.

[87] Silver City *Daily Southwest,* August 16, 1880.

[88] Silver City *New Southwest,* October 15, 1881.

[89] Albuquerque *Evening Review,* December 22, 1882; at this time W. H. Bailhache and Max Frost, Santa Fe Ring members, owned a controlling interest in this paper.

[90] Albuquerque *Morning Journal,* November 23, 1882.

[91] Santa Fe *New Mexican Review,* January 17, 1884.

[92] Albuquerque *Morning Democrat,* June 18, 1883.

[93] Silver City *Southwest Sentinel,* March 14, 1885.

[94] Las Vegas *Daily Optic,* April 26, 1886.

[95] Albuquerque *Morning Democrat* as quoted in Las Vegas *Daily Optic,* January 3, 1889. J. G. Albright, *Morning Democrat* publisher, believed himself wronged by E. G. Ross and Anthony Joseph, for the congressional delegate Joseph had supported Ross for the governorship which Albright believed rightfully should have been his.

[96] Santa Fe *Weekly New Mexican,* November 25, 1886. There is further evidence of the attitude of the *New Mexican* in its issue of December 2, 1886. Dargan, *New Mexico Historical Review,* XIV, 1939, p. 136, contends that the *New Mexican* converted

Governor Ross to statehood. The evidence presented here refutes that contention, for the acceptance of statehood by Ross antedates that of the *New Mexican.*

[97] Santa Fe *Weekly New Mexican,* December 22, 1887, January 19, 1888.

[98] *Ibid.,* March 29, 1888.

[99] Las Cruces *Rio Grande Republican,* January 7, 1888.

[100] Las Vegas *Daily Optic,* March 2, 1888.

[101] Santa Fe *Herald,* April 7, 1888. In this Congress Democrats had a majority in the House of Representatives while Republicans controlled the Senate.

[102] Las Vegas *Daily Optic,* April 7, 1888.

[103] Santa Fe *El Boletin Popular,* April 5, 1888.

[104] Socorro *Chieftain* as quoted in Santa Fe *Herald,* April 7, 1888.

[105] Santa Fe *New Mexican Review,* April 19, 1888.

[106] Las Vegas *Daily Optic,* January 3, 1889; Hillsboro *Sierra County Advocate,* January 26, 1889; Silver City *Enterprise,* February 15, 1889.

[107] Albuquerque *Morning Democrat,* June 15, 21, July 7, 1889.

[108] Las Vegas *Daily Optic,* July 5, 1889.

[109] *Ibid.,* April 26, 1886.

[110] Las Cruces *Rio Grande Republican,* September 21, 1889.

[111] Deming *Headlight,* September 7, 1889.

[112] *Ibid.,* November 30, 1889.

[113] Las Vegas *Daily Optic,* August 19, 1890; Albuquerque *Daily Citizen,* June 28, 1890.

[114] Las Cruces *Rio Grande Republican,* December 7, 1889.

[115] Albuquerque *Daily Citizen,* June 24, August 30, 1890.

[116] See Chapter V, footnote 126.

[117] See Chapter V.

[118] Beck, *New Mexico,* p. 234, maintains that many newspapers were indifferent to the question of statehood for New Mexico prior to 1902. Newspaper editors picked editorial topics keyed to the current news, and since the territories could get little more than peremptory rejections for their statehood efforts in Congress from 1892 to 1902, there were few editorials. Compare this with the congressional session in 1904 when about one-third of the *Congressional Record* is devoted to the debates over the admission of the territories. Considering the congressional reception of New Mexican statehood bids in the 1890s, interest was high and general throughout the territorial press when there was anything noteworthy occuring, but certainly not as high as it was from 1886 to 1891 and from 1903 to 1910.

[119] Socorro *Chieftain,* October 25, 1894.

[120] For examples of the use of this appeal, see Santa Fe *New Mexican,* May 5, 1902; Hillsboro *Sierra County Advocate,* November 30, 1900, March 1, 1901, October 24, 1902; Socorro *Chieftain,* October 13, 1900, August 2, 9, 1902; Silver City *Enterprise,* March 29, 1901.

[121] Territorial Governor M. A. Otero as quoted in Dargan, *New Mexico Historical Review,* XIV, 1939, p. 121. When statehood came a decade later, hundreds of miles of new railway had been constructed, millions of acres of range had been transformed into dry land and irrigated farms, and the population of the territory had almost doubled. Nevertheless, in the early years after admission as a state taxes were exceptionally high for that era. Yet the new state provided only minimal services, and its educational system lagged far behind national standards. Only after an intense drive for statehood were New Mexicans willing to accept the high taxes necessary to support state government.

[122] Albuquerque *Daily Citizen,* February 1 to September 1, 1903, *passim;* Santa Fe *New Mexican,* May 23, August 20, September 1, 3, 1903, March 5, 12, 14, 1904; Las Cruces *Rio Grande Republican,* February 12, 1904; Las Vegas *Daily Optic,* January 25, February 2, 1904.

[123] Santa Fe *New Mexican,* February 6, September 1, 3, 1903, March 8, 9, 11, May 10, 1904; Socorro *Chieftain,* August 22, 1903, January 2, 1904; Portales *Times,* September 5, 1903, January 25, 1904; Dargan, *New Mexico Historical Review,* XIV, 1939, p. 134,

states that Max Frost so well controlled some of the smaller Republican weeklies that he sent them editorials to print, which he then cited in the *New Mexican* as representative of the attitude of the press.

[124] Las Vegas *Daily Optic,* January 25, 1904; Silver City *Enterprise,* March 4, 1904; Las Cruces *Rio Grande Republican,* February 12, 1904; Santa Fe *New Mexican,* March 5, 12, 14, 1904.

[125] Hillsboro *Sierra County Advocate,* August 25, 1904; Las Cruces *Rio Grande Republican,* September 23, 1904; Santa Fe *New Mexican,* September 8, 9, 12, 15, 1904. B. S. Rodey contended that Max Frost had a major part in engineering his defeat. See Santa Fe *New Mexican,* November 11, 1904.

[126] Santa Fe *New Mexican,* October 14, 31, 1904; Las Vegas *Daily Optic,* October 11, 13, 1904; Hillsboro *Sierra County Advocate,* October 21, 1904; Albuquerque *Morning Journal,* September 15 to November 15, 1904; Albuquerque *Daily Citizen,* September 15 to November 15, 1904.

[127] Las Vegas *Daily Optic,* October 11, 14, 1904; Silver City *Enterprise,* October 14, 21, 28, 1904; Las Cruces *Rio Grande Republican,* October 21, 28, 1904.

[128] Santa Fe *New Mexican,* April 4, 16, June 28, July 2, August 11, November 30, 1904.

[129] *Ibid.,* November 28, 1904.

[130] *Ibid.,* December 19, 1903, March 3, April 6, 8, 9, 13, 1904, February 7, October 28, December 5, 28, 1905, January 3, 4, May 10, June 15, 1906. The enabling act guaranteed the payment of about $1,000,000 indebtedness of Santa Fe County and guaranteed that the capital would be left at Santa Fe for at least ten years.

[131] Las Vegas *Daily Optic* as quoted in Santa Fe *New Mexican,* June 18, 1906.

[132] Santa Fe *New Mexican,* August 11, 1906.

[133] Silver City *Enterprise,* August 24, 1906.

[134] Las Vegas *Daily Optic* as quoted in Deming *Graphic,* October 5, 1906.

[135] Carlsbad *Argus,* October 26, 1906.

[136] Tucumcari *News,* September 6, 1906.

[137] For examples, see Silver City *Enterprise,* August 3, 1906; Socorro *Chieftain,* September 1, 1906; Santa Fe *New Mexican,* September 15, 1905.

[138] Albuquerque *Opinion Publica,* June 14, 1906.

[139] Las Cruces *El Labrador,* August 10, 1906.

[140] Las Vegas *El Independiente,* October 18, 1906.

[141] Santa Fe *New Mexican,* November 7 to December 15, 1906, *passim.*

[142] See Chapter III.

[143] Santa Fe *New Mexican,* February 17, November 20, 1905, March 27, 1912; Albuquerque *Morning Journal,* February 16, November 1-7, 1905; Hillsboro *Sierra County Advocate,* November 3, 10, 1905.

[144] Albuquerque *Morning Journal,* January 1-3, September 6, 1906, January 7, 23, 25, 26, February 1, 6, 12, March 10, April 11, 1907; Santa Fe *New Mexican,* January 4, 1906; Aztec *San Juan County Index,* December 14, 1906, April 5, 1907. Herbert Hagerman was the son of J. J. Hagerman, the irrigation and railway pioneer of the Pecos Valley.

[145] Albuquerque *Morning Journal,* September 1-5, 1906; Farmington *Times-Hustler,* September 7, 1906; Santa Fe *New Mexican,* September 16, 1906. It must be said in extenuation of H. O. Bursum that he later convinced the territorial courts that instead of being short in his accounts at the prison the territory owed him a large sum. However, newspaper accounts reveal that when he left office he had taken part of the prison records with him and had burned others.

[146] Albuquerque *Morning Journal,* April 20-30, 1907; Aztec *San Juan County Index,* April 26, 1907; Aztec *San Juan County Democrat,* May 2, 1907. Hagerman did not appear to be guilty of any real malfeasance in office by which benefits accrued to him. He had, however, blundered in one instance, which was used by his enemies to ask President Roosevelt to remove him. It appears, however, that the real reason for his removal was that he seemed to be splitting the territorial Republican party.

The *Morning Journal* charged that this was the true reason that President Roosevelt asked for his resignation.

[147] Albuquerque *Morning Journal*, July 17, 18, 21, 22, 24, 26, 1908, September 1 to November 10, 1911; Farmington *Times-Hustler*, July 19, 1906; Hillsboro *Sierra County Advocate*, November 16, 1906.

[148] Estancia *News*, August 10, 1910.

[149] Las Cruces *Rio Grande Republican*, August 5, 1910.

[150] Fort Sumner *Sunnyside Republican*, August 20, 1910. Residents of the villages of Fort Sumner and Sunnyside both moved to the present site of Fort Sumner when the New Mexico Eastern (Santa Fe) railway made it a station. For a time, disputing townsmen gave it both names. The *Republican* was a proponent of Sunnyside.

[151] Las Vegas *Daily Optic*, July 5, 1910; Albuquerque *Morning Journal*, July 10, 27, 1910; Santa Fe *New Mexican*, June 29, 1910; Roswell *Record*, July 5, August 2, 1910.

[152] Albuquerque *Morning Journal*, August 20 to September 20, 1910, *passim*.

[153] Tucumcari *Sun* as quoted in Bard City *News*, October 10, 1910.

[154] Bard City *News*, October 10, 1910; Las Cruces *Rio Grande Republican*, September 9, 1910.

[155] Silver City *Enterprise*, December 30, 1910.

[156] Hillsboro *Sierra County Advocate*, January 6, 1911.

[157] Santa Fe *New Mexican* as quoted and commented about by Estancia *News*, December 16, 1910. The *New Mexican* claimed that 116 territorial papers favored and 4 opposed ratification. The Estancia *News* named 12 papers opposed, and there were at least four more than those named by the *News*. Thus, it appears that the ratio was about 110 to 16.

[158] Roswell *Daily Record*, January 13, 1911. The enabling act provided that if the constitution was defeated the convention would be recalled to rewrite it. However, the editor of the *Record* apparently believed that this would lead to a fight between parties and between conservatives and liberals and that in the end it would lead to defeat of statehood or a worse constitution.

[159] The provisions for amendment of the original constitution were so stringent that it was actually impossible to amend. The stringent restrictions were left intact with regard to voter qualifications and certain school sections to insure that Spanish-American voting rights would be protected and that the ethnic groups would never be separated in public schools. Repeated recent attempts to amend the portion of the constitution regarding voting rights to provide for absentee balloting have all failed, despite the fact that there was practically no opposition to them. In view of this, it seems that the original constitution would have been impossible to amend.

[160] Although the Flood Resolution left intact the amending process of the original constitution with regard to voting rights and education rights, many Spanish-Americans believed themselves endangered by the "Blue Ballot Amendment" and opposed it.

[161] Santa Fe *New Mexican*, September 23, 1911; Las Vegas *Daily Optic*, September 29, October 4, 1911; Albuquerque *Morning Journal*, October 17, 1911.

[162] The archbishop, out of the territory when the letter was written and released, repudiated it on the eve of the election. Of the Spanish-language papers, Mora *Combate* (November 3, 1911) was the most militant. Other examples of opposition to the "Blue Ballot Amendment" were shown by Las Cruces *Laborador*, November 3, 1911; Las Vegas *El Independiente*, October 26, 1911.

[163] Roswell *Record*, October 20, 1911.

[164] Las Cruces *Rio Grande Republican*, November 4, 1911; Nara Visa *New Mexican and Register*, November 4, 1911; Fort Sumner *Review*, October 28, November 4, 1911.

[165] Albuquerque *Morning Journal*, August 1 to November 10, 1911, *passim*.

[166] Democrats and Republicans split the two congressional seats awarded New Mexico, but Spanish-American Republicans charged with some justification that one of the Republican candidates, Elfego Baca, had been denied Anglo-American Republican votes in some areas, costing him the election (see Chapter V). Had it not

been for incidents such as this, the Republican victory might have been a clean sweep—except for Bursum.

[167] Beck, *New Mexico,* pp. 300-03.

[168] Will Irwin, *Columbia Journalism Review,* II, p. 42.

[169] See Chapter III.


CHAPTER V

[1] Santa Fe *Republican,* August 8, 1848.

[2] Albuquerque *Rio Abajo Weekly Press,* February 3, April 14, June 23, 30, September 22, 29, December 1, 1863; Santa Fe *New Mexican,* December 12, 1863; Santa Fe *Weekly Gazette,* December 31, 1864.

[3] The homeland of the Navajo was a mountainous and desert area in northeastern Arizona and northwestern New Mexico. The area around Fort Sumner, on the other hand, is an open country characteristic of the Great Plains, vastly different from the Navajo homeland. At Fort Sumner the Navajo dug irrigation canals and cleared fields almost with their bare hands but had very poor success with their farming. As a result they subsisted on army rations to which they were unaccustomed. They also believed themselves menaced by the very warlike Comanches who often ranged that far west. Because of all of the above and their close confinement, the Navajo were very unhappy at Fort Sumner despite the fact that it is a better farming and grazing country than their homeland.

[4] Albuquerque *Rio Abajo Weekly Press,* March 22, May 3, 1864; Santa Fe *New Mexican,* September 2, 1864.

[5] Santa Fe *Weekly Gazette,* February 4, July 22, December 23, 1865, November 17, 1866, May 23, 1868; Santa Fe *New Mexican,* July 14, October 27, 1866, June 9, 1868.

[6] For many years New Mexicans had raided the Navajo, taking captives as slaves. This practice was continued in the American era, and between 1858 and 1863 under authority of a legislative act hundreds of Navajo were captured and sold into slavery. Santa Fe *Weekly Gazette,* August 12, 1865, January 19, February 2, April 20, 1867; Santa Fe *New Mexican,* January 19, February 9, 1867. Beck, *New Mexico,* pp. 27-37, 191-99, gives a brief background of the New Mexico Indians and a history of this struggle; he also notes the practice of Indian slavery and says that a healthy Indian brought up to $300 at slave auctions in Santa Fe. Maurice Garland Fulton and Paul Horgan, *New Mexico's Own Chronicle* (Dallas, 1937), p. 164, state that some northwestern New Mexico villagers made contracts with the Rio Grande settlements to furnish Navajo girls as slaves at $500 a head and then would gather men for an expedition into Navajo country to capture women and children.

[7] Santa Fe *Weekly Gazette,* January 19, February 2, April 20, 1867; Santa Fe *New Mexican,* January 19, February 9, 1867.

[8] Santa Fe *New Mexican,* August 19, 1864.

[9] *Ibid.,* February 2, 1867, May 26, 1868; Santa Fe *Weekly Gazette,* May 23, 30, 1868.

[10] This incident furnishes an example of one of the relatively few times that heated competition between two territorial newspapers in the same town produced a beneficial result for society.

[11] Santa Fe *New Mexican,* September 1, 1868.

[12] Silver City *Grant County Herald,* September 22, 1877.

[13] Las Vegas *Daily Optic,* February 4, 1881.

[14] *Ibid.,* December 3, 1881.

[15] Las Vegas *Chronicle* as quoted in Silver City *Enterprise,* June 5, 1885.

[16] Hillsboro *Sierra County Advocate,* March 2, 1889.

[17] "Bits from Bippus," Albuquerque *Daily Citizen,* June 25, 1890.

[18] Santa Fe *New Mexican Review,* June 4, 1885.

[19] Santa Fe *Weekly New Mexican,* November 11, 1879.

[20] Socorro *Industrial Advertiser*, February 23, 1889.

[21] Silver City *Enterprise*, May 29, June 26, July 17, 31, 1885, September 17, 1886, November 9, 1889; Santa Fe *New Mexican Review*, June 4, 1885; Chloride *Black Range*, July 24, 1885.

[22] Santa Fe *Weekly New Mexican*, August 23, 1872. For examples of similar editorial attitudes, see Silver City *Grant County Herald*, June 24, 1876, August 19, 1878; Las Vegas *Daily Optic*, September 23, 1887; Albuquerque *Evening Review*, May 30, 31, June 28, 1882; Silver City *Enterprise*, October 23, 1885; Farmington *Hustler*, January 22, 1902.

[23] Silver City *Grant County Herald*, September 8, 1877; Silver City *Enterprise*, August 29, 1884, November 4, 1887, June 8, 1888, February 15, 1889; Las Cruces *Rio Grande Republican*, August 13, 1881; Albuquerque *Daily Democrat*, April 7, 1883.

[24] Santa Fe *Weekly New Mexican*, March 12, 1872.

[25] Las Cruces *Rio Grande Republican*, June 27, 1885, March 26, 1887; Santa Fe *New Mexican Review*, July 20, August 13, 1885; Santa Fe *Weekly Leader*, August 22, 1885. On the other hand, W. H. H. Llewellyn, agent at the Mescalero Apache Indian Reservation, was conceded to be an excellent Indian agent by many New Mexico papers, who several times noted his realistically firm but kind attitude toward his charges.

[26] It should be noted in extenuation of Colonel Hatch that in the early phases of this Apache trouble, some New Mexico troops were involved in the Lincoln County war and that part of the time Hatch and many of the troops under his command were in Colorado to aid in a war against the Ute Indians. It was during this latter period that the Apache Indians began their period of most intense raiding.

[27] Santa Fe *Weekly New Mexican*, October 4, 1879, July 12, 1880.

[28] Silver City *Daily Southwest*, May 3, 14, 20, 1880; Las Vegas *Daily Optic*, May 3, 1880, June 29, 1881; Albuquerque *Daily Journal*, August 15, 1881; Santa Fe *Weekly New Mexican*, December 6, 1879.

[29] Las Vegas *Daily Optic*, May 5, 1880; Silver City *Daily Southwest*, March 13, 20, May 19, June 7, 1880; Santa Fe *Weekly New Mexican*, April 12, 1880.

[30] Silver City *Daily Southwest*, March 20, 25, June 9, 25, July 16, 1880; Las Vegas *Daily Optic*, April 20, 1880.

[31] Las Vegas *Daily Optic*, June 4, 1880.

[32] Silver City *Daily Southwest*, April 15, 1880.

[33] Las Vegas *Daily Optic*, May 19, 1880.

[34] Silver City *Daily Southwest*, March 27, 1880.

[35] Las Cruces *Thirty-Four* as quoted in Las Vegas *Morning Gazette*, February 5, 1881.

[36] Santa Fe *Weekly New Mexican*, May 10, 1880.

[37] *Ibid.*, May 24, 1880; Silver City *Daily Southwest*, May 7, 11, 13, June 7, 1880; Albuquerque *Daily Journal*, August 15, 1881.

[38] Silver City *Daily Southwest*, March 26, 1880. Other calls for the use of volunteers were made by Las Vegas *Daily Optic*, May 5, 1880; Santa Fe *Weekly New Mexican*, April 12, 1880; Albuquerque *Daily Journal*, September 2, 8, 1881.

[39] Silver City *New Southwest*, May 14, 1881; Las Vegas *Daily Optic*, September 12, 13, 1881; Albuquerque *Evening Review*, May 3, 1882.

[40] The Apaches continued intermittent raiding, particularly in Arizona, until about 1890.

[41] Las Cruces *Rio Grande Republican*, May 3, 1884.

[42] Santa Fe *Weekly New Mexican*, July 14, 1887; Santa Fe *New Mexican Review*, December 13, 1888; Santa Fe *New Mexican*, May 29, August 31, 1906; Las Cruces *Rio Grande Republican*, August 13, 1887, December 22, 1888.

[43] Santa Fe *Weekly New Mexican*, June 15, 1875.

[44] Santa Fe *New Mexican*, May 21, June 6, July 31, September 10, 1903, March 26, May 25, 1904.

[45] Albuquerque *Morning Journal* as quoted in Farmington *Times-Hustler*, October 20, 1904.

[46] The terms Spanish-American and Anglo-American were not generally used by the press in this period. Persons of Spanish and Indo-Spanish descent were generally referred to as Mexicans in the press, while immigrants from the eastern states were commonly called Americans. Early in the twentieth century these so-called Mexicans, most of whom were native-born Americans, began to call themselves, and asked others to call them, "Spanish-Americans." Since their New Mexico ancestors had a history of over 200 years of Spanish rule compared to a period of only twenty-five years of Mexican rule, the term Spanish-American rather than Mexican-American seems justified. For convenience the writer has lumped all the Spanish-speaking people under the terms Spanish-American or Hispano and the English-speaking under the term Anglo-American.

[47] For example, among the early editors H. S. Johnson, W. H. Manderfield, William McGuiness, Louis Hommel, and A. J. Fountain married Spanish-Americans.

[48] See Silver City *Mining Life*, December 27, 1873, to October 31, 1874, *passim*.

[49] Silver City *Grant County Herald*, September 16, October 7, December 2, 1876, November 24, 1877.

[50] Hillsboro *Sierra County Advocate*, March 13, 1886.

[51] *Ibid.*, March 26, April 2, 16, 1889; Las Cruces *Rio Grande Republican*, March 3, 31, 1889. For other examples of the hostility of editors of this area toward Spanish-Americans, see Santa Fe *New Mexican*, February 16, 1888; Deming *Headlight*, April 12, August 16, 1889; Las Vegas *Daily Optic*, October 27, 1896.

[52] Las Vegas *Daily Optic*, December 28, 29, 1880, March 8, 31, November 5, 10, 1881; Albuquerque *Daily Journal*, March 3, November 8, 13, 20, 1881; Socorro *Sun*, January 1, 1881; Silver City *Grant County Herald*, January 1, 1881. J. F. Chaves was the former territorial delegate to Congress.

[53] Albuquerque *Daily Journal*, November 8, 1881.

[54] Las Vegas *Daily Optic*, November 10, 1881.

[55] Socorro *Sun* and *Miner* as quoted in Albuquerque *Daily Journal*, November 20, 1881.

[56] Las Vegas *Daily Optic*, November 20, 1879.

[57] *Ibid.*, April 11, 1884.

[58] Las Cruces *Rio Grande Republican*, September 16, 1882.

[59] Albuquerque *Daily Journal*, March 4, 1881.

[60] See Chapter IV for full details.

[61] Las Vegas *Daily Optic*, December 19, 1888.

[62] Santa Fe *New Mexican Review*, March 29, 1881; Santa Fe *New Mexican*, December 3, 1903, September 5, 1905; Las Vegas *Daily Optic*, February 17, 1890, September 29, 1910; Las Cruces *Citizen*, September 2, 1905.

[63] Land grant titles were being confirmed by congressional acts in this period, and other grant owners were anticipating future confirmation of their titles. Both types of grant owners began fencing lands that they claimed—lands commonly believed to be public domain. These fences barred the roads to wood, water, and grazing lands used for many years by other New Mexicans.

[64] Las Vegas *Daily Optic*, December 12, 1889, March 12, April 4, 8, September 12, November 1, 1890, January 21, 1891; Las Cruces *Rio Grande Republican*, March 15, May 24, August 9, 1890, April 8, 15, 1892; Albuquerque *Daily Citizen*, August 12, 1890.

[65] Las Cruces *Rio Grande Republican*, November 9, 1889.

[66] Las Vegas *Daily Optic*, March 12, 1890.

[67] *Ibid.*, April 4, 1890.

[68] *Ibid.*, April 7, 1890.

[69] Mesilla *Defensor del Pueblo* as quoted in Las Cruces *Rio Grande Republican*, August 9, 1890; Las Vegas *Sol de Mayo*, May 1, 1891.

[70] Gallup *Gleaner* as quoted in Las Cruces *Independent Democrat*, April 13, 1892.

[71] Mora *Mosquito*, June 12, 1892.

[72] Las Vegas *El Independiente* as quoted in Las Cruces *Democrata*, August 4, 1894.

[73] Las Vegas *El Independiente*, February 3, 1898.

[74] *Ibid.*, May 7, 1903, August 8, 1904.

[75] Santa Fe *New Mexican*, March 30, 1905. Other sources indicating the southern background of the southeastern New Mexico immigration were Santa Fe *New Mexican*, January 16, 1903; Socorro *Chieftain*, February 14, 1908; Albuquerque *Morning Journal*, February 4, 1907.

[76] Hagerman *Messenger* as quoted in Santa Fe *New Mexican*, May 30, 1906.

[77] Portales *Times*, October 14, 1905.

[78] Artesia *Advocate* as quoted in Santa Fe *New Mexican*, May 18, 1906.

[79] Santa Fe *New Mexican*, January 16, 1903, March 30, 1905.

[80] Las Vegas *El independiente*, July 2, 1904.

[81] *Ibid.*, March 29, 1906.

[82] Clayton *Fenix* as quoted in Santa Fe *New Mexican*, April 13, 1906.

[83] Carlsbad *Sun*, March 9, 1906.

[84] Alamogordo *Otero County Advertiser* as quoted in Santa Fe *New Mexican*, June 4, 1906.

[85] Santa Fe *New Mexican*, June 9, 1906.

[86] Roswell *Tribune* as quoted in Santa Fe *New Mexican*, February 28, 1906.

[87] The Roswell *Record* and the Carlsbad *Sun* both favored educational requirements for voting—as quoted in Santa Fe *New Mexican*, March 6, 1906.

[88] Santa Fe *New Mexican*, February 28, March 6, 1906. New Mexico had a poll tax requirement for voting in the election of 1892 but abandoned it in 1893; apparently the tax was passed onto the vote-buying politicians and raised campaign expenses excessively. See Santa Fe *New Mexican*, January 5, 12, 19, 1893; Las Cruces *Rio Grande Republican*, September 23, 1892; Las Vegas *Daily Optic*, November 16, 1892.

[89] Las Cruces *El Labrador*, August 10, 1906.

[90] Hillsboro *Sierra County Advocate*, March 1, 1905.

[91] Las Vegas *Daily Optic* as quoted and answered in Santa Fe *New Mexican*, March 2, 1906.

[92] Las Vegas *El Independiente*, October 1, 1903.

[93] Santa Fe *New Mexican*, May 29, 1906.

[94] Carlsbad *Current* as quoted in Santa Fe *New Mexican*, June 20, 1906. The *Current* further contended that the parents of Spanish-American children wished the schools to remain segregated because the children, because of language difficulty, made faster progress in segregated schools.

[95] Santa Fe *New Mexican*, April 16, 1906.

[96] Beck, *New Mexico*, p. 299; Santa Fe *New Mexican*, November 21, 1910; Oliver La Farge, *Santa Fe*, pp. 202-03.

[97] Beck, *New Mexico*, pp. 125, 131.

[98] Santa Fe *Republican*, January 1, 1848.

[99] *Ibid.*, January 15, 1848.

[100] Perhaps the enthusiasm of these editors for Protestant churches was not solely because of a Protestant bias, but because churches brought civilization and stability which encouraged further immigration.

[101] Silver City *Mining Life*, August 30, October 18, 1873.

[102] Santa Fe *Weekly New Mexican*, August 18, 1869. It was later revealed, however, that the minister had been misquoted.

[103] Albuquerque *Republican Review*, March 11, 1876; Santa Fe *Weekly New Mexican*, March 14, 1876; Mesilla *Valley Independent*, April 13, 1878; Silver City *Grant County Herald*, April 27, 1878; Las Vegas *Daily Advertiser*, May 29, 30, 1903. A close examination of the general newspaper files throughout the territorial era revealed few instances of hostility toward Catholicism by Anglo-Protestant editors except in relation to schools and the Jesuit order.

[104] Santa Fe *Weekly New Mexican*, February 23, 1878.

[105] Santa Fe *Weekly Post*, December 16, 1871, March 2, 1872.

[106] Silver City *Mining Life*, July 26, August 10, November 22, 1873.

[107] Santa Fe *Weekly New Mexican*, August 25, September 8, 29, 1874, March 9, 30, 1875.

[108] *Ibid.*, January 19, 1875, March 14, 1876; Albuquerque *Republican Review,* January 2, 9, 23, 1875, March 11, 1876; Silver City *Mining Life,* January 30, 1875.

[109] Santa Fe *Weekly New Mexican,* December 14, 1875; Albuquerque *Republican Review, January* 1, 8, 15, February 12, 1876.

[110] Santa Fe *Weekly New Mexican,* January 4, 1876.

[111] Albuquerque *Review,* June 17, September 17, 1876, November 17, December 8, 1877; Santa Fe *Weekly New Mexican,* August 15, September 26, 1876.

[112] Santa Fe *Weekly New Mexican,* January 26, 1878. Ultimately this legislative act was revoked by an act of the United States Congress.

[113] Mesilla *Valley Independent,* January 19, 26, February 9, 23, March 2, April 13, 1878; Silver City *Grant County Herald,* July 13, 1878.

[114] Las Vegas *Revista Catolica* as translated and quoted by Santa Fe *Weekly New Mexican,* February 2, 1878.

[115] Santa Fe *Weekly New Mexican,* February 2, 1878.

[116] *Ibid.*, February 8, 1879.

[117] *Ibid.*, April 19, 1880.

[118] *Ibid.*, February 8, 1884; Las Vegas *Daily Optic,* February 21, 1885.

[119] Las Vegas *Daily Optic,* April 11, 1884, April 1, 17, 1885, March 28, 1887; Hillsboro *Sierra County Advocate,* January 15, 1887; Santa Fe *Weekly New Mexican,* October 28, 1886.

[120] This minority report of the United States House of Representatives Committee on Territories is covered in detail along with press reaction to it in Chapter IV.

[121] San Marcial *Reporter* as quoted in Las Vegas *Daily Optic,* January 15, 1889; Chloride *Black Range,* February 22, 1889; Albuquerque *Daily Citizen* as quoted in Las Vegas *Daily Optic,* January 17, 1889; Las Vegas *Daily Optic,* February 7, 1889. Ten mills equal taxes of one per cent of assessed valuation.

[122] Silver City *Enterprise,* March 22, 1889; Las Vegas *Daily Optic,* February 21, 1889; Deming *Headlight,* September 7, 1889. The first two papers listed were Republican, which lends credence to this contention. W. D. Kistler, author of the Kistler school bill, was the brother of editor Russell Kistler of the *Daily Optic.* W. D. Kistler was once business manager and a co-owner of the *Daily Optic.*

[123] Las Vegas *Daily Optic,* April 23, 1889; Silver City *Enterprise,* September 26, 1890; Deming *Headlight,* October 12, 1889.

[124] Las Vegas *Daily Optic,* August 31, 1889; Silver City *Enterprise,* September 26, 1890; Deming *Headlight,* October 12, 1889.

[125] Hillsboro *Sierra County Advocate,* March 15, 1889; Socorro *Industrial Advertiser,* March 2, 9, 1889; Las Vegas *Daily Optic,* May 11, 1889, July 10, 19, 23, 1890; Kingston *Shaft,* July 19, August 2, 16, 1890.

[126] Silver City *Enterprise,* September 26, 1890. Although this would appear to answer all complaints of taxes too low to support schools, it did not, for apparently implementation was left in the hands of the legislature. The Deming *Headlight* as quoted in Las Vegas *Daily Optic,* October 5, 7, 1889, had claimed earlier that Spanish-American leaders were won over to the non-sectarian school provision by a guarantee of co-operation to prevent its implementation. In any case, the measure was apparently designed to placate Anglo-Americans, but large land grant owners such as T. B. Catron, M. S. Otero, J. F. Chaves, and Pedro Perea probably felt secure in the face of it, counting on their ability to defeat such a high tax through their political control of the school districts in which their land grants lay. On the other hand, the move could have been motivated by the congressional threat to impose amply supported non-sectarian schools on the territory. Such taxes would probably have been placed beyond the control of local bosses. Thus, the 5 per cent proposal would have the effect of halting congressional action, yet could have left school taxes in the hands of the bosses if the constitution were accepted and New Mexico became a state.

[127] Las Vegas *Daily Optic,* September 24, 1889.

[128] *Ibid.*, October 2, 1890.

[129] Las Vegas *Revista Catolica,* November 30, 1890.

[130] Silver City *Enterprise,* October 10, 1890.

[131] Las Cruces *Rio Grande Republican,* October 4, 1890.

[132] Dargan, *New Mexico Historical Review*, XV, 1940, pp. 133-87. The late Professor Dargan stated that there were various causes for the defeat of this constitution. Among them were Democratic opposition, tax provisions favorable to land grant owners, prospects of the funding of the fradulent militia warrants, Anglo-American fear that the new state government would be dominated by Spanish-Americans, and Catholic dislike of the non-sectarian public school provision. Professor Dargan, however, did not assess any one of these as the principal cause of the defeat of the constitution. The writer, on the other hand, agrees with an observer of that day: "The constitution was not defeated by any defects of the instrument, but solely upon the clause providing for free and non-sectarian public schools . . ." (Silver City *Enterprise*, October 10, 1890). This appears to be the principal cause for various reasons. Only two counties approved the constitution, Grant and Valencia. The population of Valencia County was predominantly Spanish-American Catholic, but it was the private political domain of J. F. Chaves and the scene of numerous earlier election frauds reflecting the desires of Chaves. He so ardently supported the constitution that he threatened if the Catholic church did not halt its opposition to the constitution that he would invoke against the church the federal statute forbidding any church to own more than $50,000 in property in any territory (Deming *Headlight*, August 23, 1890). Grant County, on the other hand, was the leading Democratic Anglo-American county of the territory. Thus, while Democrats no doubt helped to defeat the constitution, they must not have been too influential since they did not carry Grant County. Furthermore, it was in Grant County that Anglo-Americans had most consistently objected to Spanish-American rule in the past. Thus, the fear of Anglo-Americans that Spanish-Americans would dominate the government of the new state does not appear to have been a key cause for the defeat of the constitution. The heavy vote against the constitution in most of the predominantly Spanish-American counties also discredits the concept that fear of Spanish-American rule was an important reason for constitutional defeat and at the same time shows the measure of Democratic influence in those counties. For example, in the predominantly Democratic counties of Mora and Taos the constitution was opposed by 85 and 83 per cent of the voters, respectively. In Rio Arriba County, which was consistently Republican, the constitution was opposed by 75 per cent of the voters. Thus, Democratic opposition to the constitution apparently accounted for only about 10 per cent of the votes. If this was true, it was insufficient to defeat the constitution, which was rejected by 70 per cent of the voters. It thus appears that the non-sectarian school clause in the constitution was the key factor in its defeat. This appears to be sustained also by the actions of T. B. Catron on the eve of the election, for, as Dargan writes, Catron had a friend in Congress introduce a bill that threatened to curtail jury service of non-English-speaking citizens of United States territories to coerce Spanish-Americans to vote for statehood to avoid the effects of this law. Catron, the most influential political leader of this era in New Mexico, took this risky action only because he had learned of the Spanish-American opposition to the constitution. See also Chapter IV.

[133] Santa Fe *Daily Sun*, January 16, 1891.

[134] Las Vegas *Daily Optic*, January 19, 1891.

[135] Las Cruces *Rio Grande Republican*, January 30, 1891.

[136] White Oaks *New Mexico Interpreter*, February 20, 1891; Las Vegas *Daily Optic*, February 6, 1891.

[137] The poll tax provision was soon repealed, see footnote 88.

[138] Previously, most New Mexico schools owned neither their buildings nor a great deal of equipment but leased both. See Santa Fe *New Mexican Review*, January 12, 1893.

[139] Albuquerque *Daily Citizen*, February 27, 1891.

[140] Las Cruces *Rio Grande Republican*, July 17, 1891.

[141] The chief comments of the press concerning schools were made at the time the territorial superintendent of schools made his annual reports, when the editors complacently noted the progress that had been made since the enactment of the Paulin bill. The Santa Fe *New Mexican*, however, was a notable exception to this rule. It was

consistent in its efforts to improve schools both at Santa Fe and over the territory during the remainder of the territorial era.

[142] Santa Fe *New Mexican Review,* January 12, 1893; Santa Fe *New Mexican,* June
19, 1903.

[143] Santa Fe *New Mexican,* October 9, 1906.

[144] *El Combate,* August 15, 29, December 31, 1904; Las Vegas *El Independiente* as
quoted by Las Cruces *El Labrador,* December 30, 1904; Socorro *Defensor del Pueblo* as
quoted in Socorro *Chieftain,* June 4, 1904.

## CHAPTER VI

[1] Albuquerque *Daily Democrat,* December 22, 1882; Albuquerque *Rio Abajo Weekly
Press,* October 13, 1863.

[2] Santa Fe *Weekly Gazette,* October 19, 1867. A War Department survey in the
1850's recommended four rail routes to the Pacific Coast, two of them through New
Mexico. These two routes were often designated as the thirty-second and thirty-fifth
parallel routes because their westward track was approximately along those latitudes.

[3] Santa Fe *New Mexican,* October 5, 1867.

[4] *Ibid.,* May 25, 1869.

[5] *Ibid., November* 7, 1871; Albuquerque *Republican Review,* December 17, 1870,
October 21, 1871.

[6] Silver City *Mining Life,* June 7, 1873.

[7] Mesilla *News,* December 4, 1878.

[8] Albuquerque *Daily Journal,* November 30, 1880. A good source of information on
railroads and town growth in the southwest is Ira B. Clark, *Then Came the Railroads* (Norman, Oklahoma, 1958).

[9] Santa Fe *Weekly New Mexican,* December 2, 1886.

[10] *Ibid.,* November 18, 1886.

[11] Albuquerque *Daily Citizen* as quoted in Santa Fe *Weekly New Mexican,* July 14,
1887.

[12] Las Vegas *Daily Optic,* January 17, 1887.

[13] Tucumcari *Times,* September 3, 1903.

[14] Santa Fe *New Mexican,* October 5, 1867.

[15] Las Vegas *Gazette* as quoted in Santa Fe *Weekly New Mexican,* December 15,
1874.

[16] Silver City *Grant County Herald,* May 11, 1878.

[17] Albuquerque *Review,* December 4, 1880.

[18] Santa Fe *New Mexican,* July 20, 1900.

[19] Santa Fe *Weekly New Mexican,* June 15, 1878.

[20] Las Vegas *Gazette* as quoted in Santa Fe *Weekly New Mexican,* March 29, 1879.

[21] Santa Fe *Weekly New Mexican,* April 5, 1879.

[22] Albuquerque was similarly divided into old and new towns. Mesilla refused to
pay the price for rail connections and the station was placed at Las Cruces. Today
Mesilla is only a historic landmark, but Las Cruces is a thriving metropolis.

[23] Santa Fe *Weekly New Mexican,* September 21, October 4, 1879. L. L. Waters,
*Steel Rails to Santa Fe* (Lawrence, Kansas, 1950), pp. 56-57, states that Santa Fe
County voted a bond issue to aid the building of a line into Santa Fe. Waters makes
no mention of the Santa Fe Railroad demand for townsites at Las Vegas and Albuquerque. But he notes (pp. 247-48) that a Santa Fe subsidiary, the Arkansas Valley
Town and Land Company, between 1870 and 1886 selected sites and launched more
than 100 towns along the Santa Fe lines. Therefore it appears that the territorial
papers accounts of the demands of the railway at Las Vegas and Albuquerque are
reasonably near the truth of the matter.

[24] Las Cruces *Thirty-Four* as quoted in Santa Fe *Weekly New Mexican,* October 4,
1879.

[25] Santa Fe *Weekly New Mexican*, May 10, June 16, August 20, 1880, July 7, 1883.

[26] Albuquerque *Evening Review*, July 27, 1882; Albuquerque *Morning Journal* as quoted in Santa Fe *Weekly New Mexican*, February 14, 1884. These bonds, however, were never issued, for the line which was eventually built stopped at Santa Fe. Santa Fe County defaulted on both sets of railway bonds as did Grant County for the bonds issued to build a line connecting Silver City with the Santa Fe and Southern Pacific at Deming. However, the enabling act of 1910 provided, that the new state of New Mexico assume the debts of its counties, and it was by this means that about $1,000,000 was paid to settle for the bonds and delinquent interest.

[27] Portales *Roosevelt County Herald*, July 2, 1909.

[28] Mesilla *Valley Independent*, February 2, 1878.

[29] Santa Fe *Democrat* as quoted in Las Cruces *Rio Grande Republican*, February 4, 1882.

[30] Las Vegas *Daily Optic*, March 1, 1884.

[31] *Ibid.*, June 11, 1888.

[32] Santa Fe *Weekly New Mexican Review*, June 7, 1888.

[33] Lordsburg *Advance* as quoted in Silver City *Enterprise*, January 9, 1886.

[34] Las Cruces *Rio Grande Republican*, May 28, 1886.

[35] Albuquerque *Morning Journal* as quoted in Las Cruces *Rio Grande Republican*, February 18, 1882.

[36] Santa Rosa *Sun*, May 8, 1908.

[37] Mesilla *Valley Independent*, January 19, 26, 1878.

[38] Silver City *Grant County Herald* as quoted in Mesilla *Valley Independent*, March 2, 1878. The *Independent*, however, stated that the railway lobby arrived only after the bill favorable to railways was passed. It was later revealed in a congressional investigation (see Las Vegas *Daily Optic*, February 2, May 17, 1884) that C. P. Huntington had secured the appointment of Governor S. B. Axtell, and he, acting in Huntington's behalf, encouraged the legislature to enact this law, and apparently the law authorizing the exceptionally high rates noted. Axtell was soon removed as New Mexico governor for his actions in the Lincoln County war. However, in 1881 Huntington was able to have him appointed territorial chief justice. Axtell then favored Huntington again by upholding the tax exemption law in a test case.

[39] Silver City *Enterprise*, June 29, July 6, 1883; Santa Fe *Weekly New Mexican*, December 27, 1883, February 7, 1884; Silver City *Southwest Sentinel*, January 18, 1884.

[40] Santa Fe *New Mexican Review*, February 16, 1893; Santa Rosa *Sun*, December 4, 1908, notes that railways built seven years earlier in Guadalupe County would pay their first taxes that year.

[41] Santa Fe *New Mexican Review*, January 12, February 16, 1893.

[42] Pecos Valley Northeastern, El Paso Northeastern, and Santa Fe Central.

[43] Santa Fe *Republican*, September 10, 1847. Similar stories appeared in later issues of this paper.

[44] Santa Fe *New Mexican*, April 6, 1866.

[45] Las Cruces *Borderer*, March 23, 1871.

[46] San Pedro *Gol-9-den*, July 18, 1899.

[47] Las Vegas *Daily Optic*, December 17, 1883, to March 21, 1884, *passim*. Many considered it legally possible to do this in this period because Las Vegas lay on a Spanish land grant. Spanish and Mexican land grants did not convey the rights to minerals to the grantee. Many believed then that under United States law a mining claim could be filed on such lands. This caused a great deal of conflict until a federal court ruled that under United States laws a title to the surface carried with it the title to mineral rights as well. Probably there was a small amount of gold on the court house lot and around Las Vegas, for there are several extensive areas in New Mexico where the top soil contains $1 to $3 of gold dust per ton.

[48] *Ibid.*, December 28, 1883.

[49] Santa Fe *New Mexican* as quoted and answered in Silver City *Daily Southwest*, August 24, 1880.

[50] Las Cruces *Rio Grande Republican*, June 11, 1881.

[51] Las Vegas *Daily Optic*, July 1, 1881; Silver City *Enterprise*, July 6, 1883;

Albuquerque *Daily Journal,* April 1 to May 5, August 8, 9, 1881; Albuquerque *Morning Democrat,* June 21, 22, September 1 to October 3, 1889; Hillsboro *Sierra County Advocate,* January 20, 1893.

⁵² Chicago *Mining Review* as quoted in Silver City *Enterprise,* September 7, 1883; Las Vegas *Daily Optic,* December 10, 1879.

⁵³ Las Cruces *Rio Grande Republican,* August 27, 1881, July 28, November 3, 1883, May 17, 1884; Silver City *Southwest Sentinel,* August 24, 1883; Silver City *Enterprise,* July 6, 1883, November 1, 1891; Hillsboro *Sierra County Advocate,* February 14, 1885; Albuquerque *Daily Journal,* December 3, 1880.

⁵⁴ For examples, see Silver City *Enterprise,* July 4, 1890; Silver City *Independent,* May 12, 1903; Socorro *Chieftain,* March 3, 1900.

⁵⁵ See Chapter IV.

⁵⁶ These winters, which had been so disastrous for cattlemen of the northern Great Plains area, were only slightly colder than normal in New Mexico, and cattle losses were very light according to the Las Vegas *Daily Optic,* April 30, 1887. There was no noticeable objection to this statement by other territorial papers, and since the ranges around Las Vegas are more likely to feel the effects of winter weather than most ranges in New Mexico, it appears that the statement of the *Daily Optic* was correct.

⁵⁷ Santa Fe *Weekly New Mexican,* September 27, 1870.

⁵⁸ *Ibid.* Issues of July 18, 1873, April 13, 1875, May 2, 1876, provide other examples.

⁵⁹ Las Vegas *Daily Optic,* April 28, 1880, February 2, 1881.

⁶⁰ Santa Fe *New Mexican,* August 1, 1907. See also Chapter IV. There is no readily apparent reason for the editor's lack of interest in the sheep industry. Possibly it was because the sheepmen were principally Spanish-American and the catlemen were Anglo-American and more likely subscribers to the papers. In addition, cattlemen at one time were good customers of the papers because of their cattle-brand advertisements, see Chapter II. Under these conditions the editors were more likely to take an interest in cattlemen and to publish news of their activities.

⁶¹ Cimarron *New and Press,* January 22, 1880.

⁶² Albuquerque *Daily Journal,* April 5, 1881, January 23, October 4, November 29, 1882.

⁶³ Las Cruces *Rio Grande Republican,* March 22, 1884.

⁶⁴ Las Vegas *Daily Optic,* November 11, 1884, April 30, 1887.

⁶⁵ Cimarron *News and Press,* June 3, 1880.

⁶⁶ For examples, see San Lorenzo *Red River Chronicle,* July 15, 1882; Las Cruces *Rio Grande Republican,* June 9, 1883, April 10, 1886; Las Vegas *Daily Gazette,* August 26, 1881.

⁶⁷ Silver City *Independent,* January 1, April 25, 1899.

⁶⁸ Las Vegas *Daily Optic,* March 21, 1881; Santa Fe *New Mexican Review,* January 17, 1884; Las Cruces *Rio Grande Republican,* February 9, March 15, 1884.

⁶⁹ Santa Fe *New Mexican Review,* January 29, May 7, 1885; Las Cruces *Rio Grande Republican,* February 2, 1884; Silver City *Enterprise,* September 4, October 30, 1885. These cattle had been ordered removed from the Indian Territory by President Grover Cleveland, and their owners were seeking ranges for them in New Mexico and Arizona.

⁷⁰ Las Vegas *Stock Grower,* May 18, June 1, August 17, 1889; Albuquerque *Daily Citizen,* May 3, 1890.

⁷¹ San Lorenzo *Red River Chronicle,* October 21, November 4, 1882.

⁷² *Ibid.,* November 28, 1882.

⁷³ Silver City *Enterprise,* December 21, 1883. Although Interior Department rules, territorial courts, and a congressional act of 1885 forbade the fencing of the public domain, it was continued past 1900.

⁷⁴ Santa Fe *Weekly New Mexican,* December 20, 1880; Santa Fe *New Mexican,* August 27, 1900; Portales *Times,* May 2, November 28, 1903.

⁷⁵ Santa Fe *New Mexican,* December 11, 1905, April 17, 1906.

⁷⁶ Santa Fe *Weekly New Mexican,* August 6, 13, 1885.

⁷⁷ Socorro *Chieftain,* December 15, 1899, January 5, February 2, 24, 1900.

⁷⁸ Silver City *Enterprise,* August 16, 1901.

[79] Hillsboro *Sierra County Advocate*, February 18, 1900.

[80] Socorro *Chieftain*, August 24, September 14, 1901; Santa Fe *New Mexican*, September 13, 1905, January 5, 17, 31, 1906; Silver City *Independent*, February 19, 1907; Albuquerque *Morning Journal*, July 19, 1908.

[81] Santa Fe *New Mexican*, August 30, 1905.

[82] Santa Fe *Republican*, September 17, 1847.

[83] Las Cruces *Rio Grande Republican*, February 10, 1893, quotes Martin Amador, one of the first settlers in the Mesilla Valley, as saying that the first irrigation canal was constructed in 1849.

[84] Las Cruces *Rio Grande Republican*, January 25, 1890, stated that the irrigated area of the Mesilla Valley was as large as all other irrigated areas of New Mexico combined. This paper then stated that canals had been constructed so that 16,000 acres could be irrigated in the Mesilla Valley but that rarely were more than 5,000 to 6,000 acres ever cultivated in the same year.

[85] The first successful artesian well was drilled near Roswell in 1885 according to the Santa Fe *New Mexican*, September 24, 1885. Beck, *New Mexico*, p. 292, states that artesian waters were discovered in 1890. Probably the *New Mexican* story is correct; and since this is the only artesian water in New Mexico, this appears to be the first well. The trio who founded the Pecos Valley Irrigation and Investment Company are equally prominent for other accomplishments. Charles W. Greene was a former editor of the Santa Fe *New Mexican* and a former publisher of the Deming *Tribune* and the El Paso *Tribune*. Pat Garrett was the famous slayer of Billy the Kid, and C. B. Eddy was later to become the promoter of the El Paso Northeastern Railroad.

[86] Santa Fe *Republican*, September 17, 1847.

[87] Santa Fe *New Mexican*, March 17, 1868.

[88] Albuquerque *Republican Review* as quoted in Santa Fe *Weekly New Mexican*, April 13, 1875.

[89] Santa Fe *New Mexican*, September 10, 1885.

[90] Albuquerque *Opinion*, October 9, 1886.

[91] Socorro *Chieftain*, April 30, 1897.

[92] For examples, see Albuquerque *Daily Citizen*, June 12, 1890; Las Cruces *Rio Grande Republican*, March 18, 1892; and a series of articles by W. E. Smythe, editor of *Irrigation Age* and author of *Conquest of Arid America*, which appeared in Santa Fe *New Mexican*, August to October, 1903, *passim*.

[93] Las Cruces *Rio Grande Republican*, March 20, 1909.

[94] Las Vegas *Daily Optic*, January 20, 1890; Santa Fe *New Mexican*, August 15, 1904.

[95] Santa Fe *Weekly Gazette*, November 24, 1866.

[96] For one example, see Santa Fe *New Mexican*, July 29, 1873.

[97] Socorro *Chieftain*, December 28, 1894.

[98] Santa Fe *New Mexican*, February 11, 1904.

[99] Portales *Roosevelt County Herald*, November and December, 1910, *passim*.

[100] Santa Fe *Weekly New Mexican*, January 9, 1872.

[101] *Ibid.*, September 30, October 14, 28, 1873.

[102] Las Vegas *Daily Optic*, March 18, 1892.

[103] Santa Fe *New Mexican*, July 21, 1906.

[104] Mesilla *Valley Independent*, June 30, October 27, 1877.

[105] Las Cruces *Rio Grande Republican*, July 24, 1886.

[106] For examples, see Las Cruces *Rio Grande Republican* February 12, 19, 1887, August 10, December 21, 1889, January 3, 24, 1890; Santa Fe *Weekly Sun*, March 14, 1891.

[107] Las Cruces *Rio Grande Republican*, June 12, 1888, September 28, 1889, January 10, March 8, 1890.

[108] *Ibid.*, February 18, 1895, April 17, 1896.

[109] *Ibid.*, June 12, August 14, October 2, December 14, 1896, May 7, 1897, January 21, 1898, May 26, 1899, May 11, 1900, January 11, 1901, July 25, 1904; Hillsboro *Sierra County Advocate*, July 9, 1897; Socorro *Chieftain*, August 30, 1902; Santa Fe *New Mexican*, April 17, May 4, 1900, May 22, 1903, October 19, 1904; Silver City *Indepen-*

*dent,* January 15, 1901. The concept that the Rio Grande was navigable in New Mexico was so ludicrous that the federal courts in New Mexico could not possibly sustain an injunction on that basis. New Mexico editors cited historical sources to prove that as early as 1540 the Rio Grande in summer simply disappeared into the sandy river bed north of Elephant Butte. Eventually the case was decided on the basis that a foreign company could not construct a dam on an international river in a border area, for it might constitute a threat to national defense.

[110] Las Cruces *Rio Grande Republican,* January 13, June 15, 23, July 14, August 18, September 15, 22, 29, 1905. Apparently nothing has been written of the long struggle of the Mesilla Valley to preserve its water rights and to develop its irrigation potential, a topic worthy of further research.

[111] Silver City *Enterprise,* September 14, 1883.

[112] Santa Fe *Weekly New Mexican,* January 14, 1885, March 24, 1887; Santa Fe *Daily New Mexican,* March and April, 1887, *passim.*

[113] Las Cruces *Rio Grande Republican,* August 17, 25, November 23, 1889; Socorro *Chieftain,* February 16, August 11, 18, 1900; Alamogordo *Otero Advertiser,* December 19, 1901; Alamogordo *News,* July 15, 1905; Tucumcari *News,* October 17, 1909; Columbus *News,* January 6, 1911.

[114] Portales *Times,* March 21, 1903, to February 25, 1905, *passim.*

[115] Las Cruces *Daily News,* July 8, 1889. Later other Las Cruces papers urged such tests: *Rio Grande Republican,* July 8, 1904; *Citizen,* August 29, 1906.

[116] Socorro *Chieftain,* September 29, December 22, 1900, January 19, 1901, February 3, March 8, 1902, November 4, 1905, Februay 17, March 10, 1906, August 27, 1910.

[117] Santa Fe *New Mexican,* January 15, 1904, April 20, August 23, 1905.

[118] Portales *Times,* October 24, 1903, August 20, 1904, September 9, 1905.

[119] Portales *Times* and *Roosevelt County Herald,* May, 1909, to January, 1912, *passim.*

[120] Folsom *Idea* as quoted in Hillsboro *Sierra County Advocate,* August 23, 1889.

[121] Santa Fe *New Mexican,* December 5, 1901.

[122] *Ibid.,* December 9, 1904, August 5, 1905.

[123] Aztec *San Juan Democrat,* February 17, 1906.

[124] Albuquerque *Morning Journal,* January 8, 1907.

[125] Portales *Roosevelt County Herald,* September 18, December 27, 1907.

[126] For example, the population of Roosevelt County grew in 1900 from 350 to over 12,000 in 1910.

[127] Examples of this can be seen in almost every issue of each eastern New Mexico paper from 1909 until 1912. For specific examples see San Jon *Quay County Times,* April 3, 1908; Fort Sumner *Review,* September 25, October 2, November 13, 1909, January 28, April 15, 22, May 20, 1911; Tucumcari *News,* July 16, 1910; Cuervo *Clipper,* October 7, 1910, February 2, 1911; Santa Rosa *Sun,* February 28, May 28, 1909; Vaughn *News,* July 15, 22, September 30, November 4, 25, December 2, 1910.

[128] San Jon *Quay County Times,* April 23, 1909.

[129] Santa Rosa *Sun,* June 18, 1909; Fort Sumner *Review,* November 13, 1909.

[130] Grady *Record,* December 30, 1909; Nara Visa *New Mexican and Register,* March 10, 1910; Bard City *News,* June 22, 1910.

[131] Cuervo *Clipper,* September 15, 1910.

[132] Fort Sumner *Review,* February 11, 1911.

[133] Portales *Roosevelt County Herald,* September 17, 1904.

[134] Portales *Times,* November 14, 1903, February 6, August 20, September 24, 1904; October 20, 1906, August 24, 31, 1907; Portales *Roosevelt County Herald,* March 19, 1904, December 6, 1907.

[135] Portales *Roosevelt County Herald,* August 20, 1904.

[136] Portales *Times,* September 9, 1905.

[137] Tucumcari *News* as quoted and commented about by Logan *Leader,* November 25, 1911.

[138] Nara Visa *New Mexican and Register,* September, 1911, to January, 1912, *passim.*

[139] To illustrate the prevalence of dairying in eastern New Mexico, at one time

Roosevelt County was reputed to have more registered Jersey dairy cattle than any other county in the United States. Currently, grade-A milk produced annually in Roosevelt County exceeds $3,000,000 in value.

## CHAPTER VII

[1] Current observers believed that the Spanish-American population was little inclined to violence and outlawry, and considering the preponderance of Spanish-Americans in the population, the rarity of Spanish names in news stories concerning crime and violence indicates this to be true. Probably Spanish-Americans participated in mob and riot actions, lesser crimes, and some crimes of violence, but the names of gunmen, desperadoes, and gang members were rarely Spanish. It appears, therefore, that Anglo-American frontiersmen were chiefly responsible for the violence of this era. For editorial opinions in this matter, see Mesilla *Valley Independent,* June 30, 1877; Albuquerque *Review,* April 5, 1879.

[2] Silver City *Grant County Herald,* February 20, 1876.

[3] Santa Fe *Daily New Mexican* as quoted in Las Vegas *Daily Optic,* March 10, 1880.

[4] Santa Fe *Weekly Gazette,* September 29, 1866.

[5] Albuquerque *Review,* August 28, 1879.

[6] This had been a common practice earlier among many American newspapers. See Chapter I.

[7] Silver City *Grant County Herald,* March 21, 1875. For another example of this type of reporting, see Albuquerque *Review,* March 13, 1880.

[8] See Chapter IV.

[9] Santa Fe *Weekly New Mexican,* November 16, 1875, February 15, March 28, May 30, September 19, October 10, 1876, April 3, May 1, 22, 1877; Silver City *Grant County Herald,* November 21, 1875, February 13, 20, April 1, 1876, September 8, 1877. William A. Keleher, *The Maxwell Land Grant* (Santa Fe, 1942), pp. 76-80; hereafter cited as Keleher, *Maxwell Land Grant.* F. Stanley (pseud. of Stanley Francis Crocchiola), "O. P. McMains, Champion of a Lost Cause," *New Mexico Historical Review,* XXIV, (January, 1949), pp. 1-11; hereafter cited as Stanley, *New Mexico Historical Review,* XXIV.

[10] Pueblo (Colorado) *Chieftain* as quoted in Silver City *Grant County Herald,* February 13, 1876, and in Santa Fe *Weekly New Mexican,* April 3, 1877. In the latter, the *Chieftain* directly charged the Santa Fe Ring with responsibility for the murder.

[11] Silver City *Grant County Herald,* February 13, 1877.

[12] *Ibid.,* February 20, 1877. At the same time the relative lack of interest in all of this other violence shows that it was the political implications of the Colfax County war that interested the editors. A close study of territorial papers of this period shows little mention of these other incidents.

[13] Santa Fe *Weekly New Mexican,* November 16, 1875, February 15, May 16, 1876, February 24, April 3, May 22, 1877. The *New Mexican* weakly sought to discredit the Pueblo (Colorado) *Chieftain* by claiming its intention was to make New Mexico appear so disorderly that railways would build to Pueblo rather than to Santa Fe.

[14] Pueblo (Colorado) *Chieftain* as quoted in Santa Fe *Weekly New Mexican,* April 3, 1877; Cimarron *News and Press* as quoted in Albuquerque *Review,* September 8, 1877.

[15] Several books and many articles have been written about the Lincoln County war; the best source and the source of most of the above information is William A. Keleher, *Violence in Lincoln County: 1869-1881* (Albuquerque, 1957).

[16] Mesilla *Valley Independent,* July 14, 1877. For the background of A. J. Fountain, see Chapter I, footnote 44.

[17] Santa Fe *Weekly New Mexican,* August 21, 1877. Later, in the issue of September

11, 1877, the *New Mexican* charged that Fountain's efforts to expose criminal activities were mere sensationalism designed to gain subscribers for the Mesilla *Valley Independent*.

[18] Cimarron *News and Press* as quoted in Mesilla *Valley Independent*, September 7, 1877.

[19] For example, see Santa Fe *Weekly New Mexican*, November 23, 1875.

[20] Mesilla *Valley Independent*, October 27, December 15, 1877, April 13, 27, 1878.

[21] For examples, see Santa Fe *Weekly New Mexican*, February 9, April 20, May 25, August 17, 1878; Mesilla *Valley Independent*, April 13, May 4, 11, 1878; Mesilla *News*, June 22, 1878; Santa Fe *Rocky Mountain Sentinel* as quoted in Mesilla *Valley Independent*, August 24, 1878.

[22] For examples, see Santa Fe *Weekly New Mexican*, April 6, June 1, 15, August 10, 1878, and as quoted in Mesilla *Valley Independent*, May 11, 1878; Mesilla *News*, June 8, 15, July 20, August 3, 1878.

[23] Mesilla *Valley Independent*, February 23, 1878.

[24] *Ibid.*, March 30, 1878.

[25] *Ibid.*, August 3, 1878.

[26] *Ibid.*, August 24, 1878.

[27] *Ibid.*, March 30, 1878.

[28] *Ibid.*, April 13, 20, 27, 1878.

[29] *Ibid.*, August 24, 1878.

[30] Cimarron *News and Press*, July 21, 1881.

[31] Las Cruces *Rio Grande Republican*, July 23, 1881.

[32] Santa Fe *Weekly New Mexican*, November 22, 1879; Las Cruces *Rio Grande Republican*, February 17, March 10, 17, April 14, 1883; Silver City *Enterprise*, March 1, 1883.

[33] Santa Fe *Weekly New Mexican*, January 6, 1883.

[34] Silver City *Southwest Sentinel*, April 1, 1883.

[35] Silver City *Enterprise*, April 27, 1883.

[36] Las Cruces *Rio Grande Republican*, February 17 to May 3, 1883, *passim*.

[37] *Ibid.*, June 30, July 7, 1883; Silver City *Enterprise*, March 1, 1883.

[38] Las Vegas *Daily Optic*, February 9, 1880.

[39] *Ibid.*, February 9, 1880.

[40] Albuquerque *Daily Journal*, February 1, 1881.

[41] Las Cruces *Rio Grande Republican*, March 18, 1882.

[42] Manzano *Gringo and Greaser*, February 1, 1884.

[43] Santa Fe *Daily New Mexican*, February 27, 1881. This paper, however, was not consistent, for a year later it wrote: "Judge Lynch is an outrage but sometimes does more effectual work than all the courts combined." Quoted in Albuquerque *Daily Journal*, January 29, 1882.

[44] Albuquerque *Evening Review*, March 9, August 17, 1882.

[45] Albuquerque *Sunday Journal*, May 2, 1886. This also seems to be sustained by absence of news stories about lynching in the territory after 1885.

[46] Often vigilante groups use their power to oppress innocent enemies as well as to punish criminals. In territorial New Mexico there appeared to be only one instance of this type, the vigilance group that sought to avenge the death of A. M. Conklin at Socorro (see Chapter IV). Thus, the editors, for the most part, escaped the evil results which could have come from their sanction of vigilante action.

[47] Keleher, *Maxwell Land Grant*; F. Stanley, *New Mexico Historical Review*, XXIV, pp. 1-11.

[48] Las Cruces *Rio Grande Republican*, November 18, 1882.

[49] Raton *Independent* as quoted in Las Vegas *Daily Optic*, June 20, 1885.

[50] Las Vegas *Daily Optic*, June 20, 1885.

[51] Raton *Guard* as quoted in San Hilario *Red River Chronicle*, April 22, 1882.

[52] San Hilario *Red River Chronicle*, April 22, 1882.

[53] Raton *Range* as quoted in Santa Fe *Daily Herald*, July 28, 1888.

[54] Las Vegas *Daily Optic*, May 7, 1890. The Santa Fe *New Mexican* consistently supported the Maxwell Land Grant owners, but for the most part this appears to be

support for the Santa Fe Ring leaders such as T. B. Catron and William Breeden, who represented the Maxwell Land Grant and other grants as attorneys. Thus, this does not truly represent the attitude of the general press in this matter.

⁵⁵ Las Vegas *Daily Optic*, March 28, 1881.

⁵⁶ For example, see Silver City *Enterprise*, July 27, 1883; Las Vegas *Daily Optic*, November 29, 1882.

⁵⁷ Las Vegas *Daily Optic*, March 3, 1887.

⁵⁸ *Ibid.*, April 10, 1888.

⁵⁹ San Marcial *Bee* as quoted in Alamogordo *Otero County Advertiser*, May 1, 1902.

⁶⁰ For examples, see Santa Fe *New Mexican*, June 25, 1903, April 18, 1906; Silver City *Enterprise*, August 2, 1907; Vaughn *News*, November 18, 1910.

⁶¹ Las Cruces *Independent Democrat*, August 17, 1898; Las Cruces *Rio Grande Republican*, July 22, August 26, September 2, 1898. Although A. B. Fall, attorney for and personal friend of Oliver Lee, had no open connection with the Las Cruces *Independent Democrat* at this time, it was still considered his paper by most New Mexico editors. See Chapter II. Gibson, *Life and Death of Colonel Albert Jennings Fountain*, pp. 212-81, provides a detailed account of the murder of Fountain and the trial of Oliver Lee.

⁶² Silver City *Independent* as quoted in Las Cruces *Rio Grande Republican*, August 26, 1898.

⁶³ Eddy *Current* as quoted in Santa Fe *New Mexican Review*, August 11, 1898.

⁶⁴ Roswell *Register* as quoted in Santa Fe *New Mexican Review*, July 25, 1898.

⁶⁵ San Marcial *Bee* as quoted in Las Cruces *Rio Grande Republican*, September 9, 1898. For other examples of editorial attitudes in this matter, see Santa Fe *New Mexican Review*, April 14, September 8, 1898; Las Cruces *Rio Grande Republican*, August 26, September 2, 1898, March 4, 1899.

⁶⁶ Albuquerque *Morning Journal*, September 2, 1911.

⁶⁷ The influence of the national reform movements can be seen by the national prohibition movement sending lobbyists to the New Mexico constitutional convention, seeking prohibition or at least a local option provision in the constitution. In another instance the reformers sought to have Congress exercise its powerful control over New Mexico by outlawing gambling in the territory. The influence of the national reform movements was vigorously extended in New Mexico by the immigration of large numbers of militant southern Protestants into eastern New Mexico. In the towns of that area these people stopped public gambling, dried up some towns, and excluded the prostitutes and were doubtless encouraged in their actions by such national organizations as the W. C. T. U. (Woman's Christian Temperance Union) and the Anti-saloon League of America.

⁶⁸ Santa Fe *Weekly New Mexican*, January 18, 1876; Silver City *Grant County Herald*, January 30, 1876.

⁶⁹ For examples, see Santa Fe *Weekly New Mexican*, April 28, 1876; Albuquerque *Evening Review*, April 29, 1882; New Mexico *Methodist*, May, 1886.

⁷⁰ Silver City *Independent*, September 18, 1900.

⁷¹ Socorro *Chieftain*, June 14, 1902.

⁷² For examples of the attitude of the Santa Fe *New Mexican*, see issues of January 7, August 18, November 30, December 1, 18, 1903, November 26, 1904, April 7, 1905.

⁷³ *Ibid.*, November 26, 1904.

⁷⁴ *Ibid.*, November 6, 1905.

⁷⁵ Silver City *Grant County Herald*, May 25, 1878.

⁷⁶ Las Vegas *Daily Optic*, March 5, 1887.

⁷⁷ Deming *Headlight*, February 15, 1889.

⁷⁸ Cerrillos *Rustler* as quoted and commented on by Las Cruces *Rio Grande Republican*, February 13, 1891.

⁷⁹ Artesia *Advocate*, March 25, 1905.

⁸⁰ For the attitude of the Santa Fe *New Mexican* and the other papers quoted by it, see issues of August 24, September 11, 21, October 6, 13, 17, 18, 21, 24, 25, 30, November 2, 4, 14, 1905, January 10, April 7, May 9, July 6, 1906. For the attitudes of other New Mexico papers concerning this, see Farmington *Times-Hustler*, January 18, 1906,

December 12, 1907; Socorro *Chieftain,* November 11, 1905; Las Vegas *Daily Optic,* August 6, 1906; Carlsbad *Argus,* September 7, 1906, February 8, March 1, 1907; Portales *Times,* April 6, 1907; Albuquerque *Morning Journal,* February 11, 1907.

[81] Albuquerque *Evening Review,* February 23 to March 23, 1882.

[82] Albuquerque *Morning Democrat,* June 14, 1889. For a similar attitude, see Las Vegas *Daily Optic,* February 5, 1887, July 31, 1888, May 12, 1890.

[83] Santa Fe *New Mexican,* September 11, 1900, March 26, 1903, December 7, 1906.

[84] Las Vegas *Daily Optic* as quoted in Albuquerque *Morning Journal,* August 6, 1905. See also other issues of this paper of August 11, 12, 1905.

[85] Carlsbad *Argus,* November 27, 1908.

[86] A letter written by C. V. Dobbs to the Portales *Daily News* for its Golden Jubilee edition September 21, 1952, but not published and still in the files of the Portales *News-Tribune* tells of the expulsion of the prostitutes, but neither paper makes mention of this dramatic episode.

[87] Las Vegas *Daily Optic,* January 10, 1893.

[88] Roswell *Baptist Workman* as quoted in Santa Fe *New Mexican,* July 7, 1906.

[89] Santa Fe *New Mexican,* December 29, 1908.

[90] *Ibid.,* May 31, June 18, 1909; Portales *Times,* February 11, April 22, 1909; Portales *Roosevelt County Herald,* March 10, 1909; Roswell *Record,* July 1, 1910.

## CHAPTER VIII

[1] See Chapters III and IV.

[2] Leigh, *Free and Responsible Press,* pp. 83-85, notes that the number of American newspapers reached a peak in 1909.

[3] Advertisers, who hoped to place a message before a maximum number of readers at a minimum cost, would have received more for their money in a town with only one newspaper. Such a newspaper probably would have served most of the people of the town and the surrounding area. Advertising rates of a paper of this type, no doubt, would have included a generous profit for the publisher. On the other hand, to have equally effective advertising in towns with more than one paper, the advertiser would have had to insert the same advertisement in two or more papers. Assuming that the competing publishers sold their advertising at production costs, one would still have had to pay a great deal more to reach the same number of readers. Approximately 90 per cent of the cost of newspaper production is incurred in preparing the copy and the printing forms. The newspaper with a monopoly could print the number of papers sold by two or more competing papers for little additional cost—and even that cost would be offset by additional circulation revenue. Thus the publisher with a monopoly might allow himself a generous 50 per cent net profit over costs and still distribute the advertisers' messages at less cost per reader than two competing newspapers which sold their advertising at production costs.

[4] In recent years critics have maintained that journalists have but exchanged masters and are now dominated by business interests. But most journalists maintain that profitable newspapers are not responsive to pressure from advertisers. For example, Herbert Brucker, *Freedom of Information* (New York, 1949), p. 58, maintains that newspapers with the heaviest advertising "are the ones most willing to tell advertisers to keep their noses out of editorial matters. Only those newspapers and magazines near the financial precipice can afford to give in to advertising pressure." It is true, nevertheless, that today American newspapers reflect an attitude which is both conservative and partial to business. The exceptionally large capital necessary to publish even small newspapers today tends to place policy making in the hands of conservative businessmen. These publishers reflect the attitude of business because of common interests rather than as the result of business pressures.

[5] By assuming the power to question politicians and to recommend new policies,

the journalists had pre-empted for themselves a portion of the political leaders' power. The publishers were not delegated this power through formal election or appointment by authorized officials. The editors were exercising the right of any citizen to question public officers and to recommend public policy, and they had an unofficial mandate from those who subscribed to their papers and even more from those who read their editorials. More recently editors have been freed from some of the control that subscribers earlier exercised over them because some readers, especially those living in a town with only one newspaper usually cannot subcribe to another paper. Most publishers now enjoy and will continue to enjoy a monopoly because of the heavy capital requirements of newspaper publication and the reluctance of advertisers to patronize any paper but the one with the largest circulation.

[6] See Chapter IV.

[7] For one example of this attitude, see Silver City *Independent,* May 22, 1900.

[8] *Ibid.,* April 25, 1905.

# APPENDIX

# TERRITORIAL NEWSPAPERS

# 1834-1912

THIS COMPILATION INCLUDES the titles of 732 newspapers published in New Mexico from 1834 to 1912. Each change of title of the various newspapers has been listed separately. This figure does not correspond to the figures given for the number of newspapers in the three periods of press development described in chapters I, II, and III, because slight changes in title were ignored in those cases.

Several sources were used to compile this list. The most important source was the files of territorial papers published during this period, providing information about the paper being inspected and other papers as well. Other sources include *N. W. Ayer and Son's American Newspaper Annual* from 1880 to 1912; the *Union List of Newspapers; A Check List of New Mexico Newspapers,* prepared in 1935 by the staff of the University of New Mexico Library; Estelle Lutrell, *Newspapers and Periodicals of Arizona, 1859-1911;* "Newspapers Published in New Mexico," an unpublished manuscript compiled in 1937 by Margery Bedinger and found in the New Mexico State University Library. Despite an effort to locate and list all papers published in this era, it is probable that several were not discovered.

The arrangement of this list is alphabetical by towns and thereunder by title. Usually preliminary words designating town or frequency of publication have been deleted for brevity and clarity.

To avoid repetition of a large number of the same newspaper titles in the Bibliography of this work, the newspaper files which are marked with an asterisk in the listings below, were examined by the writer in 1963 and 1964. The files of the newspapers, which are marked with a dagger symbol, were not then available for examination but most are now available to the public. Except for duplications in holdings, these listings include all of the known files at public institutions and newspaper offices in New Mexico. In either case the last entry in the descriptive material for each paper gives the extent of the holdings and the location of the most accessible files in New Mexico. When the repositories were found to have collections which did not overlap, additional sources have been listed. Several sources have identical files for many papers, and here only the most convenient source was listed.

The largest collection of territorial newspapers is at the University of New Mexico Library at Albuquerque. The holdings of the Museum of New Mexico at Santa Fe are only slightly less extensive than those of the University. The libraries of New Mexico Highlands University at Las Vegas and New Mexico State University at University Park both have interesting collections which are largely unduplicated elsewhere. At Highlands the papers gathered during the career of T. B. Mills, territorial realtor, legislator, and publisher, have been given to the library. At Las Cruces the proprietors of the Amador Hotel haphazardly collected newspapers over several decades. Recently this collection was given to the New Mexico State University Library, where it was in the process of preparation for microfilming in 1964. The New Mexico State University Library holdings include many Spanish language newspapers of Mesilla and Las Cruces that are unavailable at other libraries. New Mexico Western University Library at Silver City and New Mexico Institute of Mining and Technology Library at Socorro have files of papers of their communities and areas that are also unique. New Mexico State library at Santa Fe has a large and varied collection of papers, many of which are not found elsewhere. Other excellent sources are the offices of county clerks throughout New Mexico. A territorial law enacted in 1889 required counties to purchase and maintain files of the newspapers published in their counties. The result has been several large holdings of newspapers. In some cases, however, the counties had neither space nor facilities to store these files, and they were eventually given to the New Mexico Historical Society, which placed them in the Museum of New Mexico. Most of these papers have been microfilmed and form the basis of collections of the Museum and the University of New Mexico, although each have made important additions from other sources. Finally, some publishers have preserved the files of their own papers and others with which their papers merged.

The newspaper files and collections listed have been examined by the writer and, except for duplications and a very few papers, included all of the files of territorial newspapers at public institutions within New Mexico. The few known papers not included were inaccessible at the time this research was conducted. The University of New Mexico then had files of ten papers that were in storage awaiting microfilming. All of the Museum of New Mexico collection was not microfilmed, and these papers along with the original papers that were microfilmed were placed in storage at the New Mexico State Library at Santa Fe.

Beneath each newspaper title in the listing additional information about each newspaper has been provided. Included, in the order of their appearance, are frequency of publication (D, daily; W, weekly; S-W, semi-weekly) , language of publication (E, English; S, Spanish; Bl, bilingual) , political affiliation, with dates of any changes (Dem, Democratic; Rep, Republican; U, unaffiliated or unknown), dates of founding and suspension (D 1901—meaning founded in December, 1901, and still in publication in January, 1912) , important personnel with the date they assumed their positions, further remarks concerning the paper or publisher, and the location and extent of the most accessible files in New Mexico. The descriptive matter will always be in this order: frequency, language, politics, years of publication, personnel, remarks, and extent and location of files in New Mexico.

## SYMBOLS AND ABBREVIATIONS USED IN APPENDIX I

| | |
|---|---|
| Ag | August |
| Ap | April |
| APL | Albuquerque Public Library |
| BI | bilingual |
| CH | courthouse |
| D | December, daily |
| Dem | Democratic |
| E | English, editor |
| ENMU | Eastern New Mexico University Library, Portales, N.M. |
| F | February |
| Ind | independent (politically) |
| Ja | January |
| Je | June |
| Jl | July |
| M | monthly |
| Mr | March |
| Mus of NM | Museum Of New Mexico, Santa Fe, N.M. |
| My | May |
| N | November |
| NMHU | New Mexico Highlands University Library, Las Vegas, N.M. |
| NMIMT | New Mexico Institute of Mining Technology Library, Socorro, N.M. |
| NMSL | New Mexico State Library, Santa Fe, N.M. |
| NMSRCA | New Mexico State Records Center and Archives, Santa Fe, N.M. |
| NMSU | New Mexico State University Library, Las Cruces, N.M. |
| O | October |
| P | publisher |
| Pub | publisher's |
| Rep | Republican |
| S | September, Spanish |
| S-M | semi-monthly |
| S-W | semi-weekly |
| Tri-W | tri-weekly (three issues per week) |
| U | unknown or unaffiliated (politically) |
| UNM | University of New Mexico Library, Albuquerque, N.M. |
| W | weekly |
| WNMU | Western New Mexico University Library, Silver City, N.M. |
| * | Used as a source by author. |
| † | Files now available, not used by author. |

EXAMPLE: Clayton *Union County Democrat.** W; E; Dem; 1893-N 1894; E and P, O. E. Smith, F 1894 Quemado de Baca; Jl-Ag 1894, CH Clayton.

TRANSLATION: The Clayton *Union County Democrat* files were examined by the author. It was a weekly newspaper, printed in English, and Democratic in political affiliation. It is known to have started in 1893 and ceased publication in November, 1894. The first editor and publisher was O. E. Smith; in February, 1894, Quemado de Baca became editor and publisher. Files for July and August, 1894, are in the courthouse at Clayton, N.M.

## ALAMOGORDO

*Banner.* W; E; Dem; D 1899-Ja 1901; E and P, W. R. Smith; see Alamogordo *Otero County Advertiser.*

*Journal (Daily).** D; E; Dem; Je 1904-Mr 1905; E and P, S. M. Wharton; see Alamogordo *Weekly Journal;* Jl 1904-Mr 1905, CH Alamogordo.

*Journal (Weekly).** W; E; Dem; O 1903-Je 1904, Mr-Ag 1905; E and P, S. M. Wharton and J. A. Haley, Ap 1904 S. M. Wharton; see Alamogordo *Daily Journal;* plant used to publish White Oaks *Eagle* earlier and Tucumcari *News* later; O 1903-Je 1904, Mr-Ag 1905, CH Alamogordo.

*News.** W; E; Rep; My 1889–; P, Alamogordo Printing Company, E, E. N. Buck, Ag 1901 W. E. Shepperd, Jl 1907 J. P. Annan, 1910 O. R. Nation, 1911 Gutherie Smith; see Alamogordo *Sacramento Chief;* Je 1899-D 1906, Ja-D 1908, CH Alamogordo.

*Nuevo Epoca.** W; Bl; U; S-D 1911; E and P, J. E. Harrison; S-D 1911, CH Alamogordo.

*Otero County Advertiser.** W; E; Dem; Ja 1901–; E and P, W. R. Smith, 1902 M. A. Morgan and C. W. Morgan, 1910 George A Byus; see Alamogordo *Banner;* Ja 1901-D 1908, Ja-D 1911, CH Alamogordo.

*Sacramento Chief.** W; E; U; Ap-My 1899; E and P, J. H. Lightfoot; see Alamogordo *News;* Ap-My 1899, CH Alamogordo.

*Southwestern Baptist.** W; E; U; F-Jl 1901; E, J. W. Newborough; F-Jl 1901, CH Alamogordo.

## ALBUQUERQUE

*Abogado Cristiano Neo Mexicano* (Methodist). S-M, 1897 M; Bl; U; 1895-1908; E and P, Thomas Harwood; moved from Socorro, became Albuquerque *Abogado Cristiano Hispano-Americano.*

*Abogado Cristiano Hispano-Americano* (Methodist). M; Bl; U; 1908-09; E and P, Thomas Harwood and T. M. Harwood; see Albuquerque *Abogado Cristiano Neo Mexicano.*

*Adobeland.†* W; E; Dem; Je-N 1891; E and P, C. E. Stivers and (?) Butler; see Albuquerque *Times;* Je 13-27, 1891, NMSU.

*Advance.** W; E; U; Ap-My 1880; E and P, A. M. Conklin; plant moved to start Socorro *Sun;* Ap-My 1880, UNM; Ap-My 1880, APL; Ap-My 1880, NMSU.

*American.* W; E; Rep; 1900-01; E and P, unknown.

*Amigo del Paiz.* W; S; U; 1853; E and P, R. H. Weightman; see Santa Fe *Amigo del Paiz.*

*Aurora* (Presbyterian). Bi-M; Bl; U; 1911–; P, Synod of New Mexico, E, H. A. Cooper; see Las Vegas *Aurora.*

*Balance Wheel.* W; E; Dem; 1911–; E and P, Hugh Collins.

*Bandera Americana.†* W; S; Rep; 1894–; E and P, Manuel Salazar y Otero, Jl 1901 P, Bandera Americana Publishing Co., F. A. Hubbell, Pres., E, Nestor Montoya; see Albuquerque *Nuevo Mundo;* 1900-08, NMSL; Ag 1901-Mr 1906, NMSU.

*Bandera de la Union.* W; S; Rep; Je-Jl 1863; E and P, H. S. Johnson.

*Barbarian.* M; E; U; 1906-07; E and P, J. H. Kaplan and E. E. Crawford.

*Bernalillo County Democrat.** W; Bl; Dem; O-N 1886; P, Bernalillo County Democratic Central Committee, E, W. T. McCreight; O 28, 1886, NMHU.

*Citizen (Daily).** D; E; Rep; Ag 1886-S 1909; E and P, C. L. Hubbs, My 1887 Thomas Hughes and W. T. McCreight, Mr 1905 W. S. Strickler, Mr 1907 W. F. Brogan; intermittently assumed title *Evening Citizen,* see Albuquerque *Tribune-Citizen;* My 1889-S 1909 (broken run), CH Albuquerque; D 1888-D 1899, APL; 1901-09 (broken), NMSL; F 1887-O 1904 (broken), NMSU.

*Citizen (Weekly).*† W; E; Rep; 1891-1909; E and P, same as Albuquerque *Daily Citizen;* Ja 1891-D 1899 (broken), APL; Ja 1891-D 1899 (broken), NMSU.

*College Advocate.** Quarterly; E; U; 1889-90; P, Albuquerque (Methodist) College, E, C. I. Mills; D 1889, NMHU.

*Combate.*† W; S; U; 1892-?; E and P, Jose Escobar; Jl 7, 1892, NMSU.

*Defensor del Pueblo.*† W; S; Dem; 1890-94; P, J. J. Herrera, E, J. Escobar; Je 1891-My 1892 (broken), NMSU.

*Democrat (Daily).** D; E; Dem; S 1882-Ja 1887; E and P, J. G. Albright; see Santa Fe *Daily Democrat* and Albuquerque *Morning Democrat;* O 1882-Ag 1886, APL; S 1882-D 1885 (broken), NMSU.

*Democrat (Morning).** D; E; Dem; Ja 1886-D 1898; E and P, J. G. Albright, Ap 1895 P, A. A. Grant, E, W. S. Burke, Je 1895 W. P. Hunter, Jl 1897 George Albright; see Albuquerque *Journal-Democrat;* Ja 1886-D 1898, APL; S 1886-D 1898 (broken), NMSL; Ag 1886-D 1898 (broken), NMSU.

*Democrat (Weekly).*† W; E; Dem; 1884-94; E and P, J. G. Albright; S 1882-Ag 1883, NMSU.

*Ecce Montezuma.* W; E; U; Mr-Ag 1884; E and P, Howard W. Mitchell.

*Estado.* W; S; Dem; S-N 1906; E and P, unknown.

*Estrella de Nuevo Mexico.* W; S; U; 1906-07; E and P, Enrique Sosa; see Los Lunas *Estrella de Nuevo Mexico* which was moved to Albuquerque.

*Estrella Mejicana.** W; S; Dem; S-N 1890; E and P, H. L. Ortiz; O 4, 1890, NMSU; O 11, 1890, NMHU.

*Golden Gate (Daily).* D; E; Rep; Je-S 1880; E and P, E. W. Deer, Jl 1880 J. A. Spradling; Spradling discontinued the *Golden Gate* to found the Albuquerque *Daily Journal.*

*Gol-9-den (Golden Nine).* W; E; U; 1891; E and P, Martha A. Hayes; see San Pedro *Golden Nine.*

*Herald (Evening).** D; E; Rep; Mr 1911—; P, F. A. Hubbell; see Albuquerque *Tribune-Citizen;* Mr-D 1911, CH Albuquerque; My-D 1911, NMSL; Mr-D 1911, NMSU.

*Hormiga de Oro.*† W; S; Rep; 1898-1904; E and P, Enrique Sosa; plant was moved to Los Lunas by Sosa to found *Estella de Nuevo Mexico;* N 7, 1903, NMSU.

*Independent.* D; E; U; My-Ag 1884; E and P, unknown.

*Indito* (Albuquerque old town).† W; S; Dem; 1900-04; E and P, (?) Armijo and (?) Martinez; 1900-01 (broken), NMSU.

*Industrial Advertiser.*† W; E; Dem; S-D 1899; E and P, J. H. McCutcheon; previously Socorro *Industrial Advertiser,* merged with Albuquerque *News;* D 23, 1899, NMSU.

*Industrial Advertiser and News.* W; E; Dem; D 1899-1909; E and P, J. H. McCutcheon.

*Journal (Daily).** D; E; Rep; O 1880-F 1882; P, Albuquerque Publishing Company, E, J. A. Spradling, F 1881 W. H. Bailhache, Mr 1881 Thomas Hughes; see Albuquerque *Daily Golden Gate* and *Morning Journal;* O 1880-F 1882, UNM.

*Journal (Morning).** D; E; Rep; F 1882-D 1886, Mr 1903–; P, Albuquerque Publishing Company to 1886, 1903 D. A. Macpherson, E, Thomas Hughes, Je 1882 W. S. Burke, S 1884 C. L. Hubbs, Ap 1885 Thomas Hughes, Je 1886 E. S. Clark, 1903 W. S. Burke, 1910 E. Dana Johnson; see Albuquerque *Journal-Democrat;* F 1882-D 1886, APL; 1907-12; UNM, F 1882-D 1886, Mr 1903-D 1911, CH Albuquerque; F 1882-D 1884, 1903-11 (broken), NMSL; F 1882-D 1886 (broken), Ap 1906-Jl 1907 (broken), Ja 1909-D 1911, NMSU.

*Journal-Democrat.** D; E; Rep; Ja 1899-Mr 1903; P, A. A. Grant, E, George Albright; successor to *Morning Democrat* and succeeded by the *Morning Journal;* Ja 1899-Mr 1903, CH Albuquerque; Ja-D 1899, APL; Ja-D 1899, NMSL; Ja 1899-N 1901, NMSU.

*Journal (Weekly).*† W; E; Rep; 1880-85; E and P, same as *Morning Journal* in this period; My 5, 1881, NMSU.

*Labor Advocate.* W; E; Labor; 1903-07; P, H. L. Dunning, E, F. M. Wyncoop, Jl 1904 E and P, (?) White and (?) French.

*Mirage.*† W; E; U; 1898-1903; P, students of the University of New Mexico; succeeded by *University of New Mexico Weekly;* Ja 1899-Je 1902, UNM.

*Miner and Manufacturer.* M; E; U; 1881-82; E and P, N. W. Smith.

*Mirror.* W; BI; U; 1879; E and P, (?) Chacon and (?) Linthieum; see Bernalillo *Mirror* and Bernalillo *Native.*

*New Age.* W; E; U; 1911; E and P, unknown.

*New Mexico and Arizona Business Directory.* W; E; U; 1882-?; E and P, unknown.

*New Mexico Democrat.* D; E; Dem; 1908; E and P, George P. Gould.

*New Mexico Mining Review.* M; E; U; Ag 1899-?; E and P, (?) Curran and (?) Stubbs.

*New Mexico News.* D; E; Dem; 1886; E and P, (?) Dunbar and W. T. McCreight.

*New Mexico Press.** W; BI; Rep; Jl 1864-D 1866; E and P, H. S. Johnson; succeeded Albuquerque *Rio Abajo Weekly Press* and was succeeded by the Albuquerque *Press;* Jl-O 1864, UNM; Jl-O 1864, APL; Jl-O 1864, NMSU.

*News* (Albuquerque old town).** W; BI; Rep; F 1885-1887; E and P, Ira Bond; former Mesilla *News* moved to Albuquerque; O 2, 9, 1886, NMHU; 1885-86 (broken), NMSU.

*News* (Albuquerque new town).† W; E; Rep; 1897-D 1889; E and P, E. W. Spencer; merged with Albuquerque *Industial Advertiser;* Ja 1897-D 1898, APL; Ja 1897-D 1898, NMSU.

*New Mexico State Democrat.* W; E; Dem; D 1910–; E and P, J. G. Albright; Albright earlier founded the Albuquerque *Daily Democrat.*

*New Mexico State Republican.* W; E; Rep; 1911–; E and P, unknown.

*Noticias.* W; S; U; 1905; E and P, unknown.

*Nuevo Mundo.*† W; S; U; 1897-Jl 1901; P, J. S. Garcia, E, J. Escobar, 1898 E and P, Mariano Armijo Y Otero; merged with Albuquerque *Bandera Americana;* 1897-1900 (broken), NMSU.

*Nugget* W; E; Pop; 1894-96 (?); P, New Mexico Farmers' Alliance, E, unknown.

*Opinion.** W; E; Rep; Jl 1886-Ja 1887; E and P, Thomas Hughes; Jl-N 1886, NMHU; Ja 8, 1887, UNM.

*Opinion Publica* (title used twice). 1–W; S; Dem; 1892-96; E and P, Pedro G. de Lama; intermittent in publication, moved to Arizona; O 1892-Mr 1895 (broken), CH Albuquerque, 1892-96 (broken), NMSU. 2–W; S; Rep; 1906–; E, J. M. Sandoval, 1907 Patricio Gonzales, 1908 Elfego Baca, 1909 M. P. Mondragon; O 1906-Mr 1907 (broken), NMSU; 1906-07 (broken), NMSL.

*Pioneer Baptist.* M; E; U; 1892-93; E and P, J. H. Thompson.

*Press.** W; BI; Rep; Ja-D 1867; E and P, Ash Upson; succeeded the Albuquerque *New Mexico Press* and succeeded by the Albuquerque *Review;* D 7, 1867, UNM.

*Pueblo* (Albuquerque old town).† W; S; U; 1900-?; E and P, Aurelio Zermeno; F 17, 1900, NMSU.

*Republican Review.** W; BI; Rep; Mr 1870-Ap 1876; E and P, William McGuiness and Transito L. Mata, Ja 1871 William McGuiness, O 1873 William McGuiness and Louis Hommel, Mr 1874 William McGuiness; succeeded by Albuquerque *Review;* Mr 1870-Ap 1876, UNM, Mr 1870-Ap 1876, APL, Mr 1870-Ap 1876, NMSU.

*Review* (semi-weekly and weekly).** S-W, Ap 1876 W; BI; Rep, Ap 1876 Dem, Mr 1881 Rep; Ja 1868-Mr 1870, Ap 1876-My 1883; E and P, H. S. Johnson, Ap 1876 William McGuiness, Ja 1881 (?) McGoodwin and (?) Williams, Mr 1881 W. H. Bailhache and McGoodwin, F 1882 W. H. Bailhache; in 1868 succeeded Albuquerque *Press,* in 1870 succeeded by Albuquerque *Republican Review,* which in 1876 again became Albuquerque *Review;* Ap 1876-D 1882, APL, Ap 1876-D 1880, S-D 1882, UNM, Ap 1876-My 1883 (broken), NMSU.

*Review (Evening).** D; E; Rep; F 1882-My 1883; P, W. H. Bailhache, E, W. F. Saunders, Ap 1883 (?) Mitchell; moved to Santa Fe to merge with the *New Mexican* to become the Santa Fe *New Mexican Review;* F-D 1882, UNM; F-N 1882, Mr-My 1883, APL; Mr 1882-My 1883 (broken), NMSU.

*Revista de Albuquerque.** W; S; Rep; S 1881-1886; P, W. H. Bailhache and (?) McGoodwin; the Spanish portion of the Albuquerque *Review* was made into a separate paper in 1881; O 1, 1881, NMHU; D 5, 1881, NMSU.

*Rio Abajo Weekly Press.*\* W; E, Jl 1863 BI; Rep; Ja 1863-Jl 1864; E and P, H. S. Johnson; predecessor of the Albuquerque *New Mexico Press;* Ja 1863- Jl 1864, UNM; Ja 1863-Jl 1864, APL; Ja 1863-Jl 1864, NMSU.

*Rio Grande Valley Irrigator.*\* W; E; U; 1887; E and P, unknown; used to advertise real estate; S 17, N 12, 1887, NMHU.

*Southwest Illustrated Magazine.*† M; E; U; 1894-97; P, George Albright, 1897 Democrat Publishing Company, E, George Albright; Je 1895-F 1896 (broken), NMSU.

*Southwestern Anti-Saloon Issue.* M; E; Prohibitionist; 1906-09; P, New Mexico and Arizona Anti-Saloon League, E, W. W. Havens.

*Southwestern Mines.*\* M; E; U; O 1905-11; E and P, Fayette M. Jones; O 1908-F 1911, UNM.

*Sun.*\* D; E; Dem; My-O 1908; P, Willis McConnell, E, C. C. Hendrick; My 18-O 8, 1908, CH Albuqueque.

*Sunshine.* W; E; U; S 1904-06; E and P, C. S. Carter, 1905 J. H. Kaplan and S. S. Pearlstine.

*Times* (weekly).\* W; E; Dem; N 1891-S 1892; E and P, J. K. Hurd and Wallace Hite, Ap 1892 Wallace Hite; successor to Albuquerque *Adobeland;* Ja-Ag 1892, CH Albuquerque.

*Times* (daily).\* D; E; Dem; S 1892-Ap 1894; E and P, Wallace Hite; S 1892-Ap 1894, CH Albuquerque; Je 14, 1893, NMSU.

*Tribune.*\* D; E; Dem; S-O 1909; P, Felix Martinez, E, Herbert T. Haywood; Martinez moved his El Paso *News* plant to Albuquerque to launch this paper which was soon merged with the Albuquerque *Citizen;* S-O 1909, CH Albuquerque; S-O 1909, NMSU.

*Tribune-Citizen.*\* D; E; Dem; O 1909-Mr 1911; P, Tribune-Citizen Publishing Co., E, William Hoffman; formed by a merger of the Albuquerque *Tribune* and *Citizen,* succeeded by Albuquerque *Evening Herald;* O 1909-Mr 1911, CH Albuquerque, 1910-11 (broken), NMSL, Ja 1910-Mr 1911, NMSU.

*Union de Albuquerque* (Albuquerque old town).† W; S; U; 1892-94; E and P, unknown; Ja 20, 1893, NMSU.

*University of New Mexico Weekly.* W; E; U; 1903–; E and P, students at the University of New Mexico; succeeded the *Mirage.*

*Voz de Nuevo Mexico.*† W; S; U; S 1893-?; E and P, (?) Baca and (?) Escobar; S 1, 1893, NMSU.

*Voz del Trabajador.* W; S; U; 1904-05; P, C. L. Hernandez, E, J. C. Guerin.

*Weekly (Albuquerque Weekly).*† W; E; U; Ap-My 1883, E and P, unknown; Ap-My 1883, UNM.

## ALMA

*Mogollon Monthly Epitomizer.* M; E; U; 1882; E and P, W. H. Lawrence.

## AMISTAD

*News.* W; E; Rep; Mr-Je 1908; E and P, W. Arthur Jones.

*Northwest New Mexico News.* W; E; Rep; 1908; E and P, W. Arthur Jones; predecessor of Amistad *News.*

*Tribune.* W; E; U; Je 1909-1910; E and P, W. M. Kinkade; merged with the Amistad *Union County Herald.*

*Tribune-Herald.* W; E; Rep; 1910–; E and P, Sam and Margaret Ridenour; successor to Amistad *Tribune* and *Union County Herald.*

*Union County Herald.* W; E; Rep; 1908-10; E and P, W. Arthur Jones; successor to Amistad *News* and merged with Amistad *Tribune.*

## AMIZETT

*Miner.* W; E; U; 1894; E and P, A. A. Foote; see Taos *Valley Herald.*

## ANGOSTURA

*Luz.*† W; BI; Rep; Ag 1900-03; P, Rio Arriba Printing Co.; moved to Espanola and remained *Luz;* 1900-03 (broken), NMSL.

## ARTESIA

*Advocate.** W; E; Dem; Ag 1903–; E and P, Gayle Talbot, Ap 1905 C. E. Biles, S 1905 J. D. Whelan, Ja 1911 Gayle Talbot, Mr 1911 J. L. Tullis; Ag 1903-D 1911, pub office (Artesia *Press*).

*Pecos Valley News.** W; E; Rep; S 1906–; P, D. L. Newkirk, E, J. F. Newkirk; S 1906-D 1907, pub office (Artesia *Press*); D 1907, NMSL; F 1910-D 1911, CH Carlsbad.

## AZTEC

*New Mexico Newsboy.* W; E; U; Je-D 1886; E and P, unknown.

*San Juan County Index.** W; E; U; 1905 Rep; 1890–; E and P, A. T. Bird, 1894 E. M. Gibson, 1896 H. B. Schwartz, 1899 Lewis C. Grove, 1904 C. S. Bailey, 1905 E. P. Wilson; Mr 1901-N 1907, UNM.

*San Juan Democrat.** W; E; Dem; Jl 1906–; E and P, G. F. Ellis and M. B. Scott, O 1906 B. O. Burt and W. B. Burt, 1909 D. H. Tobey, 1911 T. P. Maddox; S 1906-N 1907, UNM.

*San Juan Independent.* W; E; U; 1889; E and P, unknown.

*San Juan Review.* W; E; U; 1888-?; E and P, unknown.

## BARD CITY

*News.** W; E; Dem; Je 1910–; P, Charles Holding, My 1911 W. R. Haynes; Je 1910-D 1911, CH Tucumcari.

## BELEN

*Hispano-Americano.* W; BI; U; 1910–; P, (?) Baca and (?) Baca, E, A. C. de Baca.

*New Mexico American.* W; E; U; My 1903-?; E and P, F. Webb.

*Tribune.*† W; E; Rep; Ja 1907–; E and P, W. M. Berger; 1909-12 UNM; 1908-11 (broken), NMSL.

## BERNALILLO

*Mirror.* W; BI; U; 1878-79; P, (?) Chacon and (?) Salazar, E, (?) Chacon; formerly *Taos Valley Mirror* (or *Espejo*), later moved to Albuquerque as the *Mirror.*

*Native.* W; Bl; Rep; 1879-80; P, (?) Chacon and B. F. Perea, E, (?) Chacon; formerly Albuquerque *Mirror.*

*News.* W; E; U; Ag 1880-Je 1882; E and P, D. O. Dare; moved to Jemez to launch Jemez *Hot Springs Guide.*

## BLAND

*Cochiti Call.* W; E; U; 1894-95; E and P, J. H. Lightfoot; see Bland *Herald.*

*Cochiti Outlook.* W; E; U; 1898; E and P, George Marsh and Hunter Woodson.

*Herald.* W; E; U; 1895-97, 1898-1903; E and P, J. H. Lightfoot, 1896 Frank Wynkoop, My 1899 Will Ments, 1902 J. M. Hunter; former Bland *Cochiti Call* and 1897-98 Bland *Weekly Herald.*

*Weekly Herald.* W; E; U; 1897-98; E and P, Frank Wynkoop; see Bland *Herald.*

## BLOOMFIELD

*Northwest New Mexican.* W; E; U; 1886; E and P, W. L. Stevens; formerly at Farmington and later at Chama as *Northwest New Mexican.*

## CABRA SPRINGS

*Chronicle.* W; Bl; U; 1886; E and P, Louis Hommel; formerly Las Vegas *Chronicle* and later revived as Mora *Cronica.*

## CAPITAN

*Capitan (El).** W; Bl; U; Mr-D 1900; E and P, A. R. Goodloe; merged with Capitan *Miner* to form Capitan *Progress;* Ap-D 1900, CH Carrizozo.

*Farol.* W; S; Rep; 1905-07; E and P, Clement Hightower.

*Miner.* W; E; U; My-D 1900; E and P, J. H. Lightfoot and A. R. Williams, N 1900 J. H. Lightfoot and C. G. Nuckols; merged with *Capitan* to form *Progress.*

*News.** W; E; Dem; Ag 1903-Je 1908; P, S. R. May, Ap 1904 J. A. Haley; formed by merger of White Oaks *Eagle* and Capitan *Progress,* moved to Carrizozo in 1908—see Carrizozo *News;* Ag 1903-Je 1908, CH Carrizozo.

*Progress.** W; E; Dem; D 1900-Ag 1903; E and P, J. H. Lightfoot and C. G. Nuckols, Jl 1901 C. G. Nuckols, Ja 1903 Eagle Publishing Company; formed by merger *Capitan* and *Miner* became the *News;* D 1900-Ag 1903, CH Carrizozo.

## CARLSBAD
### (before 1900 Eddy)

*Argus.** W; E; Rep; 1900–; P, L. O. Fullen, 1902 W. R. Reed, E, L. O. Fullen, D 1906 W. R. Reed; see Eddy *Argus;* Ja-D 1903, Ja 1906-D 1911, CH Carlsbad; 1901-11 (broken), NMSL.

*Current.** W; 1903 S-W, 1906 W; E; Dem; 1900–; E and P, W. H. Mullane, D 1900 J. L. and C. C. Emerson, 1903 R. K. Jacks, Jl 1904 Will Robinson, 1905 E. A. Heath, Ap 1906 C. F. Drake, N 1906 W. H. Mullane; from Ag 1907 to D 1908 was *Current and New Mexico Sun;* see also Eddy *Current;* Ja 1900-D 1902, Ja-D 1906, Ja 1909-D 1911, CH Carlsbad; 1901-10 (title varies), NMSL.

*Current and New Mexico Sun.* W; E; Dem; Ag 1907-D 1908; E and P, W. H. Mullane; see Carlsbad *Current* and Carlsbad *New Mexico Sun;* Ag 1907-D 1908, CH Carlsbad.

*Eddy County Eagle.* W; E; U; 1900-02; E and P, W. C. Griffen; see Carlsbad *Miner-Stockman.*

*Miner-Stockman.* W; E; U; 1902-05; E and P, W. C. Griffen and Ed Lyons; see Carlsbad *Eddy County Eagle.*

*New Mexico Sun.* W; E; Dem; My 1905-Ag 1907; E and P, W. H. Mullane; merged with Carlsbad *Current;* Ja 1906-Ag 1907, CH Carlsbad.

*Pecos Valley Stockman.* W; E; Dem; F-S 1900; E and P, James Kibbee and Lucius Dills; moved to Roswell under same name.

*Sun.* D; E; Dem; Ja-S 1900; E and P, W. H. Mullane.

## CARRIZOZO

*News.** W; E; Dem; Je 1908—; E and P, J. A. Haley; see Capitan *News;* Je 1908-F 1911, CH Carrizozo.

*Outlook.** W; E; Rep; D-1906—; E and P, N. S. Rose, O 1909 Lee B. Chase; for a few months in 1909 was named *Southwestern Outlook,* formerly White Oaks *Outlook;* S 1906-D 1911 (broken), CH Carrizozo.

## CATSKILL

*Champion.* W; E; U; 1891; E and P, unknown; merged with Raton *Colfax County Courier.*

*Sawdust.* W; E; U; 1891; E and P, C. W. Thompson.

## CENTRAL CITY

*News.* W; E; Rep; 1908; E and P, W. Arthur Jones.

## CERRILLOS

*Beacon.** W; E; Dem; Je 1891-92; E and P, G. E. Hosmer; Je 20, 1891, NMHU.

*Chronicle (Weekly).* W; E; U; N 1882-?; E and P, D. O. Dare.

*Comet.* W; E (?); U; F 1882-?; E and P, unknown.

*Galisteo Democrat.* W; E; U; 1893; E and P, unknown.

*Prospector.* W; Bl; U; Jl 1879-81; E and P, A. V. Aoy; Aoy was a former publisher of Santa Fe and Las Vegas *Advertisers.*

*Register.* W; E; U; 1898-1903; E and P, W. A. De Busk and Wallace Walker, 1901 N. S. Rose.

*Rustler.** W; E; U; 1888-98; E and P, A. M. Anderson, 1896 F. C. Buell; N 1888-D 1891 (broken), NMHU.

## CHAMA

*Northwest New Mexican.** W; E; U; 1887-96; E and P, W. L. Stevens; was at Bloomfield earlier under same title; Ap 28, My 26, 1888, NMHU; Je 10, 17, 1893, NMSU.

*Tribune.* W; E; Rep; N 1898-1902; E and P, W. H. Hildreth.

## CHLORIDE

*Black Range.** W; E; Rep, 1896 Dem; Ja 1883-Ag 1897; E and P, V. B. Beckett, Je 1885 W. C. Thompson; see Robinson *Black Range;* My 1883-Ag 1897 (broken), NMIMT; My 1883-Ag 1897 (broken), UNM; Jl 1886-Ag 1889, NMSL; 1884-97 (broken), NMSU.

## CIMARRON

*Citizen.** W; E; Rep; Mr 1908-11; E and P, G. E. Remley; became Cimarron *News and Citizen;* Mr-S 1908, CH Raton.

*Jacksonian.* W; E; Dem; 1908; E and P, unknown.

*News.* W; E; U; O 1870-D 1874; E and P, J. F. Wightman, F 1872 Frank Springer, 1873 J. H. Koogler and W. H. H. Werner; merged with the Elizabethtown *Railway Press and Telegraph.*

*News and Citizen.* W; E; Rep; 1911—; E and P, James McVey; successor to the Cimarron *Citizen.*

*News and Press.* (title used twice)* 1—W; E; U; D 1874-O 1881; E and P, W. R. Morley, Frank Springer, and W. D. Dawson, Ja 1876 W. D. Dawson, F 1876 W. R. Morley and Frank Springer, Je 1877 Harry Whigham and Thomas Henderson, Je 1880 E. L. Sheldon, S 1881 George F. Canis and Thomas Henderson; moved to Raton as *New Mexico News and Press,* see Elizabethtown *Railway Press and Telegraph* and Cimarron *News;* Ag 1875-S 1881 (broken), UNM. 2—W; E; U; 1907-09; P, Cimarron Publishing Co.; apparently was owned by the Raton *Range;* Ja-O 1907, pub office (Raton *Range*).

## CLAYTON

*Citizen.** W; E; Rep; S 1906—; E and P, R. Q. Palmer and Louise Cliver, Ag 1910 O. A. and Josephine Foster, D 1910 G. W. Baker; formerly Clayton *Enterprise;* O 1906-D 1911, CH Clayton.

*Cricket.* W; E; U; 1895-96; E and P, E. C. Dobson; merged with Clayton *News.*

*Defensor del Pueblo.* W; BI; U; 1902-03; E and P, Gavino Garcia; successor to Clayton *Enterprise* and succeeded by Clayton *Empresa.*

*Empresa.* W; BI; U; 1903-04; E and P, Gavino Garcia; see Clayton *Defensor del Pueblo,* succeeded by Clayton *Enterprise.*

*Enterprise.** W; E; Rep, 1892 Dem, 1898 Rep; My 1888-O 1901, 1905-S 1906; E and P, G. W. James, 1889 T. W. McSchooler, Ap 1890 J. E. Curren, 1897 G. R. Guyer, 1900 S. F. Hickman, 1905 R. Q. Palmer; My 1888-O 1889 (broken), NMHU; Ja 1893-Ja 1894, CH Raton; F 1894-D 1895, F-D 1901, Ja-S 1906, CH Clayton.

*Fenix.** W; S; Rep; 1900—; E and P, N. F. Gallegos; Ja 1903-D 1911 (broken), CH Clayton; 1906-08 (broken), NMSL.

*Fruiz.* W; S; U; 1899-1902; E and P, unknown.

*Lance.* W; E; Dem; 1908-10; E and P, G. W. Guyer; formerly Folsom *Epoca.*

*Maverick.* W; E; U; 1893-95; P, Maverick Publishing Company.

*News.* (title used twice) 1—W; BI; U; 1894-96; E and P, G. W. Guyer; merged with *Cricket*. 2—W; E; Dem; 1907—; E and P, 1910 J. A. Taylor, 1911 T. C. Bryant; claimed to be a successor of Clayton *Enterprise.*

*News-Cricket.* W; BI; U; 1896-97; E and P, G. W. Guyer and C. E. Dobson; merger of *News* and *Cricket* and apparently merged with *Enterprise* in 1897.

*Union County Democrat.*\* W; E; Dem; 1893-N 1894; E and P, O. E. Smith, F 1894 Quemado de Baca; Jl-Ag 1894, CH Clayton.

*Union del Pueblo.*\* W; BI; Union People's party; 1894-95; P, Central Committee Union People's Party; S-O 1894, CH Clayton.

*Union Democrat.* W; BI; Dem; 1896-98; E and P, W. J. Eaton.

### CLEVELAND

*Jornalero.* W; S; U; 1895; E and P, unknown.

### CLOUDCROFT

*Silver Lining.*\* W; E; U; 1903-10; E and P, J. R. Wallace; Ja 1904-O 1909, CH Alamogordo.

### CLOVIS

*Chronicle.* W; E; U; 1907; E and P, unknown.

*Democrat.* W; E; Dem; 1908-11; E and P, (?) Evans and (?) Griffith, 1910 J. E. Curren.

*Journal.* (weekly) W; E; Dem; My 1909—; E and P, J. E. Pardue, Ag 1909 T. J. Mabry.

*Journal (Daily).* D; E; Dem; Ag-N 1909; E and P, T. J. Mabry.

*News. (Daily).* D; E; Rep; My 1909, Ag-N 1909; E and P, A. E. Curren.

*News.* (weekly) \* W; E; Rep; My 1907—; E and P, A. E. Curren, 1910 W. J. Curren; Ja-Je 1909, pub office (Clovis *News-Journal).*

*Pony Post.* (daily) D; E; Dem; My 1909; E and P, Harry Armstrong.

*Post.* W; E; Dem; 1908-Ag 1909; E and P, Harry Armstrong; sold paper and plant to Clovis *Journal,* which had lost its plant in a fire.

### COLUMBUS

*Courier.*\* W; E; Rep; Je 1911—; E and P, Jesse Mitchell; apparently successor to Columbus *News;* Je-D 1911, CH Deming.

*News.*\* W; E; Rep; Jl 1907-Je 1911; E and P, P. G. Mosley; apparently succeeded by Columbus *Courier;* Jl 1907-My 1911, CH Deming.

### CUERVO

*Clipper.*\* W; E; Rep; Ja 1909—; E and P, W. C. Hawkins, My 1910 A. J. Thomas; Ja 1909-N 1911, UNM.

### DAYTON

*Current.* W; E; U; 1905; E and P, unknown.

*New State Informer.*\* W; E; Dem; N 1911—; E and P, J. D. McBride; changed name from Dayton *Pecos Valley Echo;* N-D 1911, CH Carlsbad.

*Pecos Valley Echo.** W; E; Dem; Jl 1905-N 1911; E and P, J. K. and J. R. Little, 1907 R. H. and A. M. Burnett, 1908 J. D. McBride; became Dayton *New State Informer;* Ja 1909-N 1911, CH Carlsbad.

## DEMING

*Advance.* W; E; Rep; N 1891-92; E and P, F. M. Galloway; formerly the Pinos Altos *Miner.*

*Democrat (Daily).* D; E; Dem; My-Ag 1884, N 1884-?; E and P, G. E. Porter, N 1884 (?) Kayoe and (?) Obenchain.

*Duster.* W; E; U; 1894; E and P, George Lockhart.

*Graphic.** W; E; Rep; Mr 1903–; E and P, N. S. Rose, O 1904 A. L. Sangre, D 1906 C. D. Ambrose, N 1911 M. M. De Puy and W. E. Holt; successor to Deming *Herald;* Mr 1904-D 1911, CH Deming.

*Headlight.* (weekly)** W; E; Rep, S 1889, Dem; Je 1881-S 1883, Je 1886–; E and P, J. E. Curren, 1886 Ed Pennington, 1889 E. G. Ross and S. M. Ashenfelter, Mr 1893 W. B. Walton, S 1898 F. L. Shakespeare, Ja 1911 Roy Bedicheck, O 1911 J. H. Shepard; Mr 1882-Je 1894 (broken), WNMU; S 1889-D 1891 (broken), NMHU; Ap 1901-D 1911, CH Deming; 1895-1912 (broken), UNM; 1889-99 (scattered issues), NMSU.

*Headlight (Daily).** D; E; Rep, Dem N 1884; S 1883-Je 1886; E and P, J. E. Curren, N 1884 A. C. Lowery, My 1885 A. J. Loomis; weekly was not published while the daily paper was being published; Jl 23, 1885, NMHU.

*Herald.* (title used twice)** 1–W; E; U; 1883; E and P, (?) Lyndon and (?) Whitelaw. 2–W; E; Rep; Jl 1900-Mr 1903; E and P, P. J. Bennett; sold subscriptions and good will to Deming *Graphic;* Ap 1901-F 1903, CH Deming.

*New Mexico Pot-Pourri.* W; Bl; U; 1892; E and P, unknown.

*Southwestern Advertiser.* M; E; U; 1904; E and P, N. S. Rose.

*State Advocate.* W E; Rep; 1892; E and P, G. L. Shakespeare; a campaign period paper.

*Tribune.** W; E; Rep; O 1883-D 1885; E and P, Charles W. Greene; former Kingston *Tribune* and Lake Valley *Herald* moved to Deming, plant was moved to El Paso to launch the *Tribune* there; Ag 1884-Jl 1885 (broken), NMHU; D 25, 1884, NMSU.

## DES MOINES

*Swastika.* W; E; Rep; Ag 1907–; E and P, Lenore Farr, 1909 W. C. Hubbard, 1910 G. T. Berenger.

## DEXTER

*News.* W; E; U; 1905; E and P, unknown.

## EDDY
### (became Carlsbad in 1900)

*Argus.** W; E; Rep; O 1889-96; P, Pecos Valley Irrigation and Improvement Company, E, J. M. Hawkins, 1896 L. O. Fullen; apparently merged with Eddy *Pecos Valley Independent* to form Eddy *Pecos Valley Argus;* Ja-D 1890, CH Carrizozo; N 1890-O 1891, CH Carlsbad; Je 9, 30, 1893, NMSU.

*Eddy County Citizen.*† W; E; U; 1891-93; E and P, A. J. Howe; Je 13, 27, 1893, NMSU.

*Eddy County Times.* W; E; U; 1891-93; E and P, unknown.

*Current (Daily).* D; E; Dem; O 1892-94; E and P, W. H. Mullane.

*Current.* (semi-weekly and weekly)* S-W, 1895 W; E; Dem; 1894-1900; E and P, W. H. Mullane; Ja 1898-D 1899, CH Carlsbad.

*Democrat.* W; E; Dem; Ag 1896-97; E and P, (?) McEachin and (?) Barnett, 1897 I. J. Stockett.

*Pecos Valley Argus.* W; E; Rep; 1896-1900; E and P, L. O. Fullen; apparently was formed by merger of *Pecos Valley Independent* and Eddy *Argus.*

*Pecos Valley Independent.* W; E; U; 1893-96; P, James A. Tomlinson, E, Robert P. Nash; see *Pecos Valley Argus.*

### ELIDA

*News.* W; E; Dem; F 1904–; E and P, W. C. Grant and J. A. Hall, Je 1904 J. A. Hall and J. R. Darnell, 1905 J. R. Darnell, 1907 J. R. Darnell and J. A. Hall, 1908 J. R. Darnell, 1910 Henry Rankin, 1911 J. R. Darnell.

### ELIZABETHTOWN

*Argus.* W; E; U; Mr-Je 1871; E and P, E. R. Sprigman; merged with *National Press and Telegraph* six months after suspension.

*Mining Bulletin.** W; E; Dem; N 1899-Ag 1900; E and P, Lorin W. Brown and M. R. Baker; Ja-Ag 1900, CH Raton.

*Moreno Lantern.* W; E; U; My-O 1869; E and P, (?) Scanten and (?) Aiken.

*National Press and Telegraph.* W; E; U; O 1869-? 1871; E and P, J. E. Wheelock, N 1869 W. D. Dawson and Jonathan Osborne, S 1870 W. D. Dawson; suspended late in 1871 by ill health of Dawson, see *Railway Press and Telegraph.*

*New Mexico Miner.** W; E; Dem, 1899 Rep; S 1896-F 1902; E and P, J. F. Hutchinson and W. C. Burnett, Je 1897 Lorin W. Brown, S 1898 Lorin W. Brown and F. D. Morse, Jl 1899 F. D. Morse; Ja 1897-F 1902, CH Raton.

*Railway Press and Telegraph.* W; E; U; Ja 1872-D 1874; E and P, W. D. Dawson and E. R. Sprigman; formed by merging *Argus* and *National Press and Telegraph,* later merged with Cimarron *News* to form Cimarron *News and Press.*

*Thunderbolt.* W; E; U; F 1871-?; E and P, unknown.

### ENCINO

*Progress.* W; BI; U; 1909-Ag 1911; P, B. Salas, 1910 J. F. Edwards, E, B. Salas, 1910 C. E. Simpson.

### ENDEE

*Enterprise.** W; E; Rep; 1910–; E and P, Jl 1910 C. C. Hixon; formerly *Rock Island Clipper;* Ja 1912, CH Tucumcari.

## ESPANOLA

*Luz.*† W, 1909 M; S; Rep; 1903–; P, Rio Arriba Printing Company; formerly Angostura *Luz;* 1903-08 (broken), NMSL.

*Voz del Rio Grande.* W; S; U; 1909–; E and P, unknown.

## ESTANCIA

*Democrat.* W; E; Dem; 1908-11; E and P, (?) Patterson and (?) Smith.

*Herald (Daily).** D; E; U; Mr 1909-Je 1911; P, H. D. Carter, Mr 1911 Allen Barrett, E, H. D. Carter, Mr 1911 Annie M. Porter; Ap-Ag 1911, CH Estancia.

*Herald (Weekly).** W; BI; U; My 1911–; P, Allen Barrett, E, Annie M. Porter; Ag-D 1911, CH Estancia.

*News (Daily).** D; E; Ind; Ap 1911–; E and P, P. A. Speckman, Ja 1912 J. A. Constant became E and P and renamed the paper *Morning News;* Ap-D 1911, CH Estancia.

*News.* (weekly)* W; BI; Rep, 1909 U; 1904-Ap 1911; E and P, P. A. Speckman; succeeded by Estancia *Daily News;* Jl 1910-Ap 1911, CH Estancia; 1905, 1907 (scattered issues), NMSU.

*Torrance County Leader.* W; E; Rep; 1907-10; E and P, Mrs. R. N. Maxwell, D 1907 C. W. Coombs, 1909 Mrs. R. N. Maxwell.

## FARMINGTON

*Cactus.* W; E; U; 1893; E and P, Charles Day.

*Enterprise.** W; E; Rep; My 1905–; E and P, Frank Staplin, 1908 B. F. Reilly, 1909 Frank Staplin; Staplin earlier published Taos *Cressett;* Ja 1906-D 1907, UNM; 1905-12 (broken), NMSL.

*Hustler.** W; E; Rep; Ja 1901-S 1903; P, C. E. Starr and D. K. B. Sellers, Jl 1902 R. C. Prewitt, E, D. K. B. Sellers, Jl 1902 R. C. Prewitt; merged with Farmington *Times* to form *Times-Hustler;* Ja 1901-Ag 1903, UNM.

*Northwest New Mexican.* W; E; U; Je 1884-86; E and P, W. L. Stevens; moved to Bloomfield and retained same title.

*San Juan Times.** W; E; Dem; 1893-1900; E and P, H. O. Willis, Je 1894 Fred E. Holt, My 1895 V. N. Greaves, My 1898 R. C. Prewitt, Ap 1900 E. S. Whitehead; formerly Junction City *Times,* became Farmington *Times;* My 1895-Je 1900, UNM.

*Times.** W; E; Dem; Je 1900-S 1903; E and P, E. S. Whitehead, Ap 1901 William Butler; merged with Farmington *Hustler;* Je 1900-Ag 1903, UNM; My 1902-S 1903, NMSL.

*Times-Hustler.** W; E; Dem; S 1903–; E and P, William Butler; S 1903-D 1911 (broken), UNM; My-D 1911, NMSL.

## FOLSOM

*Cometa.* W; S; U; D 1909-10; E and P, Manuel B. Sisneros.

*Epoca.* W; BI; U; 1907-08; E and P, G. W. Guyer; moved to Clayton and renamed *Lance.*

*Hispano-Americano.* W; BI; U; S-N 1902; P, Rumaldo Martinez, E, J. M. Martinez.

*Idea.** W; E; U; Jl 1888-Ap 1890; E and P, J. E. Curren; renamed Folsom *Springs Metropolitan;* F-D 1889, CH Raton; S-N 1888, UNM.

*Independent.* W; E; Ind-Rep; 1897-99; E and P, B. J. Barnett.

*Leader.* W; E; U; 1909-10; E and P, H. G. Hammon.

*New Mexico American.* W; BI; U; N 1889-Ja 1890, E and P, unknown; moved to Mora as *Hispano-Americano.*

*Springs Metropolitan.** W; E; Rep, 1895 Dem; Je 1890-95; E and P, T. W. McSchooler, 1893 J. E. Curren, 1894 J. H. Griffen; Ja-D 1893, CH Raton; Ja-N 1894, CH Clayton.

*Union County Stockman.** W; E; U; O 1900-01; E and P, S. F. Hickman and Ward Thomas; Ja 1901-Ja 1902, CH Clayton.

## FORT SUMNER
### (for a time also called SUNNYSIDE by residents)

*Index.* W; E; Rep; D 1909-10; E and P, L. D. Beckwith; moved to Melrose with same title.

*Republican.*† W; E; Rep; 1908-11; P, A. Clausen and George Murphy, E, A. Clausen; until Jl 1910 was Sunnyside *Republican;* Ag 1909-Je 1910 (broken), UNM.

*Review.** W; E; Dem; Jl 1907—; P, A. Clausen, Jl 1908 J. E. Pardue and M. R. Baker, 1909 J. V. Stearnes, Ja 1911 M. P. Manzaneres, E, A. Clausen, Jl 1908 M. R. Baker; until 1909 was named Sunnyside *Review;* Jl 1909-D 1911 (broken), UNM.

*Sun (Sunnyside).* W; E; Dem; 1905; E and P, J. E. Curren; moved to Melrose as *Headlight.*

## FRENCH

*Plaindealer.* W; E; U; 1909-10; E and P, unknown.

## FRUITLAND

*Tribune.* W; E; U; 1906-07; P, William Evans and Frank Staplin, E, William Evans.

## GALLUP

*Catholic Pioneer.* W; E; U; 1905; E and P, J. G. Juliard.

*Democrat.* W; E; Dem; 1902; P, McKinley County Democratic Central Committee.

*Elk.* W; E; Dem; F-N 1890; E and P, W. T. Henderson, Eli Covert, and F. A. Blake; before and after the above dates this paper was the Gallup *Gleaner.*

*Gazette.* W; E; U; O 1887-?; E and P, W. C. Lamonte.

*Gleaner.** W, 1894 S-W, 1895 W; E; Dem; Ag 1889-F 1890, N 1890-1902; E and P, W. T. Henderson; had been Watrous *Arrow-Pioneer* and became the *McKinley County Republican;* Ag-N 1888, NMHU, My-D 1889, N 1891-Ap 1896 (broken), CH Albuquerque.

*Independent.* W; E; Ind-Dem; S 1911–; E and P, W. H. Hanns.

*McKinley County Republican.** W; E; Rep; 1902–; E and P, H. A. Pease, 1905 L. E. Gould, 1908 W. E. Schwartz, 1909 Gus Mulholland, 1911 J. E. Williams; formerly Gallup *Gleaner,* true owners Republican leaders at Gallup; Ja-D 1911, CH Gallup.

*News-Register.** W; E; Rep; D 1888-F 1890; E and P, A. M. Swan and F. A. Blake; formed by merger of Gallup *Register* and Las Vegas *News;* S 1889-F 1890, NMHU.

*Register.** W; E; Rep; Ja-D 1888; E and P, A. M. Swann; see Gallup *News-Register;* S-N 1888, UNM.

## GEORGETOWN

*Courier.* W; E; Dem; Jl 1882-Ja 1884; E and P, A. C. Lowery; moved to Kingston to become *Clipper.*

*Silver Brick.* W; E; U; S 1881-Jl 1882; E and P, Lamar P. Davis; became Georgetown *Courier.*

## GOLDEN

*Retort.* W; E; Rep; S 1881-S 1884; E and P, R. W. Webb.

## GRADY

*Gazette.* W; E; Rep; Jl-O 1909; E and P, F. C. Newing; merged with *Record.*

*Record.** W; E; Rep; Ap 1908–; E and P, T. M. Carter, Ja 1909 R. A. Chubb, O 1909 F. C. Newing, 1910 E. A. Berdell, 1911 J. C. Trickey; Ap 1908-D 1909, CH Tucumcari.

## HAGERMAN

*Irrigator.* W; E; Dem; 1895; E and P, W. H. Mullane; moved to Roswell as the *Irrigator.*

*Messenger.* W; E; Dem; 1903–; E and P, J. E. Wimberly, 1908 J. D. Mell, 1909 J. E. Wimberly.

## HILLSBORO

*Prospector.* W; E; U; O 1882-83; E and P, R. H. Jones.

*Sierra County Advocate.** W; E; Rep, Mr 1889 Dem; Mr 1885–; E and P, J. E. Curren, Ap 1887 B. M. Glasgow, Mr 1889 Allan McDonald, Ap 1891 P. J. Bennett, Ap 1900 W. O. Thompson; Mr 1885-D 1911, UNM.

*Sierra Free Press.** W; E; Dem; Mr 1911–; E and P, E. D. Tittman; Ap-D 1911, UNM.

*Skipper.* W; E; Rep; Mr 1889-?; E and P, G. W. Gregg.

## HOPE

*Penasco Valley Pess.** W; E; U; 1908–; P, Abe M. Burnett, E, R. H. H. Burnett; O 1909-D 1911, CH Carlsbad.

## HOUSE

*Pioneer News.** W; E; U; 1910–; E and P, H. O. Norris; see House *Plains News;* N 1910-D 1911, CH Tucumcari.

*Plains News.*\* W; E; Rep; Jl 1908-10; E and P, M. F. Young; name changed to House *Pioneer News;* Jl-N 1908, CH Tucumcari.

## JEMEZ

*Hot Springs Guide.* W; E; U; Je 1882-?; E and P, D. O. Dare; moved from Bernalillo where it was the *News.*

*Guide.* W; E; U; 1888-89; P, Jemez Hot Springs Library Association.

## JUNCTION CITY

*Times.* W; E; U; My 1891-92; E and P, H. O. Willis and Charles Day; moved to Farmington to launch *San Juan Times.*

## KENNA
### (earlier named URTON)

*Record.* W; E; Rep; D 1907—; E and P, W. T. Cowgill; paper earlier named Urton *Record.*

## KINGSTON

*Black Range Herald.* W; E; U; D 1886-F 1887; E and P, Jacob Mitchell; combined with Hillsboro *Sierra County Advocate.*

*Clipper.* W; E; Dem; Ja-N 1884; E and P, A. C. Lowery; sold to J. E. Curren who renamed it Kingston *Sierra County Advocate.*

*Ledge (Daily).* D; E; U; Jl 1886-?; E and P, (?) Olney and (?) King; merged with the Kingston *Percha Shaft.*

*Percha Shaft.* W (briefly summer 1886 was S-W); Rep; Ap-? 1886; E and P, J. E. Curren; merged with Kingston *Daily Ledge.*

*Percha Shaft and Ledge.* W; E; Rep; ?-D 1886; E and P, J. E. Curren; became Kingston *Daily Shaft.*

*Shaft (Daily).* D; E; Rep; D 1886-Mr 1887; E and P, J. E. Curren.

*Shaft.* (weekly) \* W; E; Rep; Mr 1887-D 1893; P, J. E. Curren, My 1887 George Frame, Mr 1889 J. P. Hyland, E, J. E. Curren, My 1887 C. F. Barr, S 1890 J. P. Hyland; moved to Rincon as the *Shaft;* Ap 1889-D 1893, UNM; Ap 1889-D 1893, NMIMT.

*Sierra County Advocate.*\* W; E; Rep; N 1884-Mr 1885; E and P, J. E. Curren; moved to Hillsboro as *Sierra County Advocate;* Ja-F 1885, UNM.

*Sierra County Democrat.* W; E; Dem; 1888; P, George Frame, E, C .F. Barr; a campaign paper.

*Tribune.* W; E; Rep; Ja-O 1883; E and P, Charles W. Greene; moved to Deming as the *Tribune.*

## KNOWLES

*News.*\* W; E; Dem; 1909—; E and P, J. H. Mullane; Ja 1910-D 1911, CH Carlsbad.

## LABELLE

*Cresset.*\* W; E; U; D 1894-O 1898; E and P, (?) Galligher and (?) Illif, 1895 Frank Staplin; moved to Taos as *Cresset;* D 1894-O 1898, UNM.

## LAKE ARTHUR

*Times.* W; E; U; 1905–; E and P, T. T. Meade, 1909 W. G. Gruber, 1911 G. W. Butler.

## LAKE VALLEY

*Herald.*\* W; E; Rep; O 1882-O 1883; E and P, Charles W. Greene; moved to Deming to start the *Tribune;* O 5, 1882, NMHU.

*New Era.* W; E; U; D-Mr 1885; E and P, J. F. Capehart; sold to J. E. Curren who renamed it *Sierra Grande Press.*

*Sierra Grande Press.* W; E; Rep; Mr 1885-Jl 1886; P, J. E. Curren.

*Times.* W; E; U; 1906–; E and P, unknown.

## LAKEWOOD

*Progress.*\* W; E; Dem; 1906–; E and P, ?, S 1906 James M. Wood; Mr 1909-D 1911, CH Carlsbad.

## LALANDE

*Leader.* W; E; U; N 1909–; E and P, C. V. Battles, Ben Sullivan, and H. O. Norris ,1910 C. V. Battles, 1911 E. D. Stoner.

*Times.* W; E; U; 1907; E and P, unknown.

## LA LUZ

*Sacramento Chief.* W; E; Rep; N 1897-Ap 1899; E and P, J. H. Lightfoot; former Tularosa *Chief,* moved to Alamogordo as *Sacramento Chief.*

## LAS CRUCES

*Borderer.*\* W; BI, S 1874 E; Dem; Mr 1871-S 1875; E and P, N. V. Bennett; S 1874 Spanish portion of paper became *El Fronterizo;* Mr 1871-D 1872, UNM.

*Citizen.*\* W; BI, Ja 1909 E; Rep; Mr 1902–; E and P, Lorenzo Lapoint, S 1909 Will Lapoint; Ap 1902-D 1911, pub office; Ap 1902-1912 (broken), NMSU.

*Defensor del Pueblo.*\* W; BI, O 1890 S; Dem; Jl 1890-N 1891; P, Ramon Bermudez and T. J. Bull, E, Pedro G. de Lama; Ag 1890-My 1891 (broken), NMSU.

*Democrata.* (title used twice)\* 1–W; S; Dem; Je-N 1894; E and P, Pedro G. de Lama and M. F. Lerma, Ag 1894 L. P. Pino and Fredrico Ochoa; Je-N 1894, NMSU. 2–W; S; Dem; F-N 1898; E and P, Pedro G. de Lama; Mr-Ag 1898, NMSU.

*Democrat.* (title used twice)\* 1–W; E; Dem; F 1899-F 1900 (?); E and P, Will Robinson, My 1899 J. I. Williams, Je 1899 C. E. Stivers; formerly Las Cruces *Independent Democrat;* My-N 1899 (broken) , NMSU. 2–W; E; Dem; 1911; E and P, unknown; a campaign paper.

*Dona Ana County Republican.*\* W; E; Rep; F 1897-Ja 1902; E and P, Fred A. Anderson, Ag 1897 John Swarts, Ja 1898 Acheson McClintock, Ag 1901 C. W. Morgan, O 1901 R. E. Mussey; name changed to Las Cruces *Progress;* Mr 1897-Ja 1902 (broken), NMSU.

*Dona Ana County Times.* W; E; Dem; F-My 1885; E and P, John F. Edwards.

*Eco del Rio Grande.*\* W; S, Ap 1875 BI; Rep; Ag 1874-Mr 1878; P, Lorenzo Lapoint, E, Lorenzo Lapoint, Ap 1875 Ash Upson, F 1876 Lorenzo Lapoint; F 1876-D 1877 (broken), NMSU.

*Eco del Siglo.*\* W; S; U; F-Ap 1882; E and P, Henry Arnold and Marcial Valdez; see Las Cruces *Thirty-Four* and *El Tiempo;* F-Mr 1882, NMSU.

*Eco del Valle.*\* W; S; Ind, My 1910 Rep; N 1905–; E and P, M. F. Lerma, My 1910 M. F. Lerma and Isadoro Armijo, Jr.; absorbed *El Tiempo* Jl 1911; D 1905-D 1911, NMSU; Ag-S 1911 (broken), NMSL.

*Empresa.*\* W; S; U; S 1896-Jl 1897 (?) ; E and P, Lorenzo Lapoint; S 1896-Je 1897 (broken), NMSU.

*Estrella.*\* W; S; Rep; N 1910–; E and P, Will Lapoint; a companion publication for Las Cruces *Citizen;* F-D 1911 (broken), NMSU.

*Flor del Valle.*\* W; S; Rep; Ja-N 1894; E and P, M. F. Lerma and Isadoro Armijo, Sr., Mr 1894 M. F. Lerma and Isadoro Armijo, Jr.; F-O 1894, NMSU.

*Fronterizo.*\* W; S; Dem; S 1874-S 1875; P, N. V. Bennett, E, Epifano Vigil; a companion paper for Las Cruces *Borderer;* Ap 29, 1875, NMSU.

*Independent Democrat.*\* W; E; Dem; Ja 1892-F 1899; P, A. B. Fall, E, L. W. Renoir, F 1892 W. R. Fall, O 1894 Allen Kelly, Mr 1896 C. E. Bull; became Las Cruces *Democrat;* F 1892-D 1898 (broken), NMSU.

*Labrador.*\* W; S; Dem; S 1896–; E and P, Pinito Pino and (?) Madrid, Ja 1897 Saloman Garcia, My 1897 F. Martinez, N 1897 M. de la Pena and Pinito Pino, 1898 Pinito Pino, My 1899 Pinito Pino and M. F. Lerma, 1901 M. F. Lerma and Jose Gonzales, O 1905 Jose Gonzales, 1908 Jose Gonzales and J. C. Rodriguez; S 1896-N 1900 (broken), Ja 1901-D 1911, NMSU.

*Liberal.* W; S; U; Je 1891-?; E and P, Fredrico Ochoa.

*Mesilla Valley Democrat.*\* W (S-W briefly in 1886); BI; Dem; Ag 1886-D 1890 (?) ; E and P, J. P. Booth, My 1887 Allan McDonald, O 1890 James M. Cole; S 1886-D 1890 (broken), NMSU.

*Metodista Neo-Mexicano.* M; BI; U; 1889-1892; E and P, T. W. Harwood; see Socorro *Metodista Neo-Mexicano.*

*Newman's Semi-Weekly.*\* S-W; E; Dem; Ap-Jl 1881; E and P, S. H. Newman and Charles Shannon; formerly Newman's *Thirty-Four,* moved to El Paso, Texas, where it soon became the *Lone Star;* Ap 2-20, 1881, NMSU.

*Newman's Thirty-Four.* S-W; E; Dem; Ja-Ap 1881; E and P, S. H. Newman and Charles Shannon; see Las Cruces *Thirty-Four,* became Newman's *Semi-Weekly.*

*News (Daily).*\* D; E; U; Ja-D 1889 (?); E and P, James Kibbee, O 1889 Charles B. Bailey; Mr-N 1889 (broken), NMSU.

*Observador Fronterizo.*\* W; S; Rep; 1888; E and P, A. J. Fountain and Pedro G. Garcia; a campaign period paper; S-O 1888 (broken), NMSU.

*Progress.*\* W; E; Rep; Ja 1902-Ja 1904; P, (?) Ferenger and F. D. Hunt, Ja 1903 Charles P. Downs, E, F. D. Hunt, Ja 1903 Charles P. Downs; formerly Las Cruces *Dona Ana County Republican,* merged with the Las Cruces *Rio Grande Republican* in 1904; F 1902-Ja 1904, NMSU.

*Progressive.* W; E; Rep; N 1910-?; E and P, E. C. Wade.

*Promotor Escolar.** W; BI; U; S 1891-? 1892; E and P, unknown; a literary publication with the objective of teaching Spanish and English to interested subscribers; S 1891-F 1892 (broken), NMSU.

*Rio Grande Gazette.* W; BI; Rep; 1869; E and P, H. W. Sherry.

*Rio Grande Republican.** W, S 1911 S-W; E; Rep; My 1881—; E and P, James A. Spradling, D 1881 A. J. Fountain, Ja 1882 C. J. Hildreth, N 1884 Paul Wagner and Charles Metcalfe, D 1891 J. P. McCrea, F 1892 J. A. Whitmore, Ja 1893 F. C. Barker, Ag 1893 J. R. McFie, Ja 1894 A. T. Hunt, N 1894 A. J. Papen, Ja 1904 C. W. Beard, Ag 1905 A. J. Papen, F 1911 O. A. and Josephine Foster; My 1881-D 1911 (broken), NMSU.

*Southwestern Farm and Orchard.†* S-M, 1896 M; E; U; My 1894-1901; P, A. T. Hunt, N 1894 A. J. Papen, E, F. C. Barker; My 1894-F 1899 (broken), NMSU.

*Thirty-Four.** W; E; Dem; D 1878-Ap 1881; P, S. H. Newman and Henry Arnold, Ja 1881 Henry Arnold, E, S. H. Newman, Jl 1880 Henry Arnold; Newman and Arnold disagreed and Newman began a new paper in Ja 1881, see *Newman's Thirty-Four;* D 1878-D 1880, NMSU; D 1878-Je 1880, UNM.

*Tiempo.** W; S; U; O 1881-Jl 1911; E and P, Marcial Valdez; absorbed by Las Cruces *Eco del Valle;* N 1882-Jl 1911 (broken), NMSU.

*Times (Daily).* (title used twice)* 1—D; BI; U; My 1889; E and P, Marcial Valdez and J. T. L. MacDonald; My 4-14, 1889, NMSU. 2—D; BI; U; Ja 1893; E and P, Marcial Valdez and E. Gandara; Ja 10-F 11, 1893, NMSU.

*Verdad.* (title used twice)* 1—W; S; Rep; 1890; E and P, Pinito Pino; a campaign period paper; S-O 1890 (broken), NMSU. 2—W; S; U; 1898; E and P, Saloman Garcia; Ja-Ap 1898 (broken), NMSU.

## LAS VEGAS

*Acorn.* (title used twice)* 1—W; BI; U; D 1869-? 1870; E and P, A. V. Aoy; became the *New Mexico Advertiser* which was later also published at Santa Fe. 2—W; BI; U; Ap-Ag 1875 (?) ; P, (?) Anchetta and (?) Maes; My 25, 1875, UNM.

*Advertiser (Daily).** D; E; Rep; My-Je 1903; E and P, Earl Lyons; My-Je 1903, UNM.

*Advertiser.* (weekly)* W; E; Rep; Mr-My, Je-O 1903; E and P, Earl Lyons; Mr-My, Je-O 1903, UNM.

*Anciano.* S-M, 1893 W; S; U; 1889-90, 1898-99; E and P, J. J. Gilcrist; a Presbyterian paper founded at La Junta, Colorado, moved to Mora in 1890 and returned to Las Vegas in 1899.

*Atrevido.* W; S; U; 1887; E and P, students at Las Vegas (Jesuit) College.

*Aurora.* W; BI; U; 1900-02, 1910-11; E and P, Noman Skinner, 1910 Benedicto Sandoval; a Presbyterian paper, moved to Albuquerque in 1911.

*Cachiporra.†* W; S; Rep; 1888; E and P, San Miguel County Republican Central Committee; O 19, 1888, NMSU.

*Cachiporrita.** S-W; S; Rep; 1890; E and P, San Miguel County Republican Central Committee; O 8-28, 1890, NMHU; O 8-28, 1890, NMSL.

*Campaign Bulletin.*† W?; E; Rep; 1880; E and P, J. H. Koogler; a Republican campaign paper; Ag 25, S 30, O 1, 1880, NMSU.

*Chronicle (Daily).** D; BI; Rep; O-N 1884; P, Louis Hommel, E, J. H. Koogler; former San Hilario *Red River Chronicle;* O-N 1884, NMHU.

*Chronicle.* (weekly)* W; BI; Rep; D 1884-? 1886; E and P, Louis Hommel; moved to Cabra Springs as *Chronicle;* N 1884-Je 1886 (broken), NMHU; O 19, 1886, NMSU.

*Clarin Mexicano.** W; S; Union People's party; 1890; E and P, unknown; a campaign paper; O 23, 1890, NMHU; O 30, 1890, NMSL.

*Democrat.* (title used twice)* 1—W; E; Dem; Ap-? 1876; E and P, J. C. Warren. 2—W; E; Dem; My-? 1890; E and P, M. W. Edwards; My-N 1890, UNM; My-O 1890, NMSL.

*Eureka.* M; E; U; N 1879-?; E and P, T. B. Mills and (?) Beecher; a real estate promotion paper.

*Examiner (Daily).** D; E; Dem, 1897 Rep; Je 1895-F 1898; P, L. R. Allen and (?) Leicham, 1896 L. R. Allen, F 1897 J. A. Carruth, E, F. J. Ellis, 1896 L. R. Allen, F 1897 J. A. Carruth; merged with Las Vegas *Daily Optic;* Ag 30, 1895, NMSU; My 13, 1897, NMHU.

*Examiner.* (weekly) W; E; Dem; Ja-Je 1895; E and P, L. R. Allen and (?) Leicham; became *Daily Examiner.*

*Fisk's Great Southwest.** M; E; U; Ag 1881-88 ?; E and P, Calvin Fisk; a real estate promotion paper; Ag 1881, N 1882, Ap-My 1886, NMHU.

*Fitzgerrell's Guide to New Mexico.** M, and at times W; E; U; 1881-88 ?; E and P, (?) Fitzgerrell; a real estate promotion paper; two issues undated, NMHU.

*Free Press. (Daily).* D; E; Rep; D 1891-D 1892; E and P, J. A. Carruth.

*Free Press.* (weekly)* W; E; Rep; Mr-D 1891; E and P, J. A. Carruth; became Las Vegas *Daily Free Press;* Mr-D 1891, WNMU.

*Gaceta.* W; S; Rep; Mr 1877-D 1878; P, J. H. Koogler, E, Louis Hommel.

*Gazette (Daily).** D; E; Rep; Jl 1879-Je 1886; P, J. H. Koogler, Ap 1883 Gazette Publishing Company (Jefferson Raynolds chief stockholder), E, J. H. Koogler, Ap 1883 W. C. Hadley, D 1883 R. B. Bryan, My 1884 J. H. Wise, S 1884 R. W. Webb, after D 1884 various short-term editors; briefly in 1881-82 was named *Morning Gazette;* Ja 1881-D 1883 (broken), UNM; F 1881-D 1883 (broken), WNMU.

*Gazette.* (weekly)† W; BI, Mr 1877 E; Rep; S 1872-O 1873, Ap 1874-Je 1886; P, Louis Hommel, Mr 1875 J. H. Koogler and Louis Hommel, D 1878 J. H. Koogler, Ap 1883 Gazette Publishing Company, E, Louis Hommel, Mr 1875 J. H. Koogler, Ap 1883 W. C. Hadley, D 1883 R. B. Bryan, My 1884 J. H. Wise, S 1884 R. W. Webb; 1883, 1888 (broken), NMSL.

*Hispano-Americano.*† W; S; U; 1892-?; E and P, Victor Ochoa; successor to *El Bravo del Valle* and *El Latino-Americano,* both of El Paso, Texas, and *El Sol de Mayo* of Las Vegas; Ap 21-O 15, 1892 (broken), NMSU.

*Homesteader.* W; E; U; ? 1909-Mr 1910; E and P, J. P. Jonquel; merged with Las Vegas *Star.*

*Independiente.** W; S; Ind, 1901 Rep; 1894–; P, E. H. Salazar, 1898 E. H. Salazar and E. C. de Baca, 1904 E. H. Salazar and Secundino Romero, S 1910 Secundino Romero, E, E. H. Salazar, 1898 E. C. de Baca, 1901 E. H. Salazar, 1904 Secundino Romero; Mr 1894-D 1911, UNM; Mr 1893-Mr 1895, Mr 1906-Ja 1907, NMSRCA; 1894-1900 (broken), NMSL.

*Labor Standard.* W; E; U; Ag 1888-?; E and P, A. D. Wallace.

*Mail.* W; BI; U, O 1871 Dem; Jl 1871-Ag 1872; P, Ash Upson and J. Bolinger, O 1871 S. H. Newman and J. Bollinger.

*Mills' Investors Review.** M; E; U; O 1887-Jl 1888; E and P, T. B. Mills and Son; real estate promotion; O 1887-Jl 1888 (broken), NMHU.

*Mills' Mexico.** M; E; U; D 1882-? 1884; E and P, T. B. Mills; advertising Mexican real estate; D 1882-Jl 1884 (broken), NMHU.

*Mining World.** M, 1881 BI-W, 1883 M; E; U; Ag 1880-? 1886; P, T. B. Mills, N 1884 J. A. Carruth, E, W. C. Hadley, N 1884 J. A. Carruth; Ag 1880-Jl 1884, UNM.

*New Mexico Advertiser (Daily).* D; BI; U; 1873; E and P, A. V. Aoy.

*New Mexico Advertiser.* (weekly)* W; BI; U; ? 1870-? 1878; E and P, A. V. Aoy; formerly Las Vegas *Acorn;* Ja 12, 1878, UNM.

*New Mexico Catholic.* S-M; BI; U; 1894; E and P, M. O. Sullivan.

*New Mexico Christian Advocate.* (Methodist) M; BI; U; ?-1881-?; E and P, Thomas Harwood; was printed at Las Vegas but datelined Santa Fe.

*New Mexico Herald.†* W; BI; Rep; Je 1879-Ja 1880; E and P, R. W. Webb and Miguel Salazar; moved to Santa Fe to become *Era Southwestern;* Je 25, Jl 2, 30, 1879, NMSU.

*New Mexico Journal of Education.†* M; E; U; 1900-11; E and P, Rupert F. Asplund; moved to Santa Fe in 1911; O 1903-1911 (broken), NMSU.

*New Mexico Livestock Journal.* W; E; U; Jl 1882-? 1883; E and P, J. A. Carruth and (?) Layton.

*New Mexico Medical Journal.* M; E; U; 1905–; P, ?, E, F. T. B. Fest.

*New Mexico Miner.* M ?; E; U; 1880; E and P, Charles Longuemare.

*New Mexico Monthly Magazine.* M; E; U; D 1881-? 1882; E and P, Richard Gerner.

*New Mexico Patriot.* W; BI; U; Mr-Ag 1875; E and P, N. Segura.

*New Mexico Stock Grower.* W; E; U; F 1884-86; E and P, R. F. Hardy and H. H. Pierce; changed name to *Stock Grower.*

*News.* (title used twice)* 1—W; E; Rep; Ap-D 1887; E and P, F. A. Blake; former Socorro *Union,* moved to Gallup to become *News-Register;* N-D 1888, UNM. 2—W; E; Rep; D 1905-? 1906; E and P, Russell A. Kistler.

*Observador.* W; S; U; 1898-99; E and P, unknown.

*Optic (Daily).** D; E; Rep, F 1898 Dem, Ap 1903 Rep; O 1879–; P, Russell A. Kistler, F 1898 Las Vegas Publishing Company, Ap 1903 J. G. McNary, O

1906 W. F. Cornell, D 1906 M. M. Padgett, E, Russell A. Kistler, F 1898 George P. Gould, Ja 1899 George Cross, Ja 1900 Russell A. Kistler, Ap 1903 J. G. McNary, D 1906 M. M. Padgett; merged with *Daily Examiner* in 1898 and *Daily Record* in 1903; N 1879-D 1911 (broken), NMHU; N 1879-D 1911 (broken), UNM; Ja 1880-D 1888, 1910-12, NMSL; 1889-1900 (broken), NMSU.

*Optic (Weekly).** W; E; Rep; Jl-O 1879, S 1880-F 1898; E and P, Russell A. Kistler; former Otero *Optic;* 1879-F 1898 (broken), NMHU; O 23-30, 1880, NMSU.

*Optic and Stock Grower (Weekly).** W; E; Dem, Ap 1903 Rep; F 1898–; P, Las Vegas Publishing Company, Ap 1903 J. G. McNary, O 1906 W. F. Cornell, D 1906 M. M. Padgett, E, same as those of *Daily Optic* in this period; formed by merger of *Weekly Optic* and *Stock Grower,* previously being published by Las Vegas *Examiner;* F 1898-D 1911, NMHU; 1910-12, NMSL.

*Pilgrim's Progress.** Quarterly; E; U; 1887-89; E and P, Calvin Fisk; real estate promotion; Winter, 1887, Fall, 1888, NMHU.

*Pointers.* W; E; U; 1879-80?; E and P, W. C. Hadley.

*Political Comet.* W ?; E ?; U; 1882; E and P, unknown.

*Real Estate and Business Index.* M; E; U; F 1880-?; E and P, A. A. and J. H. Wise.

*Record (Daily).*† D; E; Rep; O 1900-Ap 1903; P, Record Publishing Company, E, various editors for brief periods—J. F. Manning, C. P. Downs, James Duncan; merged with *Daily Optic;* 1901-03 (broken), NMSL; Ja 29, 1901, Ap 12, 1902, NMSU.

*Republican.** W; E; Rep; D 1899-? 1900; P, Republican Publishing Company, E, A. N. Brown; formerly *Sunday Morning Review* and at end of campaign of 1900 resumed that title; Ja-N 1900, UNM.

*Revista Catolica.** W; S; U; Ja 1875–; P, Jesuit Order; Ja 1890-D 1908, NMSRCA; 1878-97 (broken), NMSU.

*Revista Evangelica.* W; S; U; 1876-79; E and P, J. A. Annin.

*San Miguel County Republican.** S-W; E; Rep; O 1886-?; E and P, San Miguel County Republican Central Committee; O-N 1886, NMHU.

*Sol de Mayo.** W; Bl; Dem; My 1891-92; E and P, E. C. de Baca and E. Romero; My 1891-Mr 1892 (broken), NMSU.

*Southwest Magazine.* M; E; U; 1898–; E and P, students at New Mexico Normal University.

*Southwestern Poultry Journal.* M; E; U; Ap 1889-?; E and P, T. M. Harwood.

*Star.* W; E; U; 1909-Mr 1910; E and P, Russell A. Kistler; merged with *Homesteader.*

*Star and Homesteader.** D, My 1910 S-W; U; Mr 1910-?; P, P. Jonquel and Russell A. Kistler, E, Russell A. Kistler; Mr-Ap 1910, UNM.

*Stock Grower and Farmer.** W; E; U; 1886-F 1898; E and P, R. F. Hardy, 1891 J. N. Schick, C. U. Strong, and (ed) H. H. Pierce, 1892 L. R. Allen and H. E. Blake, 1894 L. R. Allen and C. G. Leicham, 1896 L. R. Allen, 1897 J. A. Carruth; merged with *Weekly Optic;* S 1886-F 1898 (broken), UNM; S 1886-Mr 1889 (broken), NMSL.

*Sunday Courier.** W; E; Dem; Jl-D 1888; E and P, George P. Gould; Jl-D 1888, NMHU.

*Sunday Herald.* W; E; Dem; S 1884-N 1885; E and P, James Brown.

*Sunday Morning Mountain Breeze.* W; E; U; My 1887-Ja 1888; E and P, unknown.

*Sunday Morning Review.** W; E; Rep; Je-D 1899, D 1900-? 1902; P, E. H. Salazar; see *Republican;* Je-D 1899, UNM; Je-D 1899, NMSL.

*Voz del Pueblo.** W; S; United People's Party; Je 1890—; P, Felix Martinez, E, Nestor Montoya, 1895 Felix Martinez, after 1902 E. C. de Baca and Antonio Lucero were the active editors; Ja 1891-D 1910 (scattered issues), UNM; Ja 1891-Ja 1896, NMSRCA; 1892-1902 (very broken), NMSU; F 1889-D 1911 (broken), NMSL.

## LINCOLN

*Golden Era.*† W; E; U; Jl 1884-F 1886; E and P, unknown; former White Oaks *Golden Era;* O 1884-Ja 1885, UNM.

*Independent.** W; E; U, 1887-88 Dem, 1889-91 Populist, Ja 1892 U; F 1886-O 1888, O 1889-Ja 1891, Ja 1892-Ap 1892, 1893; P, J. J. Dolan, 1887 J. K. Byers, O 1889 James Kibbee, Ja 1892 J. J. Dolan, 1893 Leslie Ellis, E, Moses Wiley, 1887 J. K. Byers, O 1889 James Kibbee, Ja 1892 Mrs. A. L. McGinnis, 1893 Leslie Ellis; former *Golden Era,* became Lincoln *News;* O 1888-D 1889, Ja-Ap 1892, CH Carrizozo.

*Liberty Banner.** W; E; Populist; Ap-Jl 1891; P, Lincoln County Farmers' Alliance, E, J. F. McDowell; former Nogal *Liberty Banner;* Ap-Jl 1891, CH Carrizozo.

*News.* W; E; U, 1897 Dem; 1894-98; E and P, (?) Norman and W. C. Thompson, 1897 J. A. Haley; former *Independent.*

*Republican.** W; E; Rep; Ap 1892-93; E and P, J. J. Dolan; former *Independent* and in 1893 reassumed that title; My 1892-Ja 1893, CH Carrizozo.

## LOGAN

*Cronica.* W; BI; Rep; Jl 1906-?; E and P, N. Faustin Gallegos.

*Leader.** W; E; Rep; Ap 1908—; E and P, Frank Nesteval, 1910 Paul Jones; My 1908-D 1911, CH Tucumcari.

## LORDSBURG

*Advance.* W; E; Dem; Jl 1883-Ag 1887; E and P, R. H. Jones, 188-? I. R. Birt.

*Western Liberal.** W; E; Rep; N 1887—; P, W. S. Dye and Don Kedzie, 1888 Don Kedzie, E, Don Kedzie; S-O 1888, UNM; Je 23, 1893, Ap 12, 1901, NMSU.

## LOS LUNAS

*Cronica de Valencia.* W; S; Rep; 1891-94; E and P, Manuel Salazar y Otero; moved to Albuquerque and became *Bandera Americana.*

*Estrella de Nuevo Mexico.* W; S; U; 1904-06; E and P, Enrique Sosa; former *Hormigo de Oro* at Albuquerque, returned to Albuquerque as *Estrella.*

*Valencia County Tribune.* W; E; U; Ja-? 1888; E and P, A. W. Webster.

*Valencia County Vindicator.* W; BI; U; 1883; E and P, unknown.

## LOVINGTON

*Leader.** W; E; Rep; Mr 1910–; E and P, Inez A. Harrington, Ap 1911 Wesley McCallister; Ap-D 1911, CH Carlsbad.

## LUMBERTON

*Independent.* W; E; U; 1895-96; E and P, Frank V. Potter.

## McINTOSH

*New Mexican Homeland.** W; E; Rep; Ja 1910-Ag 1911; E and P, H. D. Carter, My 1911 Irving Mead; Ja-Ag 1911, CH Estancia.

## MAGDALENA

*Mine and Lariat.* W; E; U; O 1890-? 1891; E and P, J. G. Davis.

*Mountain Mail.** W; E; U; Ap-D 1888; P, Whitmore and Company, E, unknown; printed in the shop of Socorro *Times;* Ap 5, 1888, NMSU; O-N 1888, UNM.

*News.* W; E; Rep; 1909–; P, J. E. Williams, 1911 (?) Edwards and N. D. Sherman, E, J. E. Williams, 1911 N. D. Sherman.

## MALAGA

*News.* W; E; Rep; 1908-10; E and P, F. G. Prouty.

## MALDONADO

*Estrella.*† W; S; U; Ja 1897-?; E and P, (?) Sanchez and (?) Medina; Ja 30, 1897, NMSU.

## MANZANO

*Gringo and Greaser.** S-M; BI; U; Ag 1883-Mr 1884; E and P, Charles L. Kusz; Ag 1883-Mr 1884, UNM.

## MAXWELL

*Maxim.* W; E; Rep; 1909-10; E and P, J. G. Smith, 1910 O. A. and Josephine Foster.

*Talisman.* W; E; U; 1906-?; E and P, unknown.

## MELROSE

*Democrat.* W; E; Dem; 1911–; E and P, W. C. Hawley.

*Enterprise.* W; E; U, 1909 Rep, 1911 Dem; 1907-Ag 1911; E and P, R. C. Edgell, 1908 A. C. Stackhouse, 1909 E. R. Peck, 1911 W. C. Hawley.

*Headlight.* W; E; U; S 1906-Ap 1909; E and P, J. E. Curren; subscription list sold to *Enterprise.*

*Index.* W; E; Rep; 1910–; E and P, L. D. Beckwith; formerly Fort Sumner *Index.*

*Southwest Baptist.* M; E; U; 1908-F 1909; E and P, O. N. McBride; moved to Portales where it became *New Mexico Baptist.*

## MESILLA

*Democrata.** W; S; Dem; S-N 1878; E and P, S. H. Newman; S-N 1878 (broken), NMSU; S-N 1878 (broken), UNM.

*Miner.** W; E; U; Je 1860; E and P, D. W. Hughes and E. B. Kelly; only one issue published; Je 9, 1860, NMSU.

*News.** W; BI; Rep; N 1873-F 1885; E and P, Lorenzo Lapoint, F 1874 Lorenzo Lapoint and Ira M. Bond, Ag 1874 Ira M. Bond; moved to Albuquerque, see *News;* F 1874-Je 1882 (broken), NMSU.

*Times.* (title used twice)* 1—W; E; O 1860-Ag 1862; P, B. C. Murray and Company, Ja 1862 Frank Higgins and B. C. Murray, E, B. C. Murray, My 1861 Frank Higgins; O 1860-Ja 1862 (scattered issues), NMSU. 2—W; E (?); Rep; Jl-Ag 1867; E and P, Everett J. Babbitt; Jl 15, 1867, Jack D. Rittenhouse collection, Albuquerque.

*Valley Independent.** W; BI; Rep; Je 1877-Jl 1879; P, A. J. Fountain, J. S. Crouch and Thomas Casad, Ag 1878 J. S. Crouch and Thomas Casad, E, A. J. Fountain, Ag 1878 J. S. Crouch; Je 1877-Jl 1879, NMSU.

## MESILLA PARK
### (was not formally given this name until about 1900)

*New Mexico Collegian.†* M; E; U; 1893-1907; E and P, students at New Mexico Agricultural and Mechanics Arts College; 1893-1907, NMSU.

*Round-up.†* W; E; U; 1907–; E and P, students at New Mexico Agricultural and Mechanics Arts College; 1907-12, NMSU.

## MIAMI

*Valley Farmer.* W; E; U; 1909-10; P, Miami Publishing Company.

## MINERAL CITY
### (sometimes known as MINERAL HILL)

*Blue Canon Drill.* W; E; U; O 1881-F 1882; E and P, J. C. Churchill; see *Drill.*

*Drill.* W; E; U; F-Ap 1882; E and P, J. W. Barney and J. C. Churchill; merger of *Blue Canon Drill* and *News.*

*News.* W; E; U; O 1881-F 1882; E and P, J. W. Barney; see *Drill.*

## MONTOYA

*Republican.** W; E; Rep; S 1907–; E and P, W. C. Hawkins; O 1907-D 1911, CH Tucumcari.

## MORA

*Anciano.* (Presbyterian) S-M, 1893 W; S; U; 1890-98; E and P, J. J. Gilcrist; before and after its time at Mora, this paper was at Las Vegas.

*Cronica.* (title used twice)* 1—W; BI; U; Je 1889-Ja 1890; E and P, Louis Hommel; successor to Mora *Democrat;* Je 13, N 2,1889, NMSU. 2—W; S; U; 1894-96; P, Mora Publishing Company, E, Jose Inez Garcia, 1895 and later, editor unknown.

*County Sentinel.* W; BI; U; 1889; E and P, unknown.

*Democrat.* W; BI; Dem; ? 1889-Je 1889; E and P, unknown but probably Louis Hommel; became *Cronica.*

*Echo.** W; BI; U; Mr-D 1890; E and P, Rafael Romero and Fernando Nolan, ? 1890 D. A. Chacon; Je-N 1890, NMHU; S 16, 1890, NMSU.

*Eco del Norte.*† W; S; U; 1907–; E and P, unknown; F-D 1911, UNM.

*Gaceta.** W; S, 1891 BI; U; Mr-N 1890, Ja-? 1891; E and P, N. Segura, 1891 A. L. Branch and C. W. Holloman; Mr-N 1890 (broken), NMHU; Ag 28, 1890, NMSU.

*Hispano-Americano.* W; BI; U; Ja-? 1890; E and P, unknown; moved from Folsom where it was *New Mexico American.*

*Mail.* S-M; BI; U; 1874; E and P, A. V. Aoy.

*Mensajero.*† W; S; U; 1910–; E and P, Benedicto Sandoval; Mr-D 1911, UNM.

*Mosquito.** W; BI, Ap 1892 S; U; N 1891-? 1892; E and P, Camillo Padilla; S 1891-Je 1892 (broken), NMSU.

*Spanish-American.* W; BI; Rep; 1908; E and P, A. S. Bushkevitz; before and after its time at Mora this paper was at Roy as *Hispano-Americano.*

*Star.* W; E; Rep; 1904-05; E and P, N. S. Rose.

### MORIARTY

*Messenger.* W; E; Rep; 1907–; E and P, George M. Flemming, Ap 1911 Harry J. Fincke.

### MOSQUERO

*Sun.* W; E; U; 1909–; E and P, ?, 1910 B. F. Brown.

### MOUNTAINAIR

*Messenger.* W; E; U; 1909–; P, Gilbert Signer and P. W. Horshor, E, Gilbert Signer.

### NARA VISA

*New Mexican.** W; E; Rep; Ja 1907-Ja 1909; E and P, V. E. McNeil; merged with *Register;* Ja 1908-Ja 1909, CH Tucumcari.

*New Mexican and Register.** W; E; Rep; Ja 1909-Ja 1912; E and P, V. E. McNeil and Harry M. Crain, Je 1909 V. E. McNeil; merged with *New Mexico News;* Ja 1909-D 1911, CH Tucumcari.

*New Mexico News.** W; E; Rep; My 1911-Ja 1912; E and P, W. Arthur Jones; merged with *New Mexican and Register* and became simply *News* (Ja 29, 1912) ; My-D 1911, CH Tucumcari.

*Register.** W; E; Rep; Ja 1907-Ja 1909; E and P, Harry M. Crain and R. C. Stubbins, Mr 1908 Harry M. Crain and W. Arthur Jones, Jl 1908 Harry M. Crain; merged with Nara Visa *New Mexican;* Ja 1908-1909, CH Tucumcari.

### NOGAL

*Liberty Banner.** W; E; Populist; F 1890-Ap 1891; P, Lincoln County Farmers' Alliance, E, J. E. Wharton, Ja 1891 J. F. McDowell; moved to Lincoln under same title, formerly Nogal *Nugget;* F 1890-Ap 1891, CH Carrizozo.

*Nugget.** W; E; Dem; Ag 1887-F 1890; E and P, J. E. Sligh, ? 1889 H. L. Harris; became *Liberty Banner;* My-N 1888, NMHU; Ja-F 1890, CH Carrizozo.

*Republican.* W; E; Rep; Ap-? 1902; E and P, C. H. Brown, ? 1902 J. H. Lightfoot.

## OBAR
### (formerly PERRY)

*Progress.** W; E; Rep; O 1908–; E and P, L. L. Klinefelter; formerly Perry *Progress* until the town changed its name; Ja 1910-D 1911, CH Tucumcari.

## OROGRANDE

*Times.** W; E; U; Ja 1906-D 1907; E and P, F. J. Arkins, Je 1907 W. R. Quarles; Ja 1906-D 1907, CH Alamogordo.

## OTERO

*Optic.* W; E; Rep; Ap-Jl 1879; E and P, Russell A. Kistler and Jay Turpen; moved to Las Vegas.

## PARK VIEW

*Progreso.* W; S; U; Ja 1895 (one issue) ; E and P, unknown.

## PERCHA

*Shaft.* W; E; U; O 1885-Ap 1886; E and P, unknown; moved to Kingston by J. E. Curren.

## PINOS ALTOS

*Miner.* W; E; U; Jl 1888-O 1891; E and P, J. C. Bayne, Ja 1889 William Cristman, Ja 1890 J. R. Hall and Charles Highgate, Mr 1891 F. M. Galloway and Milt Warner; moved to Deming as *Advance.*

## PERRY
### (became OBAR)

*News.* W; E; Rep; Ja-Je 1908; E and P, W. Arthur Jones.

*Progress.** W; E; Rep; Jl-O 1908; E and P, L. L. Klinefelter; see Obar *Progress;* Jl-O 1908, CH Tucumcari.

## PORTALES

*Herald.** W; E; Dem; My 1902-S 1907; E and P, G. F. Ellis, Ag 1903 O. E. Creighton, N 1903 Bert Robey and H. B. Ryther, Je 1905 A. S. Hornbeck, F (?) 1907 A. B. Codrington; see *Roosevelt County Herald;* F-D 1904, Ap-S 1907, ENMU, F 1904-S 1907, NMSL.

*New Mexico Baptist.* M; E; U; F-Je 1909 (?) ; E and P, O. N. McBride; moved from Melrose where named *Southwest Baptist,* according to some sources this is the ancestor of the *Baptist New Mexican* launched at Albuquerque in 1912.

*Progress.** W; E; U; Ag 1901-?; E and P, John Pipes; Ag 1, 1901, Roosevelt County Museum, Portales.

*Roosevelt County Herald.** W; E; Dem; S 1907–; E and P, A. B. Codrington, N 1907 E. A. Priest and Son, Ja 1909 E. P. Alldredge and (F 1909) O. N.

McBride, Je 1909 E. P. Alldredge, My 1911 H. B. Ryther, N 1911 J. R. Darnell; successor to Portales *Herald;* S 1907-D 1911 (broken), ENMU, Ja 1908-D 1911, NMSL.

*Times.** W; E; Rep; F 1903–; E and P, Munsey Bull, Ap 1904 W. C. Hawkins, N 1905 G. V. Johnson; Mr 1903-D 1907, Ja 1909-D 1911, ENMU, Mr 1903-D 1907, Ja 1909-D 1911, NMSL.

## PUERTO DE LUNA

*Voz Publica.* W; S; U; 1898-1903; E and P, Placido Baca y Baca; moved to Santa Rosa.

## QUESTA

*Gazette.*† W; E; Rep; 1910–; E and P, J. Matt Alvey; N-D 1912 (broken) NMSL.

## RATON

*Amigo del Pueblo.*† W; S ?; U; D 1895-?; E and P, J. B. Arellano and Jose Escobar; Ja 8, 1896, NMSU.

*Colfax County Courier.* W; E; U; D 1890-? 1891; E and P, (?) Hall and O. S. Bowman.

*Colfax Democrat.* W; E; Single-tax; 1892-94; E and P, P. H. Smith; see *New Mexican Single-Taxer.*

*Comet.** W; E; U; Ja-Je 1881, Jl 1882-Ja 1887; E and P, O. P. McMains, N 1882 Clarence H. Adams, Charles B. Adams and Edwin E. Adams, F 1886 F. R. Butler, D 1886 J. A. Hunt and A. Clausen; became the *Range;* Jl 1882-Ja 1887, pub office, Raton *Daily Range;* Jl 1882-Ja 1887, NMSL.

*Gazette.** W, 1907 S-W; E; Dem; My 1898-1905. F-? 1907; E and P, W. A. Eaton, 1902 Mrs. W. A. Eaton, 1903 W. L. Burke, Je 1905 L. E. Ellis and J. E. Lysinger; revived F 1907 by E. H. Hehmyer; Ja-D 1902, Ja 1904-Je 1905, CH Raton; 1902, NMSL.

*Guard.** W; E; U; Jl 1881-Jl 1882; E and P, (?) Newell and F. A. Lanstrum, D 1881 F. A. Lanstrum and E. Donghe; apparently O .P. McMains leased the *Comet* for a year and it was renamed *Guard;* N 1881-Jl 1882, pub office, Raton *Daily Range;* N 1881-Jl 1882, NMSL.

*Independent (Daily).** D; E; Rep, 1885 Ind; Ap 1883-Ag 1889; E and P, J. C. Holmes; Jl 1884-N 1886 (broken) , NMHU.

*Independent (Weekly).** W; E; Rep, 1885 Ind; D 1883-Ag 1889; E and P, J. C. Holmes; O 1886-My 1889 (broken), NMHU; Jl 1884-My 1889, NMSL.

*Morning Telegram.** D; E; U; F-Ap 1909; E and P, E. P. Sherman and H. R. Schneider; F-Ap 1909, CH Raton.

*New Mexican Single-Taxer.* W; E; Single-Tax; 1894-97; E and P, P. H. Smith, see *Colfax Democrat.*

*New Mexico News and Press.** W; E; Rep; O 1881-N 1882; E and P, George F. Canis and Thomas Henderson, F 1882 George F. Canis; formerly Cimarron *News and Press;* O 1881-My 1882, UNM.

*News (Daily).** D; E; U; D 1908; E and P, unknown; D 29, 1908, CH Raton.

*News (Weekly).*\* W; E; U; My-Je 1904; E and P, J. W. Bell and W. J. Wright; no known connection between daily and weekly *News;* My-Je 1904, CH Raton.

*Range (Daily).*\* D; E; Rep; O 1908-Ja 1911; E and P, O. A. and Josephine Foster, 1910 Raton Publishing Company, E, J. A. Cutler; D 1908-Ja 1911, pub office; D 1908-Ja 1911, NMSL.

*Range.* (weekly)\* W, Ja 1908 S-W, O 1908 W; E; Rep; Ja 1887–; E and P, J. A. Hunt and A. Clausen, F 1888 J. A. Hunt and T. W. Collier, My 1891 T. W. Collier, Ap 1900 F. D. Morse, 1903 C. E. Stivers, 1905 O. A. and Josephine Foster, 1910 Raton Publishing Company, E, J. A. Cutler; Ja 1887-D 1911, pub office; Ja 1887-D 1911, NMSL.

*Register. (Daily)* D; E; U; Mr-? 1884; E and P, E. E. Adams and E. C. Stone.

*Relampago.*\* W; S; U; My-Ag 1904; E and P, Carlos M. Wood; My-Ag 1904, CH Raton.

*Reporter.*\* W, Je 1894 Tri-W, Je 1897 S-W, F 1899 W; E; Dem; Ap 1890–; E and P, G. B. Beringer and A. Clausen, S 1890 G. B. Beringer, 1910 W. G. Brown; Ap 1890-D 1906, CH Raton; Ja-D 1910, pub office, Raton *Daily Range;* Ja-D 1910, NMSL.

*Republican.* D; E; Rep; 1906; E and P, O. A. Foster; Foster also published the Raton *Range.*

*Times (Daily).*\* D; E; U; O-D 1908; E and P, Leroy Kennedy; O-D 1908, CH Raton.

*Tipografica.* W; S; U; Jl-? 1902; E and P, unknown.

*Union.*\* W; S; Union People's party; Ja-N 1898; E and P, Antonio Cajal and S. M. Sanchez; F-S 1898, CH Raton.

## RED RIVER

*Mining Bulletin.* W; E; Dem; Ag-? 1900; E and P, Lorin W. Brown.

*Mining News.* W; E; Dem; 1898-99; E and P, G. B. Beringer; apparently printed at Raton *Reporter* plant.

*Prospector.*† W; E; Rep; 1900-08; E and P, Fremont C. Stevens; 1901-07 (broken), NMSL.

## RINCON

*Pointer.* W; E; U; Ag-? 1901; E and P, unknown.

*Shaft.* W; E; Rep; 1893-1895; E and P, J. P. Hyland; former Kingston *Shaft,* succeeded by Rincon *Weekly.*

*Valley Reporter.* W; E; U; 1909–; E and P, Elizabeth P. Hendrix.

*Weekly.*\* W; E; U; Ap 1895-My 1897; E and P, Rincon Publishing Company (Saloman Garcia, ed), F 1896 Fred A. Anderson; moved to Las Cruces and became *Dona Ana County Republican;* Ag 1895-My 1897 (broken), NMSU.

## ROBINSON

*Black Range.* W; E; Rep; Ap 1882-Ja 1883; E and P, V. B. Beckett; moved to Chloride and kept same name.

## ROCK ISLAND

*Clipper.* W; E; U; 1909-10; E and P, C. C. Hixon; moved to Endee and became *Enterprise.*

*Tribune.** W; E; U; My 1910—; E and P unknown; My 1910-D 1911, CH Tucumcari.

## ROSWELL

*Baptist Workman.* M; E; U; 1906; E and P, H. F. Vermillion.

*Chaves County Herald.** W; E; Rep; 1890-91; E and P, J. A. Erwin and L. O. Fullen; O-D 1890, CH Carrizozo.

*Democrat.* S-W; E; Dem; 1908-09; E and P, James D. Whelan.

*Irrigator.* W; E; Dem; 1895-96; P, W. H. Mullane, E, W. E. Orr; merged with Roswell *Register.*

*Journal (Daily).* D; E; Dem; Mr-Jl 1903; E and P, C. C. Emerson; merged with *Morning Record.*

*Journal.* (weekly) W; E; Dem; D 1902-Mr 1903; P, Emerson Brothers, E, C. C. Emerson.

*Morning News.** D; E; Dem; Ag 1911—; P, B. F. Harlow, E, Lucius Dills; Ag-D 1911, pub office, Roswell *Daily Record;* Ja-D 1912, NMSL.

*Morning Record.** D; E; Dem; Mr-S 1903; E and P, H. F. M. Bear and C. E. Mason; became Roswell *Daily Record,* an afternoon paper; Mr-Ag 1903, pub office; Mr-S 1903, UNM; Mr-D 1903, NMSL.

*Pecos Valley Register.** W; E; U; N 1888-90; E and P, J. A. Erwin and L. O. Fullen; became Roswell *Register;* N 1888-D 1889, pub office Roswell *Daily Record;* N 1888-D 1889, NMSL; Ja-N 1890, CH Carrizozo.

*Pecos Valley Stockman.** W; E; Dem; O 1900-N 1902; E and P, James Kibbee and Lucius Dills, Mr 1901 G. W. Powers, O 1901 Munsey Bull; moved from Carlsbad to Roswell; Mr 1901-N 1902, pub office Roswell *Daily Record;* Mr 1901-N 1902, NMSL.

*Practical Irrigator and Fruit Grower.* M; E; U; 1896-97; E and P, James Kibbee.

*Record (Daily).** D; E; Dem; S 1903—; P, Record Publishing Company, E, H. F. M. Bear, Ja 1905 G. A. Puckett, 1909 C. E. Mason; S 1903-D 1911, pub office; S 1903-D 1911, NMSL.

*Record.* (weekly)* W; E; Dem; Mr 1891—; P, J. D. Lea, 1899 A. A. Burnett and E. O. Creighton, 1900 E. O. Creighton, Ag 1902 H. F. M. Bear and C. E. Mason, 1903 Record Publishing Company, E, J. D. Lea, 1899 E. O. Creighton, Ag 1902 H. F. M. Bear, Ja 1905 G. A. Puckett, 1909 C. E. Mason; Jl 14, 1893, NMSU; My 1894-D 1901, My 1904-D 1911, pub office; My 1894-D 1911 (broken), NMSL.

*Register (Daily).* D; E; Rep; Mr 1903; E and P, R. S. Hamilton.

*Register.* (weekly)* W; E; Rep; 1890-F 1906; E and P, James Kibbee, 1894 C. E. Bull, 1895 J. W. Mullen, 1896 W. H. Mullane, 1898 R. S. Hamilton, 1903 C. E. Mason; O 1895-F 1906, pub office Roswell *Daily Record;* Ag 1896-F 1906, NMSL.

*Register-Tribune.** W; E; Rep; F 1906–; P, Roswell Printing Company, E, Will Robinson, S 1907 J. S. Carter, Jl 1909 Will Robinson; see *Tribune;* Mr 1906-D 1911, pub office Roswell *Daily Record;* Mr 1906-D 1911, NMSL.

*School News.* M; E; U; O 1899-?; E and P, W. L. Martin.

*Tribune.** W; E; Rep; Ja-F 1906; P, Roswell Printing Company, E, Will Robinson; merged with *Register;* Ja-F 1906, pub office Roswell *Daily Record.*

## ROY

*Hispano-Americano.* W; BI; Rep; 1905-08; E and P, A. S. Bushkevitz, 1906 H. A. Hanson, 1907 A. I. S. Hanson; formerly Roy *Observer and Reporter,* 1908 moved to Mora as *Spanish-American.*

*Observer and Reporter.* W; E; U; Ja 1904-05; E and P, A. S. Bushkevitz; see *Hispano-Americano.*

*Spanish-American.* (title used twice)† 1–M; BI; U; 1904-05; E and P, A. S. Bushkevitz; 1905, UNM. 2–W; BI; Rep; 1909–; E and P, A. S. Bushkevitz, 1910 Ervin Ogden, Sr. and Edwin C. Floersheim; former Mora *Spanish-American.*

*Roy and Solano Herald.* W; E; Rep; 1911–; E and P, A. S. Bushkevitz; former Solano *Herald* moved to Roy.

## SAN ACACIO

*Comercio.*† S-W; S ?; U; 1901-04 (?); E and P, A. R. Cordova; Jl 11, S 12, 1901, NMSU.

## SAN HILARIO

*Red River Chronicle.** W; BI; U; 1882-O 1884; E and P, Louis Hommel; formerly San Lorenzo *Red River Chronicle* moved to Las Vegas as *Daily Chronicle;* N-1882-D 1883, UNM.

## SAN JON

*Quay County Times.** W; E; Rep; Mr 1908–; E and P, I. L. Fowler; Ap 1908-D 1911, CH Tucumcari.

*Sentinel.** W; E; Rep; Jl 1909–; E and P, E. G. Little and H. W. Burton, 1910 H. W. Burton, 1910 James McVey, 1911 H. E. Adams; My 1910-D 1911, CH Tucumcari.

## SAN LORENZO

*Red River Chronicle.** W; BI; U; Je 1880-1882; E and P, Louis Hommel; moved to San Hilario under same title; Ap-O 1882, UNM.

## SAN MARCIAL

*Bee.** W; E; Rep; D 1892-1904; P, A. T. Hunt, Ap 1895 Bee Publishing Company, E, A. T. Hunt, Ap 1895 H. H. Howard; Ap 1893-Mr 1902 (scattered issues), NMSU; 1901-04 (broken), NMSL.

*Libertad.** W; S; U; 1896; P, Pablo Trujillo, E, C. T. Valdivia; Ap 15, 1896, NMSU.

*Reporter.*\* W; E; U; N 1886-1894; P, L. R. Whitmore and Company, E, J. A. Whitmore, 1892 N. A. Whitmore; Ap 14, 1888, Mr 8, 1890, NMSU; Ja 1888-D 1890 (broken), NMSL.

*Standard.* W; E; U; S 1907–; E and P, D. P. De Young, 1909 Ida M. Farrell, Ag 1911 L. J. Whiteman.

*Times.* W; E; U; 1882-83; E and P, unknown.

## SAN PEDRO

*Gol-9-den* (Golden Nine)\* W; E; U; Jl 1889-91; E and P, D. O. Dare, N 1889 Martha A. Hayes; moved to Albuquerque under same title; Jl 18, 25, 1889, UNM; S-D 1889 (broken), F 6, O 19, 1890, NMHU.

*Outlook.* W; E; U; O-N 1889; E and P, A. J. Hughes.

## SANTA FE

*American Weekly.* W; E; U; 1906; E and P, unknown.

*Amigo del Paiz.* W; S; U; 1853; E and P, S. M. Baird.

*Aurora.*\* W; S; Dem; Ag-N 1884; E nd P, Pietri Baldacci; a campaign paper; Ag-N 1884, Mus of NM; Ag-N 1884, NMSU.

*Boletin Popular.*\* W; S, 1893 BI, 1894 S; U, 1888 Rep, 1902 Dem; O 1885-1908; E and P, Jose Segura, N 1907 A. J. Loomis; absorbed by the Santa Fe *Eagle* also belonging to Loomis; Je 1, 1888, Je 21, 1889, Mus of NM; O 21, 28, 1886, Ja-S 1888 (broken), NMHU; 1886-95 (broken), NMSU.

*Bulletin.* W; E; Dem; 1903-04; E and P, Charles Hartsough.

*Capitol.*† W; E; Rep; Je 1900-04; E and P, William M. Berger; Je 1900-Ap 1903 (broken), NMSL; S 14, 1901, NMSU.

*Capitol Sun.* W; E; Dem; Mr-? 1894; E and P, Allen Kelly.

*City News.* S-W; BI; Dem; S 1874-76; E and P, H. Motley and Company.

*Clarin Mejicano.* W; S; U; Ag 1873-?; E and P, unknown.

*Crepusculo de la Libertad.* W; S; U; Ag-S 1834; E and P, Ramon Abreu.

*Democrat (Daily).*\* D; E; Dem; O-N 1880, Ja-Ag 1882; E and P, J. G. Albright; O-N 1880, Ja-Ag 1882, UNM; O-N 1880, Ja-Ag 1882, NMSU.

*Democrat.* (weekly—title used three times)\* 1—W; E; Dem; N 1880-S 1882; E and P, J. G. Albright; moved to Albuquerque as the *Daily Democrat;* Ja 6, 13, 1881, UNM; O 1880-S 1882 (broken), NMSU. 2—W; E ?; Dem; Ag-N 1884; E and P, unknown; a campaign paper. 3—W; E ?; Dem; Ja-N 1898; E and P, unknown; a campaign paper.

*Democrata.* W; S; Dem; 1857; P, S. M. Baird, E, Miguel E. Pino; a campaign paper.

*Eagle.*† W; E; U, 1910 Dem; Mr 1906–; E and P, A. J. Loomis; absorbed *Boletin Popular;* 1906-12 (broken), NMSL.

*Era Southwestern.*\* W; E; Rep; F-S 1880; E and P, R. W. Webb; formerly Las Vegas *New Mexico Herald,* became Santa Fe *Daily Democrat;* Ag-S 1880, UNM; Ag 5, S 30, 1880, NMSU.

*Estrella de Nuevo Mexico.* W; BI; U; 1892-94; E and P, unknown.

*Express (Weekly)*.† W; E; U; My-? 1887; E and P, H. P. McKevitt; see *Free Lance;* Jl 2, 1887, NMSU.

*Free Lance.*\* W; E; U; Je-? 1889; E and P, George Marsh and H. P. Mc-Kevitt, Ag 1889 George Marsh; Je-Jl 1889, NMHU.

*Gato.*\* W; S; U; My-? 1894; E and P, Enrique Sosa; My-Ag 1894 (broken), NMSU.

*Gauntlet.*† W; BI; U; F-? 1894; E and P, unknown; Je 25, 1894, NMSU.

*Gazette (Weekly).*\* W; BI; Dem, 1863 Rep, 1868 Dem; Ap (?) 1851-S 1869; P, J. L. Collins, 1857 C. P. Clever and Dav. J. Miller, 1860 J. L. Collins, S 1865 John T. Russell, E, Neville Stuart, 1853 W. G. Kephart, 1855 J. L. Collins, 1857 Samuel M. Yost, F 1859 H. S. Johnson, 1860 John T. Russell, O 1863 J. L. Collins, 1865 John T. Russell; became the *Weekly Post;* F 1853-S 1869 (broken), UNM, 1856-66 (scattered issues), NMSL; 1853-69 (broken), NMSU.

*Guia de Santa Fe.*\* W; S; Dem; 1886; E and P, unknown; a campaign paper; S 2, 1886, Mus of NM; S 2, O 9, 16, 1886, NMSU.

*Herald (Daily).*\* D; E; Dem; Jl-N 1888; P, Herald Publishing Company (Joseph Clark, Pres., H. C. Burnett, Sec.), E, George Marsh; Jl-N 1888, UNM; Jl-D 1888, NMSU.

*Herald (Weekly).*\* W; E; Dem; Ja 1888-? 1889; P, Herald Publishing Company, E, George Marsh; after advent of *Daily Herald* became *Weekly Herald;* Ja 1888-Ap 1889, UNM.

*Illustrated Monthly.* M; E; U; Ja-? 1878; E and P, (?) Williams and (?) Shaw; became *Rocky Mountain Sentinel.*

*Leader (Daily).*\* D; BI; Dem; O 1882; E and P, E. J. Simpson; O 21, 1882, UNM.

*Leader (Weekly).*\* W; E; Dem; N-? 1884, My 1885-87; P, S. W. Bear and Company, E, unknown; Je 27, 1885-F 1886, N-D 1886, UNM; 1886 (scattered issues). NMSL; N 1884-86 (broken), NMSU.

*Military Review.*\* S-M; E; U; Mr-? 1881; E and P, George A. Nunes; O 1, 1881, NMHU; O 1, 1881, NMSU.

*Miner's Home and Southwestern Mining Magazine.* W; E; U; 1881-83; E and P, unknown.

*New Mexican (Daily*—daily part of title).\* D; BI, F 1880 E, D 1881 BI, Ja 1890 E; Rep; Je 1868-D 1877, F 1880-My 1883, Jl 1885-Ja 1890; E and P, W. H. Manderfield and Thomas Tucker, F 1880 Charles W. Greene, D 1881 E. B. Purcell, Jl 1885 C. B. Hayward, N 1885 T. W. Collier, F 1887 James A. Spradling, O 1889 Max Frost; Je 1868-D 1877, F 1881-My 1883, Jl 1885-S 1887, UNM; Ja 1886-Ja 1890, Mus of NM; Jl 1868-D 1877, S 1880-My 1883, Jl 1885-Ja 1890, NMSL; Jl 1868-D 1877, F 1880-My 1883, Jl 1885-Ja 1890, NMSU.

*New Mexican (Weekly*—weekly part of title).\* W; BI; Rep; Je 1868-My 1883, Jl 1885-F 1888; E and P, W. H. Manderfield and Thomas Tucker, F 1880 C. W. Greene, D 1881 E. B. Purcell, Jl 1885 C. B. Hayward, N 1885 T. W. Collier; Je 1868-D 1880, F 1881-My 1883, Jl 1885-F 1888 (broken), UNM; O 1868-D 1880, Jl 1885-F 1888 (broken), NMSU.

*New Mexican.* (weekly—weekly not part of title)\* W; BI; Rep; D 1849-My

(?) 1850, Ja 1863-Je 1868; P, Daniel R. Rood, E, (?) Davis (Davies?) and (?) Jones, E and P, Ja 1863 Charles Leib, Ag 1863 C. P. Clever, N 1863 W. H. Manderfield, My 1864 W. H. Manderfield and Thomas Tucker; N 24, 1849, N 1863-Je 1868, UNM; N 24, 1849, N 1863-O 1868, NMSU.

*New Mexican.* (daily—daily not part of title)* D; E; Rep, Ja 1894 Dem, Ja 1897 Rep; Ja 1890—; E and P, Max Frost, Ja 1894 George Cross, Ja 1897 Max Frost, Ja 1909 Paul A. F. Walter; Ja 1890—, Mus of NM; Mr 1900-D 1911, ENMU; Ja 1900—, NMSL; Ja 1898-D 1911, NMSU.

*New Mexican Review (Daily).*  D; BI; Rep; Je 1883-Je 1885, E and P, W. H. Bailhache, Ag 1883 C. B. Hayward; Albuquerque *Evening Review* moved to Santa Fe and acquired the subscription list and good will of the *Daily New Mexican;* Je 1883-Je 1885, UNM; Je 1883-Je 1885, NMSL; Je 1883-Je 1885, NMSU.

*New Mexican Review (Weekly*—part of title until 1899).* W; BI, Ag 1890 E; Rep, Ja 1894 Dem, Ja 1897 Rep; Je 1883-Jl 1885, F 1888—; E and P, W. H. Bailhache, Ag 1883 C. B. Hayward, F 1887 J. A. Spradling, O 1889 Max Frost, Ja 1894 George Cross, Ja 1897 Max Frost, Ja 1909 Paul A. F. Walter; Je 1883-Jl 1885, F 1888-D 1899, UNM; Je 1883-Jl 1885, F 1888-D 1899, NMSU.

*New Mexico.* M; E; U; 1884-85; P, S. W. Bear and Company; My 1885, NMSU.

*New Mexico Advertiser (Daily).* D; BI; U; Ag 1877-? 1878; P, A. V. Aoy; re-placed *New Mexico Cooperator.*

*New Mexico Advertiser.* (weekly) W; BI; U; 1878-80; E and P, A. V. Aoy, My 1879 E. N. Ronquillo and Transito L. Mata.

*New Mexico Cooperator.* W; BI; U; Jl 1876-Ag 1877; P, A. V. Aoy; see *New Mexico Advertiser.*

*New Mexico Democrat.* W; BI; Dem; Je-? 1871; E and P, William Rencher; a campaign paper.

*New Mexico Journal of Education.*† M; E; U; 1911—; E, Rupert F. Asplund; moved from Las Vegas; 1911-12, NMSU.

*New Mexico Mining News.*† W; E; U; Ap 1881-? 1882; P, New Mexican Publishing Company, E, Charles W. Greene; D 21, 1881, NMSU.

*New Mexico School Journal.* M; E; U; 1898-?; E and P, unknown.

*New Mexico Union.* W; BI; Dem; Ag 1872-Ja 1874; E and P, Kirby Benedict; successor to the *Post.*

*News.* W; BI ?; Dem; Ag-S 1878; E and P, Sam Davis.

*Nuevo Mexicano.** W; S; Rep, Ja 1894 Dem, Ja 1897 Rep; Ag 1890—; E and P, Max Frost, Ja 1894 George Cross, 1897 Max Frost, Ja 1909 Paul A. F. Walter; published by the New Mexican Publishing Company; Ag 1890-D 1899, UNM; 1890-1908 (broken), NMSU.

*Palito.* W; S; U; 1909—; E and P, unknown.

*Payo de Nuevo Mejico.** W; S; U; Je-Ag 1845 (?); E and P, Donaciano Vigil; Jl-Ag 1845, NMSRCA.

*Post (Daily).* D; BI; Rep; Je 1870-Mr 1872; E and P, A. P. Sullivan.

*Post (Weekly).** W; BI; Rep; O 1869-Jl 1872; E and P, A. P. Sullivan; successor to *Weekly Gazette;* Ag 1870-Je 1872, UNM; O 16, 1869, NMSU.

*Regimental Flag.* S-M; E; U; O 1873-O 1875; E and P, (?) Eaton and (?) Arnold.

*Republican.* (title used three times)* 1—W; BI; U; Ja 1847-? 1849; E and P, (?) Hovey and (?) Davies, Ap 1848 (?) Hovey; Ja 1, 1847, S 1847-S 1848, UNM; Ja 1, 1847, S 1847-S 1848, NMSU. 2—W; BI ?; Rep; Je-Jl 1862; E and P, J. H. Holmes. 3—W; BI ?; Rep; Jl-N 1894; E and P, unknown; a campaign paper.

*Rocky Mountain Sentinel.* (daily) D; E; Dem; ?-D 1879; E and P, A. M. Williams and E. F. Pegram.

*Rocky Mountain Sentinel.* (weekly)* W; E; Dem; Jl 1878-? 1879; E and P, A. M. Williams and E. F. Pegram; N 7, 1878, UNM; N 7, 1878, NMSU.

*Sun (Daily).** D; E; Dem; D 1890-? 1891; E and P, J. H. Crist; Ja-F 1891, NMHU.

*Sun (Weekly).** W; E; Dem; Ja 1890-Ja 1894; E and P, C. C. Everhart and Wood Spradling, Ap 1890 J. H. Crist; after the start of the *Daily Sun* weekly was added to the title of this paper; Ja 1890-D 1891 (broken), NMHU; Mr-S 1891, UNM; Mr 1891-Je 1893 (broken), NMSU.

*Town Topics.* W; E; U; Ag-N 1890; E and P, W. E. Parker.

*Verdad.** W; S; U; F 1844-My 1845; E and P, unknown; probably edited by Donaciano Vigil who later edited *El Payo;* S 1844-F 1845 (broken), NMSRCA.

*Voz del Pueblo.** W; S; Dem; O 1888-Je 1890; E and P, H. L. Ortiz (E), Nestor Montoya, and E. H. Salazar, F 1889 Nestor Montoya and E. H. Salazar; see Las Vegas *Voz del Pueblo;* O 20, 1888, F-My 1889 (broken), UNM; O 20, 1888, Ap 27, Je 1, 15, 1889, NMSU.

## SANTA ROSA

*Estrella Nueva.* W; E; U; Jl-? 1910; E and P, B. Padilla and B. Casus.

*Sol.* W; S; Rep; 1911—; E and P, unknown.

*Star.†* W; E; U; F 1901-? 1903; E. G. Cooper; moved to Tucumcari as the *Times;* 1902 (scattered issues), NMSL.

*Sun.** W; BI, My 1909 E; Rep; N 1902—; E and P, F. D. Morse, Ag 1910 W. C. Burnett; N 1907-D 1911, UNM.

*Voz Publica.†* W; S, Jl 1911 BI; U; 1903—; E and P, Placido Baca y Baca, My 1911 (?) Sanchez and (?) Sena, Jl 1911 W. C. Burnett; moved from Puerto de Luna; 1908-11, (broken), UNM.

## SHAKESPEARE

*Miner's Monthly.* M; E; U; 1880-81; P, Shakespeare Gold and Silver Mining Company.

## SILVER CITY

*Eagle.†* W; E; Dem; Ag 1894-97, Ja-Ap 1900; E and P, A. J. Loomis and H. L. Oakes, 1895 A. J. Loomis, Ja 1900 A. J. Loomis and O. P. Williams; Ag 28, D 18, 1895, NMSU.

*Enterprise.*\* W; E; Rep; O 1882–; E and P, W. A. Leonard and J. A. Downs, My 1886 W. A. Leonard and J. H. Tyndale, Jl 1886 W. A. Leonard and W. A. Hawkins, Ag 1888 W. A. Leonard and Dell Cobb, Ap 1890 W. A. Leonard and J. E. Sheridan, Ap 1893 J. E. Sheridan, D 1899 L. M. Fishback, Jl 1901 Fred A. Bush; N 1882-D 1894, Jl 1898-Ag 1907, O 1909-D 1911, WNMU; S 1886-Ag 1895 (broken), NMSU.

*Grant County Democrat.* W; E; Dem; 1897-F 1898; E and P, unknown; merged with the Silver City *Independent.*

*Grant County Herald.*\* W; E; Dem; Mr 1875-Ap 1881; E and P, W. H. Eckles and A. H. Hackney (E), Ja 1877 James Mullen and A. H. Hackney, S 1877 S. M. Ashenfelter, My 1880 Cornelius Bennett, O 1880 Charles A. Newton, Ja 1881 S. M. Ashenfelter; became *New Southwest;* Mr 1875-Ap 1881, UNM.

*Independent.*\* W; E; Dem; Je 1896–; E and P, George A. Norton, F 1898 W. B. Walton; succeeded the Southwest *Sentinel;* Je 1896-D 1911, WNMU; 1901-11 (broken), NMSL; Ag 1897-N 1901 (broken), NMSU.

*Mining Chronicle.*\* W; E; U; Je 1880-D 1881; E and P, J. S. Crouch and W. H. Lawrence, Ag 1881 J. S. Crouch; merged with *New Southwest;* S 29, 1881, NMHU.

*Mining Life.*\* W; E; U; My 1873-F 1875; E and P, Owen L. Scott; succeeded by *Grant County Herald;* My 1873-F 1875; UNM.

*New Alta.* D; E; U; Ap 1880; E and P, unknown.

*New Mexico Mining Gazette.* W; E; U; Ag 1882-? 1883; E, Charles W. Stephenson.

*New Southwest.*\* W, Dec 1882 D; E; Dem; Ap 1881-Mr 1883; E and P, S. M. Ashenfelter, D-1881 James Mullen; merged with *Sentinel;* Ap 1881-Mr 1883, UNM; 1881-82 (broken), NMSL.

*People's Advocate.* W; E; Populist; 1894; E and P, unknown; a campaign paper.

*Record (Silver Record).* W; E; U; Ja 1879-? 1880; E and P, H. W. Sherry, Ap 1879 Charles W. Ruggles.

*Sentinel (Grant County).* W, briefly 1882-83 daily, Mr 1883 S-W; Dem; ? 1882-Mr 1883; merged with *New Southwest* to form *Southwest-Sentinel.*

*Silver Citizen.* (renamed *Evening Citizen* Ja 1884) D; E; U; Jl 1883-Ap 1884; E and P, Gaye E. Porter and (?) Nye; moved to Deming to become *Daily Democrat.*

*Southwest (Daily).*\* D; E; Dem; Mr-Ag 1880; E and P, S. M. Ashenfelter, My 1880 Cornelius Bennett; Mr-Ag 1880, UNM; Mr-Ag 1880, NMIMT.

*Southwest-Sentinel (Daily).* D; E; Dem; S 1887-Je 1888; E and P, A. J. Loomis.

*Southwest-Sentinel.* (weekly)\* S-W, Ja 1884 W; E; Dem; Mr 1883-S 1887, Je 1888-Je 1896; E and P, J. J. Bell, Je 1883 S. M. Ashenfelter, S 1884 C. M. Shannon, Je 1886 S. M. Ashenfelter, S 1886 A. J. Loomis, Je 1888 Charles G. Bell and Gideon D. Bantz, Ap 1890 C. L. Davenport and J. J. Bell, O 1890 Allan MacDonald and P. J. Bennett, O 1891 Allan MacDonald; became *Independent;* Mr 1883-D 1885, UNM; O 1886-Ja 1888 (broken), NMSU.

*Sun.* W; E; U; 1883-84; E and P, unknown.

*Telegram.* W; E; U; N 1880-N 1882; E and P, H. W. Sherry.

*Tribune.*† W; E; U; ? 1873-? 1874; E and P, U. C. Garrison; Ag-D 1873, UNM.

*Watchdog.* S-W; E; U; My-D 1882; E and P, unknown.

## SOCORRO

*Abogado Cristiano Neo-Mexicano.* S-M; BI; U; 1892-95; E and P, Thomas Harwood; former *Metodista Neo-Mexicano* at Las Cruces, moved to Albuquerque.

*Advertiser (Evening).* D; E ?; U; 1883-84; E and P, unknown; was published briefly at three different times.

*Bullion.** M, Jl 1883 W; E; U; Ap 1883-Ap 1888; E and P, W. N. Beal, Jl 1883 Charles Longuemare and R. M. Parker, N 1883 Charles Longuemare, My 1885 Charles Longuemare and C. J. Hildreth, F 1887 Charles Longuemare, O 1887 C. G. Leicham; moved to El Paso, Texas, using same title; Jl 1885-Ap 1887, NMHU.

*Catch as Catch Can.* W; E; U; Ap-? 1885; E and P, Will A. Henry.

*Chieftain (Daily).** D; E; Rep; O 1885-? 1889; E and P, John A. Helphingstine and William Tell De Baun, O 1886 William Tell De Baun, N 1888 R. P. Helphingstine; Jl 1886-S 1888 (broken), NMHU.

*Chieftain.* (weekly)* W; E; Rep; My 1884-O 1885, ? 1889—; E and P, John A. Helphingstine, ? 1889 R. P. Helphingstine, Ap 1890 C. G. Leicham, J. A. Whitmore, and W. S. Williams (E), S 1898 Clement Hightower, Ja 1900 Socorro Publishing Company (E. A. Drake, ed); My-S 1884 (broken), NMHU; N 1891-D 1911 (broken), UNM; N 1891-D 1911 (broken), NMIMT; 1901-11 (broken), NMSL.

*Combate.*† W; S ?; U; Ja 1898-?; E and P, Jose Escobar; Ja 8, 15, 1898, NMSU.

*Defensor del Pueblo.*† W; S; Dem; My 1905—; P, Torres Brothers Publishing Company, E, A. C. Torres; S 1905-Ja 1912 (scattered issues), NMSU.

*Eco del Socorro.* W; BI; Dem; 1881-1887; E and P, 1886 (?) Simpson and (?) Crawford; probably this paper was published in 1881 and 1882 and revived in 1886; became Socorro *Union.*

*Estrella del Nuevo Mexico.*† W; S; Rep; 1895-96; E and P, Pablo Trujillo and E. Sosa; Ag 7, 1896, Mr 26, 1897, NMSU.

*Estrella del Socorro.* W; S; Dem; Mr 1885-? 1886; P, Candalario Garcia, E, H. L. Ortiz; formerly Socorro *Star.*

*Golondrina.*† W; S ?; U; F 1898-?; E and P, L. A. Gutieriz (sic); F 12, 1898, NMSU.

*Hispano-Americano.*† W; BI; U; 1886-92; E and P, unknown; N 10, 1891-Mr 27, 1892, NMSU.

*Industrial Advertiser.** W; E; Dem; F 1889-S 1899; E and P, J. H. McCutcheon; moved to Albuquerque under same title; F-D 1889, UNM; Je 10, 1893, Ag 24, 1895, NMSU.

*May Festival Herald.* M; E; U; My-? 1887; E and P, L. Meyerhoff; a musical publication.

*Miner.*\* W, O 1881 S-W, O-D 1882 D; U; Ap 1881-Ja 1883; E and P, D. A. Beckwith, Jl 1882 W. N. Beall, D 1882 R. M. Parker; S 22, 1881, NMHU.

*New Mexico Methodist.*\* M; Bl; U; O 1885-1892; E and P, Thomas Harwood and S. W. Thornton; moved to Las Cruces as *Metodista Neo-Mexicano;* My 1886, UNM; N 1886, NMHU.

*News (Daily).* D; E; U; O 1881-O 1882 (?); E and P, G. W. McClintick, Ja 1882 R. M. Parker and Charles Longuemare; intermittent, suspended several times in this period.

*Progreso.* W; Bl; U; My-? 1887; E and P, (?) Vincent and (?) Fitch; My 17-Ag 9, 1887 (broken), NMSU.

*Republicano.*† W; Bl; Rep; 1898-Ag 1903; P, W. E. Martin, H. O. Bursum, and S. C. Abeyta, E, W. E. Martin, Mr 1899 S. C. Abeyta; 1901-03 (broken), NMSL; Mr 16, 1901, NMSU.

*Star.*\* D, N 1884 Tri-W; Bl; Dem; O 1884-Mr 1885; P, Candalario Garcia, E, Charles O'Connor Roberts, and H. L. Ortiz; became *Estrella del Socorro;* N 25, 1884, NMHU.

*Sun (Daily).*\* D; E; U; 1882-84; E and P, S. D. Holden and Mark Edwards, Ja 1883 W. N. Beall, D 1883 F. A. Blake, Ap 1884 Charles O'Connor Roberts and W. T. McCreight; intermittently in this period the *Sun* reverted to weekly publication; S-D 1883 (broken), NMIMT; Ap 16, 1884, NMHU.

*Sun.* (weekly)\* W; E; U; Jl 1880-82; E and P, A. M. Conklin and (?) Curtis, S 1880 A. M. Conklin, F 1881 R. M. Parker, S 1881 P. C. Campbell, D 1881 S. D. Holden and Mark Edwards; see *Daily Sun;* Ag-S 1880, UNM; Ap-O 1881 (broken), NMHU.

*Times (Daily).* D; E; U; Jl-? 1883; E and P, R. M. Parker and Charles Longuemare.

*Times.* (weekly)\* W; E; U; D 1887-? 1889; P, John S. Sniffen, 1888 Whitmore, Bull, and Company; briefly in O 1888 was a daily; Ja 1888-Ja 1889 (broken), NMHU.

*Union.* W; Bl; Rep; D 1886-N 1887; E and P, F. A. Blake; formerly *Eco del Socorro,* moved to Las Vegas to become *News;* Mr 3-17, 1887, NMHU.

*Verdad.* W; E; Rep; 1900, 1902; E and P, unknown; a campaign paper published in the shop of the *Chieftain.*

## SOLANO

*Herald.* W; E; Rep; 1908-11; E and P, J. F. Perry; moved in 1911 to Roy and renamed *Roy and Solano Herald.*

## SPRINGER

*Banner.*\* W; Bl; Dem; Je 1889-93; P, Hosmer Brothers, E, George E. Hosmer; Ja-D 1890, WNMU, Jl 1891-Je 1893, CH Raton.

*Colfax County Stockman.*\* W; E; Rep, 1894 Ind, 1896 Dem; Ap 1882—; E and P, John R. Woodburn, N 1883 C. F. Martin, Je 1885 H. W. Sturges and P. F. Sturges, 1888 H. W. Sturges, S 1893 J. F. Hutchinson; Jl 1885-O 1888 (broken), NMHU; Ja 1890-D 1908, CH Raton; Ja 1909-D 1911 (broken), UNM; 1904, NMSL.

*News.* W; E; U; Ap-? 1910; E and P, unknown.

*Sentinel.** W; E; Rep; F 1901-N 1902; E and P, James Corry; F 1901-Ja 1902, CH Raton.

*Statesman.* W; Rep; E; My 1911—; E and P, unknown.

*Tribune.* W; E; U; S-? 1882; E and P, unknown.

## STANLEY

*Index.* W; E; U; 1908-10; E and P, W. F. Castle.

## ST. VRAIN

*Journal.* W; E; Socialist; Ap 1909—; E and P, W. C. Tharp.

## SUNNYSIDE (see FORT SUMNER)

*Republican*—see Fort Sumner *Republican.*

*Review*—see Fort Sumner *Review.*

*Sun*—see Fort Sumner *Sun.*

## TAIBAN

*Valley News.* W; E; Dem, 1909 U; O 1908—; E and P, B. F. Edgell, 1909 E. G. Coan, 1910 J. W. King.

## TAOS

*Advertiser.* (title used twice) 1—M; E; U; 1885; E and P, unknown. 2—W; E; U; 1898-99; E and P, J. B. Wallace.

*Bien Publico.* W; S; Dem; 1911—; E and P, Vincent Thomas.

*Crepusculo.* W; S; U; N-D 1835; E and P, Padre Jose Antonio Martinez; some authorities doubt the existence of this paper.

*Cresset.** W; E; Rep; O 1898-Je 1902; E and P, Frank Staplin; merged with *Revista de Taos,* formerly LaBelle *Cresset;* O 1898-D 1900, UNM.

*County Republican.*† W; E; Rep; 1904—; E and P, unknown; 1904-05 (broken), NMSL.

*Faro Popular.* W; S; U; 1892-94; E and P, unknown.

*Herald.* W; BI, 1886 E; Rep, 1886 U; Jl 1884-? 1886; E and P, J. M. Alvey, 1886 Lorin W. Brown; became the *Taosonian.*

*Heraldo de Taos.** W; S; U; 1886-O 1888; E and P, Lorin W. Brown; see *Heraldo Taoseno;* Mr-O 1888 (broken), NMHU.

*Heraldo Taoseno.* W; S; U; O 1888-90; E and P, Lorin W. Brown; O-D 1888 (broken), NMHU.

*Monitor.* (title used twice)† 1—W; S; U; 1890-92; E and P, John Valdes, Jr.; 1890-99 (broken), NMSL. 2—W; E, 1896 BI; U; 1895-97; E and P, J. M. Martinez (E) and (?) Trujillo.

*Revista de Taos.*† W; S; U; 1902—; E and P, A. J. Baca, Je 1902 A. J. Baca and Frank Staplin, 1903 A. J. Baca, 1904 Jose Montaner; 1902-03, 1909-11 (broken), NMSL; F 20, 1904, NMSU.

*Taosonian.** W; E; U; 1887-S 1889; E and P, Lorin W. Brown; see *Valley Herald;* Jl 5, 1887, UNM.

*Valley Herald.** W; E; U; S 1889-? 1890, 1893-95; E and P, Lorin W. Brown, 1893 C. E. Griffith; in 1893 *Rio Hondo Miner* was added to title, probably the Amizett *Miner* was moved to Taos to launch this paper; S 1889-F 1890 (broken), NMHU; My 25, 1893, UNM.

*Valley Mirror.* (sometimes called *Espejo*) W; BI; U; My-? 1878; E and P, (?) Chacon and (?) Salazar; moved to Bernalillo as the *Mirror.*

*Valley News.†* W; E; Rep; 1909–; P, Jose Montaner, E, J. W. Giddings; 1910-12, NMSL.

## TEXICO

*Democrat.* W; E; Dem; O 1906-O 1907; P, Democrat Publishing Company.

*Times.* W; E; U; S 1908-Ap 1909; E and P, John Custer and J. W. Childers.

*Trumpet.* W; E; Dem, 1905 Rep; Ap 1904–; E and P, A. S. Hornbeck, Ag 1905 H. R. Putnam, 1908 Leroy P. Loomis, Ag 1911 Robert Neihaus.

## TIERRA AMARILLA

*Nuevo Estado.†* W; S; Rep; 1908–; E and P, F. L. Sosa, 1911 E. M. Valdez; 1911-12 (scattered issues), NMSL.

*Republicano.* W; BI; Rep; 1901-S 1903, 1904-07; E and P, A. L. Runyan and B. C. Hernandez, 1904 Diego Chacon.

## TIPTONVILLE

*Mora County Pioneer.* W; E ?; U; F 1881-?; E and P, J. E. Holmes and J. F. Wallace; moved to Watrous under same title.

## TOLAR

*Tribune.* W; E; Rep; Mr 1908–; E and P, J. R. Little.

## TRES PIEDRAS

*Mining Reporter.* W; E; U; S 1903–; E and P, J. D. Frazy, 1905 E. D. Seward.

## TUBAC
(after 1863 in Arizona Territory)

*Weekly Arizonian.* W; E; U; Mr-? 1859; E and P, Ephram Cross; moved to Tucson.

## TUCSON
(after 1863 in Arizona Territory)

*Arizonian.* W; E; U; 1859-1861; P, Sylvester Mowry, E, H. W. Sherry, Mr 1861 T. M. Turner.

## TUCUMCARI

*Actual Settler.** W; E; U; D 1904-Jl 1905; E and P, J. E. Curren; formerly *Quay County Democrat;* moved to Sunnyside as the *Sun;* Ja-Jl 1905, CH Tucumcari.

*News.** W; E; Rep; O 1905–; E and P, S. M. Wharton (E) and S. R. May; merged with Tucumcari *Times;* O 1905-D 1911, CH Tucumcari.

*Pathfinder.*† W; E; Rep; F 1902-Mr 1903; E and P, J. E. Curren; became *Quay County Democrat;* 1902 (scattered issues), NMSL.

*Quay County Democrat.** W; E; Dem; Ap 1903-D 1904; E and P, J. E. Curren; renamed *Actual Settler;* Ap 1903-N 1904, CH Tucumcari.

*Sun.** W; E; Dem; D 1907–; E and P, O. C. Hammons, 1910 S. T. Hopkins, 1911 R. C. Stubbins, 1912 J. W. Campbell; D 1907-D 1911, CH Tucumcari.

*Times.** W; E; Rep; Ap 1903-Ja 1907; E and P, E. G. Cooper, D 1903 A. E. Curren; merged with Tucumcari *News;* Ap 1903-Ja 1907, CH Tucumcari.

## TULAROSA

*Chief.* W; E; U; Ag 1896-N 1897; E and P, J. H. Lightfoot; moved to La Luz as *Sacremento Chief.*

*Democrat.** W; E; Dem; Ap 1899-? 1905; E and P, W. G. Davenport and (?) Longino, Ap 1903 A. J. Davis and W. G. Davenport; Ja 1903-D 1904, CH Alamogordo.

*Reporter.** W; E; U; Ap-N 1905; E and P, H. B. Fay; Ap-N 1905, CH Alamogordo.

*Valley Tribune.** W; E; Dem; Ja 1909–; E and P, W. F. Hume and J. E. Anderson, Ja 1911 J. E. Anderson; Ja 1909-D 1911, CH Alamogordo.

## URTON
### (later became KENNA)

*Record.* W; E; U; F-D 1907; E and P, J. M. Hughes; became Kenna *Record.*

## VAUGHN

*Chronicle.*† W; E; U; S 1908-? 1909; P, S. L. Kelso, E, C. H. Underwood; 1906 (broken), UNM.

*News.** W; E; Dem, S 1910 Rep, Ap 1911 U; F 1910–; P, Wester and Wester, S 1910 Haughton and O'Grady, Ap 1911 G. A. Clark, E, F. C. Wester, S 1910 R. E. Haughton, Ap 1911 G. A. Clark; F 1910-D 1911, UNM.

## WALLACE

*Watchman.* W; BI; U; My 1880-F 1882; E and P, A. V. Aoy and George Albright.

## WAGON MOUND

*Arrow.* W; BI; U; S 1885-D 1886; E and P, unknown.

*Arrow-Pioneer.* W; BI; U; F-Ag 1888; E and P, W. T. Henderson and Lon Hartigan; merger of *Arrow* and *Mora County Pioneer,* moved to Gallup as *Gleaner.*

*Combate.** W; S; Rep; O 1902-? 1910; E and P, Diego A. Chacon, Mr 1903 Patricio Gonzales, 1906 Q. A. Martinez; merged with *Sentinel;* D 1902-Ja 1905, UNM.

*Flecha (Arrow).*\* W; BI; U; D 1886-Ja 1887; E and P, W. T. Henderson; became *Arrow-Pioneer;* D 1886-Ja 1887, UNM.

*Mora County Sentinel and El Combate.*\* W; BI; Rep; 1910–; P, M. M. Padgett, E, Blas Sanchez; Mr-D 1911, UNM.

*New Mexico Settler.* W; E; Dem; Ja-Ag 1888; E and P, G. E. Hosmer.

*Sol de Mayo.* W; S; U; 1900-Mr 1902; E and P, Patricio Gonzales; became *Combate.*

*Pantagraph.* W; E; Rep; 1909–; E and P, J. Gordon Smith.

## WATROUS

*Mora County Pioneer.*\* W; E; U; 1881-85, D 1887-Ja 1888; E and P, Ap 1883 J. M. Alvey; became *Pioneer Journal* in 1885 and merged with *Arrow* in Ja 1888; See Tiptonville *Mora County Pioneer;* Ag 8, 1885, NMHU.

*Pioneer Journal.* W; E; U; 1885-Ja 1887; E and P, H. H. Green, Mr 1886 George Alvey and William Sparks; merged with *Plaindealer.*

*Plaindealer.* W; E; U; Ja-N 1887; E and P, M. Calhoun.

*Times.* W; E; U; Ap-O 1886; E and P, J. C. McNeil.

## WHITE OAKS

*Eagle.*\* W; E; Dem; 1898-Ag 1903; E and P, S. M. Wharton and J. A. Haley, 1900 S. M. Wharton; formerly *Old Abe Eagle,* merged with *Capitan Progress* to form Capitan *News;* Ja 1899-Ag 1903, CH Carrizozo.

*Golden Era.*\* W; E; U; D 1880-Jl 1884; E and P, J. H. Wise and G. W. Pritchard, Jl 1881 J. C. O. Morse, D 1881 J. E. Sligh, 1882 John A. Helphingstine, F 1884 M. S. Taliaferro; moved to Lincoln; S 1881-My 1884 (broken), NMHU.

*Lincoln County Leader.*\* W; E; Rep; O 1882-? 1894; E and P, Lee H. Ruidisille, Ja 1883 William Caffery; S 1884-N 1890 (broken), NMHU; Ja 1891-Ja 1892, CH Carrizozo; 1882-1893 (broken), UNM; Je 24, 1893, NMSU.

*New Mexico Interpreter.*\* W; E; Dem; Jl 1885-N 1891; E and P, J. E. Sligh, Ap 1887 William Watson, O 1889 J. A. Allen, Mr 1891 Mrs. A. L. McGinnis; became *Old Abe Eagle;* My 1887-Je 1891 (broken), UNM; N 15, 1889, NMSU.

*Old Abe Eagle.*\* W; E; Dem; N 1891-98; E and P, H. L. Ross and H. G. Raible, 1894 H. G. Raible, My 1896 William Watson and John Y. Hewitt, 1897 John Y. Hewitt; formerly *New Mexico Interpreter* and became *Eagle;* N 1891-N 1892, CH Carrizozo; Ag 22, 1895, NMSU.

*Outlook.*\* W; E; Rep; S 1904-D 1906; E and P, Lee H. Ruidisille; moved to Carrizozo under same title; S 1904-D 1906, CH Carrizozo.

*Scorpion.* W; E; U; 1882; E and P, unknown.

## WILLARD

*Record.* W; E; Rep; 1908–; E and P, Eugene Forbes, 1910 B. E. Pedrick.

# BIBLIOGRAPHY

IN THE PREPARATION of this work the territorial newspapers have been used extensively with most other sources being used more to furnish background and to check facts found in the newspapers. In many instances newspapers provide poor sources for historical data, for their stories often are hastily written with little attempt to verify facts. But a comparison of several newspaper accounts, taking care that opposed factions are represented, may provide reliable information, insight, and a depth of understanding unavailable in public documents alone.

With regard to politics, practically all territorial newspapers reflected a prejudiced viewpoint, particularly during political campaigns. Thus, it is essential that the conflicting stories and editorials be examined so that reasonably accurate information may be extracted from the combined sources. Most territorial editors were motivated by a desire to see New Mexico grow and prosper; therefore, information in economic matters is likely to be slanted. Again it may be necessary for researchers to compare several newspaper accounts to get reliable information. The writer has used this practice in the preparation of this work, and, as can be noted above in many instances, several sources have been cited in controversial matters.

Portions of the files of a great many territorial newspapers are available to the researcher, and all of them are valuable in one instance or another. For the convenience of those who wish quickly to find the most reliable information, however, the writer has sought to evaluate the best general historical sources during various territorial periods. Up to 1870 the Santa Fe *Republican,* the Albuquerque *Rio Abajo Weekly Press,* the Santa Fe *New Mexican,* and the Santa Fe *Weekly Gazette* provide the best information, and their reliability approximates the order assigned them above. When possible the *New Mexican* and the *Weekly Gazette* should be checked against each other.

For the 1870s the Santa Fe *New Mexican* is the best general newspaper source which covers the entire period. However, the viewpoint of this paper is prejudiced in favor of the Republican party and the official hierarchy of the territory. The Silver City *Mining Life* and the Silver City *Grant County Herald* provide good information, although the latter is prejudiced against the Republican party and the official group. The Mesilla *Valley Independent* provides the most impartial newspaper source that contains extensive information concerning the Lincoln County War. The Las Cruces *Borderer* provides good general information except in politics, where it is strongly slanted toward

Democratic views. The Albuquerque *Review* files cover most of this period, but it is a less reliable source because of its strongly Catholic bias.

From 1880 to 1890 the best general newspaper source for historical data is the Las Vegas *Daily Optic*. The Santa Fe *New Mexican* is valuable for its reprints of opposition views attacking its strong advocacy of the Republican party and the Santa Fe Ring. The Albuquerque *Morning Journal* from 1880 to 1885 is a good source of information. The Albuquerque *Morning Democrat,* on the other hand, is less valuable, being too preoccupied with the promotion of its publisher's political career and the city of Albuquerque. The best sources of information about southern New Mexico in this decade are the Silver City *Enterprise* and the Silver City *Southwest Sentinel.*

For the 1890s the Las Vegas *Daily Optic* is again the best general source. The Santa Fe *New Mexican* alternates in political coloring, since it was owned alternately by Republican and Democratic factions. The Albuquerque *Daily Citizen* is a good general source, and the Silver City *Enterprise,* the Silver City *Independent,* and the Las Cruces *Rio Grande Republican* provide reasonably accurate information about southern New Mexico.

For the period from 1900 to 1912 the Albuquerque *Morning Journal* is the best general source of information. The Santa Fe *New Mexican* continues to reflect a prejudice favorable to the Republican party and its guiding clique. It is also overly optimistic about the future of New Mexico, giving an exaggerated report about territorial economic prosperity. The Las Vegas *Daily Optic* is less reliable than in the past but still a good general source. The newspapers of this decade which provide the best information about the various territorial regions are as follows: southwestern, the Silver City *Independent;* south central, the Las Cruces *Rio Grande Republican;* southeastern, the Roswell *Daily Record;* east central, the Tucumcari *News;* northeastern, the Raton *Range;* northwestern, the Farmington *Times-Hustler.* For the Spanish-American point of view, consult *El Independiente* of Las Vegas.

## NEWSPAPERS

For newspapers of the territorial era used in the preparation of this work consult Appendix. Those papers bearing an asterisk (*) were used, and each such entry lists the approximate periods for which files are available. Listed below are newspaper sources after the territorial era.
Albuquerque *Journal,* July 7, 1933.
Clovis *News,* July 11, 18, 1912.
Clovis *News-Journal,* April 1, 1954.
Portales *Daily News,* September 21, 1952.

## UNPUBLISHED MATERIALS

At the Albuquerque Public Library, Albuquerque, New Mexico:
Goff, Harold A. "A History of the Daily Newspapers in Albuquerque."
New Mexico State University Library, University Park, New Mexico:
Bedinger, Margery. "Newspapers Published in New Mexico," 1937.
Norris, H. O. Personal interview with the writer August 30, 1963, Fort Sumner, New Mexico.
Portales *News-Tribune* information files:
Alldredge, E. P. Letter to Editor Gordon K. Greaves.
Dobbs, C. V. "Buck." Letter to Editor Gordon K. Greaves.

## BOOKS AND PAMPHLETS

Beck, Warren A. *New Mexico: A History of Four Centuries.* Norman, 1951.

Bentley, Arthur F. *The Process of Government.* Bloomington, 1908.

Chase, C. M. *The Editor's Run in Colorado and New Mexico.* Lyndon, Vermont, 1882.

Clark, Ira B. *Then Came the Railroads.* Norman, 1958.

Crichton, Kyle S. *Law and Order Limited, The Rousing Life of Elfego Baca.* Santa Fe, 1928.

Fulton, Maurice Garland and Paul Horgan. *New Mexico's Own Chronicle.* Dallas, 1937.

Gibson, A. M. *The Life and Death of Colonel Albert Jennings Fountain.* Norman, 1965.

Gregory, Winniford. *American Newspapers, 1821-1936: Union List of Files in the United States and Canada.* New York, 1937.

Hannett, Arthur Thomas. *Sagebrush Lawyer.* New York, 1964.

Hutchinson, W. H. *A Bar Cross Man: The Life and Personal Writings of Eugene Manlove Rhodes.* Norman, 1956.

Keleher, William A. *The Maxwell Land Grant.* Santa Fe, 1942.

————. *Violence in Lincoln County: 1869-1882.* Albuquerque, 1957.

Kemble, Edward C. *A History of California Newspapers: 1846-1858,* ed. Helen Harding Bretnor. Los Gatos, 1962.

La Farge, Oliver. *Santa Fe: Autobiography of a Southwestern Town.* Norman, 1959.

Lamar, Howard Roberts. *The Far Southwest, 1846-1912: A Territorial History.* New Haven, 1966.

Lasswell, Harold D. *POLITICS: Who Gets What, When, How.* Cleveland, 1958.

Leigh, Robert D. (ed.). *A Free and Responsible Press.* Chicago, 1947.

Library Staff, the University of New Mexico. *A Check List of New Mexico Newspapers.* Albuquerque, 1935.

Lutrell, Estelle. *Newspapers and Periodicals of Arizona: 1859-1911.* Tucson, 1950.

McDougal, Curtis D. *Newsroom Problems and Policies.* New York, 1947.

Mengel, Willi. *Ottmar Mergenthaler and the Printing Revolution.* Brooklyn, 1954.

Mott, Frank Luther. *American Journalism: A History, 1690-1960.* New York, 1962.

*N. W. Ayer and Son's American Newspaper Annual.* Philadelphia, 1880-1912.

Petersen, William J. *The Pageant of the Press: A Survey of 125 Years of Iowa Journalism, 1836-1961.* Iowa City, 1962.

Plucknett, R. F. T. *Taswell-Langmeads English Constitutional History.* Boston, 1960.

Tebel, John. *The Life and Good Times of William Randolph Hearst.* New York, 1952.

Truman, David B. *The Governmental Process.* New York, 1951.

Twitchell, R. E. *The Leading Facts of New Mexican History.* II. Cedar Rapids, Iowa, 1912.

Waters, L. L. *Steel Rails to Santa Fe.* Lawrence, 1950.

Weiss, A. E. (ed.). *Editor and Publisher International Yearbook, 1964.* New York, 1964.

Westphall, Victor. *The Public Domain in New Mexico.* Albuquerque, 1965.

Winkler, John K. *William Randolph Hearst: A New Appraisal.* New York, 1952.

## ARTICLES

Alvis, Berry Newton. "The History of Union County," *New Mexico Historical Review*, XXII (July, 1947).

Coan, Charles F. "The County Boundaries of New Mexico," *Southwestern Political Science Quarterly*, III (December, 1922).

Curren, Arthur E. "Pioneer Editor," *New Mexico Magazine*, XXXII (November, 1954).

Dargan, Marion. "New Mexico's Fight for Statehood," *New Mexico Historical Review*, XIV, XV, XVI, XVIII (1939, 1940, 1941, 1943).

Irwin, Will. "The Voice of a Generation," *Colliers*, July 29, 1911, reprinted under the title of "How far have we come? A view from 1911," *Columbia Journalism Review*, II (Summer, 1963).

Lugo, Dolores P. "Aoy's Gift to El Paso," *The Junior Historian of the Texas State Historical Association*, XXV (September, 1964).

McMurtrie, Douglas C. "El Payo de Nuevo-Mejico," *New Mexico Historical Review*, VIII (April, 1933).

Reeve, Frank D. "Albert Franklin Banta: Arizona Pioneer," *New Mexico Historical Review*, XXVIII (April, 1952).

Stanley, F. [Stanley Francis Crocchiola]. "O. P. McMains, Champion of a Lost Cause," *New Mexico Historical Review*, XXIV (January, 1949).

Wagner, Henry R. "New Mexico Spanish Press," *New Mexico Historical Review*, XII (January, 1937).

## PUBLIC DOCUMENTS

U. S. Bureau of the Census. *Population of the United States in 1860, the Eighth Census.* Washington, 1864.

———. *Ninth Census, Vol. I, Statistics of the Population of the United States, 1870.* Washington, 1872.

———. *Statistics of the Population of the United States at the Tenth Census, 1880.* Washington, 1883.

———. *Compendium of the Eleventh Census: 1890, Part I—Population.* Washington, 1892.

———. *Thirteenth Census of the United States: Vol. III—Population, 1910.* Washington, 1913.

# INDEX

Abiquiu, N.M., 106
Advertising, *see* Newspaper business practices
Alamogordo, N.M., 51, 54, 171; newspapers at, 54, 76, 133, 171
Alamillo, N.M., 165
Albright, J. G., 26, 28, 33, 39, 47, 88, 101-102, 199, 211, 230
Albuquerque, N.M., 5, 21, 23-24, 27-29, 39, 46, 50-51, 61, 66, 74, 109, 144, 147, 148-149, 151, 153, 171, 189, 192, 194, 200; newspapers at, 3, 5, 7, 9, 11, 13-14, 17-19, 21, 28-29, 33-37, 39-40, 42-45, 47, 59, 61-63, 65-66, 69-72, 75-78, 88, 91-93, 95, 99-103, 108-116, 118, 123, 125, 128, 137-138, 140-141, 144, 148-149, 151, 153, 158, 160, 165, 171, 176, 178, 185-186, 192-194, 199-200, 204
Alldredge, E. P., 52, 65, 219
Allison, Clay, 177
Amarillo, Texas, 51, 147
Amizett, N.M., 155
Andrews, W. R., 109, 112
Anglo-Americans (as ethnic group), 1, 17, 24, 34, 47, 51, 56-57, 59, 64, 85-87, 90, 98, 100, 117-118, 126-132, 134-136, 138, 140-141, 143-145, 154, 163-164, 175, 182, 191, 196, 198
Anton Chico, N.M., 163
Aoy, A. V., 6, 8, 11, 12, 21, 206
Apaches, *see* Indians, pacification of
Arizona, 3, 87, 127, 140, 155, 168; joint state with New Mexico, 107-112, 123, 133, 148
Armijo, Jr., Isadoro, 59, 65, 221
Armijo, Perfecto, 192
Artesia, N.M., 56, 155, 193; newspapers at, 56, 132, 133
Artesian wells, *see* Farming, irrigation

Ashenfelter, S. M., 8-9, 19, 30, 85, 87, 101, 203, 208
Associated Press, 12-13, 40-43, 47, 51, 56, 61, 67, 70, 71, 200
Axtell, S. B., 138, 179
Aztec, N.M., 32, 57; newspapers at, 32, 57, 171

Baca brothers, 128
Baca, Elfego, 59, 66, 221, 233
Baca, Ezequiel Cabeza de, *see* Cabeza de Baca
Badman image of New Mexico, 176, 190
Bailhache, W. H., 27-28, 212
Baird, S. M., 8, 84, 90, 227
Bard City, N.M., 113
Bear, H. F. M., 56, 63, 65, 220
Bedichek. Roy, 65
Belen, N.M., 48, 52, 57-58, 147; newspapers at, 57-58
Bennett, Cornelius, 88, 101, 208
Bennett, N. V., 5, 7-8, 10, 87, 99-100
Bennett, P. J., 31, 63
Berger, William, 65
Beringer, G. B., 32, 58
Bernalillo, N.M., 46, 48
Bilingual newspapers, 12-13, 16, 36, 39, 53, 59
Blue Ballot Amendment, 114
Bond, Ira M., 5, 10
Bonney, W. H. (Billy, the Kid), 182-183
Bonuses to encourage railway construction, *see* Railroads
Boston, Mass., 122
Breeden, William, 85, 187
Bull, Munsey, 52, 77, 218
Bureau of Immigration, Territorial, 78, 87, 171
Burke, W. S., 61, 101, 212